Globalization

The last two decades have witnessed an explosive proliferation of academic writings on the subject of globalization. Unusually, this has been accompanied by a high level of interest in the media to the extent that, in almost no time at all, globalization has become an accepted term in a vast number of languages throughout the world. In the blink of an eye, the term has come into such common usage that it is difficult to imagine that just over a decade ago most regarded it as a neologism. However, such widespread usage has inevitably resulted in the meaning of the concept broadening to include a whole host of issues, running the attendant risk of losing any conceptual focus it had.

Rather than claim that there exists a common concept of globalization that all parties can agree to, Glenn seeks to examine some of the conceptions and the way in which they render different interpretations of particular aspects of globalization. What is of greater interest are the differences between the approaches when the various conceptions are applied to a particular issue concerning globalization.

Globalization: North–South perspectives examines five issue areas affected by globalization: the economy; sovereignty; civil society; governance; and communication. In so doing, the book aims to articulate certain questions within each area, which we consider will allow for some judgement to be made concerning the differing perspectives on globalization. This book will be of interest to students of international political economy and politics and international relations in general.

John Glenn is a lecturer in the Department of Politics at Southampton University, UK.

Globalization

North–South perspectives

John Glenn

Routledge
Taylor & Francis Group

LONDON AND NEW YORK

First published 2007
by Routledge
2 Park Square, Milton Park, Abingdon, Oxon OX14 4RN

Simultaneously published in the USA and Canada
by Routledge
711 Third Avenue, New York, NY 10017

*Routledge is an imprint of the Taylor & Francis Group, an informa
business*

Typeset in Times by
HWA Text and Data Management, Tunbridge Wells

British Library Cataloguing in Publication Data
A catalogue record for this book is available from the British Library

Library of Congress Cataloging-in-Publication Data
Glenn, John, 1963–
    Globalization: north–south perspectives / John Glenn.
        p.   cm.
    Includes bibliographical references and index.
    1. Globalization.   2. International economic relations.
    3. North and south   I. Title.
    JZ1318G554 2007
    337–dc22   2007011516

ISBN 10: 0–415–25096–X (hbk)
ISBN 10: 0–415–25097–8 (pbk)
ISBN 10: 0–203–93919–0 (ebk)

ISBN13: 978–0–415–25096–2 (hbk)
ISBN13: 978–0–415–25097–9 (pbk)
ISBN13: 978–0–203–93919–2 (ebk)

To the staff and students of the departments of
International Studies and IPE at Tsukuba University

Contents

Boxes

Figures

Tables

Acknowledgements

Without the continual help and support of Steve Day, Jane Freedman, Rob Frith, Darryl Howlett and Nana Poku, this book would never have seen the light of day. In today's environment we are ever more reliant on those we can count on. I am lucky enough to have such friends and can only hope that I can repay their kindness one day. I would also like to take this opportunity to thank Tony McGrew and Grahame Thompson not only for their help and support, but also for their technical advice and the materials that they provided. Finally I would like to thank Ali Maharramov for his help in converting many of the tables. Without such help I doubt that this book would have ever been completed.

The author and publisher are grateful for permission to reprint extracts from the following published materials: John Glenn, 'Globalization's alternatives: competing or complementary perspectives?', *Government and Opposition,* vol. 43, no 1 (Winter 2008).

Abbreviations

AFTA	ASEAN Free Trade Agreement
AGOA	African Growth and Opportunity Act
APEC	Asia-Pacific Economic Cooperation
ASEAN	Association of Southeast Asian Nations
BCBS	Basel Committee on Banking Supervision
CACM	Central American Common Market
CARICOM	Caribbean Community and Common Market
DFQFT	Duty Free and Quota Free Treatment
EBG	Everything But Guns
ECOWAS	Economic Organization of West African States
EU	European Union
FDI	Foreign Direct Investment
G7	Group of Seven
G8	Group of Eight
GATT	General Agreement on Tariffs and Trade
GCC	Gulf Cooperation Council
GDP	Gross Domestic Product
GNP	Gross National Product
GSP	Generalized System of Preferences
HIPC	Heavily Indebted Poor Countries
IASB	International Accounting Standards Board
IBRD	International Bank of Reconstruction and Development
IMF	International Monetary Fund
IOS	International Organization for Standards
ITU	International Telecommunications Union
MAI	Multilateral Agreement on Investment
MERCOSUR	Mercado Común del Sur
MFN	Most Favoured Nation
MNC	Multinational Corporation
NAFTA	North American Free Trade Association
NATO	North Atlantic Treaty Organization
NGO	Non-Governmental Organization
OECD	Organization for Economic Cooperation and Development

OSCE	Organization for Security and Cooperation in Europe
PLM	Product Life-cycle Management
PRGF	Poverty Reduction and Growth Facility
PRSP	Poverty Reduction Strategy Paper
SADC	South African Development Community
SAP	Structural Adjustment Policy
TNC	Transnational Corporation
TRIMS	Trade Related Investment Measures
TRIPS	Trade Related Intellectual Property Rights
UEMOA	Union Économique et Monétaire Ouest-Africaine
UN	United Nations
UNDP	United Nations Development Programme
WTO	World Trade Organization

1 Introduction

> The world is becoming one at last is it not? Pleasant thought, or is it? Ah well, soon it will be a *fait accompli* and no concern of ours.[1]

The last two decades have witnessed an explosive proliferation of academic writings on the subject of globalization. Unusually, this has been accompanied by a high level of interest in the media to the extent that, in almost no time at all, globalization has become an accepted term in a vast number of languages throughout the world. As Jan Aart Scholte has pointed out, the term first appeared in a dictionary in 1961 and the terms 'globalize' and 'globalism' were coined in the forties.[2] Yet, in but a blink of an eye, the term has come into such common usage that it is difficult to imagine that just two decades ago most regarded it as a neologism. However, such widespread usage has inevitably resulted in the meaning of the concept broadening to include a whole host of issues, running the attendant risk of losing any conceptual focus it had.

It is no coincidence that the upsurge of interest in globalization in the nineties occurred simultaneously with the end of the Cold War and the full development and implementation of the Internet. In the 'heartwarming afterglow of the breaching of the Berlin Wall' it looked as if, in ideological terms at least, the world would finally be unified.[3] The simplicity of the Internet and its high utility meant that its spread occurred at such a breakneck speed that the world became electronically connected seemingly overnight. With the advent of the Internet and fibre optics, information not only about things but other parts of the world could be transferred, literally at the speed of light, giving us knowledge of remote places and events that are occurring elsewhere as they unfold – 'we can acquire a sense of the world without moving very far at all. We can travel vicariously through the "electronic highways" which now encircle the globe, and through them garner a level of knowledge about the rest of the world which would surpass that of even the most seasoned nineteenth-century traveller'.[4] Under such conditions, talk of the world finally becoming a 'global village', a new imagined community going beyond the nation-state's borders – to paraphrase Benedict Andersen – a village in which people rarely meet each other face to face but know each other through remote contact, was therefore understandable.[5]

However, the broad application of globalization to a host of modern phenomena has given further grist to the mill of those sceptics that question whether globalization is happening and of those that argue that if it is happening, then it is not something of recent origin but has been occurring for a very long time. True, much of the interest in the subject can be attributed to the usual *fin de siècle* desire to identify the moment as a unique watershed in human history. Certainly, many of the processes associated with globalization have been identified in earlier generations. As the quote at the beginning of this chapter indicates, the idea of a unified world had already gained currency by the fifties and by the beginning of the sixties the idea that we lived in an era of the 'global village' had been proposed by that most prescient of authors, Marshall Mcluhan.[6] At a much earlier stage, in the twenties, we can also find resonance of the much talked about rapidity of modernity. George and Ira Gershwin's *Fascinating Rhythm* (1924), originally titled *Syncopated City*, reflected the new society that was in continual motion and the impact of this hustle and bustle of city life on the individual,

> Oh, how I long to be the man I used to be!
> Fascinating rhythm,
> Oh, won't you stop picking on me?

Just as we are able to identify the terminology in earlier generations, we can identify much of the phenomena related to globalization with much earlier developments. In fact, it is the argument of this book that several of the processes associated with globalization have been around for centuries, indeed, where trade is concerned, we may speak of millennia. Today's globalization should be regarded as a particular epoch with some constitutive elements similar to previous periods and other constitutive elements that are rather different. Although many of the transformations associated with globalization can be attributed to the continuing repercussions of capitalism, there are many changes that are particular to the contemporary period, such as: the end of the Cold War; the re-emergence of neo-liberalism on the political stage; and the communications revolution. Therefore, just as continuities can be identified, so too can changes. The logic may be that of capitalism, but each historical epoch has a grammar all of its own. Such changes are grounds enough for regarding the study of globalization as an enterprise worth pursuing.

In recognizing that globalization encapsulates both changes and continuities, the following section identifies underlying and proximate causes. In addition, it identifies certain facilitating factors that have enabled globalization to occur as quickly as it has done. It is argued that, on the one hand, capitalism and technology represent the main underlying causes of globalization. American hegemony, the end of the Cold War and the emergence of neo-liberal ideology, on the other hand, all represent proximate causes. This classification could of course be challenged. If American hegemony continues for several more centuries and it continues to support the international financial institutions and free trade regime that it played a central role in founding, then there would be a strong argument in favour of describing the United States' international policies as an underlying cause. Similarly, rather than regarding the influence of neo-liberal economic policy as a fairly recent phenomenon, one could argue that 'embedded liberalism' and the Keynesian Welfare State represented a temporary hiatus; that liberal economic policies are the norm rather than the exception. Although this may be true, the manner in which these policies manifest themselves in neo-liberalism and the extent to which they are implemented across the world lend support to the argument that it should be regarded as a proximate cause.[7]

Underlying causes

Technology

One change that is most commonly associated with globalization is the revolution in technology. The impact has been so great, many now refer to the microprocessor technology that enabled these changes as the 'third revolution', thereby implying that the micro-chip will have as deep an impact on our societies as the harnessing of steam and electricity did for industrial purposes.[8] Yet the seeds of this 'third revolution' were planted in earlier decades. The replacement of vacuum tubes by the semiconductor transistor at the Bell Laboratories in 1947 paved the way for the huge advances in the miniaturization of electronic devices that we are still witnessing today. By 1965, progress in miniaturization was such that it led the co-founder of Intel, Gordon Moore, to speculate that computing capacity would double every 18 months or so (or more precisely the number of transistors and resistors that could fit on the same size silicon chip would double in density). This guesstimate has proven to be relatively accurate over time and thus what was a rough and ready rule of thumb has become known as Moore's law.[9] The late sixties witnessed a further breakthrough, as much conceptual as technological, with the invention of the microprocessor. Rather than designing several physically separate devices, the microprocessor brought them together in one integrated circuit. Although the first project using a microprocessor was started in 1968 to be used in the F-14A Tomcat, it was the mass production of such devices by Intel in 1971 that would eventually lead to the development of IBM's personal computer range first launched in August 1981.

Similarly, the Internet has its origins in the US Defense Department's desire in the sixties to establish a digital communications network that would survive a Soviet nuclear attack. By 1969 the Defense Advanced Research Projects Agency (DARPA) had created the Advanced Research Projects Agency Network (ARPANET) which would eventually evolve into the Internet. Even by the mid-eighties the use of this network was limited to a privileged few – the military, scientists, librarians, engineers, etc. However, the creation of the World Wide Web by a team at CERN in Switzerland and its eventual release in 1991 led to the easy to use, publicly available Internet that we now know.

The advent of personal computers, the Internet, electronic mail, the mobile phone, etc. have altered the way in which millions conduct their daily affairs.

Box 1.1   Underlying causes of globalization

Technology

The impact of recent technology has been so great, many now refer to the microprocessor technology that enabled these changes as the 'third revolution', thereby implying that the micro-chip will have as deep an impact on our societies as the harnessing of steam and electricity did for industrial purposes. The advent of personal computers, the Internet, electronic mail, the mobile phone, etc. have altered the way in which millions conduct their daily affairs. Our world seems to be shrinking before our very eyes as new communication technologies have led to time–space compression allowing us to span the world in the blink of an eye.

Such technology has also changed the nature of the supply chain. It has enabled manufacturers to move to flexible production techniques that allow for far greater variety and far less wasteful stockpiling of materials through the application of the 'Just in Time' philosophy. Although this idea had been applied prior to the advent of EDI and EPOS, these innovations have led to the development of ultra efficient supply chains. As a result, companies are increasingly moving away from the idea of the vertically integrated organization encompassing all of the activities relating to a product. Increasingly, companies prefer to outsource much of the production activity to external suppliers – 'organizations are now focusing on their "core business" – in other words the things they do really well and where they have a differential advantage. Everything else is "out-sourced" – in other words it is procured outside of the firm. So, for example, companies that once made their own components now only assemble the finished product'.[1]

Capitalism

Capitalism is understood here as an economic system that arose from a confluence of factors around the fifteenth and sixteenth centuries. This included the mass detachment of labour from the land which may have 'freed' many from bondage and servitude but also dispossessed them of, what was at the time, the dominant means of production, leaving them with nothing but their labour-power to sell. The means of production became privately owned thus producing a new form of economic relations with production facilities owned and controlled by the few, employing wage labourers to produce the goods to be sold. These changes also involved a move to a full market economy with goods being produced in order to be exchanged rather than for direct consumption. The new mode of production was such that producers could no longer meet their own needs from their own economic activities, thus creating a complex market based economic system through which producers were bound together by the exchange of their products among one another. But the development of a market economy also introduced competition between the various producers of similar goods leading to pressures to either innovate (producing higher quality or new variations of the product in question) thereby temporarily increasing profits or to reduce input costs of material or to reduce their labour costs. In accomplishing the latter, the owner of the means of production extracts further surplus value from workers through various means, such as, extending their hours, reducing their wages or deriving greater efficiency from the hours worked.

Our world seems to be shrinking before our very eyes as new communication technologies have led to time–space compression whereby 'space is annihilated by time'. Today, space is traversed electronically in a finite amount of time giving the appearance of simultaneity, so that, 'it is now feasible to contact a remote area regardless of distance and the time delay is negligible'.[10] This perception that we are living in an ever shrinking world has been reinforced not only by new technologies but also by increases in more traditional technologies, such as air travel which currently conveys 1.6 billion passengers per year.[11] Similar advances have occurred in the shipment of goods; for example, the first container ships held just under sixty containers whereas the latest versions can hold 9,000 and it is future projected that in the future the cargo of one ship alone will be enough 'to fill a line of trucks 68 miles long'.[12] With such large increases in capacity come vast decreases in per unit transport costs, spurring the globalization of production. As David Held *et al.* have pointed out, technology has thus facilitated the density, reach and speeding up of contemporary communications in all spheres (or as they put it, the velocity, intensity and extensity).[13]

But, similarly, there is continuity and change in this sphere. In fact, the phrase 'space is annihilated by time' was originally coined by Marx a century and a half ago.[14] As one author has pointed out, the emphasis on speed has been exaggerated – the actual increase in speed of electronic transmission between remote computers is not actually that great when one compares it to the advent of the telephone and the telegraph.[15] However, the volume of information that can be transmitted has increased exponentially. This increase in volume capacity is a result of fibre optic cable and microprocessors. Compared to the copper telephone wire that could transmit one page worth of information in a second, a single strand of fibre optic can carry '90,000 volumes in a second'.[16] Microprocessors allow for this information to be broken up into packets that are actually physically transmitted along different lines and then recompiled by the end user's computer, thereby increasing the volume of information transmitted at any given time. However, in spheres other than communication, the continual improvements in computing have led to incredible advances in processing speeds and storage capacity introducing efficiency improvements in a whole range of activities. What used to take a week to do by a roomful of computers in the fifties can now be done in a fraction of the time by a single mainframe computer. Although it is therefore important to distinguish between improvements in volume and speed in relation to communications, in other areas we are indeed witnessing a revolution in both the speed of data processing and storage capacity for that processed information.

These technological advances have not only brought about a quantitative change in our ability to monitor and analyse but also a qualitative change in the social sphere as well. It has been argued that the heightened 'speed' and frequency of long distance interactions have led to a new imagined community, the 'global village', a village in which people rarely meet each other face to face but communicate with each other through remote contact.[17] Such interactions can be of a material kind in which economic transactions are conducted to deliver goods from elsewhere but also personal communications have become faster and more frequent especially since recent advances in electronic media. The nature of this contact has also changed from a one-to-many relationship to a many-to-many relationship. A particular interest group can not only 'narrowcast' their agenda to those concerned through their web site but can also communicate between themselves and to other groups with an unparalleled ease. Once again change and continuity can be identified. Transnationalism – 'contacts, coalitions, and interactions across state boundaries that are not controlled by the central foreign policy organs of governments' – is not new.[18] However, such transnational relations now involve an unprecedented multiplicity of groups and intensity of interaction, both of which are likely to increase even further as time goes by.

There is also another new aspect to this revolution in technology. The content of information has also changed radically. It is not only possible to send and receive text and numerical data but also to transmit images, thus enabling us to obtain knowledge of remote places and events as they unfold – '[W]e can acquire a sense of the world without moving very far at all. We can travel vicariously through the "electronic highways" which now encircle the globe, and through them garner a level of knowledge about the rest of the world which would surpass that of even the most seasoned nineteenth-century traveller'.[19] Once again, this is not as unusual as it first appears. Television broadcasting and, before that, cinema newsreels provided us with similar indirect experiences. However, the sheer volume and specific nature of Internet-based information, the shift from broadcasting to narrowcasting, enables the user to gain a particular and detailed knowledge of almost anything or anywhere. Certainly, the ability actually to carry out complex tasks remotely using a combination of state of the art communications and robotics as demonstrated by the case of transatlantic surgery is unprecedented.[20]

In manufacturing and retail, advances in technology were expected to change the face of business forever. Such enthusiasm led the founder of Intel to declare that '[I]n five years' time all companies will be internet companies, or they won't be companies at all'.[21] Indeed, many companies, whose products are ideally suited to this new environment, have changed the manner in which they conduct business because of the Internet. However, although the Internet has proved to be a cheap and effective way of selling products, consumer habits have ensured that rumours of the demise of the high street shop have been greatly exaggerated. Indeed, the most successful marketing strategies have been those combining the Internet with retail stores ('bricks and clicks'). Such strategies have tended to appeal to a wider audience than those based solely on the Internet not only because it provides two different consumer environments but also because it increases consumer confidence simply by providing a physical location for customers to go to if they have a difficulty that needs addressing. But whichever method companies have opted for ('bricks and clicks' or just 'clicks'), the Internet has proved to be an excellent and cost-effective method of advertising, selling or simply providing information on their products.

Electronic media have had an equally strong impact upon manufacturing with the invention and implementation of Electronic Data Interchange (EDI) and Electronic Point of Sale (EPOS) data. The former involves the 'electronic movement of standard business documents such as purchase orders, bills and confirmations between businesses'.[22] The latter stores sales data at the point of sale (the till) and transfers this data to the head office on a daily basis thereby providing immediate sales figures that can be used to ascertain levels of stock both in the shop and at the warehouse. This allows a retail store's stocks to be replenished using daily deliveries, thereby freeing up much needed shop space for its intended purpose – selling.

Such technology has also changed the nature of the supply chain. It has enabled manufacturers to move away from so called Fordist production techniques that rely heavily upon the standardization and mass production of parts and commodities (i.e. you can have any model car that you want – as long as it's black and a Model-T). This form of production is being increasingly replaced by flexible production techniques that allow for far greater variety and far less wasteful stockpiling of materials through the application of the 'Just in Time' philosophy. Originating in Japan, 'Just in Time' (*kanbanhoushiki*) is based on the idea that 'no products should be made, no components ordered, until there is a downstream requirement'.[23] Although this idea had been applied prior to the advent of EDI and EPOS, these innovations have led to the development of ultra-efficient supply chains. For example, Benetton, the Italian clothes manufacturer/distributor, employs an innovative dyeing process that enables the factory to dye small batches of garments (rather than the large-scale processes previously used). This, combined with daily electronic sales data, EDI and the use of airfreight has resulted in a factory-to-store delivery time of just eight days regardless of the distance involved.[24]

In addition to the changes in actual production techniques outlined above, companies are increasingly moving away from the idea of the vertically integrated organisation encompassing all of the activities relating to a product. Increasingly, companies prefer to outsource much of the production activity to external suppliers – 'organizations are now focusing on their "core business" – in other words the things they do really well and where they have a differential advantage. Everything else is "out-sourced" – in other words it is procured outside of the firm. So, for example, companies that once made their own components now only assemble the finished product'.[25]

This is primarily because the labour intensive aspects of production at the bottom end of the supply chain have lower yields of value added compared to those activities at the top end of the supply chain such as sales, marketing and customer service – 'bulk or volume production which is concentrated at the lower end of the chain yields lower value-added than specialised, high-tech products which are concentrated at the higher end of the value chain'.[26] Although this is the main reason for the increasing degree of out-sourcing witnessed today, it has been greatly facilitated by both EDI and EPOS. The use of EPOS and the standardization of orders, bills, confirmations, etc. through electronic transfers between the 'brand' company and its suppliers ensures that information flows freely and quickly between the firms involved with a smaller probability of error whilst generating what appears to be a seamless environment similar to that of a vertically integrated company.

For some, the ever-increasing application of such technology has given rise to 'a truly global economy, an economy with the capacity to work as a unit in real time on a planetary scale'.[27] Although many would agree with this, Castells' additional claim that we are now living in an informational society, which is a new stage of development beyond industrialism, remains controversial. Although there are many definitions of industrialism, Giddens has produced a general description of it as 'the use of inanimate sources of material power in either production or in processes affecting the circulation of commodities' combined with the 'mechanization of production and other economic process' such that 'there are routinized processes creating a "flow" of produced goods'.[28] Earlier, it was pointed out that the innovations in micro-electronics and information technology has had such a deep impact that it is frequently referred to as the 'third revolution' of industrialization. The use of such a term implies that just as steam and electricity had a revolutionary effect upon our productive capacities, the relatively recent innovations in technology have had a similar impact. Few would disagree with such an assertion, however, Castells' argument is far more radical, that these innovations have led to a new form of development, a stage beyond industrialism in which 'the source of productivity lies in the technology of knowledge generation, information processing, and symbol communication. To be sure, knowledge and information are critical elements in all modes of development…However, what is specific to the informational mode of development is the action of knowledge upon knowledge itself as the main source of productivity'.[29]

Castells thus makes a distinction between economies that are information based and an informational economy in which 'the cultural-institutional attributes of the whole social system must be included in the diffusion and implementation of the new technological paradigm, as the industrial economy was not merely based on the use of new sources of energy for manufacturing but on the emergence of an industrial culture, characterized by a new social and technical division of labour'.[30] This is a controversial claim, and for many the fundamentals of industrialism remain unchanged by these technological innovations. True, the application of information processing to improve further information networks and data processing is becoming increasingly important in order to enhance their efficiency. But, the objective of such improvements continues to be increased productivity or more efficient services as an integral part of industrialism.

Capitalism

Technological advancement has certainly facilitated the increased interconnectedness of the world and to a growing 'consciousness of the world as a single place', but these changes have not taken place in an economic and political vacuum.[31] In terms of economics the dominant mode of production is capitalism and in its current form it is one based upon a liberal free trade order. Contemporary political space may be constituted by a plethora of nation-states but the political and economic spheres are not congruent. Economic activity by citizens of one state are not normally confined to that state's borders, but instead can freely engage in investment, speculation and trade across borders in their pursuit of profit. This is re-enforced by the relatively free flow of information and temporary movement of people (for business and tourism purposes) between the majority of states in the world. Technological advances do not in themselves create the world we now live in, their application depends upon the political and economic space in which we reside. History is littered with examples of technological advances that were not applied to their full potential because of the different circumstances under which they were created. One of the best examples of this is the curtailment of the voyages to Africa, India and the Middle East by the Chinese explorer, *Zheng He*. Despite having superior ships to those of European explorers and setting sail 87 years before Columbus in 1405 A.D., the Chinese Emperor saw little benefit to these costly travels to far off lands from which nothing could be learnt (as was the common belief at the time).

Although capitalism and industrialism are closely tied to one another and together create a dynamic impetus for social and economic change, initially it is best to consider them separately. The first key element of industrialism is the 'use of inanimate sources of material power in either production or in processes affecting the circulation of commodities'. The second aspect is that this production process utilizes various inanimate sources of energy to enable machines to accomplish certain tasks regularly. Industrialism thus entails mechanized processes of production using inanimate sources of power to create goods on a mass scale 'in a centralized work-place'.[32]

The term capitalism, however, remains essentially contested. It is understood here as an economic system that arose from a confluence of factors around the fifteenth and sixteenth centuries. These factors included the mass detachment of labour from the land which may have 'freed' many from bondage and servitude but also dispossessed them of, what was at the time, the dominant means of production, leaving them with nothing but their labour-power to sell. The means of production became privately owned, thus producing a new form of economic relations with production facilities owned and controlled by the few, employing wage labourers to produce the goods to be sold. These changes also involved a move to a full market economy with goods being produced in order to be exchanged rather than for direct consumption. The new mode of production was such that producers could no longer meet their own needs from their own economic activities, thus creating a complex market-based economic system through which producers were bound together by the exchange of their products among one another. But the development of a market economy also introduced competition between the various producers of similar goods leading to pressures to either innovate (producing higher quality or new variations of the product in question) thereby temporarily increasing profits or to reduce input costs of material or to reduce their labour costs. In accomplishing the latter, the owner of the means of production extracts further surplus value from workers through various means, such as, extending their hours, reducing their wages or deriving greater efficiency from the hours worked.

It is therefore important to distinguish this new mode of production from simple trading activity which has occurred throughout the millennia. The advent of this particular economic system brought with it a huge rupture in social, economic and political relations creating wage labour, the ownership of the means of production in the hands of a few and competitive market relations requiring continual innovation and reductions in cost. One of the central consequences of capitalism has been the movement of economics to the centre stage of human affairs, at the expense of most other social relations. This 'Great Transformation' had the effect of turning traditional practices of communities on their head because capitalism entailed 'the control of the economic system by the market' and this has an 'overwhelming consequence to the whole organization of society: it means no less than the running of society as an adjunct to the market. Instead of economy being embedded in social relations, social relations are embedded in the economic system'.[33]

Such an economic system provides one of the central dynamics behind the process of globalization. Several consequences arise from the development of a competitive market economy. First, accumulation of capital becomes the central pursuit of those owning the means of production. Although of course some profits are siphoned off for consumption, the nature of the economic system means that much of the profit has to be re-invested either in research and development (to produce product improvements or new innovatory products) or in the production facilities in order to increase the quality and quantity of current products. If not, companies would continue to lose portions of market share to their competitors – 'the development of capitalist production makes it constantly necessary to keep increasing the amount of capital laid out in a given industrial undertaking, and competition makes the immanent laws of capitalist production to be felt by each capitalist, as external coercive laws'.[34] Second, as was indicated earlier, market competition is said to produce pressures on companies to reduce costs, including labour costs. If possible, production plants, *ceteris paribus*, are relocated to sites where labour is low and the requisite skills are available. Indeed, evidence for such a tendency is readily available in the daily broadsheets, for example, British

Telecom recently (2006) announced that over two thousand call centre jobs will be moved to Bangalore where wages are less than a seventh of the British equivalent; and, in 2002, the vacuum cleaner company, Dyson, announced it was moving to Malaysia, closing up shop and shedding 800 jobs in the process – a year later the same company announced that it had doubled its profits as a result of its decision.[35] Competition also means that capitalists will endeavour to reduce the costs of transporting both component parts to the assembly plant and the cost of getting the finished product to the point of sale. In addition, it is imperative that circulation time (time between a commodity being produced and being sold to the user) be reduced as much as is feasibly possible. There is therefore a strong incentive to invest in new forms of transport that will enable a speeding up of this process, although, of course, the benefits of shortening circulation time will be considered in the context of the additional costs that might be incurred.

The difficulty for any company is that they all too quickly become victims of their own success and sooner or later are confronted with the prospect of market saturation. Several options are then available including, as we have already seen, further innovations. Another, is to create 'new social wants and needs, developing entirely new product-lines'. Viewed from this perspective, it is no coincidence that ever greater portions of companies' budgets are today taken up by advertising. Finally, companies have the option of expanding their markets overseas. It is this expansionary dynamic combined with the imperative to reduce circulation time, that led Marx to make the oft-cited observation that '[W]hile capital must on one side strive to tear down every spatial barrier to intercourse, i.e., to exchange, and conquer the whole earth for its market, it strives on the other side to annihilate this space with time'.[36] Moreover, where markets do not exist, it is said that capitalism has to create them, where 'money is not the community, it must dissolve the community...[to] draw new continents into the metabolism of circulation'.[37]

Capitalism, with its imperative to reduce labour and circulation costs, to cut circulation time and to expand into markets farther and farther afield thus forms one of the key dynamics of globalization. Capitalism remains, as yet, an unspent force continually changing the world we live in. As such, many of the changes associated with globalization have their roots in this 'Great Transformation'. However, identifying capitalism as one of the major forces of change does not mean that it is the only source. Nor does it imply that this process is linear and uninterrupted in nature. In any given period, capitalism operates within a context particular to that time, within a specific political space and at a particular technological level.

Proximate causes

American hegemony

The end of the Cold War has given rise to much talk of the unique international environment that states now find themselves occupying. The demise of the only other superpower has created a rather unusual 'unipolar moment' in which the

Box 1.2   Proximate causes

American hegemony

After the Second World War, the United States established a unique set of multilateral institutions that continue to this day. If anything, they have become more influential as time passes. This is because the nature of the free trade regime that the United States created had the potential to create a global economy, albeit one controlled and monitored by the hegemon. Liberal free trade regimes were nothing new; however, the form that the regime took under the aegis of the United States was rather unusual, based upon a series of multilateral institutions. The universalism inherent within its foundational code that policies should be based on generalized principles of conduct has had a profound impact upon the development of the global system spinning an economic web that 'attracts others' and 'makes it hard for them to leave' and thereby promoting ever greater economic integration.[1]

The end of the Cold War

The events of 1991 transformed the political, economic and military landscape that had remained relatively unchanged since the Second World War. The August coup of that year not only triggered off a series of events leading to the dissolution of the Soviet Union but also signalled a conclusive end to the Cold War and the collapse of the bipolar structure, which at one time seemed like a permanent fixture of the post 1945 international environment.

Neo-liberalism

Although the post-Second World War multilateral institutions promoted 'an internationalist, market-orientated order', at the time, they allowed for 'mechanisms, safeguards and escape clauses through which states would not be forced to sacrifice domestic social policies in order to maintain international equillibria'.[2] However, the final decades of the last century witnessed a fundamental change in the principles under which the international monetary and trade regimes mentioned above operated. Embedded liberalism was replaced by what Robert Cox has called 'the internationalizing of the state' whereby '*national* policies and practices have been adjusted to the exigencies of the world economy of international production'.[3] In other words, the previous policies that had been pursued for over three decades, i.e. state intervention in the economy, the mixture of public and private enterprises, and the welfare state were shunned in favour of the purported self-regulating mechanism of the free market, 'an economy directed by market prices and nothing but market prices'.[4]

1   W. R. Mead, *Power, Terror, Peace, and War: America's Grand Strategy in a World at Risk*, New York: Alfred A. Knopf, 2004, pp. 23–5. See also J. Nye, 'Soft Power', *Foreign Policy*, vol. 80, Fall 1990, pp. 153–71.

2 J. Kirsher, 'Keynes, capital mobility and the crisis of embedded liberalism', *Review of International Political Economy,* vol. 6:3, 1999, pp. 317–22. John Ruggie popularized the term in his 'International regimes, transaction, and change: embedded liberalism in the postwar economic order', *International Organization,* vol. 36:2, 1982.
3 R.W. Cox, *Production, Power and World Order: Social Forces in the Making of History,* New York: Columbia University Press, 1987, pp. 253–65.
4 K. Polanyi, *The Great Transformation,* p. 43.

United States, in terms of economic and military power, stands head and shoulders above any other state and is likely to do so for the foreseeable future.[38] Hence the current preoccupation with the new American century by pundits and think tanks alike; and the growing concern felt by secondary powers such as China and Russia over the United States' dominance in the international sphere. With a population of just 300 million, yet an annual GDP currently registering over $12 trillion combined with a military capability that can achieve full spectrum dominance against any competitor, it may be more accurate to follow the former French Foreign Minister Hubert Védrine and describe it as a *hyperpuissance*. Whether it wants to or not, America has a major influence on the world economy to the extent that, '[A]cross the whole spectrum of commercial, social, financial and monetary policy, it is ultimately Washington's politicians and their advisers who set the rules for global integration, even if they are often not themselves aware of it'.[39] The current shape and the future evolution of globalization therefore very much depend upon the type of economic policies adopted by the one remaining superpower.

Although to describe the second superpower as Upper Volta with missiles is both inaccurate and misleading; in truth the Soviet Union was always the poorer cousin. This was so even before *zastoi* under Brezhnev and the economic decline that accompanied his leadership. Indeed, today's talk of *hyperpuissance* looks more like a case of *déjà vu* – after the Second World War the United States already bestrode 'the world like a colossus; neither Rome at the height of its power nor Great Britain in the period of its economic supremacy enjoyed an influence so direct, so profound, or so pervasive'.[40] With greater economic and military capabilities, the United States set out to contain Communist influence and establish as wide a sphere of influence across the world as was feasibly possible.

In 1944 at Bretton Woods, New Hampshire, the United States and its allies established the International Bank of Reconstruction and Development (IBRD – a core element of today's World Bank) and the International Monetary Fund (IMF). A little later in 1947 following a failed attempt at creating an International Trade Organization (ITO), the General Agreement on Tariffs and Trade (GATT) came into being. Although not a formal organization, successive trade rounds were convened and major tariff reductions mainly amongst the OECD countries agreed upon. GATT eventually evolved into the WTO in 1995. By underpinning these agreements and international institutions, the United States established a unique set of multilateral institutions that continue to this day. If anything, they have become more influential as time passes. This is because the nature of the free trade regime that the United States established had the potential to create a global economy, albeit one controlled and monitored by the hegemon. Liberal free trade regimes were nothing new; however the form that it took under the aegis of the United States was rather unique, based upon a series of multilateral institutions.

Whereas international/regional organizations prior to the Second World War had tended to be more bilateral than multilateral in nature, after the war, the US set about establishing monetary, trade and security regimes based on multilateralism. Prior to this, such regimes were based more on a conglomeration of bilateral agreements rather than on multilateralism, which differs from the former in that 'it coordinates behavior among three or more states on the basis of generalized principles of conduct'.[41] For example, the most-favored-nation rule under which GATT operated meant that once an agreement to reduce tariffs on imports is made between two states it must apply to all states. Similarly, the North Atlantic Treaty Organization (NATO), although regional in nature, is based on the collective security principle of 'one for all and all for one', i.e. that if any member state is attacked it is seen as an attack on all. This, it is argued, was quite intentional. After two World Wars in the first half of the twentieth century, the United States realized it 'could not be just another great power playing the old games of dominance with rivals and allies. Such competition led to war, and war between great powers was no longer an acceptable part of the international system. The Americans were replacing Great Britain at a moment when the rules of the game were changing for ever. The United States was going to have to attempt something that no other nation had ever accomplished ... to build a system that could at least potentially put an end to thousands of years of great power conflicts'. The result was the creation of a multilateral trade order that brought great benefits to its allies, spinning an economic web that 'attracts others' and 'makes it hard for them to leave' and thereby promoting ever greater economic integration.[42]

Several reasons have been put forward to explain why the United States sought to replace the empires of old by a very open multilateral world order: the bipolar world placed a premium on intra-systemic accord and integration; American ideology; and that it reflected the economic form (i.e. transnationalism) that best suited its interests.[43] But, whatever the reasons for the United States' promotion of multilateralism, the universalism inherent within its foundational code that policies should be based on generalized principles of conduct has had a profound impact upon the development of the global system, 'the cold war's ultimate effect had been one of integration, not world disintegration, and although it created deep fissures between East and West, this served the purpose of integration within the West, stimulated an attempted incorporation of the Third World into the First, and may potentially contribute to a single global system in the cold war's aftermath'.[44]

It may be argued that American influence is finally on the wane. Certainly, if one were to use the annual balance of payments deficit in goods and services (totalling approximately $700 billion in 2005) solely as evidence, then one might conclude that this were the case. However, there are several reasons for caution when using such figures. First, it is estimated that imports from US foreign affiliates constitute approximately one-third of the current trade deficit. Second, the sales of goods produced by US foreign affiliates actually in the country concerned or through exports from that country are not registered as exports for the US. Yet, these sales are of the magnitude of '$2,900bn, roughly three times the value of US exports'.[45] The decline of US hegemony may therefore be greatly exaggerated and its influence on the future course of globalization may remain substantial.

The end of the Cold War

It is easy to forget just how dramatic the events of 1991 were and the way in which they transformed the political, economic and military landscape that had remained relatively unchanged since the Second World War. The August coup of that year not only triggered a series of events leading to the dissolution of the Soviet Union but also signalled a conclusive end to the Cold War and the collapse of the bipolar structure, which at one time seemed like a permanent fixture of the post-1945 international environment. The Cold War between the United States and Europe, on the one hand, and the Soviet Union and the Eastern bloc on the other, was never quite as immutable as it appeared. As Fred Halliday has pointed out, it is more accurate to depict the Cold War in terms of several phases during which the tension between the two sides oscillated in intensity.[46] But, whilst political relations at times may have improved, the military threat, even towards the end, was so great that it was difficult to comprehend. The nuclear arsenal of the US amounted to over 30,000 warheads and the Soviet Union's was approximately 40,000. It is highly likely that if this adversarial confrontation that lasted almost half a century had erupted into war, it would have led to the mutual annihilation of each side or even perhaps the end of life on this planet.

Although the Cold War divided the world into two blocs competing on the military, economic and ideological level, analysts have also identified certain aspects within the western sphere of influence that contributed to the processes of globalization. The United States, using the fact that it now possessed the strongest economy in the world, carefully set about establishing a new liberal free trade regime. This free trade regime encouraged the development of a world economy, yet, paradoxically, the United States also encouraged further political fragmentation of the world by advocating the dissolution of former empires. According to one author on the subject, this dismantling of former empires represented 'the most important single change in world politics in recent centuries. The dominant nation-state-empires of the nineteenth and early twentieth centuries were overthrown. With them went the core of the interstate system – which lay in interimperial relations rather than in Westphalian ideas of sovereignty – and the classic meaning of the nation-state'.[47]

The disappearance of outright confrontation and the scaling down of conventional and nuclear forces is but one aspect of the changes since 1991. But it is possible to identify both change and continuation. The end of the Cold War and the dissolution of the Soviet Union have led to a remarkable reduction in military tension and the disappearance of ideological competition. But there is also continuation – the multilateral regime that used to be based solely in the western bloc has now spread eastwards across the Eurasian continent. The northern hemisphere has since that time experienced a rapid consolidation and expansion of the multilateral regimes set up at the end of the Second World War. The Conference on Security and Cooperation in Europe that had managed the scaling down of conventional forces in Europe has evolved into the Organization of Security and Cooperation in Europe with 30 members and 50 participating states. Stretching from Vancouver to Vladivostok its remit now includes, amongst other things, confidence and security building measures, preventative diplomacy, and the monitoring of human rights and elections. Since the end of the Cold War, NATO has also expanded its membership from 16 to 26 to include Eastern Europe and it is likely new rounds of negotiations will lead to further expansion to include a few of the twenty-three countries that now cooperate under NATO's Partnership for Peace Program.

However, it should be noted that although multilateralism is based on the principle of equal treatment for all states this does not necessarily lead to equality in outcomes. Indeed, treating unequal entities equally can lead to great disparities. This has often been the case for less developed states that have struggled to compete on a level playing field with developed states because they lack the economic wherewithal. This also appears to be the case for many of the states of the former Soviet Union. As will be discussed below, the IMF, World Bank and the European Bank of Reconstruction and Development have been instrumental in shaping the form of development that these eastern states have taken through the provision of loans and the promulgation of the neo-liberal economic model. However, the first decade of the envisaged brave new world has failed to live up to expectations. It is only the former Eastern bloc countries (Poland, Hungary, Slovakia and the Czech Republic) that are now fully recovering from the decade-long economic transition.[48] If 1989 is taken as the benchmark, the rest of the region is still suffering from the effects of the Soviet Union's disintegration. Many countries, such as Russia, the Baltic States, Kazakhstan and Kyrgyzstan, are operating, in real terms, at approximately two-thirds of their GDP levels in 1989. Others are faring much worse; for example, Moldova and Georgia are operating at just over a third of 1989 GDP levels.[49]

This has resulted in startling increases of poverty within the region. Even if we only concern ourselves with those states that have experienced a reduction in output of 30 per cent the deterioration is difficult to comprehend. Taking a poverty line of $120 PPP per capita per month at 1990 prices and comparing the percentage of the population in poverty in 1987–8 with 1998 we find that: for Russia the percentage in poverty has risen to over half the population compared to a quarter in 1992; for Kazakhstan, the percentage in poverty has increased from 5 per cent to 50 per cent (1996); in Kyrgyzstan, from 12 per cent to 84 per cent.[50] In terms of inequality, we find that: in Russia (1998) the richest 10 per cent had a 38 per cent share of consumption whilst the poorest decile had 1.7 per cent; in Kazakhstan

(1996) the richest 10 per cent had a 26.3 per cent share of consumption compared to 2.7 per cent for the poorest 10 per cent; in Kyrgyzstan (1997) the richest 10 per cent received 31.7 per cent of national income and the poorest decile received 2.7 per cent of the national income.[51] It would appear that although the world has undergone incredible changes since 1991, it has become more uniform in terms of inequality and poverty with the majority of countries from the former Soviet Union experiencing massive increases in both these aspects.

The emergence of neo-liberalism

Although Polyani's description of unfettered capitalism, outlined earlier, is an accurate one, it has often been tempered and harnessed by the state to ameliorate attendant social strains. The political space within which capitalism operated after the Second World War was founded on a triad of cornerstones: the welfare state; nationalization of key industries; and the Bretton Woods system. The post-war Welfare State had, amongst other things, sought to: redistribute via taxation a certain degree of surplus accumulation in order to ensure basic levels of provision for the vulnerable in society; set acceptable levels of minimum wages; and provide a wide range of social services to the population. State subsidies for nationalized industries and Keynesian demand management via state expenditure ameliorated the worst effects of economic downturns. At the international level, the Bretton Woods system, agreed upon in 1944, was established to ensure international economic stability and promote a liberal trading regime. The International Monetary Fund would provide short-term credit to states suffering from a balance of payments deficit. The International Bank of Reconstruction and Development, on the other hand, provided long-term loans for major infrastructural projects. This system was further strengthened after the General Agreement on Tariffs and Trade was established in 1947 to manage trade and reduce tariffs between countries.

A combination of international monetary and trade regimes, the welfare state, a mixed economy of public and private ownership plus Keynesian demand management thus served to control and ameliorate the worst excesses of capitalism. In contrast to Polyani's description of disembedded liberalism, i.e. 'unfiltered international market forces' unfettered by political and societal constraints, this post-Second World War arrangement has been described as 'embedded liberalism' in which 'postwar institutions would support an internationalist, market-orientated order, but would allow for mechanisms, safeguards and escape clauses through which states would not be forced to sacrifice domestic social policies in order to maintain international equillibria'.[52]

However, the final decades of the last century witnessed a fundamental change in the principles under which the international monetary and trade regimes mentioned above operated. Embedded liberalism was replaced by what Robert Cox has called 'the internationalizing of the state' whereby '*national* policies and practices have been adjusted to the exigencies of the world economy of international production'.[53] In other words, the previous policies that had been pursued for over three decades, i.e. state intervention in the economy, the mixture of public and private enterprises, and the welfare state were shunned in favour of the purported self-regulating mechanism of the free market, 'an economy directed by market prices and nothing but market prices'.[54] But in reality 'capital has outgrown its own need for national regulation and developed a productive capacity befitting world markets – the corporate sector has faced increasingly limited avenues for further accumulation ... No longer for the most part national in character, capital is able to move to wherever the advantages are greatest'.[55]

Economic downturns, according to neo-liberalism, would be naturally overcome by the market through the self-adjustment of prices to reflect the laws of supply and demand. In this regard, employment would be treated no differently to any other commodity. Historically, under Keynesian economic management, stimulating economic growth via, amongst other things, increased government expenditure, reduced unemployment created by an economic downturn. However, neo-liberalism argued that unemployment would naturally decline once wages had decreased to reflect the new levels of supply and demand. In addition, state-owned enterprises were viewed as economically inefficient and therefore privatized by floating them on the stock exchange. This not only increased government revenues but also conformed to neo-liberal arguments promoting the idea of minimal state intervention.

This neo-liberal orthodoxy has become known as the 'Washington consensus', such is the uniformity of opinion and aggressive promotion of neo-liberal economic policies not only by the US government but also by the 'International Monetary Fund, World Bank, think tanks, politically sophisticated investment bankers, and world finance ministers – all those who meet each other in Washington and collectively define the conventional wisdom of the moment'.[56] This consensus developed in the eighties and was promoted most vigorously by the Reagan Administration in the United States, the Thatcher Government in Britain and the Labour Government in New Zealand; they argued for a minimal state, lower taxes and the promotion of free market principles entailing 'privatization of public services and public assets, liberalization of trade, finance and production, deregulation of labour and environmental laws and the destruction of state activism generally in the public realm'.[57]

Two points are worth mentioning at this stage. Although this reassertion of liberal principles represented a change from the principles of Keynesian economic management, one can also argue that in some ways they are a continuation of pre-war policies of disembedded liberalism. It may be that we are currently witnessing a continuation of the great transformations generated by capitalism and that 'embedded liberalism' was but a hiatus brought about as a result of four main factors: the pre-war collapse of liberal world economic order; the human sacrifice during the Second World War and the ensuing change in attitude amongst the population; the success of the war economy; and the Cold War economic and social competition with the Soviet Union. In other words, the rebirth of unadulterated liberalism based on free trade and free markets may represent long term continuation rather than contemporary change. However, the manner in which these policies manifest themselves in neo-liberalism and the extent to which they are implemented across the world lend support to the argument that it should be regarded as a proximate cause.

Second, when implemented, these neo-liberal policies have met with varying degrees of success in the industrialized countries. In terms of welfare spending, it is unclear whether efforts at reducing budgets in this area have actually resulted in real decreases in expenditure. In the case of Britain, public social expenditure as a percentage of GDP increased from about 18 per cent in 1980 to 24.7 per cent in 1998. At the same time, it appears that 'levels of tax for most families were higher at the end of the Thatcherite period than they had been at its start'.[58] With the election of a Labour government in 1997 and especially so after their re-election in 2001 social expenditure has increased markedly.[59] In the case of the United States, the level of social expenditure has been relatively stable during the same period, increasing marginally by just over one percentage point. The rest of Europe has been more wary of adopting the neo-liberal model wholesale, but has in general agreed to the liberalization of trade, finance and production. It is argued by globalists that such global liberalization should, through the pressures of economic competitiveness, bring about a degree of convergence in taxation and expenditure levels of states at similar levels of development. However, in 2000, the actual individual expenditures of countries varied considerably; for example, Japan's expenditure as a percentage of GDP was 31.9 compared to Sweden's 52.5.[60] Indeed, if we look at the long term trend, government expenditure as a percentage of GDP has increased in the industrialized countries by almost 20 per cent in just 35 years.[61]

In addition, the move towards a minimal state has had a rather paradoxical outcome. True, in the economic realm the state has reduced its commitments through privatization of state enterprises, private finance initiatives for major infrastructural projects and the general disavowal of responsibility for economic affairs. But state power in other areas has tended to increase in those countries that have implemented neo-liberalism. This is no simple coincidence. Polyani, for example, argued that the state was instrumental in developing the so-called free market and that historically 'political interventions' have been 'constitutive of, rather than external to, the market economy'.[62] Those states that sought to introduce neo-liberalism had to overcome those who sought to challenge the implementation of such policies and to do so they had to increase the power of the state, whether this be through increased centralization, the introduction of employment and anti-union legislation to enforce labour deregulation, stronger police forces to monitor and control the disaffected or a combination of these and other actions:

> In the normal course of things markets become embedded in social life. They are circumscribed in their workings by intermediary institutions and encumbered by social conventions and tacit understandings. Among these intermediary institutions, trade unions and professional associations have long been central in standing between individuals and market forces. Constructing a free market demands that these social institutions be weakened or be

destroyed ... Only a strong centralized state can wage war on such powerful intermediary institutions.[63]

Even for those industrialized countries that have promoted neo-liberalism most vigorously, the degree of success in attaining the desired outcome has therefore been rather varied. The industrialized states have found it more difficult than expected to reduce their expenditure and taxation rates, but in the areas of privatization of public assets, the contracting-out of public services, the reduction of barriers to trade, finance and foreign direct investment they have been more successful. Domestically, these countries have reduced the extent of the state by privatizing previously public-owned enterprises and, internationally, they have concluded global agreements to further liberalization in the three areas mentioned above.

The effects of neo-liberalism have been most pronounced in the developing states of the South who have had little choice but to implement such policies wholesale, mainly at the behest of the IMF. It is to the developing states that we need to turn to understand the full impact of neo-liberalism upon the global economy. At the same time as the United States was restructuring its own economy internally it was promoting similar policies through the IMF and World Bank:

> The IMF is the linchpin in the implementation of the neo-liberal vision of development. Going beyond its original mandate to provide short-term balance-of payments support, it has coordinated with the World Bank since the early 1980s to reform national economies so that they better reflect the dominant vision of market-led rather than state-led development.[64]

Despite the fact that 'embedded liberalism' was never 'fully extended to the developing countries', the eighties can be said to constitute a watershed in terms of the relationship between the international financial institutions and the developing world.[65] In 1980, the World Bank agreed to lend Turkey, which had just experienced a military coup, $200 million on condition that it adopt a stringent programme of economic reform which explicitly rejected 'the social compromises which were the considered response of democratic societies to the chaos of World War II'.[66] Since then, countries seeking help with balance of payments deficits or loans for large-scale infrastructural development were subject to increasingly strict conditions upon their economic policies. The impact of neo-liberalism is therefore most pronounced in the economies of the South, primarily because they have had to adopt such policies wholesale.

This conditionality entailed a series of economic reforms, or so-called Structural Adjustment Policies (SAPs), thus ensuring the adoption of neo-liberalism by the majority of less developed states. So, unlike the industrialized countries that had adopted such policies, the South was given little choice as to whether or not to accept. Refusal of the recommended economic reforms could result in a full-blown financial crisis and as a result most leaders reluctantly implemented such policies, often without the requisite political mandate from their populations. A pertinent example of the constraints that state leaders can find placed upon them is the situation that confronted Thailand immediately after the Asian financial crisis of 1997. Many of the difficulties that faced these countries were as a result of capital flight following a loss of confidence in several of the Asian markets. This massive haemorrhaging of financial capital away from these markets was made easier by earlier recommendations of the IMF and World Bank for the lifting of restrictions on capital movements. Despite this, the IMF's conditions for a $16 billion rescue package included, amongst other things, raising value added tax to ten per cent, the speeding up of privatization, foreign ownership of Thai banks and the balancing of the budget.[67]

Although it is not possible to isolate and separate out other possible causal factors and ascertain the precise impact of neo-liberal policies in the last two decades, the correlation is highly compelling. Unfortunately, it is not only levels of inequality that have been adversely affected. Structural Adjustment Policies have targeted states' social spending in order to balance budgets with the predictable result of having a deleterious impact upon the welfare of the 4.4 billion in developing countries. This, in a population where 'almost three-fifths lack basic sanitation, one-third have no safe drinking water, one-quarter have inadequate housing, while one-fifth are undernourished and the same proportion have no access to modern health services'.[68]

In global terms, then, the neo-liberal revolution has had a far-reaching but varied impact. Yet, it is also clear that there are several aspects that appear again and again. In the last two decades there has been a rash of privatizations of formerly public owned enterprises as well as increased contracting-out of public services; for example, by 1992 'more than 80 countries around the world had privatised some 6,800 previously state-owned enterprises'.[69] In developing countries, welfare spending has been slashed in order to balance the budget, despite the fact that much of the population are already living in poverty. Inequality has increased both between states and, in most cases, within states. In addition, global unemployment and underemployment has risen. In 1994 there were an estimated 120 million unemployed world wide and 700 million underemployed. After the Asian crisis of 1997 the world witnessed a rapid increase in unemployment to an estimated 150 million and 900 million under-employed.[70] This is not because states are failing to follow IMF and World Bank neo-liberal economic prescriptions, but precisely because they are following such policies to the letter.[71]

Facilitating factors

The development of abstract systems

The globalized nature of the world, argues Anthony Giddens, has meant that, increasingly, previous relationships, which involved close encounters of a direct kind in which we meet others face to face, are being replaced by indirect contact with remote persons. As Giddens put it, 'the advent of modernity increasingly tears space away from place by fostering relations between absent others'.[72] Today, operations are no longer focused at the local level, where the objective was to serve a limited population with immediate needs. Modern production is spread over large intervals of time due to long-term industrialized planning and does not involve one local site but many spatially distant sites. Generally, modern production is no longer geared to the satisfaction of a community's immediate needs. Instead, it is designed to fulfil consumption at a distant site by an unknown user, so that, 'increasingly we produce what we do not consume, and we consume what we do not produce'.[73] At the same time, the global nature of the financial system has resulted in capital created in one area being re-invested in a multitude of facilities and enterprises situated in other, often very distant, sites. Social activities are geared towards producing items not for immediate local needs but towards producing commodities that satisfy the desires of absent others who in all likelihood one will never meet. Globalization has therefore radically altered the manner in which we conduct our lives in the sense that 'locales are thoroughly penetrated by and shaped in terms of social influences quite distant from them. What structures the locale is not simply that which is present on the scene; the

Box 1.3   Facilitating factors

Cartographic and temporal frameworks

The creation of cartographic and temporal frameworks enabled the mapping of a state's domain and the eventual uniform representation of the globe. The mapping of the world abstracted the local and represented it by its place in the world, its shape, location and size in comparison to other areas. Time became independent of any one place with the advent of clocks and watches. Western expansion across the world thus brought with it a uniform measurement of both time and space that eventually became universalized.

Symbolic tokens

The use of money as a symbolic token meant that producers using money could exchange their goods for money which could be later swapped for other necessities. Thus economic transactions no longer needed to take place in a personal face to face manner and therefore the restrictions of space became less important. At the same time, the second part of the exchange process wherein the producer receives other goods to consume for those traded is deferred until the producer wishes to gratify their needs. Money as a symbolic token has now gone a stage further as a result of electronic accounting with digitized financial transactions being substituted for the physical presence of money.

Expert systems

Expert systems include the design and construction of almost everything in the construction and production industries: houses, bridges, roads, aircraft, cars etc. They are defined as '[S]ystems of technical accomplishment or professional expertise that organise large areas of the material and social environments in which we live today'.[1] Expert systems disembed social relations by 'providing "guarantees" of expectations across distanciated time and space'.[2] Such systems are applied across the world and are accepted and implemented because they have been scientifically tested and are seen to 'generally work as they are supposed to do'.[3]

International institutions

One major branch of international institutions is concerned with establishing international standards for governments and companies to adhere to. Standard setting ranges from technical specifications ensuring product safety, communication protocols and compatibility through to establishing basic auditing and legal requirements in the field of commercial activity. The creation of such regulatory frameworks thus greatly facilitates further globalization by providing the necessary environment for the free exchange of people, information, finance and goods.

1 A. Giddens, *The Consequences of Modernity*, p. 27.
2 Ibid., p. 28.
3 Ibid., p. 29.

"visible form" of the locale conceals the distanciated relations which determine its nature.'[74]

For Anthony Giddens one of the defining aspects of globalization, then, is this disembedding of human relations, the 'lifting out of social relations from local contexts of interaction'.[75] Compared to their traditional counterparts, modern societies, it is argued, exhibit a high degree of, what he terms, 'time–space distanciation'.[76] Previously, our daily interactions were mainly confined to our local areas, and communication with others was through face to face encounters of a direct kind. Today, however, such interactions are predominantly with remote persons through indirect contact. Several developments enabled this. In the Middle Ages, time was linked to the local region because clock setting was still based on noon, i.e. when the sun was at its highest point for that area. At the same time, daytime hours often differed to nighttime hours and the length of daytime hours varied over the course of the year; for example, in thirteenth century England, 'a daytime hour in summer was more than twice as long as a daytime hour in winter'.[77] However, in the same century, Abul-Hassan al-Marrakushi of Cairo introduced the idea of twenty-four equal length hours. Although the invention of the mechanical clock occurred around 1270, it was so inaccurate that time still had to be set by noon of each day locally. It was only at the end of the eighteenth century that clocks became accurate enough to allow the creation of uniform time that no longer relied upon 'socio-spatial markers'. Similarly, the mapping of the globe and the eventual agreement (1884 in Washington) to create a uniform representation of time based on Greenwich mean time with every 15 degrees of the 360 degrees of longitude representing one hour, 'established space as "independent" of any particular place or region'.[78] Western expansion across the world brought with it this uniform measurement of both time and space that eventually became universalized.

This process of disembedding social relations from their local surroundings has also been facilitated by the introduction of abstract systems, of which there are two main variants. There are those that Giddens labels symbolic tokens defined as 'media of interchange which can be "passed around" without regard to the specific characteristics of individuals or groups that handle them'.[79] The best example of this is money, which is used as a symbolic representation of what a product is worth in comparison to other products circulating within society. Money has a deeply significant impact upon economic relations because producers are no longer hindered by the necessity of taking their goods to the market and bartering them for other goods. Producers using money exchange their goods for coinage which can be later swapped for other necessities. Thus economic transactions no longer need to take place in a personal face to face manner and therefore the restrictions of space become less important. At the same time, the second part of the exchange process wherein the producers receive other goods to consume for those traded is deferred until the producers wish to gratify their needs. Money as a symbolic token has now gone a stage further as a result of digitization with digitized financial transactions being substituted for the physical presence of money. This is nowhere more apparent than in foreign exchange services where the daily turnover has now reached over $1.8 trillion.

The second type of abstract system is what Giddens calls expert systems which are defined as '[S]ystems of technical accomplishment or professional expertise that organise large areas of the material and social environments in which we live today'.[80] This involves the design and construction of almost everything in the construction and production industries: houses, bridges, roads, aircraft, cars etc. Expert systems disembed social relations by 'providing "guarantees" of expectations across distanciated time and space'.[81] Such systems are applied across the world and are accepted and implemented because they have been scientifically tested and are seen to 'generally work as they are supposed to do'.[82]

These abstract systems have become so much part of our daily lives that they are taken for granted, yet '[E]very time someone gets cash out of the bank or makes a deposit, casually turns on a light or a tap, sends a letter or makes a call on the telephone, she or he implicitly recognises the large areas of secure, coordinated actions and events that make modern life possible'.[83] The introduction of abstract systems brought with it the possibility of developing interactions beyond the local to a global level. But these new forms of interaction require a high degree of trust.

In this sense trust is said to be 'related to absence in time and in space. There would be no need to trust anyone whose activities were continually visible and whose thought processes were transparent, or to trust any system whose workings were wholly known and understood'.[84] Such interactions therefore involve two forms of trust, trust in those you are communicating with, i.e. trust in faceless others, and trust in the abstract systems that we have developed over time.

Giddens' objective is actually far greater than one would assume from the short adumbration outlined above. In fact, Giddens claims that globalization cannot be explained by reference to the usual sociological approaches derived from, amongst others, Marx, Weber and Durkheim. Rather he argues that societies should be analysed by investigating the way in which they organize 'time–space relations'. Rosenberg argues that Giddens identifies two ways in which such relations can be organized, 'both quantitatively (meaning how far they stretch social relations across these two dimensions) and qualitatively (meaning how the variety of social systems organise time and space "so as to connect presence and absence")'.[85] As we have seen, it is argued that in pre-modern societies, time was connected to place and usually identified by natural occurrences; and place was not defined abstractedly, but in terms of the locality in which one went about one's daily life. What is unique about modernity is that time and space are separated. The mapping of the world abstracted the local and represented it by its place in the world, its shape, location and size in comparison to other areas. Time became independent of any one place with the advent of clocks and watches.

According to Giddens, this separation of time and space is 'crucial to the extreme dynamism of modernity'.[86] The above sections, however, have depicted these aspects of globalization as facilitating factors rather than as central elements. As Justin Rosenberg points out, Giddens is attempting not just to create a theory of globalization but create a globalization theory. There is an important distinction between the two. The former attempts to explain phenomena associated with globalization, such as time–space distantiation, by identifying certain causal processes that generate these phenomena, and these causal processes precede the phenomena associated with globalization and are therefore ordinal in nature. Globalization theory, on the other hand, identifies several of the phenomena commonly associated with globalization, such as the reordering of time and space, as causal processes in their own right. This book argues that the elements of modernity identified by Giddens, such as the creation of cartographic and temporal frameworks as well as symbolic tokens, are best understood as facilitating factors rather than causal processes of the first degree.

International institutions

One major branch of international institutions is concerned with establishing international standards for governments and companies to adhere to. Standard setting ranges from technical specifications ensuring product safety, communication protocols and compatibility, through to establishing basic auditing and legal requirements in the field of commercial activity. The first such body, the International Telecommunication Union, was established as early as 1865 and is concerned with, amongst other things, managing allocations of the radio spectrum to interested parties and developing international telecommunication protocols thereby ensuring a seamless global network of communications to the end-user. Similarly, the International Organization for Standardization (1947) which currently has representatives from 157 countries, promotes the recognition of international technical standards for a vast array of products ranging from film speeds to digital file storage. Other institutions ensure basic standards for travel and shipments; the Warsaw Convention (1929), for example, ensures that companies comply with basic standards concerning the issuance of air tickets and liabilities. In the financial field, the International Accounting Standards Board (previously the International Accounting Standards Committee 1973) now has members from over 100 countries, thus promoting international standardization in financial reporting. Finally, the conclusion of the Uruguay Round of trade talks resulted in the Trade Related Intellectual Property Rights Agreement, promoting the uniform protection of intellectual property amongst member states, including agreements on patents, brand names and copyrights. The creation of such regulatory frameworks thus greatly facilitates further globalization by providing the necessary environment for the free exchange of people, information, finance and goods.

However, as can be seen from the last example, the role of international institutions is not merely confined to regulatory frameworks facilitating globalization. Several are actively engaged in the promotion of neo-liberal economics encouraging states to relax their controls concerning trade, finance and investment. True, as Jan Aart Scholte points out, some of the more ambitious attempts at doing so, such as the IMF's efforts at getting its members to permit the free flow of capital across borders and the OECD's endeavour to establish a Multilateral Agreement on Investment (MAI) based on the non-discrimination of domestic and international capital, ended in failure.[87] But these organizations have promoted such liberalization either through membership criteria or, in the case of the IMF, through applying such conditions to the loans it provides. From this perspective, the growing tendency towards global governance is deeply worrying because the decision-making procedures and outcomes of these institutions, more often than not, reflect the interests of the 'leading states, particularly the United States, and such states represent other interests, notably those of global capital'.[88] Although this is not seen as something entirely new, its proponents argue that there has been a significant increase in the last few decades not only in the intensity of transnational interactions but also in the disparity of power relations. This disparity is said to traverse a complex network of relations encompassing states, class, corporations, NGOs, etc. and operate both within such categories (e.g. state to state) and across such categories (e.g. corporations to state).

Defining globalization

The last section identified the main elements that have given rise to the increasing interest in globalization. Several of these events and processes are fairly new developments. But equally, some of these are actual processes that have existed for some time but have intensified in the last few decades. Given the multifaceted nature of globalization indicated by the summary above, it is unsurprising that manifold definitions of globalization also exist. This section uses several of these definitions to demonstrate the wide-ranging diversity of opinions on the subject.

Not unexpectedly, each of these definitions more often than not reflects the approach adopted by the writer and the particular elements of globalization that they wish to emphasize. For example, one of the most prolific writers on the subject, Anthony Giddens, focuses on the sociological aspects of globalization. Much of Giddens' globalization literature shares the earlier concerns of John Burton for redrawing the cognitive map of the world. His 'cobweb model' sought to reconceptualize our understanding of the world by replacing the conventional state-centric map with an image that illustrated more appositely the complex linkages within and between a multitude of different transnational organizations and companies.[89] But in addition, Giddens seeks to bring to our attention the global ordering of socio-economic relations stemming from the globalization of productive and financial processes; in particular, the so-called distanciated nature of these interactions.

From Giddens' description of globalization it is apparent from the above that, for him, one of the defining aspects of globalization is the disembedding or, 'lifting out of social relations from local contexts of interaction'.[90] He therefore defines globalization as, 'the intensification of worldwide social relations which link distant localities in such a way that local happenings are shaped by events occurring many miles away and vice versa'.[91]

As a result of the annihilation of space we are ever more conscious of living in a global village. Others, therefore, regard globalization primarily as a subjective feeling, arguing that 'a crucial variable in such considerations is the scope and depth of consciousness of the world as a single place. When we speak of contemporary globalization we are very much concerned with matters of consciousness, partly because that notion carries reflexive connotations. Globalization does not simply refer to the objectiveness of increasing interconnectedness. It also refers to cultural and subjective matters'.[92] However, that is not to say that a consciousness of living together in one world has not come about because of the increasing interconnectedness that modernity has brought with it. Rather, this subjective feeling has its concrete foundations in the objective interactions that now surround us. Martin Shaw takes a similar line and also distinguishes between globalization, i.e. the processes involved in creating a global world, and the actual end condition of globality which is taken to 'mean not just transformed conceptions of time and space but the new social meaning that these involved. I propose that we understand this as the development of *a common consciousness of human society on a world scale*'.[93]

From an alternative perspective, the growing tendency towards global governance is deeply worrying because the decision-making procedures and outcomes of these institutions more often than not reflect the interests of the dominant powers.[94] The idea that this political space is also highly hierarchical in nature is not seen as something entirely new; for example, those previously writing on transnationalism and interdependence acknowledged that '[E]ven in domains characterized by complex interdependence, politics reflects asymmetrical economic, social, and environmental interdependence, not just among states but also among non-state actors, and through transgovernmental relations'.[95] However, it is argued that there has been a significant increase in the last few decades not only in the intensity of transnational interactions but also in the disparity of power relations. Such writers therefore define globalization as 'the processes whereby power is located in global social formations and expressed through global networks rather than through territorially based states'.[96] In a similar vein, others have endeavoured to incorporate power relations into Giddens' notion of the distanciated nature of global interactions so that globalization is said to refer 'to a process (or set of processes) which embodies a transformation in the spatial organization of social relations and transactions – assessed in terms of their extensity, intensity, velocity and impact – generating transcontinental or interregional flows and networks of activity, interaction, and the exercise of power'.[97]

This latter definition has the merit of emphasizing that globalization is a set of processes that are leading to the transformation of social relations, an intensification and/or reconfiguration of power relations without necessarily claiming that this is leading or has led to the generation of supra-territorial entities. However, any mention of these processes leading to (potentially at least) an increasing consciousness of the world as a single place is missing – an aspect that most people would associate with the processes of globalization. We need to acknowledge that the fact 'that human lives are increasingly played out in the world as a single place' is therefore changing the way we view that world.[98]

Book structure

The next chapter examines the 'great debate' between the three main schools of thought with regard to globalization: the globalists; sceptics; and transformationalists. The initial enthusiasm for the concept of globalization led to many a grand claim that proved difficult to substantiate, such as: the end of the nation-state: the decline of the Welfare State, the immanent development of supra-national institutions. Such claims can best be understood in the context of the times with the end of the Cold War and the advent of the Internet – an easily accessible telecommunications system open to all, potentially at least. The sceptics therefore provided a healthy corrective to such over-enthusiasm. Such research questioned whether the current era really represents as great a rupture with past historical epochs as we were led to believe. Indeed, there appear to be many similarities of our contemporary condition with that of the 'belle époque' before the First World War.

On the other hand, the chapter also argues that it is important to identify what really is new about the current economic system. It concludes, amongst other things, that for several of the most industrialized countries, trade levels are now at unprecedented levels. Equally significant is that, unless something completely unforeseen occurs, the tendency is for this trading activity to increase to ever greater levels. At the same time, qualitative changes in the types of trade carried out have also occurred with substantial increases in intra-industrial trade between the OECD countries. In the world of finance, we are currently witnessing unprecedented levels of daily foreign exchange turnover. The introduction of new financial instruments, such as futures, options and swaps have produced a far more complex and integrated financial world than we have hitherto known. The chapter therefore concludes that, in the last few decades, there are quantitative and qualitative changes that are worthy of study.

Chapter Three examines several competing views concerning the geographical delimitation of globalization: regionalization; triadization; and the involutionist perspective. In so doing, this chapter revisits the involutionist perspective arguing that, in relation to the developing countries' relative share of world trade and investment shares, the use of the term globalization should be questioned. Yet the chapter challenges the portrayal of these perspectives as competing conceptions and instead argues that each perspective furnishes us with a partial view of a larger process. In relation to trade, involution of the world economy is indeed the most apt description. However, in terms of FDI, stasis better describes the contemporary international economy. The chapter then turns to the trade and investment patterns within the triad, corroborating earlier findings that each leg of the triad is increasingly trading more with their neighbours than with each other, but that inter-triad FDI is indeed increasing. Three main factors are presented in order to explain the contemporary patterns of trade and investment associated with involution, regionalization and triadization: product differentiation; vertical specialization; and the continuing concentration on primary product production in much of the developing world.

Significantly, the chapter finds that South-East Asia and East Asia plus some individual countries, such as Mexico, have managed to become embedded in the supply chain for higher value-added manufactured goods in the low-, medium- and high-technology sectors, and this is reflected in their shares of world exports, supplying both intermediate and final products to the northern industrialized core. As a result, South–South trade has increased substantially and now constitutes just under half of all of the developing world's trade. However, East Asian trading activity accounts for two-thirds of this South–South trade mainly as a result of vertical specialization with countries providing intermediate products within a larger production process. Given that there has been a shift in favour of higher technology exports worldwide, it is likely that we will see a further marginalization of those countries that do not, or cannot, engage in such activity.

Chapter Four therefore considers the advantages and disadvantages of developing states adopting an export growth strategy as part of their economic policy. One of the central problems confronting developing states is the relative decline in the terms of trade for primary products. The more of these products that are traded, the more supply there is on world markets and the concomitant decline in demand leads to a fall in value relative to other goods. On the other hand, rents accrue to those businesses in the secondary and tertiary sectors that produce relatively scarce goods, thus obtaining relatively higher prices and better profits. The challenge is therefore not only to move up the business chain to the secondary and tertiary sector, but also to be able to offer goods that others cannot, either in terms of quality or novelty. In examining East Asia, some writers view state intervention as a critical element in a country's economic development. The setting of high trade tariffs, the provision of cheap loans and the granting of industrial licences (thereby limiting competition) to certain industries are all said to provide a positive environment for embryonic industries. But in the case of East Asia, this state intervention has been made conditional upon productivity gains in the sectors concerned thus stimulating continual improvements in both productivity and the quality of the final product.

The chapter considers whether the 'developmental state model' can continue to be a successful model for states to follow if ever more countries follow this path or will it lead to a downward spiralling of prices as more and more industries compete in the same product sector? At the present time (2007), as a result of the huge demand by the Chinese economy, many primary commodities are witnessing large increases in their relative prices. This, combined with the debt cancellation of several highly indebted poor countries and the promises of increased aid, provides at least some hope to the developing states. For some, the answer lies in regional trade agreements that complement the economies of each country while not exposing them to the full competition of the world market. For others the way forward is to concentrate on innovation and the higher profits associated with such ventures. Although others will soon copy these new products the objective should be to attain continual innovation thereby keeping one step ahead of the competition. The investment and trading investment environment is a harsh one, doubly so for those countries trying to take off economically. Given the current climate, developing states have limited options, one of which is to adopt highly selective investment and trading strategies whilst simultaneously endeavouring to alter the current trading regime.

Chapter Five identifies four types of state responses to the pressures of globalization: the competition state; compensatory state; catalytic state; and the virtual state. The competition state, it is argued, has actively undertaken a restructuring of its regulatory, distributive and redistributive capabilities. In terms of taxing, regulating and establishing the macroeconomic conditions for the state (regulatory), governments now concern themselves with ensuring non-inflationary growth and a business-friendly regulatory framework. [99] In terms of direct state ownership of production (i.e. control of the production and distribution of goods), governments have relinquished or are relinquishing direct ownership of production, concentrating instead on improving infrastructure. [100] As a result, state functions have been reconfigured and geared towards attracting capital. Redistributive functions do remain, but in a restricted form. Moreover, the focus of such expenditure is upon developing human capital, ensuring a healthy, well-educated, skilled workforce. The state has undertaken this restructuring in order to become pro-business in orientation, thus competing with other states for finance and investment from around the world.

In contrast to this approach, there are those that argue that states are placing ever greater emphasis upon their redistributive functions, directing their resources towards compensating those workers adversely affected by greater economic openness. Still others argue that these changes are leading the state *qua* virtual state to take advantage of global outsourcing in order to continue providing the population with high levels of social welfare at a reduced cost. In other words, by imitating the practices of multinational companies, these mimetic states are seeking to reduce their costs by assigning many of their functions to private service providers. Linda Weiss, on the other hand, emphasizes the transformative capacity of the state, concentrating upon the successful cooperative collaboration between government and business. In so doing, she turns the 'globalization and the decline of the state' debate on its head, arguing that state *qua* catalytic state has in several ways acted as the midwife of globalization.

The chapter concludes that several characteristics from these classifications can be identified when considering the industrialized states. Some have sought to help their industries stay ahead of the game by facilitating off-shore production and overseas investment. Others have sought to curtail the upward trend in state spending by parcelling out key tasks to private service providers. Most have ensured that they continue to possess high quality infrastructure and a highly skilled workforce in order to attract investment. However, current figures indicate that fears of a decline in welfare spending and the redistributive functions of the northern states are, by and large, unfounded. In contradistinction, the competition state model is most appropriate for the restructuring that states of the South are currently undertaking (with the exception of the East Asian states). The structural adjustment policies recommended by the IMF that they have implemented involved the privatization of many services and the selling off of many previously publicly owned industries. Historically, compared to the North, there has been far less regulation concerning employment of labour and this remains the case today. In addition, because much of their expenditure is dedicated to servicing their debts, they lack the economic wherewithal to provide high levels of welfare or to compensate workers for unemployment or low wages. In other words, the states of the South have experienced the greatest changes in their regulatory, distributive and redistributive capabilities.

Chapter Six considers the changing patterns of poverty and inequality of the last few decades. Although these figures indicate that there have been increases in poverty levels, for example, in Sub-Saharan Africa, Latin and Central America, the chapter argues that globalization is not the sole explanation of these changes. Other factors include education levels, highly unequal land distribution and population growth. However, the chapter concludes that, although the causes of inequality and poverty are complex, in many cases the high levels of debt of these states, structural adjustment and the worsening terms of trade have had a negative impact upon poverty levels and upon intra-state and inter-state inequality.

Chapter Seven examines the various arrangements between states at the international level, arguing that global governance is essentially Janus-faced in nature. It is argued that through collective action and the aggregation of their capabilities, northern states possess the wherewithal to monitor and control the plethora of economic activities that have blossomed at the international level in the last few decades. Indeed, there is good evidence that these states have actively promoted economic globalization, at least in some aspects, in a very similar manner to those states labelled by Linda Weiss as 'catalytic states'. Many of the industrialized states have played an astute political game of double standards. Through international or regional bodies (for example, the IMF, World Bank, OECD, etc.), they have actively promoted economic liberalization, yet blamed the very forces that they have chosen to unleash for the economic woes within their borders.

Politicians have been more than willing to sidestep their responsibilities and shift the blame onto the faceless forces of globalization thereby depoliticizing many critical (and very political) decisions concerning the economy. Thus far, the industrialized states have been able to maintain both the share of international trade and of foreign direct investment. Although many northern countries have suffered from economic dislocation, these states possess the economic wherewithal to compensate their workforces and re-orientate their economies to these challenges. By and large, opposition to liberalization has not thus far been of sufficient strength to force a reversal of such policies. Despite there being good arguments for greater control of the economic sphere and for some form of redistributive taxation (redistributed to the developing nations) to be applied to the super-profits accrued by international financial institutions, this is unlikely to happen in the near future. But if globalization were to impact significantly on the economic well-being of large sections of the population in the North, then it may well be that we witness a roll back of the economic liberalization that we have witnessed in the last few decades and for a far greater level of control to be imposed on such activities. Concerning the industrialized states, more governance may be better, but is unlikely in the near future

In contrast, the chapter concludes that, in regard to the developing states of the South, the main international financial institutions need to address the issues of representational justice, procedural justice and the outcomes of the policies currently pursued (output legitimacy). Currently, there are moves to increase the voting power of several developing states in both the IMF and World Bank, but thus far the reforms have been inadequate. Although the constitutional basis of the WTO is such that all states are represented, reforms are required to ensure greater procedural justice. Full and free access to impact assessment information concerning proposed trade agreements to all member-states should be made compulsory. In addition, the transaction costs involved in bringing a case to the Dispute Settlement Body are clearly unaffordable for most of the developing states. The creation of a legal advice council providing public legal assistance with the running costs paid by all members on an ability to pay basis would go a long way in the right direction.[101] In the long term, improved input legitimacy and procedural fairness will produce fairer outcomes and improve the output legitimacy of these institutions.

This book therefore seeks to add to the current globalization debate by examining both North and South perspectives on globalization, rather than one or the other. Although the OECD industrialized countries and the developing states share some of the pressures and effects arising from globalization, there are also significant differences worthy of examination. Several of the core industrialized states have actively pursued a course of economic liberalization, whereas many developing states have been compelled to adopt them as part of the structural adjustment policies recommended by the IMF. The benefits of open trade and encouraging foreign direct investment have not, thus far, been overly negative for most industrialized countries. They have continued to attract roughly the same relative portion of world FDI as in the past and have successfully restructured their economies to (and protected certain vulnerable sectors from) a more open trade system. Unlike developing states and despite much talk of the decline of welfare provision in the industrialized countries, they continue to possess the economic wherewithal to dedicate extremely high levels of their GDP to ensure the welfare of their citizens.

Yet, the same is not necessarily true for developing states; they are struggling with the forces of globalization. The book therefore examines world patterns of trade and investment to illustrate that this is the case. Many developing states that have simply adopted export-led strategies have not reaped benefits from doing so. The 'developmental states' of East Asia are often held up as successful models of this approach. The book therefore examines in detail the actual policies that were adopted by these states, concluding that the state was in fact heavily involved in guiding the economy and engaged in highly selective trading strategies. In comparison with the North, much of the pressure on the South actually arises from the international financial institutions and their overly zealous promotion of structural adjustment. The book concludes, therefore, that the major international institutions are in dire need of reform. Greater autonomy needs to be given to the developing states whose leaders, in turn, need to adopt feasible long-term economic strategies aimed at diversifying their economies and encouraging investment. The voice of the South will only truly be heard when its countries have greater representation at the international level and a greater say in how their economies are to be run.

2 Globalization: myth or reality?

As with all concepts within the social sciences, globalization is a highly contested issue with opinions ranging across a broad spectrum. At the one end are those who view it as 'a process that will result in the melting away of national boundaries and the unification of mankind in one peaceful and prosperous community'. Yet, at the other end of the spectrum, there are those who view it as 'the source of all the ills that inflict the poorest – and collectively the most populous – countries and/or social groups'.[1] Despite this diversity of opinions, several scholars have identified three main schools of thought in the globalization debate: the globalists, sceptics and transformationalists.[2] As Anthony McGrew points out, one of the major fault lines that divide the three schools of thought is the issue of historical continuity and change: the globalists argue that 'it represents a new historical conjuncture'; the sceptics 'dismiss the idea of globalization as a contemporary myth'; while the transformationalists view contemporary economics as 'a process of on-going transformation'[3] As will become apparent, the globalists and sceptics are situated at the opposite end of the spectrum, while the transformationlists attempt to develop the middle ground between the other two competing schools. This chapter adopts such a classification. Inevitably, pigeonholing scholars in such a manner runs the danger of caricaturing their positions. A warning thus accompanies this three-fold classification and should be regarded more as a heuristic device rather than as a perfect depiction of the range of views that exist on the topic of globalization.

The globalists

Writers within this school view contemporary economic relations as qualitatively different from those of previous historical epochs. Unsurprisingly, this group emphasizes the increasing level of interactions across states that has led to a complex web of political, social and economic relations in today's world – 'national boundaries no longer act as "watertight" containers of the production process...Today, fewer and fewer activities are orientated towards local – or even national – markets ... And because of the increasingly complex ways in which production is organized across national boundaries, rather than contained within them, the actual origin of individual products may be very difficult to determine'.[4] In the economic realm, it is argued that two trends are apparent as a result of this.

First, the volume of international finance, trade and production has increased to such an extent that these activities are said to now cut across the borders of nations such that a truly integrated economy has emerged. Equally importantly, the manufacturing process itself now encompasses a plethora of production sites integrated across the world consisting of 'producer-driven commodity chains (in industries, such as, automobiles, computers, aircraft, electrical machinery), and buyer-driven commodity chains (in industries such as garment, footwear, toys, housewares). What is fundamental in this web-like industrial structure is that it is territorially spread throughout the world, and its geometry keeps changing.'[5] From the globalist's point of view the spatial configuration of the production process has altered radically. Gone are the days of national production geared towards the local needs of the population, the contemporary world is one based upon 'production chains and networks configured at a multiplicity of geographical scales, from the local through to the global. Such networks are the structures through which different parts of the world are connected together through flows of material and non-material phenomena in a system of differential power relationships'.[6]

Second, it is argued that this has impacted upon the autonomy of the state itself, drastically reducing its ability to control such economic flows. Globalists point to the increasing economic wherewithal of companies compared to the overall economic activity occurring within states. Table 2.1 compares the overall sales of some of the major companies of the world with the GDP of several states. If one ranks the sales of major corporations in 2002 with the GDP of the world's 193 states, the top corporation's sales – in this case Wal-Mart – was greater than the

Table 2.1 Sales of top corporations compared to the GDP of countries, 2002

World ranking	Country or corporation	GDP/sales (US$ billions)
19	Wal-Mart	246.5
20	Sweden	229.8
21	Austria	202.9
22	Norway	189.4
23	Poland	187.7
24	General Motors	186.8
25	Saudi Arabia (2001)	186.5
26	Exxon Mobil	184.5
27	Turkey	182.9
28	Royal Dutch/Shell	179.4
29	BP	178.7
30	Denmark	174.8
31	Indonesia	173.0
32	Ford Motor	163.9
33	Hong Kong, China	161.5
34	Daimler Chrysler	141.4
35	Greece	132.8

Source: S. Anderson and J. Cavanaugh, *Field Guide To The Global Economy* (New York: New Press, 2005). Available online http://www.ips-dc.org (accessed 17 December 2005).

Box 2.1   The globalists' perspective

The globalists cite the following as some of the evidence that globalization is dramatically altering the world in which we live:

1   The total sales of many TNCs are higher than the GDP of many countries of the world.
2   Gross cross-border equity flows alone reached $2.5 trillion by the mid-nineties.
3   The sheer quantity of money transacted daily on foreign exchanges across the world, around $1.8 trillion a day, renders the nation-state incapable of even controlling its own currency.
4   In just over two decades, the United States has experienced an eighteen-fold increase in FDI stock reaching a total of almost $1.5 trillion by 2004. The United Kingdom has also been one of the main recipients of FDI with current inward stocks standing at $770 billion.
5   Where trade is concerned, the globalists argue that levels have now surpassed the 'belle époque' at the end of the nineteenth century.

As a result of this increasing cross-border activity in the spheres of finance, trade and production, the globalists argue that a shift of focus away from the state towards global financial companies and TNCs is therefore required. Concerning the latter, the phenomenal improvements in computer power in the last few decades means that these companies no longer have to worry so much about coordinating a vast array of activities. The internet combined with the latest computers allows for just in time deliveries regardless of the distance involved. As a result, these transnational corporations direct investment and production on a world-wide basis, with limited regards for national boundaries or any particular allegiance to a nation-state.

GDP of Sweden, Austria, Norway or Poland. Moreover, this was not an exception to the rule: altogether out of the top 100 countries and corporations 52 were corporations.[7] The fact that the total sales of these companies are higher than the GDP of many countries of the world calls into question our assumption that the nation-state is the most important unit of analysis within the global system. These corporations are a major source of employment within the various countries that they operate in; they control much of the production, movement of goods and technological innovation within a state's borders. Their wealth, combined with these factors, imply that they are important and highly influential actors on the world stage. Because they believe that 'only two forces matter in the world economy, global market forces and transnational companies, and that neither of these is or can be subject to effective public governance', globalists argue that a shift of focus away from the state and towards these transnational entities is therefore required.[8]

Where trade is concerned, the globalists compare the 'belle époque'at the end of the nineteenth century with today's trading activity. Economists generally agree that from 1890 until the onset of the First World War the international system exhibited a hitherto unprecedented level of openness. However, as can be seen from Table 2.2, the volume of trade today far exceeds that of the 'belle époque'. For example, the United States, Canada, Australia and New Zealand currently export 39 times the amount that they exported in 1913; Western Europe now exports almost 20 times the level; and Asia has experienced a 69-fold increase in the amount it exports. Globalists also point out that these increases are not only apparent in the absolute measures of volumes of trade but are also apparent in relative measures concerning trade to gross domestic product ratios. This represents a more accurate picture of trade activity because it is a measure of trading activity as a proportion of the total economic activity (total value of goods and services produced) within the country concerned.

If one compares merchandise exports to GDP ratios in 1998 (Table 2.3) with those just before the First World War (both in 1990 prices), the globalists argue that we have experienced a significant increase in trading activity. Some of the largest increases with regard to industrialized countries have been associated with those countries that were less open than their counterparts. For example, Japan's merchandise exports to GDP ratio has increased more than five-fold since 1913 and France's openness has increased by three-and-a-half-fold.[9]

In addition, the globalists argue that the sheer quantity of money transacted daily on foreign exchanges across the world renders the nation-state incapable of

Table 2.2 Volume of world exports compared to 1913 (constant prices)

	1913	1950	1973	1990	1998
Western Europe	100	95	605	1250	1948
Western Offshoots	100	229	927	2080	3907
Eastern Europe and USSR	100	169	1459	1905	2717
Latin America	100	231	606	1280	2622
Asia	100	183	1625	3857	6889
Africa	100	201	665	679	1055

Source: A. Maddison, *The World Economy: A Millennial Perspective*, Paris: OECD, 2001, Table F-3. Western offshoots refer to the US, Canada, Australia & New Zealand.

Table 2.3 Ratio of merchandise exports to GDP, 1913–98 (1990 prices) (multiplied by two)

	1913	1950	1973	1998
France	15.6	15.2	30.4	57.4
Germany	32.2	12.4	47.6	77.8
Japan	4.8	4.4	15.4	26.4
Netherlands	34.6	24.4	81.4	122.4
UK	35.0	22.6	28.0	50.0
USA	7.4	6.0	9.8	20.2

Source: A. Maddison, *The World Economy: A Millennial Perspective*, Paris: OECD, 2001, Table F-5.

even controlling its own currency, '[W]ith the speed and volume of transactions in the global capital market, national governments cannot control exchange rates or protect their currencies, and political leaders increasingly find themselves at the mercy of people and institutions making economic choices over which they have no control'.[10] Kenichi Ohmae cites the case of the Japanese government in March 1986 and January 1987 – which injected $16 billion to prevent the free fall of the dollar, but nothing happened – as evidence that in 'a fundamental sense, money supply has moved beyond the control of any single government'.[11]

This is one of the globalists' stronger points. In the last few decades international finance has experienced increasing levels of commodification in areas such as foreign exchange, derivatives and securities. Commodification in this book refers to the creation of objects for the main purpose of exchange with the objective of obtaining additional value over and above that of the original capital invested. The development of floating exchange rates, derivatives and securities, it is argued, has led to the further commodification of financial instruments such that '[T]rade in these "articles"… [has become] a means of accumulation in its own right, and the financial assets … [have become] … to some degree divorced from "real" assets'.[12] This diversification of financial instruments, combined with the electronic age, has led to a bewildering array of exchanges occurring with increasing rapidity twenty-four hours of the day. Moreover, '[A]ll the current prices in every stock exchange can be pulled up at any moment at any place in the world, and trigger buying and selling at prices which are in turn immediately communicated round the globe as so many bits and bytes'.[13] This is nowhere more true than in foreign exchange services where over $1.8 trillion worth of currencies are traded every day. To put this into perspective, if a trillion dollars were physically stacked they would be 20 miles taller than Mount Everest.[14] The globalists therefore argue that this financial activity has led to a highly integrated and interdependent world, so that it is 'possible that falling interest rates in the USA will push up share prices on the other side of the world … For that very reason, anyone who wants to borrow money or raise capital – whether a government, a corporation or a house builder – immediately enters into worldwide competition with every other potential debtor'.[15]

Shortly after the collapse of the Bretton Woods System in 1971, the major economies of the world moved to a floating exchange regime as opposed to the fixed exchange rate regime that was in place previously. However, this has led to high degrees of speculative foreign exchange dealings unrelated to trading activity in goods and services. Although the fluctuations in currency rates are usually fairly small, exchanging large volumes of money from one currency to another can still make significant profits. The vast increases in foreign exchange turnover (Table 2.4), therefore, have less to do with businesses buying currencies for actual use (though of course this constitutes some of the turnover) and more to do with currency speculation (buying a currency in the expectation that its value relative to other currencies will increase) and, even more so, currency arbitrage (profiting from differences in the value of a currency in two or more currency markets by buying in one market while simultaneously selling in another). Indeed, it has been

Table 2.4 Daily foreign exchange turnover

Year	Average daily turnover $US billions	
	Current prices	Constant prices (April 2004)
1989	590	650
1992	820	840
1995	1,190	1,120
1998	1,490	1,590
2001	1,200	1,380
2004	1,880	1,880

Source: G. Galati and M. Melvin, *BIS Quarterly Review*, December 2004, Table 1.
Decline between 1998 and 2002 largely due to introduction of the Euro and the more recent gap between current and constant exchange rates is largely due to the depreciation of the dollar.[1]

Note
1   Exchange rates at constant prices for non-US dollar currencies were calculated by converting into original currency at average exchange rates for April of that survey year and then converting into dollars at average April 2004 rates. Refer to G. Galati and M. Melvin, 'Why has FX Trading Surged? Explaining the 2004 triennial survey', *BIS Quarterly Review*, Basel: Bank for International Settlements, December 2004, p.68.

estimated that currency exchange related to 'transactions in "real" goods fell from 90 per cent in the early 1970s to around 2 per cent in the late 1990s'.[16]

Such high levels of financial flows are also seen in the area of investment, which, it is argued, is 'interconnected worldwide, from banks to pension funds, stock exchange markets and currency exchange'.[17] As Table 2.5 indicates, the increase in cross-border transactions in bonds and equities (defined as gross purchases and sales between residents and non-residents) has increased exponentially, particularly since around 1985, reflecting the move towards full liberalization of many of the OECD states' capital accounts at the end of the seventies and during the eighties.[18] The amounts involved in the bonds and equity markets are quite staggering, with gross cross-border equity flows alone reaching $2.5 trillion by the mid-nineties.[19] Because of this high degree of financial integration with investors being able to move their money to wherever they will receive the highest return, it is said that 'monetary policies and interest rates' have also become interdependent.[20]

In addition to this, globalists point to the striking growth of transactions in derivatives (futures, options and swaps) and loan securities. Concerning the latter financial transactions, rather than waiting for loans to mature and simply profiting from the interest charged to their clients, these days financial institutions offer securities based on an array of outstanding debt that is owed to them. This involves selling a package of claims that give the right to 'the lender to receive regular interest and capital from their borrowers' on the open market. These securities may be 'either "non-recourse", in which case the buyer of the securities from the mortgage firm bears the risk of non-payment by the borrowers, or with recourse to the mortgage lender'.[21] The future repayment of debt has thus become a commodity in its own right bought and sold on the open market, thus converting '*expected cash flow*, wherever and whenever it might occur, into instant spending power'.[22] Essentially, this enables financial institutions to receive income immediately, thus

Table 2.5   Cross-border transactions in bonds and equities* (percentage of GDP)

	1980	1985	1990	1992	1993	1994	1995	1996	1997	1998
USA	9	35	89	107	129	131	135	159	213	230
Japan	8	62	119	72	78	60	65	79	96	91
Germany	7	33	57	85	170	158	172	200	257	334
France	5	21	54	122	187	197	187	258	314	415
Italy	1	4	27	92	192	207	253	470	677	640
Canada	9	27	65	114	153	206	187	251	355	331

Source: Bank for International Settlements, *69th Annual Report*, Table VI.5, p. 118.

Note

* Gross purchases and sales of securities between residence and non-residence.

allowing them to either lend to an even greater number of clients or to diversify and invest the money in other financial instruments.

Concerning derivatives, such operations are highly complex but the most significant aspect of this type of security is that investors are only required to commit a small proportion of their capital to such investments, as the initial payment represents just a portion of the overall market value of the asset in question (primary products, currencies bonds, shares etc.). The initial down payment is derived from the value of the item concerned – hence the term 'derivative'. Futures provide the investor with the possibility of conducting 'a transaction at an agreed price on a specified future date'.[23] Buying such a contract gives the buyer assurance that they can buy a set quantity of a product at a pre-established price (for example, to buy a primary product for 'x' amount) on the specified date, thus providing a 'hedge' against possible future fluctuations in prices. Options, on the other hand, provide the buyer 'the right, but not the obligation, to buy or sell a financial instrument, commodity or some other underlying asset at a given price, at or before a specified date'.[24] However, whether this right is exercised or not is entirely at the discretion of the holder of such a contract. Finally, a swap 'is an exchange of cash payment obligations'; for example, where one party wishes to swap their fixed rate loan for a floating rate loan with another party, they agree to meet each other's interest rate commitments.[25]

In essence, then, these innovations in global finance have produced a multiplying effect in financial markets by offering the opportunity to invest, often in order to hedge against the risk of fluctuations in the price of a commodity, while permitting investors to retain the greater proportion of their capital for other financial transactions. Although such types of investment on a wide scale have been available since the establishment of the Chicago Options Exchange in 1972, these activities were further stimulated by financial deregulation in several key economies followed by the revision of the OECD's 'code of liberalisation of capital movements' in 1989 to promote investment in various forms of finance across member states.[26] By 1995, the amount involved in such operations totalled $1.2 trillion a day.[27]

From the globalists' perspective, the sheer volume of transactions of these various financial instruments has made it difficult, if not impossible, for states to monitor international financial activities. But, in addition, it has dramatically

Table 2.6 FDI inward stock (millions of dollars)

	1980	1985	1990	1995	2000	2004
France	25,925[a]	36,701	86,845	191,434	259,775	535,201[b]
Germany	36,630	36,926	119,618	192,898	271,611	347,957[b]
Japan	3,720	4,740	9,850	36,658	50,322	96,984
Netherlands	19,167	24,921	68,731	116,049	241,328	428,803[b]
UK	63,014	64,028	203,905	199,772	438,631	771,658
USA	83,046	184,615	394,911	535,553	1,214,254	1,473,860[b]

Source: UNCTAD, *World Investment Report 2004: The Shift Towards Services,* Annex Table 2.7:Ratio of merchandise trade to GDP (exports and imports) at current prices.
Notes:
a   Stock data prior to 1989 are estimated by subtracting flows
b   Estimated

increased the overall economic wherewithal of these institutions *vis-a-vis* the core industrialized states. For the G7, with the exception of Japan, the holdings of these institutions dramatically increased in the nineties so that by 1998 for the US, UK, Canada and France, these financial institutions' assets either equalled or exceeded the GDP of the country concerned. For the United States and the United Kingdom their holdings were more than '200% of gross domestic product'.[28]

Globalists also point to the high degree of foreign direct investment stock (overseas investment in which the investing company has a direct managerial role) that has built up over time (Table 2.6). For example, in just over two decades, the United States has experienced an eighteen-fold increase in stock reaching a total of almost $1.5 trillion by 2004. The United Kingdom has also been one of the main recipients of FDI with current inward stocks standing at $770 billion, reflecting its economy's traditionally open nature in terms of finance, trade and production. Other industrialized countries experienced similar increases. Japan also experienced large increases relative to initial investments, but the overall size of investment stocks continues to be relatively low at 2.1 per cent of GDP (2003) reflecting the less open nature of its economy.[29]

For globalists this level of investment is significant because, for them, it indicates that the structure of production has fundamentally altered. Companies are increasingly slicing up the supply chain, producing parts wherever the process is cheapest and then shipping them to assembly plants that make the final product. Falling costs of communication and freight transportation, it is argued, have encouraged companies to develop truly global production systems. For the globalists, the transnational corporation is the main catalyst for this reconfiguration, developing global chains of 'transactionally linked sequence of functions in which each stage adds value to the process of production of goods and services'.[30] In 2006, the chief executive of IBM, Samuel Palmisano, gave support to this view by arguing that truly transnational (as opposed to multinational) companies were emerging, that were developing:

strategy, management and operations to integrate production – and deliver value to clients – worldwide. That has been made possible by shared technologies and shared business standards, built on top of a global information technology and communications infrastructure. Because new technology and business models are allowing companies to treat their functions and operations as component pieces, companies can pull these pieces apart and put them back together in new combinations.[31]

The phenomenal improvements in computer power in the last few decades mean that these companies no longer have to worry about the coordination of such activities, allowing for just in time deliveries regardless of the distance involved. An increasing number of companies now use Product Life-cycle Management software not only to design and manage their products, but also to coordinate tasks across the globe, for example: Rolls Royce uses 'PLM to facilitate around-the-clock development by engineering teams in Britain, India and America' to produce engines for Airbus; Dassault Aviation, producers of the first aircraft to be 'designed entirely in a virtual environment' used PLM to coordinate the design and production between the 27 sub-contractors they used; and General Motors uses such software to coordinate activities between its 19 design centres and 32 production sites.[32]

The globalists therefore argue that the contemporary period has moved beyond the realm of internationalization, that 'globalization today defines a new epoch in human history'.[33] In so doing, they make a crucial distinction between internationalization and globalization. The former is said to refer 'to a process of intensifying connections between national domains' but one in which 'the principal entities are national economies'.[34] The latter, on the other hand, is said to involve a qualitative shift from this condition of internationalization to a situation in which:

> the key activity is the orchestration of investment flows by transnational corporations across the globe. As the major players, transnational corporations direct investment and production on a world wide basis, with limited regards for national boundaries or any particular allegiance to a nation-state, simply a concern to secure a profitable return on their activities. Moreover, the markets that are important are global rather than national.[35]

Under a condition of internationalization, then, when considering the web of contemporary economic activity, although the importance of multinational companies is acknowledged, the main referent object remains the nation-state. In a globalized economy, the main referent object for analysis shifts from the nation-state to the transnational companies and their global network of interlinked production, marketing and sales. Those arguing the latter case point to the fact that transnational companies' share of world trade stands at two-thirds of total world trade, with intra-firm trade alone constituting approximately one-third of total world trade.[36] Globalists view these companies as transnational in nature, representing 'genuine footloose capital, without specific national identification and with an internationalized management, and at least potentially willing to locate and relocate anywhere in the globe to obtain either the most secure or the highest returns'.[37]

Such differences between the globalists and the other two schools are readily apparent in the writings of Kenichi Ohmae who argues that in four key areas the world has become more globalized (or the four I's as he labels them). First, investment is no longer constrained, it has become truly footloose and fancy-free. An ever increasing number of states are liberalizing their capital accounts allowing for the free flow of investments to wherever the opportunities are most favourable. At the same time, the type of investment has changed, previously 'the flow of cross-border funds was primarily from government to government or from multilateral lending agency to government', but in the contemporary era this has been dwarfed by private investment.[38]

Second, information technology has given rise to 'a truly global economy, an economy with the capacity to work as a unit in real time on a planetary scale'.[39] Third, industry now locates and re-locates 'to serve attractive markets wherever they exist and to tap attractive pools of resources wherever they sit'. Ohmae argues that, as a result of the shortened shelf life of technological goods, companies now have to market such products simultaneously across the world. For example, in the case of electronics, replacement models are developed in a matter of just a few months. It is therefore important to launch the product in all regions while the demand is still there. In addition, the increasing complexity of technological products means that companies are unable to produce all of the constituent components in-house. There is therefore now a much greater degree of out-sourcing of multiple aspects of a company's production process. Finally, individual consumers now have far better access to information about the products that they wish to buy and therefore seek access to these commodities regardless of where they were made – '[P]eople have become more informed and clever, as a real consequence of living in a truly global information era. And now governments have become the major obstacle for people to have the best and the cheapest from anywhere in the world'.[40]

In the inter-linked economy of the United States, Europe and Japan it is said that a new type of multi-national company is emerging. As a result of the above mentioned outsourcing of much of their production processes and the increased level of intra-firm trade across countries, multi-national companies are losing their national character and no longer have a true home base. New technologies have enabled companies to 'contract out their production, economising on endowments of plant, equipment, and land. "Just in Time" methods bring materials to the plant when a specific process occurs, saving on storage and warehousing costs'.[41] In addition, strategic alliances between firms, regardless of their country of origin, are becoming more commonplace. Ohmae argues that, because of technology, the variable cost of labour is of diminishing importance. Thus, in today's world, companies are more concerned with reducing their fixed costs and one way of doing this is to develop strategic alliances with their would-be competitors. Fixed costs can be reduced, for example, if companies agree to use each other's sales and distribution networks rather than setting up their own independent network.

There is some evidence to support this, for example UNCTAD has reported that 'IBM (United States) has alliances with Thomson-CSG (France) to market microprocessor chips, with Toshiba (Japan) to cooperate in the development of static random access memory chips, with Siemens (Germany) for work on advanced dynamic random access memory chips, and with Toshiba and Siemens to develop a new 256 megabyte chip...Renault (France) and Volvo (Sweden) have an alliance to produce automobiles and trucks. Nestlé (Switzerland) and Coca-cola (United States) are cooperating to distribute canned hot drinks through vending machines'.[42] In addition, there were about '1,760 cross border inter-firm agreements (R&D partnerships excluded) concluded in 1990, rising to 4,600 just five years later'.[43]

Furthermore, because of the burgeoning costs of Research and Development it is becoming increasingly common for companies to pool their research resources or for them to make constituent components for each other's products. In the globalized economy, a multi-national company's 'actual operations are conducted with other firms: not only with the hundreds or thousands of subcontracting and ancillary enterprises, but with the dozens of relatively equal partners with whom they cooperate and compete at the same time in this new brave economic world where friends and foes are the same'.[44] These research and development partnerships are not as substantial in number compared to general inter-firm agreements and stood at about 500 in 1994, but strategically they have great significance because such activity is closely associated with a company's future continuing success.[45]

Although the globalists are united by their vision of an economically integrated world, it is noteworthy that some of the main writers, such as, Manuel Castells and Kenichi Ohmae acknowledge that this only applies at the moment to the triad: the United States; Europe; and Japan. But the general tone of the globalists' argument implies that this will expand beyond the so-called inter-linked economy of the triad to 'encompass most East European countries, most of the Asian newly industrialized economies (NIEs), and some Latin American countries'.[46] Significant differences within this group are also apparent. On the one hand, Ohmae views the above developments in a very positive light. Ohmae's perspective is strongly coloured by neo-liberalism and he therefore believes that the invisible hand of the market will ensure the most efficient and therefore cheapest possible price of goods available to the consumer. By each pursuing their own self-interests the general interest of all will be served, the market is therefore viewed as a self-regulating mechanism. Out of this theory of the market arises the principle of *laissez faire*, or more accurately, *laissez-faire les hommes, laissez-passer les marchandises* – allow individuals to pursue their interests (free of government control), and let commodities circulate freely. In other words, the market should be left unhindered by government intervention to provide the best and most efficient provision of goods via unfettered competition. The general assumption underpinning such arguments, then, is that any form of government intervention leads to distortions in the market and therefore pricing policies that do not reflect the best possible outcome for the consumer. Ohmae believes that the increasing economic interaction across states is creating near perfect market conditions in which there is unrestricted competition between companies – '[I]n today's borderless economy the workings of the "invisible hand" have a reach and strength beyond anything Adam Smith ever could have imagined'.[47] Ohmae believes that in this global market consumers can only benefit from this situation as they can now choose the best value items from across the world, as a result he argues that '[M]ultinational companies are truly the servants of demanding consumers around the world'.[48]

Ohmae says little about the way in which the growth of power of these transnational companies has affected labour relations. If these companies really are free to relocate anywhere in the world, then presumably this has weakened the hand of organized labour and their demands for improved working conditions and higher wages. Similarly, he claims that as a result of economic globalization the power of nation-states is in terminal decline, yet omits how this may negatively impact upon the welfare of much of the population. One of the main functions of the modern nation-state has been, up to now, the redistribution of wealth through taxation. If its capacity to do so has diminished, then presumably this has negative implications for the welfare of the poorest segments of society.

Other globalists take exception to this rosy view of the globalization process. For instance, although Castells believes that we are now living in a global informational society, he is far less optimistic about the ramifications of such change. To the contrary, he argues that the increasing use of technology and informational processes in the economy is exacerbating the division between the 'have-nots' and 'have-lots'. A new international division of labour is said to be in the making, creating a four-fold division between 'producers of high value, based on informational labour; the producers of high volume, based on lower-cost labor; the producers of raw materials, based on natural endowments; and the redundant producers, reduced to devalued labor'.[49] Those less well trained and less well educated are now finding themselves marginalized, unable to find stable employment but instead confined to poorly paid temporary or part-time work, if and when they can find it, globalization 'proceeds selectively, including and excluding segments of economies and societies in and out of networks of information, wealth, and power...the crisis of the nation-state, and of the institutions of civil society constructed around it during the industrial era, undermines institutional capacity to correct social imbalances derived from unrestricted market logic... there is more than inequality and poverty in this process of social restructuring. There is also exclusion of people and territories which, from the perspective of dominant interests in global, informational capitalism, shift to a position of structural irrelevance'.[50]

The sceptics

At the other end of the spectrum of the globalization debate lie the sceptics. This group of scholars question many of the claims of the globalists. They present an alternative picture of the world, one in which levels of international trade, production and finance of much earlier periods are comparable (if not higher) to today's level of integration. In particular, they also challenge the globalist's vision of relatively unfettered trade across borders and their claim that today's multi-national companies are footloose and fancy-free, regularly relocating their production facilities to wherever the operating costs are lowest. If this were so, they argue, then we should also experience convergence in both the price of products and also in wage levels. This patently is not the case, they argue, because if it were, 'then how do we explain that German workers continue to earn almost double that of those in the US or eleven times that in Thailand? ... why does there continue to be such large variation among national economies not only in the rewards to labour, but in profit margins as well?'.[51] Additionally, they point to the fact that the prices of goods vary considerably across the world. If unfettered trade really existed, then local companies would be forced to compete with their international counterparts; therefore, we should expect greater price convergence between states than is currently observed.

In offering this alternative analysis, the sceptics call into question the globalists' assumption that the power of the state is waning. If one believes that today's corporations are really more influential than most states and that they are truly footloose entities that are free to move from state to state, then political fatalism may follow. Democratic states, through political representation of citizens' interests, have traditionally channelled at least some of the economic benefits of capitalism toward the public good through redistributive and minimum wage policies. If the globalists are correct, then this invaluable political control of economic activity occurring within the borders of a state by the population via the state's representative institutions is in danger of disappearing. As Hirst and Thompson argue, '[O]ne key effect of the concept of globalization has been to paralyse radical reforming national strategies to see them as unfeasible in the face of the judgement and sanction of international markets ... "Globalization" is a myth suitable for a world without illusions, but it is also one that robs us of hope'.[52] The sceptics argue that states continue to be significant actors on the world stage, with the means to control the activities within and across their borders. Hence the title of Paul Hirst and Grahame Thompson's well known critique of globalization – *Globalization in Question: The International Economy and the Possibilities of Governance*.

Moreover, they argue, the core industrialized states have been active participants and the key architects behind economic globalization. For example, the OECD code of liberalization of capital movements has been instrumental in promoting the free flow of investments between these states. Although initially the code primarily encouraged foreign direct investment between OECD members (from the early sixties), it gradually expanded its remit so that: in 1973 it included collective investment securities; in 1984 it established conditions of reciprocity concerning FDI so that a member country can 'invest or establish in another member country under conditions similar to those granted by its own country'; and in 1989 encouraged further capital account liberalization by including new forms of financial instruments, such as swaps, futures and options.[53] Sceptics

Box 2.2   The sceptics' perpective

The sceptics cite the following evidence questioning the level of globalization in today's world:

1   States have been active participants and the key architects behind economic liberalization.

2   If trade figures are recalculated using current prices, rather than constant prices, then the trade levels of the core industrialized states during the 'belle époque' were greater than they are today.

3   Although there has been a steep increase in levels of FDI in the last two decades or so, these corporations have a readily identifiable 'major national location of assets, production and sales' and therefore can be said to retain 'a clear national home base'. These corporations are therefore still best described as *multinational companies* rather than *transnational companies*[1]

4   In relation to finance, they argue that the cost of money has not converged because significant differentials in real interest rates remain.

5   Much of the cross-border flows in bonds and equities represent financial churning by investors in search of quick returns; a different picture emerges if one examines the pattern of holdings of bonds and shares by various financial institutions. The evidence indicates that foreign holdings continue to represent just a portion of overall investment (varying from 10–30%).

The sceptics therefore conclude that rather than living in a fully globalized economy, the contemporary era is still best described as an international economy in which 'the principal entities are national economies'. Such an international economy, it is argued, 'is well short of dissolving distinct national economies in the major advanced industrial countries, or of preventing the development of new forms of economic governance at the national and international levels'[2]

1   P. Hirst and G. Thompson, *Globalization in Question*, 1999, pp. 2, 9, 11.
2   Ibid., 1999, pp. 4, 8.

---

therefore point to the continuing importance of states' involvement in the management of the financial and monetary systems. This is not to say that they do not recognize the changing nature of such regimes. Indeed, they further divide the usual dichotomy of the Bretton Woods system/post Bretton Woods system so that the latter is split into the 'floating rate dollar standard', the establishment of the European Monetary system in 1979 and the Plaza and Louvre accords in 1985 and 1987.[54]

If international trade, finance and production relative to states' GDP have not increased considerably in the last few decades, then the impact of globalization upon the capabilities of the state will be less significant than first thought. Some sceptics go further and argue that financial investors and multinational companies find strong states an attractive proposition as they recognize that the state provides certain collective goods, such as a country's infrastructure. Moreover, it does so in a more efficient manner than the private sector does by using its advantage in economies of scale.[55] Others argue that rather than states being merely passive actors in the process of globalization (or internationalization as they would see it) developed states, in particular, have actively encouraged certain changes, 'economic integration is being advanced not only by corporations but also by national governments'. These 'catalytic' states have promoted trade tariff reductions and encouraged offshore relocation of production facilities by offering incentives to 'finance overseas investment, promote technology alliances between national and foreign firms, and encourage regional relocation of production networks'. Rather than viewing the process of economic globalization as leading to the decline of state autonomy vis-à-vis its control of large corporations operating within its borders, some sceptics argue that '"globalization" is often the by-product of states promoting the internationalisation strategies of their corporations, and sometimes in the process "internationalising" state capacity'.[56]

As we saw earlier, the sceptics argue that we should distinguish between trends towards greater internationalization and a fully globalized economy. The latter is said to exist when '[T]he international economic system becomes autonomized and socially disembedded, as markets and production become truly global. Domestic policies, whether of private corporations or public regulators, now have routinely to take account of the predominantly international determinants of their sphere of operations. As systemic interdependence grows, the national level is permeated by and transformed by the international ... Socially decontextualised global markets would be difficult to regulate, even supposing effective cooperation by the regulators and a coincidence of their interests'.[57]

If such a fully globalized economy existed, the sceptics argue that several consequences would follow. First, transnational corporations would become the most important economic actors on the world stage, they would be 'genuine footloose capital, without specific national identification...potentially willing to locate and relocate anywhere in the globe to obtain either the most secure or the highest returns'. Second, because of this potential mobility, these corporations would set up their sites of production and/or services to those areas that offered the requisite labour skills at the lowest cost. Therefore we would witness a 'further decline in the political influence and economic bargaining power of organized labour'. Finally, regulation would become increasingly difficult in a fully globalized economy. If regulations in any particular country were not to the liking of major transnational corporations, they could simply relocate to countries with more lax regulations. Coordinated global governance would be unlikely as key states would come under increasing pressure to opt out and those that believe that they benefit from the current situation would be reluctant to cooperate.[58]

However, the sceptics argue that rather than living in a fully globalized economy, the contemporary era is still best described as an international economy in which 'the principal entities are national economies'. Such an international economy, it is argued, 'is well short of dissolving distinct national economies in the major advanced industrial countries, or of preventing the development of new forms of economic governance at the national and international levels'.[59]

Several factors lead these authors to such a conclusion. First, they argue, the current period of economic openness is not that different to other periods in history; for example, the levels of trade between the world's major economies is not historically unprecedented.[60] In addition, if the defining element of globalization is a 'global economy, an economy with the capacity to work as a unit in real time on a planetary scale', then, the sceptics argue, this began with the installation of intercontinental telegraphic communications in 1866 and the spread of this technology connecting the main industrial centres by the turn of the century.[61] Second, the core industrialized countries continue to attract the vast majority of the world's FDI. Although there has been a steep increase in levels of FDI in the last two decades or so, these corporations have a readily identifiable 'major national location of assets, production and sales' and therefore can be said to retain 'a clear national home base'. These corporations are therefore still best described as multinational companies rather than transnational companies.[62] In addition, in contradistinction to Ohmae who emphasizes cooperation and strategic alliances between these corporations, Hirst and Thompson view them as being 'involved in a deadly competitive game, one in which they deploy all manner of business strategies to exclude some competing players from their networks whilst locking others firmly into them'.[63] Finally, trade, investment and financial flows occur mainly within the triad of the United States, Europe and Japan and therefore, 'the G3 have the capacity, especially if they coordinate policy, to exert powerful governance pressures over financial markets and other economic tendencies. Global markets are thus by no means beyond regulation and control'.[64] The following section examines some of these claims in detail.

As we have seen above, the sceptics argue that the claim that we now live in a globalized world can be challenged on a variety of fronts. In terms of finance, the sceptics do recognize the enormous increase in foreign exchange turnover and the proliferation of derivatives accompanied by large volumes of trading in these relatively new financial instruments. However, they argue that in other important respects international finance has not changed as much as the globalists' argument would imply. Their first point concerns the sensitivity of the various stock markets around the world and the contemporary risk of 'contagion' whereby the collapse of prices in one country leads to a domino effect leading to the rapid collapse of prices everywhere. Although this is true, the sceptics point out that such sensitivity has been around since at least 1870.[65]

Second, with regard to financial market integration, if investors can move capital from country to country unhindered, then we would expect that returns on that investment would be the same (investors would seek the highest returns available while borrowers would seek the lowest cost loans and interest rates across the world would tend towards equilibrium). In Linda Weiss' apt phrase, the cost of money should converge.[66] One way of measuring whether or not this is actually occurring is to compare national interest rates on various investment instruments. In so doing, the sceptics argue that uncovered interest rate parity has not been established (covered interest rates counter exchange rate fluctuations by forward selling of the currency concerned and charging a higher interest rate for any losses this might involve, whereas uncovered interest rate parity on investments is achieved when returns are equal without having to factor in forward exchange rate fluctuation).[67] In addition, they argue that real interest rate parity (in which the reduction in returns due to inflation is taken into account) between countries seemed 'far from established by the mid-1990s'.[68] In other words, 'a *currency premium* remains, consisting of an exchange risk premium plus expected real currency depreciation. This means that, even with the equalization of covered interest rates, large differentials in *real* interest rates remain'.[69] National variation is thus still apparent, an unaccounted-for anomaly if state borders really have become completely permeable to capital flows. However, as we will see shortly, the transformationalists counter these claims by pointing to long-term trends in real interest rates which do indicate that, although parity has not been attained, a certain degree of convergence is evident. Moreover, they question whether it is realistic to expect that such a result will ever pertain given the vagaries of the market.

Finally, the sceptics point to the continuing correlation between domestic savings and national investment. In a truly integrated global economy, they argue, one would expect the two to diverge as 'investment will flow to the highest yielding opportunity' in markets across the world.[70] However, they point to the seminal article by Feldstein and Horioka published in 1980 and several succeeding works that indicate that the historical correlation between domestic savings and national investment is still relatively high in the OECD countries, although it has declined from the immediate post-war high of 89 per cent (1960–74) to 67 per cent between 1991 and 1995.[71] Similarly, others have found that there exists a relatively low degree of investment overseas; for example, in 1990 the 'Japanese had only 1.9 percent of their equity in foreign stocks, while US investors held 6.2 percent of their equity portfolio overseas. The British, by comparison, held 18 percent of their portfolio abroad'.[72]

Such home-based investment is an economic oddity in an era of few capital account restrictions because transaction costs are relatively low; diversification into other markets would provide a certain degree of risk reduction.[73] Economists have attempted to explain this in various ways. One of the main explanations is that investors may still perceive that foreign investment is a more risky venture than domestic investment, or they may be concerned about possible capital controls by states in the future.[74] Another is that the data include both private and public investment. Once investment by the state is excluded, the correlation between the two is significantly reduced. Sceptics concede that this is the case, but argue that 'the effect is likely to be relatively small; the essential paradox remains'.[75] Another contending explanation is that if rates of return on investments within the OECD are converging, then there is little incentive for investors actually to go beyond their domestic borders when considering where to put their funds. But, according to the sceptics, this argument is undermined by the fact that there was a general resynchronization of business cycles amongst the OECD countries in the late eighties and early nineties. Such differences would have resulted in investment opportunities (i.e. higher rates of return) in those countries whose economies were doing better than others. Yet, the correlation between domestic savings and national investment remained.[76]

As we saw in Table 2.5, cross-border transactions in bonds and equities have reached unprecedented levels in recent years. However, much of this represents financial churning by investors in search of quick returns; a different picture emerges if one examines the pattern of holdings of bonds and shares by various financial institutions. The data indicates two main findings. First, that national patterns of investment continue to vary and, second, that for 'most countries the foreign securities holdings by their institutional investors were in the 10–30 percent range'. Although there were some countries with slightly higher rates of foreign investment, the proportions were not significantly higher in cases such as Ireland (35 per cent) and New Zealand (34 per cent). However, Hong Kong's rate was very high with international securities constituting 60 per cent of overall pension fund investments.[77] In addition, the proportion of various overseas financial assets owned by households remains relatively low at about 10 per cent, leading Hirst and Thompson to conclude that 'people's financial wealth still remains a domestic affair: it stays at home'.[78]

One of the most controversial counter-claims made by the sceptics is that the level of trade between states in the contemporary era is not historically unprecedented. In making their case, the sceptics refer back to the 'belle époque' from 1878 to 1914 when the Gold Standard was in operation (i.e. during the period when most of the major economies' currency was fixed to the price of gold). At the time, the Bank of England's guarantee of sterling's convertibility into gold whenever and wherever coupled with zero tariffs on manufactured imports helped promote greater free trade between countries.[79]

At the time of writing, the merchandise trade figures available to Hirst and Thompson only went up to the year 1995. It can be seen from Table 2.7 why the sceptics therefore reached such a conclusion. At that time, a comparison of levels of merchandise trade in 1913 and 1995 indicated that, for some of the major economies of the world, trade to GDP ratios were not that different. Indeed, in some cases (Japan, Netherlands and the UK) trade to GDP ratios were lower in 1995 than they were in 1913. However, more recent figures employed by Thompson suggest that, for many of the major economies merchandise trade to GDP ratios now exceed those of 1913. However, the sceptics would point out that for several of these economies the difference is not that great. In addition, for the largest economy, the United States, the 1913 level was very low and it still remains relatively low at about 20 per cent. Similarly, in the case of the second largest economy in the world, Japan, the ratio has declined by more than half and

Table 2.7   Ratio of merchandise trade to GDP (exports and imports) (current prices)

	1913	1950	1973	1995	2000
France	35.4	21.2	29.0	36.6	47.0
Germany	35.2	20.0	35.2	38.8	55.8
Japan	31.4	17.0	18.2	14.2	15.2
Netherlands	103.6	70.2	80.0	83.4	107.0
UK	44.6	32.0	39.4	42.6	43.0
USA	11.2	7.0	10.4	19.0	20.8

Source: G. Thompson, 'Economic globalization?', in D. Held (ed.), *A Globalizing World? Culture, Economics, Politics*, London: Routledge, 2000. (All figures divided by 2 to facilitate comparison)[1]. © Routledge 2000. Reprinted with the permission of Routledge.

Note
1 Refer also to P. Hirst and G. Thompson, *Globalization in Question*, 1999, p. 63.

is currently even lower than that of the United States at just over 15 per cent (both figures for exports and imports).

This debate is further complicated by the fact that trade figures are fairly poor indicators for establishing how much of a state's economic activity is involved in trading. This is because trade figures are sales figures and, as such, include the value added to products by other countries. If a country imports many of the components for the final assembly of a product, such as a car, these costs have not been subtracted from the export figures for this product. Gross domestic product, on the other hand, is the aggregation of value added to products by the economic activity within a country. Such calculations intentionally factor out the value added to a product or service by other companies in order to avoid double-counting. Using trade figures thus produces an exaggerated account of the amount of domestic production and services traded between countries.

Readers may be puzzled when comparing Table 2.7 with the earlier table of trade to GDP used by the globalists which gave much higher levels of trading activity (Table 2.3). The major difference is that the sceptics use trading figures given in current prices, whereas the globalists use figures given in constant prices. Measuring trade in constant prices involves using the value of products in a given year (in this case 1990) and applying this same value to the volume of trade in other years. Measuring trade using current prices, on the other hand, gives the value of those sales according to the prices that could be obtained for those items in the year concerned. Why should the figures differ significantly for the two forms of measurement? Constant price calculations use general price levels in a given year. However, 'productivity in the export sector is systematically greater than it is in the economy as a whole'.[80] The prices of traded goods do not, therefore, increase as rapidly as do those of domestic goods. By using the national price of any given year and multiplying trade volumes for all years by this factor, thus risks exaggerating the extent to which trade has increased. Hirst and Thompson therefore argue that their figures present a more accurate picture of the degree of openness in the world economy and in fact Angus Maddison has, in other work, used current price data that corroborate their findings.[81]

Two other aspects of trade are also worth examining at this point. First, in terms of the North–South divide, the sceptics argue that trading activity and the distribution of foreign direct investment remain concentrated in the core industrialized countries. Although the common perception of economic globalization is one of greater trade openness leading to an increasing amount of traded goods being exported from the developing countries to the industrialized states, this is not borne out by the most recent data. As will be seen in Chapter Three, in relation to world merchandise exports, the industrialized countries' share is approximately the same as it was in the 1960s. The pattern for world trade in services has recently changed, however, so that the industrialized countries' share has declined from 79.1 per cent in 1980 to 73.2 per cent of world trade in 2002.

In terms of foreign direct investment, the sceptics agree that the recent period has witnessed a rapid increase in the levels of this type of investment; for example, they assert that, '[B]etween 1985 and 1990, FDI grew at an average rate of 30 percent a year, an amount four times the growth of world output and three times the growth rate of trade'.[82] By establishing sites within a country/free trade zone, firms can escape the tariffs that would otherwise be levied if they had chosen instead to export their goods or services to the area or country in question. In this way, FDI has become 'an effective substitute for trade'.[83] They also point out that much of this type of investment involves mergers and acquisitions rather than the development of new production sites, for the OECD FDI inflows are 'predominantly (i.e. more than 50 per cent) for mergers and acquisitions' involving a change of ownership but not necessarily changing the productive capacity within a country.[84] In addition 'the major part of global FDI is directed towards technically "non-productive" assets or speculative ventures and financial services – golf courses, real estate, hotels, department stores, banking and insurance'.[85] Moreover, the measure of FDI flows includes 'changes in the shares, loans and retained earnings of affiliated companies that are operating abroad'.[86]

Some also point out that, although in the last few decades FDI/GDP ratios have increased significantly; total investment levels as a proportion of GDP were also very high during the 'belle époque'. It has been estimated that Great Britain's overseas lending was on average 5.2 per cent of GNP during the period 1870–1913, with France (between 2–3 per cent) and Germany's (below 2 per cent) significantly lower.[87] However, there are problems in establishing the type of investment that was involved in overseas transfers. Michael Edelstein distinguishes between portfolio investment (government bonds and company stocks) and direct investment, identifying the latter as those investments that had a controlling stake of 30 per cent or more. In so doing, he estimates that 'the widely held belief that 80 percent or more of gross UK overseas investments in the nineteenth and early twentieth centuries were portfolio in character may be exaggerated but not by very much'.[88] This proportion varied from continent to continent with Sub-Saharan Africa receiving more direct investment than the norm, but generally speaking, the majority of investment was not therefore direct.

Second, the sceptics question whether FDI actually has much effect upon either labour standards or the taxation capabilities of highly industrialized states.

In terms of the former, they point to evidence suggesting that MNCs 'typically adapt to national patterns; they are not aggressive change agents'. Rather than attempt to lower wages and reduce workers' rights by threatening to exit the country concerned, the average MNC (although there are of course exceptions) usually follows the national standards that are already established. In relation to the supposed downward spiral of labour standards as a result of 'regime shopping' by MNCs it has been found that, at least in the case of American FDI, the 'wider adoption of ILO conventions is positively and highly significantly correlated with extent of FDI' and 'investment significantly increasing with union density'.[89] This may not be the same, however, in the case of less developed countries, 'if a country or industry has high labor standards and accommodative labor relations, the MNC adopts the high road; if a country or industry has low labor standards and confrontational labor relations, the MNC tends toward the low road'.[90]

As we saw in the last section, countries have experienced a rapid increase in the absolute amounts of direct investment they receive. But the figures the globalists use are absolute measures. If one compares annual foreign direct investment flows to the total fixed capital investment within a country, a rather different picture emerges (Table 2.8). This gives us a more tangible grasp of how significant a role such investment plays in the economies of various states/regions because it is compared with the total investment in durable assets within a country for any given year. But even then, some difficulties arise. For example, some of the large increases witnessed at the end of the millennium reflected an unusually high degree of merger and acquisition activity. Taking this into account, we can see that inward FDI flows have increased, but the rates represent about a tenth of overall annual gross fixed capital formation. FDI in today's world represents an important source of investment for countries but, as the sceptics point out, its significance should not be overstated.

Furthermore, Hirst and Thompson also argue that 'most MNCs have an average of about two-thirds of their sales and a higher proportion of their assets in a major region like North America or Europe'. Research and development activities, which provide both strategic market advantage and ensure continuing profitability, are conducted mainly within a firm's home country (70 per cent or above). In addition, although MNCs accounted for 'about 40 per cent of world output in

Table 2.8   Inward FDI flows as a percentage of gross fixed capital formation, by region

Region/economy	1992–97[a]	1998	1999	2000	2004
World	5.2	10.6	16.0	19.8	7.5
Industrialized countries	4.2	9.9	16.2	21.3	6.1
Developing economies	7.9	12.3	14.7	14.9	10.5
Africa	6.5	8.3	11.6	8.8	12.5
Latin America and Caribbean	10.1	17.4	25.6	21.1	15.5
Asia and the Pacific	7.4	10.6	11.3	13.3	9.1
Central and Eastern Europe	6.9	15.2	19.3	18.3	9.5[b]

Source: UNCTAD, *World Investment Report 2004: The Shift Towards Services,* Annex Table B.5 and *WIR 2005: Transnational Corporations and the Internationalisation of Research and Development,* Table B.3 ([a]annual average, [b]2003 figures).

1990...the share taken by their subsidiaries and affiliates abroad was only 7 per cent'. For the sceptics, then, MNCs remain embedded within their home country which serves as their main production and consumer base. They argue that this makes commercial sense for such businesses because they can take 'advantage of a solid core business in a major region of the wealthy industrial world and the benefit of trade and production through subsidiaries and affiliates outside the home territory'.[91] In addition, such companies are often reliant upon 'hot-spot "clusters" of related assets and specialized infrastructure...these immobile resources are comprised of a dense network of specialised, often small, independent enterprises that supply crucial inputs and are difficult to replicate elsewhere'.[92]

With regard to this debate, Linda Weiss has developed three useful criteria by which to assess the current period of globalization: its novelty; its magnitude; and its distribution.[93] In terms of novelty, the sceptics argue that a more accurate measure of trade is one that uses current as opposed to constant prices. If one uses the former measurement, a different picture emerges concerning the level of contemporary trading activity compared to the period preceding the First World War, one that indicates that the level of openness today is not unprecedented. In terms of magnitude, the sceptics would agree that in sheer volumes of trade or in terms of the total value of foreign direct investments the amounts in question are unprecedented. However, the sceptics argue that such measurements need to be compared with a state's overall GDP. In addition, much of the foreign direct investment activity involves mergers and acquisitions rather than investment in new production facilities. In terms of distribution, rather than trading activity and foreign direct investment being spread across the globe, these activities continue to be concentrated in the industrialized countries, particularly the triad. Rather than the contemporary period witnessing the rise of truly transnational corporations, their assets, sales and research and development activities remain centred in their country of origin. The evidence presented by the sceptics thus calls into question the image of a novel era of globalization and instead depicts multinational companies as still embedded within nation-states that continue to monitor, regulate and tax their activities.

The transformationalists

The final group to be considered here, the transformationalists, occupy the middle ground between the globalists and sceptics. Although they do not believe that we are currently living in a globalized world, they do believe that the world is more integrated and that the level of interactions, particularly of the economic kind, between a variety of units (states, corporations, multilateral organizations etc.) are unprecedented – '[G]lobal economic activity is significantly greater relative to domestically-based activity than in previous historical periods and impinges directly or indirectly on a greater proportion of national economic activity than ever before'.[94] In presenting their argument, they, like the sceptics, introduce alternative ways of quantitatively measuring certain aspects of globalization. At the same time, they also point to qualitative changes that have occurred in the last few decades which, they argue, are central to our understanding of globalization. In addition, the transformationalists not only bring to the debate new interpretations of available data, they also provide an alternative interpretation of what is meant by globalization.

The transformationalists' perspective therefore differs fundamentally from that of the globalists and sceptics in a number of ways. They criticize both schools for a 'tendency to conceptualise globalization as prefiguring a singular condition or end-state, that is, a fully integrated global market with price and interest rate equalization'.[95] The globalists, on the one hand, tend to argue that we (or, more accurately, those within the triad) now live in a truly inter-linked economy, one in which the borders of states no longer represent barriers to finance, trade and production. The sceptics, on the other hand, take this model of a perfectly liberalized global economy and then proceed to demonstrate the many ways in which this differs from contemporary reality. The transformationalists argue that in terms of finance, trade and production the world is becoming more globalized and, furthermore, that in all these areas it has gone beyond any levels that we have experienced in the past, even those during the so-called 'belle époque'. There is reasonable evidence to suggest, they argue, that this has 'produced significant international convergence in wages for groups of workers with similar skill levels'.[96]

This may seem very close to the globalists' position; however, there are several important differences. Although, the transformationalists argue that the world has become more globalized, they do not try to compare today's world with some ideal type global economy in order to gauge whether we do or don't live in a world of 'perfectly integrated international markets'.[97] Of course, such models are needed in order for us to understand better the world; and the transformationalists, like most social scientists, employ them in their analyses. But it is misleading to argue, as the sceptics do, that we do not live in a globalized world because several aspects of the contemporary economy do not match that of some idealized model. As they see it, this is a mistaken enterprise. Such models rarely, if ever, converge perfectly with reality. For example, they argue, '[N]ational markets may well fall short of perfect competition but this does not prevent economists from characterizing them as markets with various forms of "imperfections"'.[98] In addition, they do view globalization as an evolving process, but not one that will eventually reach some specified end-point in history. Social, political and economic relations involve highly complex interactions and history is replete with examples of key turning points where identifiable trends are reversed or suddenly take a different turn because of unexpected events. They therefore prefer to view globalization as a complex of open-ended processes with identifiable tendencies for any given historical epoch, but that these processes are always subject to new and sometimes unexpected contingencies. In response, the sceptics point out that if we are to be able to gauge where we are in such a process then we need to specify some end-point on which to base such a judgement, even if it is an 'ideal-type' economic end-point.[99]

Box 2.3 The transformationalists' perspective

The transformationalists point to the fact that:

1 The comparison between GDP and the total sales registered by MNCs is misleading. Instead they compare the GDP of countries with the total value added to the products that MNCs sell. Such an analysis indicates that these corporations are extremely important with regard to the well-being of a country's economy and that this significance is growing.

2 With regard to the convergence in the cost of money, they argue that there is evidence of covered interest rate parity.

3 The high correlation between domestic savings and investment is changing and the proportion of overseas investment is growing.

4 The proportion of foreign direct investment by companies from the developing world has increased significantly in the last two decades and now stands at over 10% of the region's GDP.

5 When calculating the level of world trade to GDP for industrialized countries, the fact that much of the economic activity is related to government provision (and therefore not related to trade) needs to be taken into account. Trade as a proportion of private GDP indicates that trading activity is now far greater than in previous periods.

6 In addition, the number of states trading with each other has increased significantly from 64% in 1960 to 95% in 1990.

7 The declining cost of transport and communication will ensure that these increases in trade and FDI will continue for the foreseeable future.

The transformationalists agree that there is little evidence for the globalists' case concerning the withering away of the state, but they do believe that the processes of globalization have brought certain pressures. They therefore argue that we are currently witnessing not the extinction of the state but its reconstitution.

Significant differences are also apparent concerning the relationship between the state and multinational companies. Transformationalists agree with the sceptics that comparing the total sales of corporations with the GDP of countries produces a misleading picture by exaggerating the importance of corporations in comparison to states. The weakness of the globalists' analysis (refer to Table 2.1), what one writer has referred to as an 'elementary howler', is that it fails to compare like with like by using corporate sales and GDP.[100] GDP aggregates the value-added by the various economic activities conducted within a country. In so doing, it avoids the problem of double-counting by subtracting the costs of any materials or external services incurred by a company from its total sales. But Table 2.1 simply compares GDP with corporate sales, failing to take into account the amount these firms pay to other companies for goods and services, thereby inflating the economic significance of these firms. For the sceptics, there are therefore 'very few truly mammoth global companies that could "threaten" countries'.[101]

A more accurate picture is produced if one compares the GDP of countries with the total value added by the economic activities of the corporations concerned (Table 2.9). By using this more accurate comparison, the ranking of corporations in the top 100 corporations/countries of the world is lowered. The top-performing corporation continues to be Wal-Mart, but it is now ranked 44th (as opposed to 19th) and all other corporations are also ranked lower down the scale. The transformationalists would therefore agree that the globalists have overstated the economic influence of such entities, but they would also point out that, even if this alternative measure were used, 37 corporations appear in the top 100 listing.[102] In addition, they point to the fact that intra-firm trade, (trade within a company) now constitutes approximately a third of total world trade and inter-firm trade (trade between companies) makes up another third.[103] The majority of trading activity is therefore dominated by corporate economic activity.

Table 2.9   Value added of top corporations compared to the GDP of countries, 2002

World ranking	Country or corporation	GDP/Value added (US$ billions)
40	Malaysia	89.7
41	Colombia	81.3
42	Philippines	74.7
43	Chile	70.5
44	Wal-Mart Stores	67.7
45	Pakistan	61.6
46	Peru	53.5
47	Algeria	53.3
48	Exxon	52.6
49	Czech Republic	50.8
50	New Zealand	50.0
51	Bangladesh	47.1
52	UAE	46.5
53	General Motors	46.2
54	Hungary	45.6
55	Ford Motor	45.1
56	Mitsubishi	44.3
57	Mitsui	41.3
58	Nigeria	41.1
59	Citicorp	39.1
60	Itochu	38.4
61	Daimler/Chrysler	37.5
62	Royal Dutch Shell	37.3
63	BP	37.0
64	Romania	36.7

Source: M. Wolf (6 February, 2002), 'Countries still rule the world', *Financial Times*, p.17, cited in D. Held and A. McGrew, *Globalization/Anti-globalization*, Figure 4.1.

In terms of finance, the transformationalists both agree and disagree on the points raised by both the globalists and sceptics. They also point to the unprecedented volume of trading in foreign exchange, securities and derivatives in the last few decades and agree that this presents a challenge to states in terms of monitoring and controlling such activities. They also cite evidence indicating that a convergence in returns for the same assets in the main capital markets has occurred – as would be expected if capital is free to invest anywhere at any time (if returns were not roughly the same for similar types of investments in the major economies, then investors would simply shift their capital to the country offering a higher return). Of course, the question then arises as to why investors should bother to move their money internationally if the returns on their investments are approximately the same. The transformationalists argue that they do so in order to ensure a steady flow of returns over the year because 'business cycles may not be synchronized'.[104]

They also conditionally agree with the globalists concerning the convergence of national interest rates, but only in terms of covered interest rate parity. In other words, when calculating the differences in interest rates between countries, it is necessary to factor in future fluctuations in currency exchange rates. For example, if government A offers a higher interest on their bonds compared to government B, investors also need to factor in whether country A's currency will depreciate relative to country B's currency. Interest rate parity is said to hold when any gain through differences between interest rates is offset by changes in the current and forward exchange rates of the currencies concerned. The transfomationalists argue that, if interests rates are expressed in a common currency there is evidence of convergence (of covered interest rates) among the OECD countries – 'when currency can be sold forward, any difference between rates is exactly offset by the difference between the current and forward rate for the period the asset is held, so that returns are equalized when expressed in a common currency'.[105] In addition, although in the short term real interest rates do not obtain, they cite recent analysis revealing that at '5–10 year horizons, however, the empirical evidence becomes far more supportive'. For the transformationalists this is evidence that over the longer term there is 'some convergence in the costs of capital' for the core industrialized countries.[106] . It should be noted that neither of the above necessarily applies to the case of developing countries because of the variation in risk concerning the possibility of defaults on loans and high inflation.

However, they do agree with the sceptics on two points concerning these issues. First, 'investors tend to display a bias towards holding domestic assets' and also there is a high correlation between national savings and investment rates.[107] However, they also point out that there are some indications that this 'historical relationship between national investment and saving ratios' may be changing.[108] In addition, rather than just pointing to the relatively low level of overseas investment by pension funds as the sceptics do, they would presumably argue that just as important is the overall trend towards greater investment overseas. It may still be true that most industrialized countries' exposure to overseas liabilities is below 30 per cent, but the proportion of overseas investment has grown quite significantly in the 1990s (Table 2.10). Second, these international financial markets do not operate in a vacuum. They would agree with the sceptics that the liberalization of capital accounts was initiated at first in the core industrialized countries who later encouraged similar deregulation in both the developed and developing world via the OECD and IMF. Moreover, these financial institutions 'still rely on national and international regulatory authorities for their effective operation'.[109] But, they point out, although states may have been instrumental in developing the liberalized financial system that we now have, they question whether even concerted action by the major states can put the genie back into the bottle.

A major difference between the transformationalists and the sceptics concerns the form of measurement they adopt in relation to FDI and portfolio investments, with the latter emphasizing investment flows and the former emphasizing investment stocks that have built up over time. In terms of global production, the transformationalists point out that, in the last two decades, inward FDI stock as a percentage of GDP in the industrialized countries has increased at least four-fold (1980–2003); Latin America and the Caribbean have experienced a similar increase; Africa has fared less well experiencing a three-fold increase; the ratio of inward stock to GDP for Asia and the Pacific has less than doubled, although the level was already high in 1980 and by 2003 it was 30 per cent. In terms of distribution, the transformationalists also note that such investment activity is not solely confined to multinational corporations from the highly industrialized countries setting up businesses and production facilities in the less developed countries. They note that companies from less developed countries, particularly from Asia and Latin America, are also investing abroad. Although the figures are

Table 2.10 Overseas investment by pension funds

Country	1994	1999
USA	9%	11%
Canada	16%	17%
United Kingdom	24%	25%
Netherlands	17%	36%
Switzerland	19%	23%
Germany	5%	9%
France	6%	9%
Denmark	8%	9%
Japan	7%	21%
Australia	15%	21%
Singapore	0%	0%
Hong Kong	50%	69%

Source: Rolf Banz and Sarah Clough, 'Globalization Reshaping World's Financial Markets'. Singapore's low level of overseas investment is due to domestic restrictions on its Central Provident Fund.[1]

Note

1   R. Banz and S. Clough, 'Globalization reshaping world's financial markets', *Journal of Financial Planning*. Available on line at http://www. fpanet.org/journal/articles (accessed 17 January 2006). Original table from Intersec Research Corporation. With reference to Singapore, refer to P. Hirst and G. Thompson, *Globalization in Question*, 1999, p. 45.

far less than the level of outward FDI stocks from the industrialized countries, it is still significant that such investment has increased more than three-fold in two decades (Table 2.11).

Sceptics may reply that these figures are percentages of GDP, and a more accurate representation of the impact of foreign direct investment upon domestic economies is to compare such investment with overall capital formation. However, it is noteworthy that sceptics, such as Hirst and Thompson, used the same form of measurement using figures up to 1995 – at that time the data indicated that FDI stocks had increased but not dramatically since the 1980s.[110] However, Table 2.11 indicates that since that time, FDI stocks as a proportion of GDP have increased substantially. Moreover, transformationalists point out that this measure understates the total final investment associated with FDI because it fails to include the domestic sources of funds, 'the capital mobilized by local borrowings and the equity shares of partners'.[111] It is estimated that FDI stocks actually only represent 'approximately 25 per cent of total investment in international production'. Neither do these figures indicate how much of the profits from the multinational's affiliates are reinvested in the country concerned, nor how much capital was provided for such ventures by various financial institutions.[112]

If the total stocks of foreign capital held by countries (stocks, bonds etc.) are compared to world GDP, then a more emphatic picture emerges. For 1870,

Table 2.11 Inward and outward FDI stocks as a percentage of GDP, by region

Region/economy	1980	1985	1990	1995	2000	2002	2003
World							
Inward	6.6	8.3	9.3	10.2	19.3	23	21.7
Outward	5.8	6.6	8.6	10	19.1	22.6	24.0
Industrialized countries							
Inward	4.9	6.2	8.2	8.9	16.6	20.5	20.5
Outward	6.2	7.3	9.6	11.3	21.4	25.8	27.3
Developing economies							
Inward	12.4	16.3	14.7	16.3	29.3	31.9	26.4
Outward	3.6	3.6	3.8	5.7	12.4	12.6	12.7
Africa							
Inward	8.2	9.8	10.9	15.4	24.6	27.0	27.8
Outward	2.2	4.1	5.3	7.3	8.6	7.6	6.2
Latin America and Caribbean							
Inward	6.5	11	10.4	11.7	25.6	34.4	34.1
Outward	6.5	7.7	5.5	5.2	7.9	10.5	13.1
Asia and the Pacific							
Inward	17.6	20.7	17.8	18.7	31.7	31.5	30.3
Outward	1.0	1.1	2.6	5.8	15.1	14.0	13.4
Central and Eastern Europe							
Inward	..	0.2	1.3	5.4	19.2	24.8	23.7[a]
Outward	..	..	0.4	0.9	3.7	6.4	6.0[a]

Source: UNCTAD, *World Investment Report 2004: The Shift Towards Services,* Annex Table B.6 and *WIR 2005: Transnational Corporations and the Internationalisation of Research and Development,* Table B.3 ([a]2003 figures).

Obstfeld and Taylor calculate that 'foreign assets were just 7 percent of world GDP; but this figure rose quickly, to just below 20 percent in the years 1900–14 at the zenith of the classical gold standard. During the interwar period, the collapse was swift, and foreign assets were only 8 percent of world output by 1930, 11 percent in 1938, and just 5 percent in 1945. Since this low point, the ratio climbed slowly to 6 percent in 1960, then dramatically to 25 percent in 1980, 49 percent in 1990, and 92 percent in 2000. Thus, the 1900–14 ratio of foreign investment to output in the world economy was not equalled again until 1980 and has now been approximately quintupled'.[113]

In addition, such quantitative measures, the transformationalists argue, fail to take into account major qualitative changes that have occurred in the last few decades. Traditionally, FDI was largely 'horizontal' in nature, involving the setting up of production sites to overcome trade barriers and/or to take advantage of knowledge/skill intensive clusters within the industrial triad.[114] However, in recent decades 'vertical' FDI that slices up the supply chain locating the different stages of production wherever they are cheapest has become increasingly important. Rather than production sites concentrating on the manufacturing and assembly of constituent components to create a final product in one factory (or one country), improvements in technology facilitating improved coordination and reductions in transport costs have enabled them to divide the production process across countries and even continents.

There has also been a sharp increase in the practice of 'out-sourcing'. 'Vertical' FDI implies that the suppliers of the component parts of a product continue to be at least partly owned and directly managed by the company in question. But rather than investing in setting up their own service or production plant and directly managing the business, corporations are increasingly procuring the required components or services from independent sources. It is argued that, as a result, greater emphasis is now placed on the core functions of managing the supply chain and final assembly rather than concentrating on 'in-house' manufacturing of a product from start to finish. For example, although Nike is regarded as example *par excellence* of a large multinational company, it actually employs only '9000 people, while nearly 75000 people are employed by its independent subcontractors'.[115] In a similar fashion to that of 'vertical' FDI, the growth of 'out-sourcing' heralds a new form of business structure, one in which the upstream linkages of suppliers and the downstream linkages to the final customer have become stretched across continents.[116]

With regard to trade, the previous sections have demonstrated how the globalists and sceptics emphasize different methods for calculating trade levels that, in turn, influence their conclusions. The transformationalists add several new dimensions to this debate. The first point they make is that the trade figures used by the sceptics represent merchandise trade and therefore do not include trade in services (because only since 1980 has reliable data been available). But the transformationalists argue that trade in services 'now constitutes well over 20 per cent of total world trade'.[117] Moreover, using ratios of merchandise trade to GDP will lead to an inaccurate picture of the economy because GDP includes services.[118] For both of these reasons, excluding services therefore leads to an underestimation of contemporary levels of trade.

Second, trade/GDP ratios underestimate the importance of trade to the domestic economy because '[W]hile the merchandise to GDP ratio was roughly comparable to what it is today, trade is now much larger as a share of tradable goods production'.[119] For example, GDP includes several elements of state activity that are not usually associated with trade (although an argument could be made that this in itself is changing). The transformationalists therefore argue that trade/private GDP ratios are more accurate because they involve a comparison of overall trade with economic activity more closely connected to trade.[120] For the industrialized countries, the difference between these two forms of measurement has become particularly important since the Second World War and the advent of the Welfare State. Since 1960, on average, the industrialized countries have increased government expenditure by almost 20 per cent, from 30 per cent of GDP to nearly 50 per cent of GDP in 1995.[121]

This alternative form of analysis indicates that, for several of the industrialized countries since the seventies, trade as a proportion of overall (private) economic activity has actually increased markedly (Table 2.12). Since 1955, all of these countries have witnessed significant increases in the proportion of trade to private GDP, with the exception of Japan. The two biggest economies, the United States and Japan, have the lowest ratios, reflecting both the overall size of their economies but also the relatively lower amount of state expenditure as a proportion of their GDP. When compared to the figures given by Hirst and Thompson, it can be seen that these figures consistently indicate higher levels of trading activity for all countries. Using these figures, the transformationalists argue therefore that, once state spending is taken account of, trade has in fact increased significantly for most of the industrialized countries.

Referring once again to Weiss' triptych, in terms of novelty, the transform- ationlists regard today's level of integration as unprecedented in terms of finance, trade and production. Furthermore, although reversible, current trends indicate that this economic integration is continuing at an ever more rapid pace. They also point to data that indicate that the number of countries trading with each other has increased, (using a constant sample of 68 countries) from around 64 per

Table 2.12 Ratio of trade to private GDP

	1955	1960	1965	1970	1973	1975	1980	1985	1990	1995	1999
France	32	28	28	36	40	44	56	62	56	58	64
Japan	24	22	20	22	22	28	32	28	22	20	22
Netherlands	–	114	108	112	114	124	120	132	116	110	–
UK	54	50	46	54	60	68	66	72	64	72	66
USA	10	12	12	14	16	20	24	20	24	28	28
Sweden	54	56	54	62	68	74	86	94	82	94	110

Source: IMF, *International Financial Statistics*, Online at http://ifs.apdi.net/imf.[1]

Note
1   Private GDP is defined here as GDP less government consumption expenditure.

cent in 1960 to over 95 per cent in 1990.[122] It may still be true that '[E]conomic interactions fall away dramatically with distance', but this increase in trading is at least partly spurred on by improvements in technology and the falling costs of communication in a variety of fields.[123] This is not only facilitating greater levels of integration in the economic sphere but also enabling an intense network of personal relations to develop, thus increasing the 'scope and depth of consciousness of the world as a single place'.[124] However, enmeshment in this global trading system remains uneven, with Africa trading with noticeably fewer countries than the world average. With regard to magnitude, the transformationalists would agree with the sceptics that such measurements are only meaningful if they are relative. But they would point out that the value-added of some of the major corporations of the world equals that of many states; that FDI has increased significantly in the last two decades and inward directed stocks now stand at about 20 per cent of GDP for the industrialized countries and 25 per cent for developing countries; trade has increased rapidly and now surpasses even the high levels experienced in the 'belle époque'.

At the same time, the transformationalists recognize that the distribution of economic activity is extremely uneven and centred on the triad. However, they do point out that several developing regions of the world are increasing their share of world trade and are attracting ever greater levels of investment. They also point to the fact that this investment is no longer one way, with several developing regions investing in economies other than their own. In addition, they argue that the effects of globalization are not limited to any one region of the world; it is cutting 'across national and geographic boundaries bringing on board within the core, segments of the Third World and relegating segments and groups in both the traditional core of the system and in the Third World to peripheral status'. For Ankie Hoogvelt, this is creating a tripartite division within states. The developed countries are said to be experiencing the emergence of a 30/30/40 society in which: only 40 per cent enjoy full job security, 30 per cent are employed but do not enjoy stable employment and another 30 per cent are effectively unemployed. Hoogvelt argues that less developed countries are experiencing a similar process but in this case the

Table 2.13 Declining cost of transport and communications

	Sea freight[a]	Air transport[b]	Trans-Atlantic phone calls[c]	Computers (1990 = 100)
1930	60	0.68	245	–
1940	63	0.46	189	–
1950	34	0.30	53	–
1960	27	0.24	46	12,500
1970	27	0.16	32	1,947
1980	24	0.10	5	362
1990	29	0.11	3	100

Source: *Human Development Report 1999: Globalization with a Human Face*, Oxford: Oxford University Press, 1999, Table 1.3. ([a]average ocean freight and port charges per ton, [b]average revenue per passenger mile , [c]3 minutes NY/London). Cited in D. Held, A. McGrew, D. Goldblatt and J. Perraton, *Global Transformations*, 1999, p. 170.

amount of people excluded is 'approaching 50 per cent, with the middle group a narrow band of between 20 and 30 per cent'.[125]

Although the transformationalists argue that there is little evidence for the globalists' case concerning the withering away of state capabilities, they do believe that the processes of globalization have brought certain pressures to bear upon the state. Multinationals are not as footloose as they are often depicted. Relocation to new countries have attendant relocation costs and, particularly in the high-technology and service sectors, they depend upon pools of skilled labour, a well-developed infrastructure and reliable high-quality suppliers in the local area. However, if the advantages still outweigh the costs, then there is some probability that these companies would relocate. Similarly, financial institutions have the opportunity to invest in low taxation countries, but they may prefer lower risk ventures in higher taxation countries with the more reliable legal systems and business practices that they are accustomed to. However, the potential does exist for companies to relocate and for financial institutions to shift their investments and this in itself may have an impact upon state policy. Redistribution of wealth by states through taxation on corporate profits may thus be constrained because policy makers fear that it will prompt large-scale disinvestment in their economies.

A question also arises concerning the state's actual ability to monitor, audit and tax corporations in today's world successfully. Given that intra-firm trade currently constitutes approximately one-third of total world trade there is much room for multinational companies to engage in transfer pricing.[126] Because this type of exchange, in effect, constitutes an internal trade regime with the prices of components set by the company itself, such prices may not reflect true market prices. Instead, companies can set arbitrary prices for components in order to take advantage of the differences in corporation tax between countries, artificially reducing profits in high taxation countries and increasing them in countries that offer lower tax rates.

According to the globalists, many states have now become so integrated into the global trading system that similar constraints are also felt in this area. Trade protection would result in similar policies being implemented by other countries and would have dire consequences for domestic export-orientated businesses. A policy considered to be a traditional element of a state's economic armoury is thus becoming a less and less feasible instrument in today's world. Although it is likely that the overall economic benefits outweigh the losses, it should also be noted that one consequence of the reduction in trade tariffs between countries is that state revenue from this type of taxation will normally decrease which will also have an impact upon a state's redistributional policies.

However, for the transformationalists, this does not imply the extinction of the state but its reconstitution. As they see it, globalization has brought with it certain pressures, particularly in the area of welfare provision. But rather than the state being a passive bystander, it is in the process of actively reforming itself, '"re-engineering" its power, functions and authority'.[127] Globalization, it is argued, has 'inspired a transformation in the role of the advanced industrialised state away from its previous incarnations as a social democratic welfare state or industrialisation-driven developmental state, and towards a competition state'.[128] Such competition states seek to enhance their economic performance through emulation and innovation. They continually monitor each other's economic performance, emulating the best models in order to enhance their own competitiveness. At the same time, emphasis is also placed on improving the 'quality of the institutional and policy environment for fostering an entrepreneur-driven enterprise culture capable of generating new sources of innovation, employment and prosperity'.[129] To that end, there has been a noticeable move away from cradle to grave social welfare towards the state investing in 'human capital and technical skills – to make national economies more competitive – as against the provision of "passive" welfare benefits'.[130]

States are also responding to the challenges of a more open world economy by actively engaging in multilateral institutions. At the international level, for example, states are actively participating in trade talks in order to ensure that their interests are represented and are members of various international financial institutions tasked with helping manage the world economy and monitoring the plethora of financial transactions that are occurring on a daily basis. At the regional level, states are also collaborating and pooling their resources, and are developing economic blocs thereby increasing their bargaining power at the international level. As a result, we are currently witnessing the growth of 'powerful new non-territorial forms of economic and political organisation in the global domain'.[131] But rather than this leading to the hollowing out of the state, the transformationalists argue that the state uses its sovereignty as a 'bargaining resource', sacrificing certain aspects of state power in order to gain influence and increased capabilities in other areas.[132]

Conclusion

This chapter has described how the three main schools of thought associated with globalization differ in their interpretations of how open the world economy is today. Much of this debate focuses on the levels of cross-border flows of finance, trade and FDI. In so doing, there is a danger of presenting the arguments of each of the schools as if no internal disagreements existed within them. Of course, differences of opinion do exist within each school of thought. Moreover, overlaps between the schools also exist. For example, Hirst and Thompson, when establishing the differences between an international and a global economy, clearly state that the 'opposition of these two types for conceptual clarity conceals the possibly messy combination of the two in reality'.[133] At the other end of the spectrum, Peter Dickens, while supporting the view that we are witnessing growing levels of economic globalization, also argues that the 'state remains a most significant force in shaping the world economy' and, moreover, '[A]ll the elements in the production network are regulated within some kind of political structure whose basic unit is the national state but which also includes such supranational institutions as the International Monetary Fund or the World Trade Organization, as well as regional groupings such as the European Union or the North American

Free Trade Agreement'.[134] Therefore, it is important to remember that variation is also apparent within each school and that overlaps between these schools exist.

However, despite some overlaps between some of these writers, this chapter has indicated that major differences are apparent between these three schools of thought. Each school views the world economy differently in terms of novelty, magnitude and distribution. The globalists regard today's world economy as markedly different in magnitude compared to those of previous periods of history. Although it is conceded that the unprecedented levels of trade and investment are currently confined to the triad, they argue that it will shortly 'encompass most East European countries, most of Asian newly industrialized economies (NIEs), and some Latin American countries, if they adopt ILE polices'.[135] As we have seen, the sceptics take issue with all three of these claims producing evidence that indicates that the world was as globalized at the end of the nineteenth century. They do concede, however, that recent decades have witnessed a marked increase in FDI but this has largely been confined to the core industrialized countries, plus a handful of developing states. The transformationalists, on the other hand, agree with the globalists that the levels of trade and investment exceed those of any other period throughout history. But because this is an ongoing process it is more accurate to describe the world as globalizing rather than globalized. Furthermore, such a process is potentially reversible, contingent upon political, social and economic events.

Certainly the sceptics have provided a much needed counter-balance to some of the overstatements in the globalists' thesis. Much of the increasing levels of trade, finance and FDI flows can be explained by the gradual lifting of protectionist restrictions after the Second World War. The sceptics therefore remind us that globalization is not a phenomenon unique to the contemporary world and a similar situation did indeed exist prior to the First World War, but was brought to a halt as protectionist sentiment mounted across the industrialized world. However, the most recent figures, particularly concerning trade and FDI do indicate that, for the industrialized countries, these activities are increasing very rapidly indeed. Concerning trade, these levels have gone beyond the levels witnessed in the 'belle époque'. Even the sceptics' merchandise trade figures indicate that the contemporary period is beginning to exceed that of the Gold Standard period (out of the five countries chosen, Japan is the exception). However, using merchandise trade to GDP ratios underestimates the real level of trading activity. In addition, one needs to take into account the prodigious growth in state spending in the core industrialized countries since the 1960s. By using trade to private GDP ratios, the transformationalists provide us with a more accurate picture of the proportion of tradeable goods exchanged between countries in today's world.

The debate between these three schools is not just limited to arguments concerning the magnitude of financial, trade and FDI flows, but by implication raises the question of how economically integrated the world is. Have levels of cross-border investments reached such an extent that the economic condition of one country is now inextricably linked to other countries? Have corporations restructured their production processes across the globe to such a degree that their core operations can no longer be associated with one country? Has the content of trade changed radically in the last few decades, thus reflecting the increasing complexity of supply chains? As we have seen, each of these schools differs in their answers to these questions. In qualitative terms, the globalists and transformationalists agree that the global economy is witnessing a fundamental restructuring. As to the degree to which this restructuring has already occurred, of course they disagree. But in comparison, the sceptics question whether there is greater openness and/or integration both in quantitative and qualitative terms. The sceptics are therefore set apart from the other two schools by their questioning whether the international economy has really changed fundamentally over the last century. However, the other two schools do see evidence of such change but differ as to how much change we have thus far experienced.[136]

At least some of these qualitative differences ultimately question the validity of the use of quantitative figures comparing the contemporary period of globalization with the 'belle époque'. Paul Krugman has identified at least four qualitative differences between these two periods, all of which the globalists and transformationalists would probably agree on.[137] Krugman argues that there has been a substantial increase in intra-industrial trade, i.e. trading of similar goods between countries. Before the First World War most merchandise trade for the industrialized countries involved the import of raw materials and the export of manufactured goods. However, similar goods now constitute a large part of trade which he argues is probably a result of the increasing complexity of manufactured products so that, in any given category, a large variety of similar yet distinguishable goods exist. As previously mentioned, there is also a tendency for contemporary services and production to be divided into discrete segments geographically separated from each other leading, to amongst other things, a substantial increase in the volume of inter-firm trade. Robert Feenstra provides an excellent example using the case of the Barbie doll – '[T]he raw materials for the doll (plastic and hair) are obtained from Taiwan and Japan. Assembly...has now migrated to lower-cost locations in Indonesia, Malaysia, and China. The moulds themselves come from the United States, as do additional paints used in decorating the doll'.[138] Recent analyses of several OECD countries (G7 plus Australia, Denmark and the Netherlands) estimates that the degree of 'vertical specialization' constitutes approximately 21 per cent of overall trade for these countries and for countries such as South Korea, Ireland and Taiwan the level is about 30 per cent.[139] Using an expanded data set in later work, some of the same researchers found that vertical specialization exports 'accounted for 30% of the growth in the overall export/GDP ratio' of the countries concerned.[140] For several less developed countries, this figure is probably much higher because they have actively sought to embed themselves in this new network and, in addition, smaller economies are more likely to be involved in such vertical specialization than larger countries because the latter 'find it easier than small ones, for scale economy reasons, to retain production of every stage'. This may explain, for example, why 'at least half of US–Mexican trade could be due to vertical specialization'.[141] Such qualitative changes highlight the weakness of relying purely on levels of trading activity, trade has undergone, and is undergoing, dramatic changes. Contemporary trade characteristics are thus significantly different to those of the 'belle époque'. The sceptics are right to draw some parallels with earlier periods, but it is equally important to take note of the qualitative changes that have occurred – to recognize that history rhymes rather than repeats itself.

3 How global is globalization?

The last chapter concluded that the transformationlists' depiction of globalization was the most accurate of the three schools. In terms of levels of trade and finance and production (FDI) we have witnessed significant increases in the last few decades and that this trend is set to continue for the foreseeable future. It was also pointed out that the qualitative changes that have occurred in all three areas during this period have been as important as the quantitative increases. In the sphere of finance the development of innovatory instruments, such as futures, options and swaps has attracted high levels of investment in such derivatives, but just as importantly it has provided investors with the opportunity to retain a greater proportion of their capital for further financial transactions (which may or may not include investing in a greater number of derivatives). In terms of trade and production, it was argued that: there has been a substantial increase in intra-industrial and intra-firm trade; the slicing up of the supply chain has also led to a substantial increase in the volume of inter-firm trade; this geographical reconfiguration of the supply chain also partly explains the rise of so-called 'supertrading economies'.[1]

Much of the debate surrounding these three schools of thought (the globalists, sceptics and transformationalists) centres mainly on the industrialized economies. Yet globalization is portrayed in the literature as involving an increasing number of countries becoming ever more integrated into the global economic system. Although the intensity of interaction is not seen as homogenous, the implication of such integration is that, over the *longue durée* a greater degree of uniformity will pertain. For example, Jan Aart Scholte emphasizes the supraterritorial nature of economic activity, and the existence of 'supraterritorial production' involving 'intra-firm trade within a global company as well as, if not more than, international trade between countries. Through so-called "global sourcing", a producer draws the necessary inputs from anywhere in the world'.[2] Others have argued that '[F]or everybody ... "globalization" is the intractable fate of the world, an irreversible process; it is also a process which affects us all in the same measure and in the same way'.[3] Such pronouncements are given some support by the various annual international trade and investment reports. In 1992 the *United Nations World Investment Report*, reflecting on the fact that by 1990 FDI flows amounted to $225 billion, stated that in the latter half of the 1980s there had been 'a massive outpouring of foreign direct investment'.[4] Yet this figure was to be dwarfed by the six-fold increase that was to occur in the nineties, with FDI inflows reaching a total of $1.3 trillion at the end of the millennium, although since then it has declined to $560 billion.[5] The cumulative effect of this investment has been that by the year 2000 the total value of FDI stock reached $6 trillion. The fact that '[O]ver 60,000 TNCs now own more than 820,000 affiliates abroad' and that the 'ratio of foreign affiliates' sales to global GDP was almost 50 per cent' gives grist to the globalists' argument that a truly global network of production has developed.[6]

This chapter examines whether globalization, understood as the intensification of economic relations between states, is the dominant pattern of the contemporary world system, or whether alternative models of economic interaction depict our current condition more accurately. In this respect, three main perspectives directly challenge the view that we currently live in a more globalized world arguing, instead, that this growing interconnectedness is geographically delimited. These are: regionalization; triadization; and the involutionist perspective.[7] The first perspective argues that economic activity is becoming ever more concentrated within clearly identifiable geographical regions. The second argues that, rather than the dominant trend being the intensification of regional economic activity, the increasing interdependence of the three main economic blocs (the European Union, Japan and the United States) is the most significant development in the contemporary era. The third perspective argues that, rather than experiencing

Box 3.1 Regionalism, regionalization and triadization

Regionalism

Refers to 'a formal process of intergovernmental collaboration between two or more states'.[1]

Regionalization

Refers to the process of economic integration between two or more states in terms of trade and investment.

Triadization

Refers to the increasing interdependence of the three main economic blocs (the European Union, Japan and the United States/NAFTA).

Economic involution

Refers to the intensification of economic relations between the core industrialized countries and a relative decline in the levels of trade and investment between this core and the less developed periphery.

1 J. Ravenhill, 'Regionalism' in J. Ravenhill (ed.), *Global Political Economy*, Oxford: Oxford University Press, 2005, p. 117.

an expansion and intensification of global economic relations, we are in fact currently witnessing the intensification of economic relations between the core industrialized countries and a relative decline in the levels of trade and investment between this core and the less developed periphery.

These three perspectives are often seen as mutually exclusive yet this may not necessarily be the case. Instead, each perspective may be providing us with a partial view of a larger process. This chapter therefore evaluates the claims of all three perspectives and argues that they are not entirely incompatible, but rather the veracity of their claims depends upon the particular type of economic activity under investigation.[8] In addition, the chapter argues that the trends identified can be largely explained by three central dynamics of the international economy: the continuing concentration on primary product production in much of the developing world; the increase in intra-industrial trade between OECD countries; and the increase in intra-firm trade/vertical specialization both between OECD countries and also between the OECD and certain developing countries, mainly located within East Asia.

Core–periphery relations

In the 1970s, several authors argued that a new international division of labour was emerging as a result of firms taking advantage of cheaper skilled and unskilled labour around the world.[9] However, such arguments were countered by evidence that trade and investment remained mainly in the core industrialized countries.[10] However, since the 1970s both trading activity between East Asia and the industrialized countries and investment in that region have gathered pace. Recent work by Ankie Hoogvelt has pointed to an involution of trade and capital such that levels of trade and investment between the industrialized countries is intensifying, but that such activities between the industrialized and developing world are declining in comparison to total world trade and investment. However, East Asia is the exception to this trend. Both the outsourcing of production tasks and the development of production facilities abroad by companies in order to take advantage of cheaper production costs are viewed as major driving forces of globalization. Yet this international division of labour is highly regional in nature, concentrated for the main part in East Asia.

If we examine the global economy in terms of core and periphery, it is claimed by those advocating the involutionist argument that, in relative terms, the industrialized countries of the core are attracting an ever-greater proportion of world investment and trade whereas the opposite is true of the less industrialized countries.[11] Rather than seeing the contemporary era as one in which there is an increasing 'enmeshment of national economies in global economic transactions', these writers see an intensification of economic interdependence between the industrialized countries and at one and the same time greater marginalization of most developing countries.[12] Thus, for example, Ankie Hoogvelt argues that we are currently witnessing 'a significant re-distribution of trade participation *within* the core, the graduation of a small number of peripheral nations with a comparatively small population base to "core" status, but above all to a declining economic interaction between core and periphery, both relative to aggregate world trade and relative to total populations participating in the network'.[13] Hoogvelt explains that such an involution involves 'an intensification of trade and capital linkages within the core of the capitalist system, and a relative, selective, withdrawal of such linkages from the periphery'.[14] She further clarifies one of the key points of the involutionist argument, that it refers to the *relative* shares of world finance and trade received by the core industrialized countries and the peripheral developing economies, not to absolute measures of increases in volumes of trade and finance. The following section examines these claims in relation to foreign direct investment and both merchandise trade and trade in services.

Foreign direct investment

In terms of FDI, Hoogvelt points out that the developing world has received a declining proportion of world FDI – 'up to 1960, the Third World had received half of the total direct investment flows; this percentage had declined to one-third in 1966, and to one-quarter in 1974. By 1988–9 it had dropped still further to 16.9 per cent'.[15] Such findings led Hoogvelt to the same conclusion as that attributed to Fidel Castro, i.e. 'that there is one thing worse than being exploited by the multinationals, namely *not* being exploited by the multinationals'.[16] However, it can be seen from Table 3.1 that the end of the eighties marked a low point in FDI inflows to developing countries. From a low of 17.5 per cent of world FDI inflows during 1988–90, the proportion of inflows accruing to the developing world has since risen reaching a peak of 35.9 per cent. However, there are two reasons to exercise caution in relation to these figures. They are highly sensitive to mergers and acquisitions in the northern core; for example, an extremely high level of mergers and acquisitions within the industrialized bloc accounts for a very low reading of FDI flows in 1999–2000. Second, the large inflows that we are currently witnessing reflect the economic upturn and the huge appetite of China for primary resources which have prompted (a possibly short term) greater investment within this sector. But if we compare the 2003–5 figure with 1970 (26.8 per cent), it

Table 3.1 Distribution of world FDI inflows, 1979–2005 (percentage)

Region	1979–1980	1988–1990	1998–2000	2003–2005
Industrialized countries	79.7	82.5	77.3	59.4
EU	39.1	40.3	46.0	40.7
Japan	0.4	0.04	0.8	0.8
United States	23.8	31.5	24.0	12.6
Developing countries	20.3	17.5	21.7	35.9
Africa	2.0	1.9	1.0	3.0
Latin America and Caribbean	13.0	5.0	9.7	11.5
Asia and Pacific	5.3	10.5	11.0	21.4
South-East Europe and CIS	0.02	0.02	0.9	4.7

Source: UNCTAD, *World Investment Report 2006*, Table 1.1.

would appear that the eighties represented an extremely low point in FDI inflows to developing countries and that the level returned to similar levels at the turn of the millennium and has since increased substantially – but a portion of this increase is probably a temporary trend.[17]

A less volatile measurement is inward FDI stock representing the cumulative totals of inflows. From Table 3.2 it can be seen that the developing world has maintained a level around 30 per cent of world share (if one includes Central and E. Europe – Table 3.2). If this is compared to figures for 1960 (32.3 per cent) and 1973 (27.1 per cent), rather than a steady involution of foreign direct investment, it can be seen that inward FDI stock is currently at similar levels to that of the seventies.[18] Although, as Hoogvelt rightly points out, this certainly does not represent a 'monumental turnaround in fortunes', it is not quite involution either.[19]

However, as can be seen from Table 3.2, the distribution of FDI within the developing world is extremely uneven. The top five developing countries (in terms of inward FDI stock) alone account for almost 60 per cent of FDI inward investment in the developing world.[20] The division of FDI into industrialized and developing blocs thus hides as much as it reveals. Despite the relatively stable share of FDI inward investment for the developing world stabilizing at about 30 per cent, this mainly accrues to East Asia and Latin America with China (22 per cent), Hong Kong (16.4 per cent), Mexico (7.3 per cent), Singapore (6.5 per cent), Brazil (5.6 per cent), Malaysia (2.6 per cent), Indonesia (2.5 per cent), South Korea (2 per cent) and Thailand (1.6 per cent) being some of the main recipients.[21]

Critics might point out that this is a relative measure to what the rest of the world is receiving and that in absolute terms, FDI stocks in the developing world have increased several fold since 1980.[22] In addition, if we measure inward FDI stocks relative to GDP, then, since 1980, Africa has increased its inward stock from around 8 per cent of regional GDP to just over 25 per cent (2003). Furthermore, Africa's performance in the last two decades, in terms of attracting inward FDI stock would appear to be slightly above the developing world's average (from 12.4 per cent of GDP to 31.4 per cent in the same period). As a percentage of its GDP, inward FDI stock has tripled in the last two decades for Africa, whilst for the developing world as a whole it has increased two-and-a-half times.[23]

Table 3.2 Regional distribution of inward FDI stock (percentage)

	1990	1995	2000	2002	2003
Industrialized countries	71.7	68	65.9	68.5	69.2
Western Europe	40.8	40.5	39.1	41.7	42.9
North America	26.0	22.0	23.4	23.4	22.2
Developing countries	28.1	30.6	31.9	28.4	27.7
Africa	2.6	2.6	2.3	2.0	2.0
America	6.0	6.7	8.4	7.9	7.9
Asia	19.4	21.3	21.1	18.4	17.7
Central and Eastern Europe	0.1	1.3	2.3	3.1	3.2

Source: UNCTAD, *World Investment Report 2004*, Table B.3.

However, two counter-points should be noted. First, the involutionist hypothesis is based upon a relative measure of world shares of trade and investment. Second, some caution needs to be taken with these figures. Most obviously, if a country has a low level of GDP, then inward FDI stock may appear large, although in absolute terms the amount may be relatively smaller compared to that of other recipients. In addition, if during the same period GDP has not grown as strongly as in other regions, then paradoxically it will appear that those regions with slower growth are attracting relatively greater and greater levels of inward FDI stock, thereby painting a far rosier picture than reality. Between 1990 and 2003, the GDP of East Asia and the Pacific grew by 7.2 per cent and of South Asia grew by 5.5 per cent compared to: Latin America and the Caribbean (2.7 per cent); Middle East and N. Africa (3.2 per cent); Sub-Saharan Africa (2.7 per cent); and high income countries (2.25 per cent).[24] The actual increases in FDI in East Asia and in the industrialized core, in absolute terms, were therefore much higher than elsewhere in the developing world.

In relation to the involutionist perspective, we can thus say that the eighties represented a period of large FDI inflows to the industrialized core and, as a result, the level of FDI stocks in the core increased relative to those of the developing world, but since then FDI inflows to the developing world have picked up so that stocks have stabilized at levels comparable to those of the earlier decades of 1960 and 1970. Stasis, rather than involution may be a better description for FDI inflows and levels of inward stock. However, within the developing bloc, the greatest share has accrued to Asia. Latin America's share has stabilized, but Africa's diminutive share has shrunk still further.

Trade

Recent data indicate that in the case of shares of world trade, Hoogvelt's involution perspective is quite apt. Table 3.3 indicates that at least some of the Eastern European and the former Soviet Union countries are slowly recovering their share of world trade. But the fortunes of the countries within this group have been mixed, with countries such as Ukraine, Moldova, the Caucasus and Central Asia still suffering from the effects of the dissolution of the Soviet Union. Others have made a relatively

Table 3.3 Shares of world merchandise exports, 1948–2003

Year	1948	1953	1963	1973	1983	1993	2003
World trade	100.0	100.0	100.0	100.0	100.0	100.0	100.0
Developed world	62.9	63.8	66.6	70.8	63.7	72.0	64.5
Central Europe/Baltic States/CIS[a]	6.0	8.1	11.0	9.1	9.5	2.9	5.5
Developing world	31.1	28.1	22.5	20.1	26.8	25.1	30.0

Source: WTO, *International Trade Statistics: 2004*, Table II.2.

Note
a   Figures are significantly affected by (i) changes in the country composition of the region and major adjustment in trade conversion factors between 1983 and 1993, and (ii) the inclusion of the Baltic States and the CIS mutual trade between 1993 and 2002.

early recovery and are now producing above their 1989 levels, such as, Poland, Hungary, Czech Republic and Slovakia.[25] But taken as an economic bloc, this group has still not recovered its share of world trade. The developing area's share has increased from 22.5 per cent in 1963 to 30 per cent in 2003, and the industrialized countries' share now constitutes 64.5 per cent of world trade.[26] Within this broad economic bloc the shares of various regions has changed quite radically over time. The United States' share of world exports has halved from its post-war (1948) high of 27.3 per cent to 13.7 per cent. On the other hand, Western Europe's share has increased from its post-war low of 31.5 per cent to 43.1 per cent and, similarly, Japan has increased its share from 0.4 per cent to 6.5 per cent.[27] Similarly, much has changed within the bloc of developing countries, principally the export boom in Asia, which has witnessed more than a doubling in its share of world exports from its low point in the early seventies. Much of this is as a result of China's vertiginous growth, but taking this into account the rest of Asia has, over 40 years, increased its share of world merchandise exports significantly (Table 3.4).[28]

Although Table 3.3 would seem to imply that stasis rather than involution is a more appropriate term to apply to the developing countries' position within the world trade system, it is apparent from Table 3.4 that there has been a major realignment of shares of world merchandise exports in the developing world and several long-term trends beginning in the sixties are discernible. First, both Hoogvelt and Castells are correct to point out the deleterious decline in Africa's position *vis-à-vis* world exports, to the extent that it is now more accurate to further subdivide developing countries into 'third' and 'fourth' worlds.[29] Since the sixties, Africa's share of merchandise exports has halved and is approximately a third of what it was just after the Second World War. However, the devastation in the core wrought by the Second World War meant that there was an unusually

Table 3.4 Developing countries' share of world merchandise exports (percentage)

	1948	1953	1963	1973	1983	1993	2003
World	100.0	100.0	100.0	100.0	100.0	100.0	100.0
Asia (excluding Japan)	**13.2**	**11.6**	**8.9**	**8.5**	**11.1**	**16.2**	**19.6**
China	0.9	1.2	1.3	1.0	1.2	2.5	6.0
India	2.2	1.3	1.0	0.5	0.5	0.6	0.8
Six East Asian traders[a]	3.0	2.7	2.4	3.4	5.3	9.2	9.7
Latin America and							
Caribbean	**12.3**	**10.5**	**7.0**	**4.7**	**5.8**	**4.4**	**5.2**
Mexico	1.0	0.7	0.6	0.4	1.4	1.4	2.3
Brazil	2.0	1.8	0.9	1.1	1.2	1.1	1.0
Argentina	2.8	1.3	0.9	0.6	0.4	0.4	0.4
Africa	**7.3**	**6.5**	**5.7**	**4.8**	**4.5**	**2.5**	**2.4**
South Africa[b]	2.0	1.7	1.5	1.0	1.0	0.7	0.5
Middle East	2.0	2.7	3.2	4.1	6.8	3.4	4.1

Source: WTO, *International Trade Statistics,* 2004, Table II.2.

Notes
a   Hong Kong, Malaysia, South Korea, Singapore, Taiwan and Thailand.
b   Beginning with 1998, figures refer to South Africa only and no longer to the Southern African Customs Union.

high demand in the core for goods from the periphery; it is thus more accurate to take the sixties as the comparator. In the case of Latin America and the Caribbean, from this period, their share has dropped by 2 per cent to 5.2 per cent. However, taking the region as a whole masks the true reality of the situation, which is that Mexico's membership of NAFTA has led to a vast increase in its trading activity. If one excludes Mexico, then Latin America and the Caribbean's share of merchandise exports has also halved in the last 40 years and is a third of its 1953 figure. In sum, the majority of developing countries have witnessed a deleterious decline in their share of world merchandise exports. The major success story is East Asia, which now accounts for almost two-thirds of developing countries' merchandise exports.

A similar pattern is also apparent for the developing world's shares of services exports (Table 3.5). Africa and the Americas are experiencing a decline in their proportion of world services exports, but not as severely as in the case of merchandise exports. Once again, the success of Asia is apparent with a 16.8 per cent share of world services exports, but China is responsible for a far lower share of services exports. Two other points are noteworthy. In the last 20 years, a significant shift in favour of North America has occurred within the industrialized bloc, with Europe losing more than 10 per cent of its share of world services exports. In addition, over the same period, the developing bloc has made a fairly significant gain (4.7 per cent) in its overall proportion of world services exports, unlike the pattern apparent in Table 3.4 above for world merchandise exports. They have thus made important inroads into the high value-added sector, currently representing just over 22 per cent of world exports in services. However, the gains can be attributed mainly to East Asia.

When analysing such figures, Hoogvelt claims that '*all* the gains, and more, may be attributed to just four "Tiger" economies in East Asia, namely, Hong Kong, Korea, Taiwan and Singapore'.[30] But this masks the impressive increases in trade in several other developing countries; for example, since 1960: Thailand's share of world merchandise trade has increased from one third of a per cent to 1.1

Table 3.5 Services exports (percentage, by region)

Region	1980	1990	2000	2002
World	100	100	100	100
Developing countries	**17.9**	**18.1**	**23.1**	**22.6**
Africa	3.5	2.6	2.2	2.1
America	4.8	3.8	4.1	3.7
Asia	9.5	11.7	16.8	16.8
South, East and Southeast Asia	6.8	9.5	14.2	14.6
Less China	6.3	8.8	12.2	12.2
Central and Eeastern Europe	–	–	**3.6**	**4.2**
Industrialized countries	**79.1**	**79.9**	**73.2**	**73.2**
North America	14.3	20.1	22.2	20.2
Europe	57.6	52.7	44.0	46.9
Others	7.2	7.1	7.1	6.1

Source: UNCTAD, *Development and Globalization*, 2004, Table 4.2A.

per cent; Malaysia from 0.63 per cent to 1.28 per cent; and Mexico from 0.74 per cent to 2.37 per cent. Significantly, these gains are not confined to trade in primary products with each of these countries' share in world exports of manufactures increasing rapidly in the last two decades, from 1980 to 2004: Thailand increased its share from 0.1 per cent to 1.1 per cent; Malaysia from 0.2 per cent to 1.5 per cent; and Mexico from 0.4 per cent to 2.4 per cent.[31] In terms of world service exports, once again success is not limited to the four Asian Tigers with Thailand's share of world service exports increasing from 0.1 per cent in 1980 to 1.1 per cent in 2004; Malaysia's increasing from 0.2 per cent to 1.5 per cent; and Mexico's increasing from 0.4 per cent to 2.3 per cent.[32] Although these two S.E. Asian countries' economies were devastated by the Asian crisis of 1997–8, they are slowly recovering and their recent growth rates have been impressive (since 2003 they have registered above 6 per cent GDP growth).[33] Compared with other developing countries, their growth and trade shares are still very significant. The figures above may not seem all that striking, but their growth is put into perspective when one considers that an 'Asian Tiger' such as Singapore currently has a share of world merchandise trade of 1.9 per cent.[34] Moreover, when one bears in mind that it is estimated that a one per cent increase in Africa's share of world trade would generate $70 billion in foreign exchange gains for this region and that the whole of Sub-Saharan Africa constitutes only 1.3 per cent of world trade in goods and services, these increases are very significant indeed.[35] This is not to dispute Hoogvelt's general conclusion that there has been an involution of the developing countries' share of world trade. But the higher than average performance of other economies should be included, while acknowledging that most developing regions suffered a decline in their shares of world trade.

Regionalization or triadization?

Two other perspectives are presented in the contemporary globalization literature. On the one hand, there are those that argue that 'the vast majority of manufacturing and service activity is organized regionally, not globally'.[36] On the other hand, there are those that argue we are witnessing the development of a truly inter-linked economy based upon the United States, European Union and Japan.[37] These two perspectives, the intensification of economic activity within regional blocs and the growing economic interdependence between the three major economic areas, are often portrayed as competing alternatives to that of globalization, yet as this section will demonstrate the former best describes current world trading patterns while the latter best describes world patterns of foreign direct investment.

Regionalism and regionalization

The nineties not only witnessed the deeper integration of the European Union with its adoption of a single market framework in 1992 and the adoption of a common currency by a majority of its members in 1999, but also the creation of several other regional trade agreements. In 1991, Argentina, Brazil, Paraguay and Uruguay established the South American common market, MERCOSUR. In 1992, the ASEAN Free Trade Agreement (AFTA) was created and quickly expanded to include not only the original ASEAN member states but also Vietnam (1995), Lao and Myanmar (1997) and Cambodia (1999).[38] In the same year, the South African Development Community (SADC) was created and now includes Angola, Botswana, Democratic Republic of Congo, Lesotho, Madagascar, Malawi, Mauritius, Mozambique, Namibia, South Africa, Swaziland, Tanzania and Zimbabwe. Finally, in 1994 the North American Free Trade Association (NAFTA) was created between the United States, Canada and Mexico, thus superseding the US–Canada Free Trade Agreement of 1989. These agreements thus joined the ranks of a whole host of other regional frameworks, such as the Central American Common Market (CACM 1961), the Caribbean Community and Common Market (CARICOM 1973), the Economic Organization of West African States (ECOWAS 1975), the Gulf Cooperation Council (GCC 1981) and also the trans-regional non-discriminatory trade promotion of the Asia–Pacific Economic Community (1989).[39] These arrangements vary in their intensity and scope with some constituting simply a free trade area (free movement of goods and services), others going further representing a customs union (common set of trade policies towards non-members) and some working towards establishing a common market (free movement of both people and money within the region). In 2000, the West African Economic and Monetary Union (UEMOA, 1994), comprising Benin, Burkina Faso, Cote d'Ivoire, Mali, Niger, Senegal, Togo and Guinea-Bissau, established a common monetary zone. However, only the European Union has established fully both a common market and common currency (although the latter does not apply to all members).[40]

There are several reasons for this proliferation in regional trade arrangements. Historically, the motives for establishing several of these arrangements were just as much to do with politics as they were to do with economics. In the Cold War period, the European Community and ASEAN helped ameliorate inter-state rivalries and promote stability in areas of strategic importance. But since the end of the Cold War, this security imperative has faded rapidly into the background, although it has been at least partially replaced by new security concerns (terrorism, trafficking, the environment), some of which are reflected in these regional frameworks.[41] However, in today's world it is unlikely that the security imperative is the only reason for the establishment of these new regional agreements.

The question thus arises, given the promotion of multilateral free trade by successive rounds of GATT and the establishment of the WTO, why has the number of such regional arrangements increased? Although scholars remain divided on this issue, one of the main reasons may be that it provides the economies of scale that are beneficial to companies residing within the countries concerned while protecting them from the (possibly more acute) competition from other regions. In addition, such regional arrangements may include the reduction of tariffs in sectors where agreement has been difficult to reach at the global level. It may also reflect the frustration at the slow progress of tariff reductions negotiated through the WTO – it is often quicker to negotiate a deal with one's neighbours, particularly in areas that have proven to be difficult at the international level. Finally, the growth of such arrangements may be part of a larger bargaining ploy. This is not to say that these regional trade frameworks do not have an internal logic of their own, but they also need to be seen in the larger strategic context of the multilateral trade negotiations carried out under the auspices of the WTO. The possibility of states settling for greater regional trade in place of multilateral arrangements can be used for political leverage at the international level. For example, part of the reason that the Clinton administration sought a multi-track approach to trade incorporating bilateral, regional and multilateral trade agreements was because of the frustratingly slow pace of the Uruguay Round of trade talks. It was felt that the possibility of the United States opting for bilateral and regional arrangements would act as a spur ensuring quick completion of the multilateral negotiations. In addition, such regional arrangements can also be a defensive reaction and balance to regional cooperation in other parts of the world.[42] For example, a recent study concluded that the probability of agreeing such arrangements increased under three conditions, 'when: (1) GATT/WTO membership rises; (2) a multilateral round is taking place; (3) parties have recently been involved in a GATT/WTO dispute in which they lost'.[43] In general, then, regional arrangements may have additional objectives above the stated reason of enhancing economic links. Furthermore, these arrangements may arise as a *reaction* to changes in the multilateral trading environment or they may be created in order to *influence* the multilateral trade negotiations.

Such regionalism should be distinguished from regionalization. The former is said to refer to 'a formal process of intergovernmental collaboration between two or more states'.[44] Several authors have argued that there has been a recent growth in these regional agreements. However, unlike the initial phase of regionalism in the 1950s and 1960s, scholars have argued that the current period is witnessing the birth of a new type of regionalism that is no longer solely based upon free trade but represents 'a multidimensional process of regional integration which includes economic, political, social and cultural aspects'.[45] Regionalization, on the other hand, refers to the process of economic integration between two or more states in terms of trade and investment. Usually the two are linked, but it is not always the case that this is so. For example, in 1987, prior to the US–Canada Free Trade Agreement, '66 per cent of all of Canada's outward stock of FDI was in the United States, but by 1996 this had fallen to 54.4 per cent', while in the same period outward FDI to the European Union increased from 16.9 per cent to 20.3 per cent.[46]

The key question is how the two (regionalism and regionalization) relate to globalization. As Björn Hettne has pointed out, these processes 'are going on simultaneously, they deeply affect the stability of the Westphalian state system, thus contributing to both disorder and (possibly) a new global order. The question is how they actually relate. Are they distinct and homogenous; are they mutually supporting and reinforcing each other; or are they incompatible and contradictory'.[47] Hettne replies in the negative when he asks whether 'the two processes of globalization and regionalization are articulated within the same larger process of global structural change'.[48] This chapter argues that in part regionalism can be understood as a reaction to the pressures of globalization but each regional framework has also been driven by individual internal dynamics promoting a move towards greater cooperation. However, most of the time, these agreements have countered globalization by promoting greater trade and investment within a delimited geographical area; as Hettne puts it, the 'difference between regionalism and the infinite process of economic integration is that there is a politically defined limit to the former process'.[49]

For Hettne, the new round of regionalism that is occurring at the moment is a reaction to globalization that has resonance with earlier attempts to ensure that some of the gains of capitalism were redistributed. Particularly during the Cold War period, states moderated the more severe consequences of a market economy through various forms of capital control and social protection. However, because the power of capital is that much greater in a globalized world, states now cooperate at the regional level in order to achieve a similar outcome – 'globalisation implies market expansion; regionalism is a neomercantilist regulation of the turbulence generated by this emerging global market; nation-states cannot handle this crisis the way they did in the 1930s, so the regulation of capitalism is more likely to manifest itself on the regional level this time'.[50]

Several points need to be noted in response to this assertion. Certainly, this is one of the reasons behind the recent growth in regionalism, but as we have seen there are also several other factors that should be taken into account. In addition, the increasing levels of regional trade and investment, i.e. *regionalization*, may not necessarily be driven completely by *regionalism*. Intra-industrial trade and the slicing up of the supply chain are two identifiable trends of the contemporary era that explain globalization. Yet, they are also some of the main dynamics driving regionalization. Thus regionalization and globalization can indeed be regarded as being 'articulated within the same larger process of global structural change'.

We are thus confronted with an apparent paradox. Regionalization and globalization can be partly attributed to common factors: greater specialization and a concomitant rise in intra-industrial trade; rising levels of vertical FDI to take advantage of the best and cheapest production; and, finally, out-sourcing of production to overseas companies that has the same objective as vertical FDI, but does not require direct managerial control of those facilities. However, at the same time inter-regional horizontal FDI amongst the triad, initially to overcome trade barriers and to take advantage of clusters of industrial specialization continues. How then to explain the increasing levels of trade within regions? Certainly the trend towards regionalism exhibited by states is a major factor, but several other factors may also help account for economic regionalization, thus making it difficult to ascertain the actual effect of regionalism. First, partly in response to such regionalism, companies have sought to establish production bases within the various regional blocs that have been created. This in itself has led to a reduction of inter-regional trade as more and more companies overcome regional trade barriers by directly investing in the regions concerned (refer to Tables 3.7 and 3.9). Previously, such MNCs were major advocates of multilateral free trade. However, now that they have established themselves in the key industrial heartlands this issue has become less pressing – 'they tend to give more importance to the lowering of intra-regional barriers to economic activity as a whole than to any perceived risk of higher inter-regional barriers to trade'.[51]

Second, despite the much vaunted 'death of distance' associated with the communication revolution and the steady decline in transport costs, proximity to one's trading partners remains important to the extent that the 'distance variable is the most consistent and significant of the variables explaining international trade'. This has become increasingly important as more and more companies adopt Just in Time production systems and firms place a premium on the ability of suppliers to adapt quickly to changing demands in markets dominated by shifting consumer preferences, 'flexible specialization systems makes regional production networks ever more important…Propinquity means lower costs and greater opportunities for matching needs and capabilities'.[52] Finally, other factors such as similarities in the legal, political and cultural fields as well as transnational migrant networks may also promote trade within regions.[53]

The increase in intra-regional trade may thus be explained by several factors that are also closely associated with globalization. Although regionalization is viewed here as reducing the degree of globalization, because they share several common dynamics it may be that in the future we may see a further increase in globalization at the expense of regionalization. This may occur if further improvements are made in the areas of communication and transportation in terms of speed and cost. We may then see, for example, a similar change in the composition of trade from inter-industrial to intra-industrial on a wider geographical scale. However, this would also require the political will to allow greater free trade and thus a reversal of the current trend towards greater regionalism. Whatever the actual causes may be, for many of the RTAs, the proportion of trade between RTA partners relative to their total trading activity, has generally increased (Tables 3.6 and 3.8). However, there are others, such as the Economic and Monetary community of Central Africa (CEMAC), the Common Market for Eastern and Southern Africa (COMESA) and the Economic Community of Central African States (ECCAS), where this is not the case.

Table 3.6 Intra-regional export shares

	1970	1980	1985	1990	1995	2001
CACM	26.0	24.4	14.4	15.4	21.7	15.0
Andean Group	1.8	3.8	3.2	4.2	12.2	11.2
CARICOM	4.2	5.3	6.3	8.1	12.1	13.4
MERCOSUR	9.4	11.6	5.5	8.9	20.3	20.8
ECOWAS	2.9	9.6	5.1	8.0	9.0	9.8
SADC	4.2	0.4	1.4	3.1	10.6	10.9
UEMOA	6.2	9.9	8.7	12.1	10.3	13.5
ASEAN/AFTA	22.4	17.4	18.6	19.0	24.6	22.4

Source: WTO, *World Trade Report 2003*, Table 1B.12. Cited in J. Ravenhill, 'Regionalism', p. 139.

Regionalization or triadization in the inter-linked economy?

Trade

Although regionalization is apparent in many areas of the world (in terms of trade), does the same hold true for the so-called inter-linked economy? As can be seen from Tables 3.7 and 3.8, merchandise trade within and between each leg of the triad constitutes a significant proportion of their overall trade. The data indicate that we are currently witnessing an increasing concentration of trade confined within each leg of the triad and a diminishing proportion of trade between the three legs of the triad. In other words, regionalization is the dominant tendency as opposed to triadization where trade is concerned.

Referring to Table 3.7 on inter-triad merchandise trade, Western Europe includes both the European Union and the rest of Europe. The table indicates how much trade each leg of the triad conducts with the other two legs as a percentage of its total trading activity. First, there is an identifiable trend indicating that inter-triad trade has decreased since 1963. On the other hand, intra-bloc trade is increasing. If Mexico is included in the North America economic bloc, then trade within this group has increased by over 10 per cent in the last 40 years. But these figures hide the importance of the United States as a trading partner for its two neighbours. In 1997, 86 per cent of Mexico's merchandise exports went to the United States and by 2003, approximately the same percentage of Canada's exports were going there. The same could not be said for trade between Canada and Mexico; in 2003 only 0.6 per cent of Canada's exports were destined for the latter.[54] The decline of imports to Japan from the rest of the triad may be explained in part by the bursting of its bubble economy and its increased trade with the rest of Asia.

Table 3.7 Inter-triad merchandise trade, 1963–2003 (percentage of total trade)

	1963	1973	1983	1993	2003
USA and Canada	32.7	30.1	31.6	32.3	26.2
Western Europe	12.3	10.9	10.9	11.25	10.55
Japan	44.5	43.2	39.8	45.5	37.4

Source: WTO, *Selected Long-term Trends*, Geneva, 2004, Tables II.3, 4 and 5.

Table 3.8 Intra-bloc merchandise trade, 1963–2003 (percentage of total trade)

	1963	1973	1983	1993	2003
NAFTA	32.5	37.9	35.8	38.0	42.1
EU (15)	54.1	60.8	57.6	61.8	61.9
Japan with Asia	31.6	33.1	31.8	40.2	49.1

Source: WTO, *Selected Long-term Trends*, Geneva, 2003, Tables II.3, 4 and 5[1]

Note
1   North America includes Mexico. Asia includes New Zealand and Australia.

Third, in all cases, the amount of imports to each leg of the triad from Africa and Latin America as a proportion of total merchandise imports declined considerably. For example, in 1963 Latin American exports constituted: 17 per cent of imports into North America (excluding imports from Mexico); 6.2 per cent of imports by Western Europe; and 8.4 per cent of Japanese imports. By 2003, these figures had declined sharply for all three blocs, so that Latin American exports constituted: just 5.8 per cent of imports to North America (excluding Mexico); 2 per cent of Europe's imports; and 2.5 per cent of Japan's. This therefore corroborates the claims made by the involutionist perspective outlined above. On the other hand, imports from Asia have increased significantly, particularly where Japan and North America are concerned. Not all of this is as a result of China's growth; Hong Kong, Malaysia, South Korea, Singapore, Taiwan and Thailand accounted for 9.7 per cent of merchandise imports to North America and 16.6 per cent to Japan. In terms of intra-triad trade we are therefore witnessing a general reduction of trade between the three major economic blocs (as a proportion of total trade) and increasing trade levels within each regional economic bloc. In addition, it is East and South-east Asia that are primarily benefiting from the triad's trade with the rest of the world.[55]

Foreign direct investment

With regards to FDI, the pattern of investment between the triad is rather lop-sided with much greater levels of investment occurring between the European Union and the United States than between Japan and the other two areas (Table 3.9). Japan's levels of outward FDI stock are much lower than those of the other two, with a total stock of about $400 billion dollars compared to almost $2 trillion for the European Union and $1.1 trillion for the United States (all figures for 1999). The combined total represents approximately 76 per cent of world outward FDI stock. Of the European Union's total outwardly directed FDI stock, just over a quarter resides in the United States, but less than one per cent (0.9 per cent) is invested in Japan. For the United States, an even stronger link with Europe emerges with 45 per cent of outward FDI stock invested in Europe, although its investment in Japan is also stronger at just over 4 per cent. Although Japan's levels of outward FDI

Table 3.9 FDI stocks among the triad (percentage of outward FDI stock)

	EU 1985	*Japan 1985*	*USA 1985*	*EU 1999*	*Japan 1999*	*USA 1999*
USA	37.4	3.8	Intra-NAFTA (30.0)[a]	45.2	4.4	Intra-NAFTA (18.0)
EU (15)	N/A	1.1	Intra-EU 27.5	(40.5)[b]	0.9	28.2
Japan	15.9	N/A	36.4	18.8	to Asia (33.5)[b]	43.7

Source: *World Investment Report 2001 & 2003*: A. Rugman, *The End of Globalization*, p. 120. [a]1986, [b]1996 EU data only includes Austria, Finland, France, Germany, Italy, Netherlands, Sweden and United Kingdom.

stock are much lower, in fact 44 per cent is invested in the United States and 19 per cent in the European Union. Compared to 1985, the United States and Japan have significantly increased their direct investments in the triad as a proportion of their overall world investments. Moreover, the amounts quoted above are also of a different magnitude to those of 1985. At that time, the European Union had a total outward stock invested in the United States totalling some $128 billion, by 1999 this had increased by four times to $554 billion. Similarly, the United States' investment in Europe has increased by over five times from $89 billion in 1985 to $512 billion, and Japan's investment in the United States has increased over ten times from $16 billion to $177 billion.[56]

Comparing recent inter-triad trade and investment patterns it is clear that for the United States and Japan, investment in the other two legs of the triad dominates, while for the EU regional investment is very high as a result of the ongoing process of integration.[57] The high levels of intra-triad investment may at first glance appear to contradict the commonly held position that the assets, sales and employment of MNCs are regionally based. For example, in terms of sales, it is estimated that for the majority of MNCs 70–80 per cent of transactions continue to be within the home country and the neighbouring region.[58] However, the data displayed in Table 3.9 does not include the investment activity within the home country itself, because we are interested in how much outward FDI stock resides within the home region and how much resides in the other two legs of the triad. Many of these overseas sites may be aimed at replacing trade and overcoming non-tariff barriers. These types of company therefore not only engage in marketing and distribution but also produce the goods within the other two legs of the triad. For example, in the case of automobiles and chemicals, 'over 90 per cent of products produced in each of the triad regions is sold within that region'.[59] But also, within the triad, rather than engaging in significant production activities many affiliates of the parent company are engaged solely in the handling of final goods or nearly completed products which are then marketed and distributed within that leg of the triad.[60] This is particularly true for 'consumer electronics and high value-added goods with low transport costs' (in fact distance is still 'the most consistent and significant of the variables explaining international trade').[61] In sum, the regionalization versus triadization debate is thus more accurately described as greater trade regionalization *and* growing triadization in terms of FDI stock, but the activities of these affiliates are often quite different to those of affiliates based in developing countries.

Changing patterns of global trade

Three trends have been identified: a growth in regionalization with each leg of the triad trading less with each other and more within their economic bloc; growing triadization in terms of FDI; and, excluding East Asia and South-East Asia, the developing world's share of trade has decreased. Yet, a quick glance at the World Bank's trade statistics indicates that the majority of developing countries have increased their trade/GDP ratios. For instance, in the last decade Sub-Saharan

Africa has increased its trade activity relative to GDP from 40.8 per cent to 55.3 per cent and South Asia from 16.5 per cent to 24.2 per cent.[62] However, the developing world's relative share of world trade has declined bar South-East and East Asia plus a few individual countries such as Mexico. There are three main reasons for this: the continuing concentration on primary product production in much of the developing world; the increase in intra-industrial trade between OECD countries and the increase in intra-firm trade/vertical specialization both between OECD countries and also between the OECD and certain developing countries, mainly located within East Asia.

However, separating out these various aspects of trade is notoriously difficult. Intra-industry trade involves trade in similar yet distinguishable goods (niche markets) including some intra-firm trade. Intra-industry trade now constitutes a large part of overall trade and is a result of the increasing complexity of manufactured products so that in any given category, despite the similarity of the goods, companies are able to maintain a market share through specialization.[63] There has also been a tendency in the last few decades for contemporary services and production to be divided into discrete segments geographically separated from each other leading to, amongst other things, a substantial increase in the volume of intra-firm trade involving the trade of intermediate (as opposed to finished) products. Traditionally, FDI was largely 'horizontal' in nature, involving the setting up of production sites to overcome trade barriers and/or to take advantage of knowledge/skill intensive clusters within the industrial triad.[64] However, in recent decades 'vertical' FDI that slices up the supply chain locating the different stages of production wherever they are cheapest has become equally important. As a result, several less industrialized countries have been able to participate in the labour-intensive aspects of production.

'Vertical' FDI implies that the suppliers of the component parts of a product continue to be at least partly owned and directly managed by the company in question. But rather than investing in setting up their own service or production plant and directly managing the business, corporations are increasingly procuring the required components or services from independent sources. It is argued that, as a result, greater emphasis is now placed on the core functions of managing the supply chain and final assembly rather than concentrating on 'in-house' manufacturing of a product from start to finish. In a similar fashion to that of 'vertical' FDI, the growth of 'out-sourcing' heralds a new form of business structure, one in which the upstream linkages of suppliers and the downstream linkages to the final customer have become stretched across continents.[65] The industrialized countries and a select few from the developing world have thus become enmeshed in a network of production chains involving a 'transactionally linked sequence of functions in which each stage adds value to the process of production of goods and services'.[66]

Table 3.10 maps recent changes in intra-industrial trade for the OECD countries; for the majority, intra-industry trade as a percentage of total manufacturing trade is now at 65 and above.[67] As a result of this general tendency for intra-industrial trade to increase amongst industrialized countries, the relative share of this type of trade as a proportion of world trade has increased substantially in the last few decades. From 1953 to 1997 intra-industrial trade increased from 37.1 per cent to 49.2 per cent and trade between industrial and non-industrial groups declined by over 10 per cent from 43.2 per cent to 32.5 per cent (indicating that relative trade between the producers supplying raw materials and the industrial sector using them has declined sharply).[68] More recently, Eastern European countries have experienced large increases in intra-industrial trade. In the last few decades these countries have been major recipients of FDI, indicating that one important source of this increase in trade is from intra-firm trade.[69]

The second aspect of trade considered here is the trend toward establishing vertical supply chains, usually involving the relocation of low value-added production activities outside of the industrialized core while retaining high valued-added activities within the core. Companies are increasingly slicing up the supply chain, producing parts wherever the process is cheapest and then shipping them

Table 3.10 Manufacturing intra-industry trade of OECD countries (percentage of total manufacturing trade)

	1988–91	*1992–95*	*1996–2000*
Czech Republic	n. a.	66.3	77.4
Slovak Republic	n. a.	69.8	76.0
Mexico	62.5	74.4	73.4
Hungary	54.9	64.3	72.1
Germany	67.1	72.0	72.0
United States	63.5	65.3	68.5
Poland	56.4	61.7	62.6
Portugal	52.4	56.3	61.3
France	75.9	77.6	77.6
Canada	73.5	74.7	76.2
Austria	71.8	74.3	74.2
United Kingdom	70.1	73.1	73.7
Switzerland	69.8	71.8	72.0
Belgium/Luxemburg	77.6	77.7	71.4
Spain	68.2	72.1	71.2
Netherlands	69.2	70.4	68.9
Sweden	64.2	64.6	66.6
Denmark	61.6	63.4	64.8
Italy	61.6	64.0	64.7
Ireland	58.6	57.2	54.6
Finland	53.8	53.2	53.9
Korea	41.4	50.6	57.5
Japan	37.6	40.8	47.6
New Zealand	37.2	38.4	40.6
Turkey	36.7	36.2	40.0
Norway	40.0	37.5	37.1
Greece	42.8	39.6	36.9
Australia	28.6	29.8	29.8
Iceland	19.0	19.1	20.1

Source: OECD, 'Intra-Industry and intra-firm trade', *OECD Economic* Outlook, vol. 71, 2002, Table VI.1.

to assembly plants that make the final product. Falling costs of communication and freight transportation have encouraged companies to 'slice through national boundaries and transcend them in a bewildering array of relationships that operate at different geographical and organizational scales'.[70] Rather than production sites concentrating on the manufacturing and assembly of constituent components to create a final product in one factory (or one country), improvements in technology facilitating improved coordination and reductions in transport costs have enabled them to divide the production process across countries and even continents.

However, as was explained above, this 'vertical specialization' not only involves intra-firm trade but also out-sourcing to other companies. As a result, to capture the true levels of this type of activity attempts have been made to gauge the level of imported goods entering a country that are used as inputs for products that are then exported to other countries. Using this as a measure, recent analysis of several OECD countries (G7 plus Australia, Denmark and the Netherlands) estimates that the degree of vertical specialization constitutes approximately 21 per cent of overall trade for these countries and for countries such as South Korea, Ireland and Taiwan the level is about 30 per cent.[71] This may explain, for example, why 'at least half of US–Mexican trade could be due to vertical specialization'.[72] Using an expanded data-set in later work, some of the same researchers found that vertical specialization exports 'accounted for 30 per cent of the growth in the overall export/GDP ratio' of the OECD countries concerned.[73] For several less developed countries, this figure is probably much higher because they have actively sought to embed themselves in this new network and, in addition, smaller economies are more likely to be involved in such vertical specialization than larger countries because the latter 'find it easier than small ones, for scale economy reasons, to retain production of every stage'.[74] Such qualitative changes highlight the weakness of relying purely on levels of trading activity; trade has undergone, and is undergoing, dramatic changes.

However, because the supply chain is now international in nature, many of the materials that are used in production of these products are actually shipped in so that the knock-on benefits for other local industries are highly limited. For example, despite the exports of garments and textiles from Bangladesh increasing exponentially, growing from a mere $1 million of export earnings in the late 1970s to $4.2 billion by the late 1990s, only 4 per cent of the fabric is supplied locally.[75] The fact that many of these factories are embedded in a wider productive process is also reflected in the ratio of domestic value added to these products compared to export value. In the case of Bangladesh, which is not an unusual case, this is about '25–30 per cent of the value of exports'.[76] High volumes of trade are thus associated with these global production chains, but these production processes can and often do operate separately from the local economy.

Vertical specialization also partly explains the increase in South–South trade alluded to by the transformationalists.[77] South–South trade has indeed rapidly developed so that by 2001 it constituted 11 per cent of world merchandise trade.[78] Moreover, in 1965 South–South trade accounted for just a quarter of the developing world's total trade, whereas in 2003 this had risen to 43 per cent.[79]

Box 3.2 Types of international trade and investment

Intra-firm trade

Trade occurring between the various divisions of a company. There has been a tendency in the last few decades for contemporary services and production to be divided into discrete segments geographically separated from each other leading to, amongst other things, a substantial increase in the volume of intra-firm trade involving the trade of intermediate (as opposed to finished) products.

Intra-industrial trade

Intra-industrial trade involves trade in similar yet distinguishable goods (niche markets). Intra-industrial trade now constitutes a large part of overall trade and is a result of the increasing complexity of manufactured products so that in any given category, despite the similarity of the goods, companies are able to maintain a market share through specialization.

Horizontal FDI

Refers to the investment by MNCs in production sites concentrating on the manufacturing and assembly of constituent components to create a final product in one factory (or one country). Often this is in order to overcome trade barriers and/or to take advantage of knowledge/skill intensive clusters within certain countries.

Vertical FDI

Vertical FDI refers to the slicing up of the supply chain locating the different stages of production in disparate geographical locations. But vertical FDI still implies that the suppliers of the component parts of a product continue to be at least partly owned and directly managed by the company in question.

Outsourcing

Refers to the increasingly common practice of companies procuring the required components or services from independent sources. It is argued that, as a result, greater emphasis is now placed on the core functions of managing the supply chain and final assembly rather than concentrating on 'in-house' manufacturing of a product from start to finish.

However, once again much of this increase is accounted for by the growth of East Asia; two-thirds of all South–South trade can be accounted for by this region. But even more significantly, this trade reflects the enmeshment of this region in the international manufacturing trade network and its increasing involvement in vertical specialization. Much of this East Asian South–South trade thus involves countries undertaking only a section of the overall production process before re-exporting to their neighbours for further work.

The third explanation for these changing trade and investment patterns is that the majority of developing countries have failed to diversify their exports into the manufacturing and service sectors (Table 3.11). For example, in 2001 manufactured goods still only constituted 30 per cent of all merchandise exports for Africa – compared to almost 70 per cent for Asia. Even though this figure is low, it masks the fact that some countries are even more dependent upon the primary sector; for example, coffee 'alone accounts for 60–80 per cent of export earnings for Ethiopia and Burundi'.[80] The decline in the terms of trade for primary commodities first highlighted by the United Nations' Economic Commission for Latin America in the 1950s is continuing unabated. In 2000, for example, 'prices for 18 major export commodities were 25 per cent lower in real terms than in 1980. For eight of these commodities, the decline exceeded 50 per cent'. For some commodities the decline was over 70 per cent: cocoa (71.2 per cent); sugar (76.6 per cent); and Tin (73 per cent).[81] Between 1980 and 2003 the decline in terms of trade was 1.3 per cent per annum for the whole of the developing world. As a result of the reliance on primary commodities, between 1980 and 2001, African exports experienced the worst decline in terms of trade (30 per cent followed closely by the Americas) compared to industrialized countries, who enjoyed a 17 per cent improvement in their terms of trade.[82]

Interestingly, Ankie Hoogvelt has added to this perspective, arguing that the active role played by the IMF and World Bank ensures that the terms of trade deteriorates even further for those countries exporting primary commodities. Hoogvelt argues that '[C]ommodity specialisation and debt go hand in hand. Both the World Bank and the IMF have used their leverage on indebtedness to require that production be concentrated on commodity exports. The consequence of this has been a flooding of the commodity markets which forced prices downward'.

Table 3.11 Distribution of merchandise exports by commodity group

Region	Year	All Food items	Agricultural and raw materials	Ores and metals	Fuels	Manufactured goods
Developing countries						
Africa	1960	32.9	41.8	10.5	4.1	10.3
	2001	12.8	4.5	4.8	46.1	30.6
The Americas	1960	40.6	18.7	5.3	31.9	3.4
	2001	16.8	2.3	6.1	15.4	58.0
Asia	1960	18.9	30.0	1.9	30.0	18.8
	2001	5.3	1.7	2.9	14.5	69.3
Oceania	1970	31.7	49.4	–	1.0	17.4
	2001	16.4	3.7	22.9	13.4	36.5
Central and Eastern	1960	14.3	13.6	2.1	12.4	56.8
Europe	2001	4.6	2.6	4.8	22.3	55.7
Industrialized	1960	13.7	12.8	3.3	4.0	64.7
countries	2001	7.4	1.8	2.6	4.7	79.7

Source: UNCTAD, *Development and Globalization*, 2004, Table 4.2D.

The result, Hoogvelt argues, is that the terms of trade for Sub-Saharan commodities 'fell more rapidly than for any other region of the globe'.[83]

The following argues that South-East Asia and East Asia's success in capturing such a large portion of world trade and investment is in large part due to their success in capturing a significant portion of the world market in both the secondary and tertiary sectors. In terms of the latter, it has already been pointed out that Asia's share of world trade in services has increased dramatically in the last two decades and now stands at 16.8 per cent (Table 3.5). In addition, placing greater emphasis on secondary production has had positive economic benefits for these countries. Much of their success may be related to the geopolitics of the Cold War, but it also had much to do with the various forms of intervention associated with these 'developmental states'.

If we compare the distribution of exports by commodity group across regions, it is readily apparent that the most significant change in the last 40 years has been Asia's shift away from primary commodities to the production of manufactured goods. In 1960, manufactured goods constituted less than a fifth of its overall exports, but by 2001 this had grown to almost 70 per cent. This was mainly at the expense of food items, agricultural commodities and fuels. The export profile of Latin America and the Caribbean has also altered dramatically during this time, although two points need to be kept in mind. First, the data for the American continent are rather skewed as a result of Mexico's large trading volumes which constituted 45 per cent of Latin America and the Caribbean's exports in 2002, largely as a result of its membership of NAFTA.[84] As a result this region's export profile changed considerably from 1990 when manufactured goods constituted about 31 per cent of merchandise exports to 2001 when they constituted 58 per cent.[85] Second, as is explained below, Asia, particularly East Asia, has been far more successful at capturing the export market in medium- to high-technology goods (again with the exception of Mexico) and is one of the main reasons for its high share of world merchandise exports.

Other countries, for example those in South Asia, have successfully increased textiles and clothing as a proportion of their merchandise exports. But for Sub-Saharan Africa, on the other hand, the proportion of textiles and clothing did not significantly change and remained extremely low at 2 per cent of overall merchandise exports; fuel and mineral extraction continued their predominance. In the 1990s, as a percentage of merchandise exports, textiles and clothing continued to constitute but a few per cent for a large number of African countries. As we have seen, primary products have experienced worsening terms of trade *vis a vis* the manufacturing sector, but on the other hand textiles and clothing are labour intensive thus providing employment for greater numbers of people. Yet these countries have been unable to take advantage of the benefits that accrue from shifting part of their production base to labour-intensive manufacturing.

The emphasis on labour-intensive manufacturing has therefore helped certain countries improve their economic prospects and the nature of the work has absorbed relatively large segments of the population thereby keeping poverty rates at a lower rate than they otherwise would have been. However, if further improvements are to be sought, then a shift towards production in the higher-technology sectors, as has occurred in East Asia, is required. The structure of East Asian and Pacific exports is instructive in this regard. In 1991, textiles and garments constituted only 19 per cent of overall exports. For South Asia, on the other hand, total manufacturing constituted 67 per cent of exports, but in this case textiles and clothing made up 37 per cent of exports. The export economy of South Asia is still dominated by low technology, whereas East Asia's export profile is more evenly distributed, with high-technology goods constituting a relatively high proportion of exports. In fact, within the developing world, East Asia 'accounts for more than two-thirds of all manufactured exports and more than three-quarters of exports in high-growth technology sectors such as electronics'.[86]

The shift in emphasis towards manufactured goods in South-East and East Asia reflects a general change in the pattern of world trade in the last few decades (Table 3.12). Since 1985, world 'manufactured exports grew nearly three times faster than primary exports' so that by 1998 primary products represented just 11.5 per cent of world exports compared to 21.7 per cent in 1985. Surprisingly, the growth of industrialized countries' primary product exports was approximately three times that of developing countries during the same period resulting in a decline in developing countries' overall share of world primary exports from 52.1 per cent in 1985 to 39.7 per cent in 1998. This could be as a result of 'the expansion by developed countries of agricultural exports because of subsidies, dumping of food stocks or bringing new land into cultivation, or their faster technological progress'.[87]

The increase in manufactured exports, as a proportion of world trade, has not been uniform across all sectors. As a proportion of world exports, resource-based manufactures have declined while the share of low-, medium- and high-technology manufactures has increased. The growth of high-technology manufactures has been the greatest; for both industrialized and developing countries they have increased from 12.4 per cent in 1985 to just over 21 per cent of world exports in 1998 (Table 3.12). Unlike the primary export sector, the developing world's share of low-, medium- and high-technology exports has grown since 1985. Once again the high-technology sector has led the way with developing countries increasing their share of world exports in this area from 10.7 per cent in 1985 to 27 per cent in 1998, nearly 17 per cent in just 13 years. But in addition, the developing world's share of low-technology exports grew from 26.7 per cent to 34.5 per cent

Table 3.12 Share of world merchandise exports by sector 1985 and 1998

	1985	1998
Primary products	21.7	11.5
Resource-based exports	21.1	14.5
Low-technology exports	13.7	15.8
Medium-technology exports	30.2	32.8
High-technology exports	12.4	21.1

Source: S. Lall, 'The technological structure and performance of developing country manufactured exports', 2000, Table 2.

and its share of medium technology exports almost doubled from 8.3 per cent to 15.3 per cent in the same period.[88]

The data also show that, in the same period, the developing world has increased its share in the production of electronic manufactures from 14 per cent to 34.2 per cent and that its share of textile manufactures remains high at approximately 49 per cent of world textile exports.[89] However, if this data is disaggregated by region, it becomes very apparent that the major share of exports in these sectors is highly limited to one major region, East Asia, which, as a result, increased its share of developing countries' manufactured exports from 56.9 per cent in 1985 to 69 per cent in 1998 (Figure 3.1).[90] As was mentioned earlier, much of South Asia has successfully re-oriented its industry so that labour-intensive manufacturing, such as textiles, now dominate their export sector. However, it still represents but a small proportion of the developing world's manufactured exports, for example, its textiles still only constitute 12 per cent of the developing world's manufactured exports. By comparison, if one includes Taiwan, Singapore, Hong Kong and South Korea in the East Asian category, the region dominates the low (70.2 per cent), medium (63.8 per cent) and high (85.5 per cent) technology sectors.[91]

To summarize, the developing countries' share of merchandise trade is now at approximately the same level as it was 40 years ago. But this is not because of a relative increase in exports of primary commodities, for this sector the developing countries' share declined from 52.1 per cent in 1985 to 39.7 per cent in 1998. Rather it is as a result of the strong performance of East Asian countries and their success in technological products, which mainly explains the rise in the developing world's share of export manufactures from 16.4 per cent in 1985 to 23.3 per cent in 1998.[92] On a regional basis, the rest of the developing world has experienced a decline in their world share of manufactured exports, although there are individual strong exporters within these groupings, such as Mexico, Turkey and Brazil. If

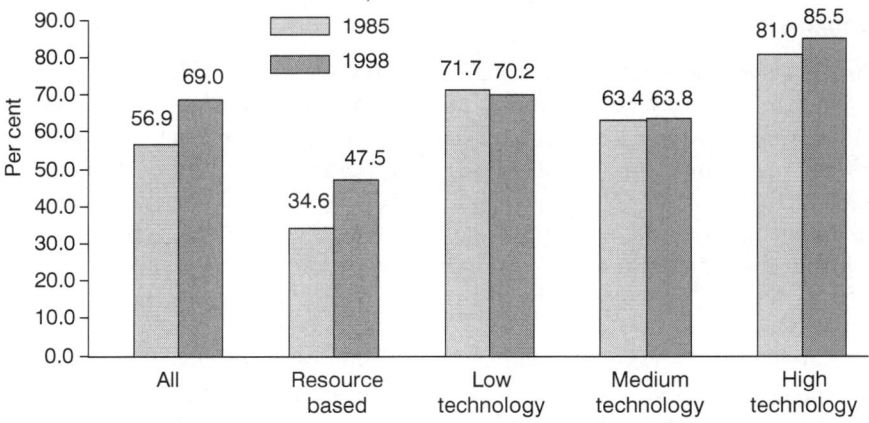

Figure 3.1 East Asia's share of developing countries' manufactured exports (Source: Based on data from S. Lall, 'The technological structure and performance of developing country manufactured exports', 2000, Table 40).

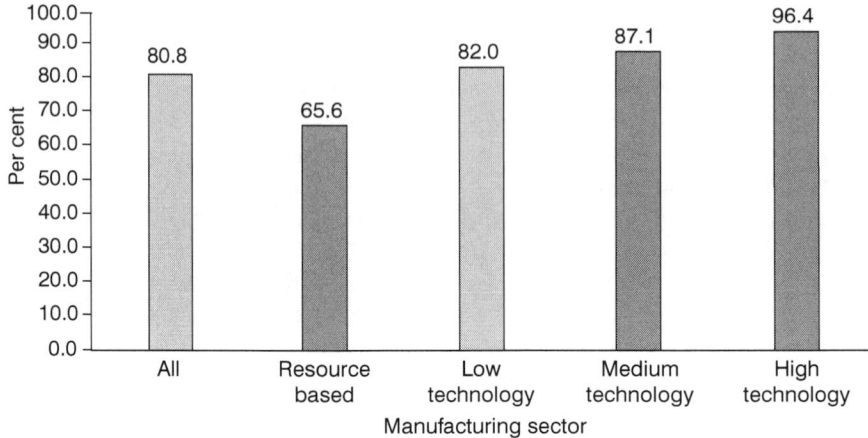

Figure 3.2 Top ten developing countries' share of manufactured exports (Source: S. Lall, 'The technological structure and performance of developing country manufactured exports', 200, Table 4)

one disaggregates the data down to the top ten countries in each of these sectors, the clustering is even more pronounced. The top ten exporters of manufactured products in the developing world account for over 80 per cent of the developing world's export manufactures (Figure 3.2). Apart from Mexico and Brazil, these ten exporters are all in East Asia. In the high-technology sector, the top ten exporters make up a staggering 96.4 per cent of the developing world's exports. Of course this includes the four Asian tigers (Hong Kong, Taiwan, Singapore and South Korea), but Malaysia, China, Mexico, the Philippines, Thailand and Brazil alone constitute 47 per cent of the developing world's high technology exports.[93]

Conclusion

This chapter examined whether globalization, understood as the intensification of economic relations between states, is the dominant pattern of the contemporary world system, or whether alternative models of economic interaction depict our current condition more accurately. The data presented certainly challenges the traditional notion of globalization and the pattern that has emerged is one of multiple and somewhat overlapping layers. The chapter challenges the idea that regionalization, triadization and the involutionist view are competing conceptions offering incompatible perspectives of the world economy. On the one hand, the industrialized triad are trading relatively more with their neighbours while at the same time trade between the triad as a proportion of overall merchandise trade has declined. However, each leg of the triad is investing relatively more in terms of their total FDI in the other two legs. At the same time, with the exception of East Asia, the developing world's share of world trade has declined significantly. In terms of merchandise exports, East Asia's share has increased rapidly since the fifties (and at a later stage South-East Asia) whereas Latin America's has halved. Africa's share has also more than halved since the fifties and has the lowest share of world exports at some 2.4 per cent. If one takes the developing world as a whole, then in terms of the proportion of world inward FDI stock, stasis best describes the last few decades of economic activity.

What lies behind these emerging trade and investment patterns? Although the figures are open to interpretation, it is likely that the changing trade patterns within the northern industrialized bloc are mainly explained by the increasing levels of regional intra-industrial trade and vertical specialization. Which of these is most important will depend upon the region under investigation. For example, the increase in Mexico's trade with the United States is largely due to companies relocating their production sites to Mexico's maquiladoras, to the extent that vertical specialization now accounts for about half of all trade between these two countries. For Europe, on the other hand, intra-regional trade has increased both as a result of further product differentiation leading to high levels of intra-industrial trade, but also more recently because of the relocation of production sites and out-sourcing within the European Union to countries with lower production costs such as Ireland and Eastern Europe. A similar scenario is also being played out with Japan and its neighbours. Japan's relatively low level of intra-industrial trade reflects its trade surpluses with other major trading nations. However, recent increases can be partly explained by Japan's increasing emphasis on vertical specialization. Recent analysis suggests that, for many of these countries, vertical specialization now constitutes at least one-third of overall trade.[94]

The chapter also demonstrated that, if we concentrate solely on outward FDI stock rather than including home country investment/assets, then there is a bias towards investing in the other legs of the triad rather than within the region (although unsurprisingly the EU is the exception in this regard). Countries often attract FDI because of their cheaper labour costs, but this factor does not always apply with regard to trade between the three major economic blocs. Some of these overseas production sites may be aimed at replacing trade and overcoming significant non-tariff barriers. These types of companies not only engage in marketing and distribution but also produce goods within the other two legs of the triad. But also for these economies, intra-firm trade is very high, for example in the case of Japan and the United States it accounts for at least a third of total merchandise trade. This can be partly explained by the fact that rather than engaging in significant production activities, many affiliates of the parent company are engaged in the handling of final goods or nearly completed products which are then marketed and distributed within that leg of the triad.[95] But also this FDI within the triad may occur to take advantage of research clusters or to have production sites close to markets. In other words, the reasons for investment very much depends on the type of production companies are engaged in.

Several explanations for the patterns of trade and investment regarding the South present themselves: debt crises; under-investment in infrastructure; mismanagement of the economy; corruption, civil strife, etc.[96] However, this chapter has concentrated upon three main explanations. The decline in the developing countries' relative share of world trade can be partly explained by the worsening terms of trade for primary commodities *vis-à-vis* the secondary and tertiary sectors and the continuing concentration on primary product production in much of the developing world. However, to concentrate solely on this aspect would ignore the qualitative changes in trade: both the increase in trade specialization and the slicing up of the supply chain. As we have seen, most intra-industrial trade and FDI remain within the northern core. This has a significant impact upon the data. Although most developing countries have increased their trade relative to GDP, their relative share of world trade has declined not only because of the worsening terms of trade, but because intra-industrial trade within the northern core constitutes so much of world trade. In addition, companies from one leg of the triad seek to take advantage of the large markets, labour specialization, research and development facilities and high-quality infrastructure that their counterparts can offer. Thus regionalization and triadization also partly explain why economic involution is occurring.

Although East and South-East Asia continue to supply large volumes of basic commodities, such as textiles, they have also managed to become embedded in the supply chain for higher value-added manufactured goods in the low-, medium- and high-technology sectors, and this is reflected in their shares of world exports, supplying both intermediate and final products to the northern industrialized core. East Asian trading activity now accounts for two-thirds of this South–South trade mainly as a result of vertical specialization with countries providing intermediate products within a larger production process. These countries are therefore not only involved in producing final products for exporting abroad, but have become embedded within complex global production chains. Given that there has been a shift in favour of higher technology exports worldwide and a move towards increasing levels of vertical specialization, it is likely that we will see a further marginalization of those countries that do not, or cannot, engage in such activity.

4   Trade liberalization and economic growth

The last chapter described several aspects of contemporary trading patterns: the tendency towards greater trade regionalization; the triadization of FDI; and the continuing dominance of the North in relation to world shares of trade and investment; plus the increasing share of relative trade accruing to East Asia. As was pointed out, this does not imply that the trading volumes of other countries have not increased. The last 20 years have seen a substantial reduction in tariffs in most countries around the world. The greatest reductions have been in South Asia, followed by Latin America and the Caribbean and then East Asia and the Pacific (Figure 4.1).[1] At the same time, the volume of world merchandise trade has grown at a much faster rate than world output. For example, from 1980 to 2004, the value of world merchandise exports increased four fold; whereas world GDP less than doubled. As a result of this general growth of trade, by 2002 'trade in goods and services as a share of world output reached 54 per cent, up from 31 per cent in 1980'.[2] So it is not that trading activity has not increased for most countries in the world, but that some are trading relatively more than others.

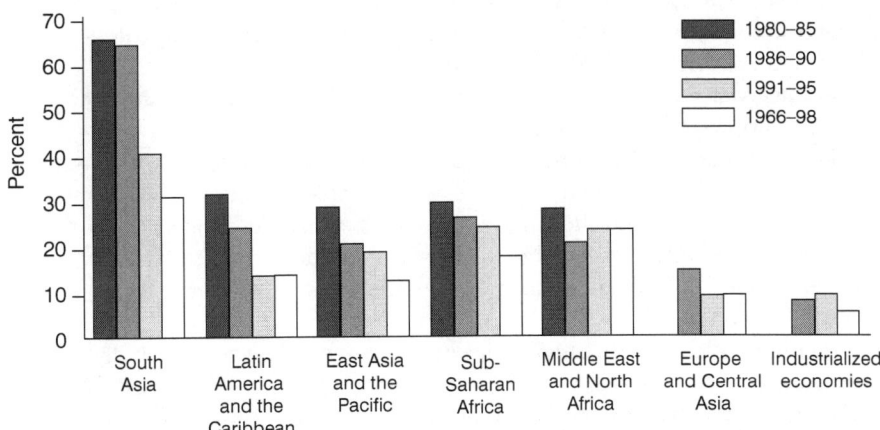

Figure 4.1 Average unweighted tariffs by region (Source: World Bank, *Globalization, Growth, and Poverty*, 2002, Figure 4. © World Bank 2002. Reprinted wth the permission of the World Bank.)

As to what is fuelling this increase in trade, several possibilities present themselves: regionalization; the growth and spread of multi-national companies; successive trade rounds of GATT/WTO; trade liberalization policies promoted by the IMF and World Bank. In truth, it is probably a mixture of all of these factors. However, this chapter examines the structural adjustment policies of the IMF and, in particular, their promotion of trade liberalization and export-led growth. The assumed connection that growth will automatically follow full trade liberalization is questioned. However, it is argued that one should not conclude from this that countries should not adopt an export-orientated approach, but that this should be carried out in stages and should be implemented as part of a wider set of measures aimed at boosting economic growth. An alternative model is therefore put forward, one based on the developmental state of East Asia whereby states pursue selective trade liberalization while at the same time steering the economy through its developmental phase.

Structural adjustment and the Washington consensus

In the introduction of this book it was argued that by the 1980s a certain view of how best to promote economic growth began to prevail amongst policy-makers, the so-called 'Washington consensus'. Prior to this period, it was quite usual for states to intervene in the economy in a variety of ways, for example: the establishment of a minimum wage to ensure basic welfare for the general population; raising tariffs to protect certain sectors of the economy; the nationalization of key industries to ensure supplies at reasonable prices; controls on capital flows to prevent currency speculation, etc. In certain aspects this was also true for states in the South. In seeking to develop rapidly, many of these states sought to establish production in certain industries through the pursuit of import substitution. State funding was often made available in order to defray the high start-up costs and at the same time these embryonic industries were protected from external competitors behind high import tariffs to give them time to establish themselves. A certain level of subsistence was ensured through government market boards regulating the price of certain critical foodstuffs, such as bread and rice.

However, the neo-liberalism that underpinned the 'Washington consensus' viewed such state intervention as creating market aberrations leading to the inefficient production and allocation of resources within these countries. Far better, it was argued, to allow consumers to buy freely and for producers to compete in an open market. As a result of such market pressures each country would end up specializing in those economic sectors that they were most efficient in. Allowing the free flow of capital investment, it was argued, would also benefit developing countries. Given that one of the main comparative advantages of these countries is their low wages and abundance of low-skilled workers, companies would begin to relocate their production sites to these areas. Incidentally, this mechanism was thought also to lead to lower levels of inequality within the countries of the South as demand for low-skilled but relatively cheap labour would increase eventually leading to higher wage levels.[3]

The effects of neo-liberalism have been most pronounced in the less developed countries of the South who have had little choice but to implement such policies wholesale, mainly at the behest of the IMF and the World Bank. It is to the less developed countries, often referred to as the 'South' that we need to turn to understand the full impact of neo-liberalism upon the global economy. At the same time as the United States was restructuring its own economy internally it was promoting similar policies through the IMF and World Bank:

> The IMF is the linchpin in the implementation of the neo-liberal vision of development. Going beyond its original mandate to provide short-term balance-of-payments support, it has coordinated with the World Bank since the early 1980s to reform national economies so that they better reflect the dominant vision of market-led rather than state-led development.[4]

In 1980, the World Bank agreed to lend Turkey, which had just experienced a military coup, $200 million, on condition that it adopt a stringent programme of economic reform which explicitly rejected 'the social compromises which were the considered response of democratic societies to the chaos of World War II'.[5] Since then, countries seeking help with balance of payments deficits or loans for large-scale infrastructural development were subject to increasingly strict conditions upon their economic policies.

This conditionality entailed a series of economic reforms, or so-called Structural Adjustment Policies (SAPs), thus ensuring the adoption of neo-liberalism by the majority of less developed states. So, unlike the industrialized countries that had adopted such policies, the South was given little choice as to whether or not to accept. Refusal of the recommended economic reforms could result in a full-blown financial crisis and as a result most leaders reluctantly implemented such policies, often without the requisite political mandate from their populations. Such reforms included at least some of the following:

1   Move to a floating or pegged exchange rate
2   Trade liberalization
3   Elimination of non-tariff barriers
4   Removal of restrictions on finance and investment flows – deregulation
5   Dismantling of market boards and other price intervention by government
6   Cancelling/reduction of subsidies
7   Privatization and/or closure of state enterprises
8   Reduction of budget deficit through reduction and/or reorientation of public expenditures
9   Interest rate increases to control inflation[6]

As Caroline Thomas points out, although the term structural adjustment was used to describe such reforms there were in fact several discrete stages associated with this process: stabilization; structural adjustment; and export-led growth.[7] Given the history of rampant inflation in many countries of the South, reducing it to reasonable levels was (and is) regarded as the top priority. Several mechanisms were introduced to reduce the money supply: a reduction in government spending (which would also lower budget deficits); high interest rates; the establishment of floating or pegged exchange rates signalling an abstention from competitive devaluation.[8] The second phase involved structural adjustment proper, including: the selling to private interests of previously nationalized industries and the closure of inefficient enterprises; the cancelling/reduction of subsidies to both private and nationalized industries; abstention of price intervention by the government. The final stage had the objective of promoting export-led growth by: liberalizing trade (reduction of tariffs); eliminating non-tariff barriers to trade; removal of restrictions on finance and investment from abroad thereby providing an investor-friendly environment for those seeking a low-cost base from which to produce and export.[9]

Why promote such policies? Underpinning such reform attempts is the belief that increases in trade promote growth, which in turn is said to lead to a reduction in poverty. The arguments for greater trade liberalization are usually based on Ricardo's principle of comparative advantage: trade between countries leads to each country specializing in the industries that are relatively more efficient. However, as Joseph Stiglitz and Andrew Charlton point out, this argument for free trade is based upon a more efficient allocation of resources rather than upon growth *per se*, although of course the end result of comparative advantage should be an increase in overall output for all parties involved. In addition, trade is said to promote growth in a variety of ways. First, integration into the world trade system provides export opportunities for domestic firms; larger markets imply that companies will thus benefit from increases in economies of scale thereby increasing returns on their initial investment. Second, a country benefits greatly if innovations are disseminated rapidly throughout a given industry bringing increased efficiency and a competitive edge against rivals. Trade liberalization should lead to more rapid and wider dissemination of technical know-how, but in addition the specialization that is said to follow from trade liberalization also leads to a more rapid 'spillover' from one firm to another. Finally, industry is said to benefit not only from cheaper inputs, but also 'a larger variety of inputs, which can sustain not only more efficient production but a faster pace of innovation'.[10]

However, many developing countries have been pursuing trade liberalization, yet have experienced reductions in the value of trade in their primary products as a result of the overall decline in terms of trade of these commodities.[11] The terms of trade problem was first highlighted in the 1950s by the United Nations' Economic Commission for Latin America headed by Raul Prebisch. The Commission identified that there had been a long-term decline in prices of primary commodities (extracted minerals and agricultural products) relative to manufactured products. This decline has continued unabated, in 1990 manufactured goods still only constituted 30 per cent of all merchandise exports for Africa, compared to almost 70 per cent for Asia.[12] Even though this figure is low, it masks the fact that some countries are even more dependent upon the primary sector; for example, coffee 'alone accounts for 60–80 per cent of export earnings for Ethiopia and Burundi'.[13]

Box 4.1 Comparative advantage explained

Principle underlying trade first elaborated by David Ricardo. Comparative advantage explains how two states can both gain from trade even if one of them can produce all of the goods more efficiently than the other. Although one country may possess an absolute advantage in the goods to be traded, both countries can receive a net benefit if each concentrates upon their comparative advantage. Consider the following situation where the US and South Korea both produce steel and cameras, but the US produces both more efficiently:

Country	Labour input	Total goods produced
US	100 workers	1000 units of steel
South Korea	100 workers	400 units of steel
US	100 workers	500 camera units
South Korea	100 workers	400 camera units

Total: 1400 units of steel and 900 camera units

If each concentrates on the area of production that they are relatively better at (relatively more efficient) and engage in trade to make up for their loss of production in the industries from which labour has been withdrawn, both will benefit. In this case, the US is twice as productive in its steel industry than in its camera industry, so it should shift more of its labour resources to steel and South Korea should specialize in cameras:

Country	Labour input	Total goods produced
US	110 workers	1100 units of steel
South Korea	80 workers	320 units of steel
US	90 workers	450 camera units
South Korea	120 workers	480 camera units

Total: 1420 units of steel and 930 camera units

To make up for the reduction in available cameras the US imports 50 units from South Korea, but this still leaves South Korea with 30 additional camera units. Likewise, South Korea makes up for its drop in steel production by importing 80 units from the US, yet even after exporting these units the US has produced an extra 20 units of steel. Each country has made up for their shortfall in their less efficient industries by importing the additional units and both have increased their industrial output in their specialized area.

Box 4.2 Trading concerns of developing states

1   Developing states are concerned that if they engage in full trade liberalization they will end up specializing solely in primary commodity exports, or at best primary commodities and some resource-based products/low-technology manufactures.

2   There has been a general decline in terms of trade of primary commodities *vis-à-vis* manufactured goods. Over the long term, these countries would therefore have to export increasing quantities of their commodities in order to pay for the same basket of imports as before.

3   This would be exacerbated if several countries endeavoured to increase exports of the same product/commodity ('fallacy of composition').

4   Primary production and resource-based products/low-technology manufactures may have the benefit of being labour intensive but they have lower yields of value-added compared to higher technology products and services.

5   Although the principle of comparative advantage and the benefits said to accrue from free trade may be theoretically sound, in practice this is not what happens. Rather than industrialized countries specializing in certain areas, they have maintained their dominance across the full spectrum of economic activities, heavily subsidizing certain industries (such as agriculture) in order to do so.

Between 1980 and 2000, for example, 'prices for 18 major export commodities were 25 per cent lower in real terms than in 1980. For 8 of these commodities, the decline exceeded 50 per cent'. For some commodities the decline was over 70 per cent: cocoa (71.2 per cent); sugar (76.6 per cent); and tin (73 per cent).[14] As a result of reliance on primary commodities, between 1980 and 2001, African exports experienced the worst decline in terms of trade (30 per cent) followed closely by the Americas compared to Asia (22 per cent) and to developed countries, which enjoyed a 17 per cent improvement in their terms of trade.[15]

There are several explanations as to why those involved in the primary sector are seeing ever-diminishing returns for their commodities. The 1950 UNCLA report indicated four main reasons for the worsening terms of trade. First, it pointed to the income inelasticity of demand for foodstuffs – despite increases in personal income, the demand for basic foodstuffs increases relatively little compared to that for manufactured goods and services. Second, synthetic materials are increasingly replacing raw materials in the manufacturing process. Third, refined production processes have reduced the input of raw material required to manufacture completed products. Finally, the report pointed to the lack of organized labour, which in turn has led to the continuation of low wages in the developing world whereas labour demands have led to a steady increase of wages in the developed world.

Developing states are therefore concerned that if they engage in full trade liberalization they will end up specializing solely in primary commodity exports, or at best primary commodities and some resource-based products/low-technology manufactures. This would have several implications for their future development. The first concern is that the general decline in terms of trade of primary commodities *vis-à-vis* manufactured goods. Over the long term, these countries would therefore have to export increasing quantities of their commodities in order to pay for the same basket of imports as before. Second, this may be exacerbated by several countries endeavouring to increase exports of the same product/commodity (fallacy of composition).[16] Third, primary production and resource-based products/low-technology manufactures have the benefit of being labour intensive but they have lower yields of value-added compared to higher technology products and services, such as sales, marketing and customer services. Finally, although free trade and comparative advantage may be theoretically sound, in practice this is not what happens. Rather than industrialized countries specializing in certain areas, they have maintained their dominance across the full spectrum of economic activities, heavily subsidizing certain industries (such as agriculture) in order to do so.

As we will see below, several states have therefore opted for a managed process of economic integration into the global system. This has involved, amongst other things, export-oriented growth while at the same time setting relatively high tariffs on products that compete with embryonic industries that the country is endeavouring to establish as leading exporters. In addition, many of these countries have provided subsidies and cheap credit to these companies, thus substantially reducing their costs. In terms of international investment, these states have tended to make entry conditional upon either developing joint ventures and/or demanding high levels of domestic content in the final product. Once their economies have taken off and the country is successfully exporting to the rest of the world, a gradual process to full trade liberalization occurs.

Trade liberalization – the historical record

Those who are in favour of further trade liberalization view the emerging pattern of global production and the decline in poverty as evidence for their theory. This line of argument is followed by David Dollar and Aart Kraay and is also evident in the World Bank's *Globalization, Growth, and Poverty* of which David Dollar was an editor.

Such writers argue that there have been three major periods of globalization as illustrated in Figure 4.2: a first wave lasting from 1870 to 1914; a second wave from 1945 to 1980; and a third wave from 1980. It is argued that the first wave was characterized by the exchange of manufactured products in the industrialized North for primary agricultural and mineral commodities from the South. The establishment of these extractive industries initially required large inputs of capital, thus explaining the historically unprecedented levels of foreign capital stock that built up in the South. Although this trade and investment is said to have

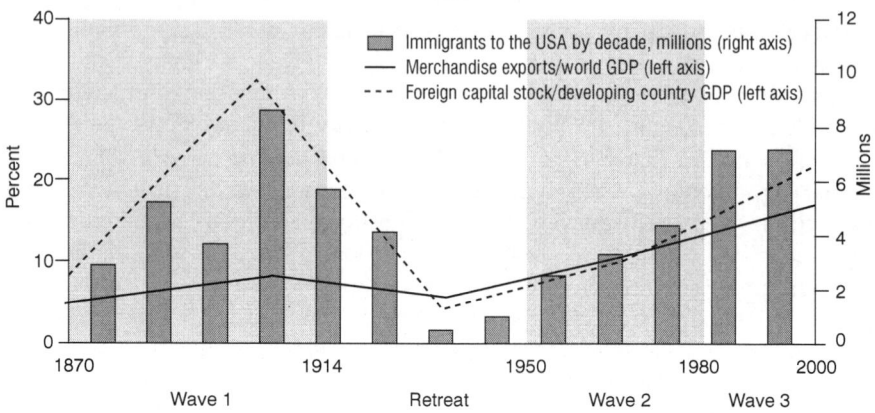

Figure 4.2 Three waves of globalization (Source: World Bank, *Globalization, Growth, and Poverty*, 2002, Figure 1.1 © World Bank 2002. Reprinted with the permission of the World Bank)

had a positive effect on poverty reduction, it was not enough to offset the increase in poverty due to population growth and it should be noted that during this period inequality grew sharply. According to the report this trade pattern continued during the second wave but with a reduced level of capital investment and movement of labour. But the most significant change was the development of an intra-North trading system of large-scale reductions in the tariffs associated with manufactured goods between these countries. North–South trade remained but was stymied because 'barriers facing developing countries had been substantially removed only for those primary commodities that did not compete with agriculture in the developed countries'.[17] As a result, the OECD countries experienced convergence in incomes over this period, but the inequality gap between the North and South continued to worsen.

However, this, it is claimed, changed as a result of the third wave of globalization that began around 1980. According to the report, since this time the world has witnessed an unprecedented level of global integration (said to involve migratory flows as well as trade and capital flows). These authors argue that the pattern of production and trade in the South has dramatically changed, that in 1980 manufactured goods represented only 25 per cent of their exports compared to 80 per cent in 1998. In addition, commercial services constituted a mere 9 per cent of exports in 1980, but by 1998 this had expanded to 17 per cent. In this third wave, those countries that have globalized (those that 'have doubled their ratio of trade to income over the past two decades') have seen their per capita growth rate expand steadily from '1 per cent in the 1960s, to 3 percent in the 1970s, 4 percent in the 1980s, and 5 percent in the 1990s' thereby outstripping growth in the OECD countries.[18] However, the remaining two-thirds of developing states experienced a decline in their trade to GDP ratios and overall also experienced a decline in their GDP per capita growth rate. Thus, '[T]he accelerated growth of recent globalizers is consistent with other cross-country statistical analyses that find that trade goes hand-in-hand with faster growth'.[19]

Several writers have questioned the purported link between trade openness and growth. One criticism has centred on the choice of countries; the report selects 24 developing countries that experienced large increases in their trade to GDP ratios in the last two decades. Critics argue that this selection involves a process of '"weeding" of the "bad" from the "good"'. In fact there were many other countries that pursued liberalizing policies and should have been included, but either experienced reductions in the value of trade in their primary products as a result of the overall decline in terms of trade of these commodities (and) or experienced balance of payment difficulties that led these states to contract their economies.[20] That many of the countries labelled as globalizers actually have maintained higher tariff rates than the so-called non-globalizers has also raised questions over the selection criteria. Although the tariff rates of the globalizers decreased by 22 per cent in the last two decades compared to 11 per cent for the non-globalizers, in the 1980s the former had tariff rates of 57.4 per cent declining to 34.5 per cent during the 1990s, while the latter had a rate of 30.6 per cent declining to 20.3 per cent (these figures are weighted by population to take into account the fact that the globalizers include some of the most populous countries).[21] The report includes in their list of globalizers: China, Mexico, Argentina, the Philippines, Malaysia, Bangladesh, Thailand, India and Brazil. Yet, as can be seen from Table 4.3, in the 1980s, India, Brazil, Bangladesh, and China were in the top ten group of countries with the highest tariffs – not something you would normally associate with the term 'globalizer'.

Therefore, although the IMF claims that '[P]olicies toward foreign trade are among the more important factors promoting economic growth and convergence in developing countries' and, as we have seen, bases its policies on such claims, it has proved to be difficult to establish a robust link between trade openness and growth.[22] Some of these difficulties are related to the problem of measuring trade openness. This can be done indirectly by measuring trading volumes but growth in volumes may or may not reflect reductions in tariffs. But concentrating simply on tariffs will fail to account for the raft of non-tariff barriers that countries use. In order to circumvent such difficulties, Jeffrey Sachs and Andrew Warner apply a set of criteria in establishing whether a country is open or not. Countries were excluded if they had: tariff rates greater than 40 per cent; non-tariff barriers covering more than 40 per cent of imports; a socialist economy; a state monopoly on major exports; and a high black market premium (percentage differential between the official and black market exchange rate).[23]

However, Francisco Rodriguez and Dani Rodrik argue that the link between trade openness and growth is heavily dependent upon the latter two criteria and these reflect other factors other than trade openness. The analysis on state monopoly of major exports contains a selection bias because it reflects geographical location (Africa) rather than anything else so that the only conclusion that can be drawn is that 'African economies have grown more slowly than the rest of the world during the seventies and eighties'.[24] Likewise, rather than a high black market premium reflecting the effect of trade restrictiveness upon growth, it may reflect economic instability/macroeconomic imbalances which may be responsible for the low growth of such countries. Rodriguez and Rodrik therefore argue that the slow growth attributed by Sachs and Warner to trade restrictions may actually be caused by other factors such as geographical location and prolonged economic instability. In surveying some of the key papers, such as the association of trade liberalization and income convergence between countries, the two authors identify similar weaknesses in the approaches adopted, concluding that there has been a tendency to 'greatly overstate the systematic evidence in favor of trade openness'.[25]

As others have pointed out, such critiques should not be taken to imply that the opposite argument has more merit, i.e. that closing an economy would be good for growth. However, it does suggest that the link between trade and growth is difficult to establish and strong assertions should be treated with caution.[26] The *Globalization, Growth and Poverty* report itself acknowledges that it is '[D]ifficult to establish a link between openness and growth in a rigorous manner'.[27] Despite acknowledging the various papers that have questioned the link between trade and growth, the report still concludes that there is such a link. Similar claims have also been made in research papers by some of the authors of the report, asserting that 'openness to international trade accelerates development'.[28] Moreover, they argue that the incomes of the poorest in the countries that they investigated also increased as a result of such growth, a claim that we will examine further in Chapter Six.

An alternative analysis has been offered by Branko Milanovic (who also works at the World Bank) in which growth is divided into two periods: the first begins in 1960 and lasts until 1978, representing the period of import substitution; the second runs from 1978 to 1998, representing the period of high globalization (and concomitantly the period of structural adjustment and, later, the Soviet bloc's transition to a market economy). In so doing, a very different picture emerges, one in which the growth rate of GDP grew at a far faster rate in the second wave of globalization than in the third wave of globalization (Table 4.1). Comparing the 1960–78 growth rates with 1978–98 for each region gives (the latter are stated in parenthesis): Africa 1.5 per cent (0.1 per cent); Asia 4 per cent (3.6 per cent); Latin America 2.8 per cent (0.8 per cent); Eastern Europe 5.1 per cent (–1.1 per cent); whereas the developed countries had growth rates of 2.9 per cent (1.6 per cent).[29] Using such regional comparisons, rather than picking only the best performers renders a very different picture of what is happening globally. First, it is clear that the latter two decades have witnessed a global downturn, global GDP per capita was a mere 1.1 per cent compared to 3.4 per cent between 1960 and 1978. Second, that the developed countries still far out-stripped the developing countries; despite this global downturn their overall growth rate was at least twice that of the other countries. But also the period identified by Dollar and Kraay as the third wave of globalization was actually a period in which, generally speaking, the economic growth of the less developed world declined significantly.

The final criticism of this analysis is that a clear distinction needs to be made between economic liberalization and economic integration.[30] This is an important distinction because many commentators have noted that countries that are often

Table 4.1 Population-weighted regional GDP per capita levels and growth rates, 1960–98[a]

	GDP per capita (in 1995 international prices)			Growth rate of GDP per capita (% p.a.)	
	Year 1960	Year 1978	Year 1998	1960–78	1978–98
Africa	1,539	2,007	2,033	1.5	0.1
Asia	963	1,945	3,967	4.0	3.6
Latin America	3,297	5,460	6,353	2.8	0.8
Eastern Europe/FSU	2,206	5,361	4,290	5.1	−1.1
WENAO	9,792	16,438	22,594	2.9	1.6

Source: B. Milanovic, 'The Two Faces of Development', 2003, Table 3.
Notes:
[a] Each country is one observation, but each observation is weighted by country's population.
WENOA = Western Europe, North America and Oceania

referred to as success stories integrated into trade and financial markets before they liberalized their current and capital accounts by significantly reducing trade tariffs and controls on capital movements. Critics of the Dollar and Kraay study point out that dividing countries into globalizers and non-globalizers simply by the growth of trade volumes is misguided because '[T]rade volumes are the outcome of many different things, including most importantly an economy's overall performance'.[31]

The cases of India and China

China and India are often seen as good examples of countries that have liberalized and, as a result, benefited from above average growth.[32] Certainly, Indian growth rates in the last quarter of a century have been impressive, registering an average GDP growth rate of 5.6 per cent from 1984 to 2004 and above 8 per cent (on average) in the last few years.[33] This is both impressive when one compares it to previous growth rates of 3.5 per cent for the preceding two decades (1960–62 to 1980–82) and compared to the growth rate of high income countries which averaged just 2.25 per cent per annum from 1990 to 2003.[34] But even these high growth rates are overshadowed by the extraordinary acceleration of China's economy which has managed to sustain an average GDP growth rate of 9.2 per cent from 1994 and 9.4 per cent for the 10 years prior to that.[35] However, their growth patterns have been somewhat different with each registering their highest growth in their traditionally strong sectors: industry in the case of China; and services in the case of India (Table 4.2).

As the saying goes, success is the father of many, failure the bastard of none. So it would seem for both India and China. As a result of their strong growth, these countries are often cited by both those advocating growth through greater trade liberalization and by those that are sceptical of such claims. For instance Jagdish Bhagwati argues that India and China both 'shifted to outward orientation roughly two decades ago, and this contributed to their higher growth in the 1980s and 1990s. China adopted aggressively outward-orientated economic policies

Table 4.2 Structure of the economies of India and China (percentage of GDP)

	China			India		
	1984	*1994*	*2004*	*1984*	*1994*	*2004*
Agriculture	32.0	20.2	15.2	35.2	30.4	21.2
Industry	43.3	47.8	52.9	26.2	27.1	27.0
Services	24.7	31.9	31.9	38.7	42.5	51.8

Source: World Bank, *India at a Glance and China at a Glance*, 2005.

in 1978. India also began opening its insular economy in a limited fashion in the 1980s and more systematically and boldly in the 1990s … No country in the world had growth as rapid as China's, and fewer than ten (and, except for China, none with poverty rates and population size comparable to India's) had a growth rate exceeding India's during these years'.[36] Similarly, the World Bank's *Globalization, Growth and Poverty* Report argues that globalization 'is a complex process that affects many aspects of our lives. The terrorist attacks on the United States on September 11 were one aspect of globalization. Rapid growth and poverty reduction in China, India, and other countries that were poor 20 years ago is another'.[37]

Others question whether India and China are really the showcases of trade liberalization that they are made out to be. Dani Rodrik, for example, points out that in both of these cases their impressive growth rates actually preceded their move towards greater free trade by about ten years. During the 1980s India's tariff average was 91 per cent and in fact 'tariffs were actually higher in the rising growth period of the 1980s than in the low-growth 1970s'.[38] Although China's tariff average was much lower, it was still very high at just over 42 per cent. Both lowered their tariffs in the succeeding decade, with India experiencing a radical reduction of over 40 per cent.

By 1991, as a result of high levels of public debt (as a result of substantial increases in state spending), much of it financed from abroad (external debt tripled from 1980 to 1990) alongside a growing current account deficit, India was confronted with a financial crisis.[39] Responding to this crisis, its leaders implemented a series of economic reforms so that foreign investment restrictions were relaxed and trade tariffs were severely reduced. In addition, the so-called 'license Raj', the system of permits and controls that businesses had to comply with, experienced a radical overhaul such that '[I]ndustrial licensing was finally removed for new and old projects, whether for creation of expansion of capacity or for product diversification'.[40]

However, Rodrik and Subramanian argue that India's strong growth rates actually started in the 1980s as a result of previous reforms under Indira and Rajiv Ghandi that were pro-business and focused on 'raising the profitability of the established industrial and commercial establishments' rather than pro-market policies involving economic liberalization.[41] The reform of the 'license Raj' in 1985/6 included: '[E]liminating the licensing of 25 categories of industries'; including 22 industries that were 'previously restricted by the Monopolies and

Table 4.3 Tariff averages for 1980s and 1990s (per cent)

Country	1980s	Country	1990s
Bangladesh	94.5	Pakistan	56.8
India	91.0	India	50.5
Pakistan	72.2	Bangladesh	39.8
Burkina Faso	60.8	Rwanda	38.4
Sudan	53.6	Cambodia	35.0
Brazil	46.7	Thailand	33.9
Benin	42.8	Sudan	33.5
China	42.4	Bahamas	32.0
Egypt	41.6	Egypt	31.4
Suriname	40.0	China	31.2

Source: Dani Rodrik, Comments on 'Trade, Growth, and Poverty', 2000, Table 1.

Trade Restrictive Act (MRTP)'; greater product diversification of industry was allowed through the introduction of 'broad-banding'; and, finally, allowing companies to 'expand their capacity up to 133 per cent of that reached in any of the previous years'.[42] These reforms, it is argued, thus gave a significant boost to businesses by increasing their profits 'without threatening them with real competition'.[43] The policies were designed to 'get industry "used" to competition internally, only then to expose it to the rigours of free external competition'.[44]

In the case of China, it is argued that not only was its economy protected by relatively high tariffs but also that the state continued to run a large section of the economy. Branko Milanovic states that '[A]lmost one-third of China's industrial output is still produced by state-owned enterprises, and almost 20% of GDP, a fraction higher than in any country in the world save for North Korea, Cuba, and a few former Soviet republics'.[45] Moreover, it is argued, the Chinese state has not only played an instrumental role by protecting embryonic industries through tariffs and maintaining a major stake in industry, but also by developing an environment that promoted the production of goods that were far more complex technologically than would be normally expected for a country at its stage of development. It did so through a variety of measures, including: requiring foreign investment to 'enter into joint ventures with domestic firms' thus promoting the diffusion of technologies and managerial know-how; intellectual property rights were not fully enforced allowing 'producers to reverse engineer and imitate foreign technologies'; high levels of domestic content were also required for some industries investing in the country, thus encouraging the growth of locally-based sources of high quality supplies.[46]

For these writers, India and China are of interest not because they are classic examples of liberalization. Rather, they view these two countries as cases of gradual reform implementing selective policies in order to compete in international markets. They thus conclude that, 'the relevant question for policy makers is not whether trade is good or bad: countries that achieve rapid growth also see trade accounting for a growing share of GDP. The question is the correct sequence of policies and how much priority deep trade liberalization should receive early in the reform process. China and India suggest the benefits of a gradual, sequenced approach'.[47]

It should be noted that these writers are not arguing that states should not participate in trade; as a recent UN report points out, '[N]o country has developed successfully by turning its back on international trade and long-term capital flows... imported capital goods are likely to be much cheaper than those manufactured at home ... Exports in turn, are important because they permit purchases of imported capital equipment'.[48] However, they do argue that the World Bank and IMF place too much emphasis on the role of trade as a generator of rapid growth. The above cases of India and China indicate that what is more important is the provision of conducive domestic economic conditions that provide the necessary stimuli for growth, 'leadership committed to development and supporting a coherent growth strategy counts for a lot more than trade liberalization – even when the strategy departs sharply from the "enlightened" standard view on reform'.[49]

Bringing the state back in?

Adopting the structural adjustments outlined in the first section has resulted in, amongst other things, a decline in the influence of the state in a wide range of activities. The denationalization of industries, the abolition of price controls and market boards, reductions in state spending, the cancellation or reduction of subsidies, etc. reduced the scope of state involvement in the economies of these countries. At the same time, the move towards a pegged or floating exchange rate, trade liberalization and the freeing up of capital flows effectively limited the range of macro-economic policies that the state could pursue. This approach has been criticized because of its negative effects for some of the most poor and vulnerable in these societies and, in the vast majority of cases, has not led to the growth rates promised. Critics also point out that the policies prescribed by the World Bank and the IMF are not the ones that were followed by the industrialized states themselves during their early stages of economic development, '[I]n reality, the relationship between trade openness and growth is likely to be contingent on a host of internal and external factors. That nearly all of today's industrial countries embarked on their growth behind tariff barriers, and reduced protection only subsequently, surely offers a clue...it is also true that no country has developed simply by opening itself to foreign trade and investment. The trick has been to combine the opportunities offered by global markets with strategies for domestic investment and institution building, to stimulate domestic entrepreneurs.'[50] What is good for the goose should be good for the gander.

Indeed, after the East Asian financial crisis of 1997, even some within the IMF and World Bank agreed that there was a need for some type of state control on capital flows. As a result of the economic slowdown in the region the short-term capital that had been used to help fuel the growth of these countries stampeded out of the region. Although the amount of money borrowed by these countries in the years before the crash meant that at some point there would be a need for some type of correction (net private capital flows to the region increased from

Box 4.3 The East Asian economic crisis

Although the economic crisis of 1997 began in East Asia, its ramifications were felt across continents (particularly the former Soviet bloc and Latin America). The reversal of fortunes was staggering; between '1994 and 1996 net private inflows into Indonesia, Korea, Malaysia, Thailand and the Philippines grew from US$48 billion to US$93 billion'. Yet once the confidence of the markets had been lost, capital exited at an alarming rate so that the same 'figure for 1997 was minus US$12 billion'[1] Although at the time much of the fault for the collapse of these economies was blamed on 'crony capitalism' several structural contradictions meant that such a collapse was highly probable at some stage.

Most of the states in the region had pegged their currencies to the US dollar, thereby providing a high level of security for those seeking to invest (although not all followed this path; the value of the South Korean Won, for example, was based on a market average rate under a managed floating exchange regime). Much of the investment pouring into these countries was on a short term basis. This was sustainable as long as growth and profits remained high. Because of the surfeit of financiers wishing to invest, when the loan term expired borrowers had no difficulty acquiring new capital.

However, the competitiveness of these countries' exports had come under pressure from: the huge devaluation of the Chinese yuan in 1994 (50 per cent decline in its value); the decline in the exchange rate value of the yen; and the appreciation of the dollar from 1995 onwards. Because most of the currencies were pegged to the dollar, demand for their exports began to decline. This was exacerbated by the fact that much of the investment was directed towards speculative accumulation in stocks and property, rather than further modernization of the production base in order to improve upon the quality and price of their exports. A fundamental contradiction thus emerged: extremely high levels of investment flowed into East Asia, yet at the same time demand for their products was declining. By the beginning of 1997 this slow down started to show up both in the economic figures and also in a string of loan defaults. Investors' confidence rapidly vanished and a vast outflow of capital followed as they shifted their money to safer shores.

1   R. Higgott, 'The Asian economic crisis: a study in the politics of resentment', *New Political Economy*, vol. 3:3, 1998, p. 339.

$48 billion in 1994 to $93 billion in 1996), the financial investors overreacted precipitating a meltdown.[51] But because these countries had earlier liberalized their capital accounts there were no mechanisms in place to prevent or slow down the financial exodus.[52] As Jagdish Bhagwati has commented, 'it is hardly plausible that the miracle would have vanished precipitously. As capital accumulated relative to labor, the future return to capital would decline only slowly, except in the most singular circumstances. But what happened in reality was that the economies *crashed*'.[53]

The volatility that can accompany capital account liberalization may not just be limited to the East-Asian crisis. A recent large-scale survey by Geoffrey Garrett examined the varying effects of tariff reductions and capital liberalization upon high-, middle- and low-income countries. It was found that capital account liberalization had a negative impact upon economic growth for medium- and low-income countries because 'financial liberalization in the absence of the kind of developed domestic capital markets and prudential regulations that only exist in the advanced industrial democracies is a recipe for volatility, unpredictability, and boom and bust cycles in capital flows'.[54] In addition, a recent report by the IMF found that 'there is evidence that international investors do engage in herding and momentum trading in emerging markets, more so than in developed countries. Recent research also suggests the presence of contagion in international financial markets ... countries that are in the early stages of financial integration have been exposed to significant risks in terms of higher volatility of both output and consumption'.[55]

Although there appears to be a new consensus forming at the World Bank and IMF that some controls on capital flows by developing states may be necessary, a fundamental reassessment of the positive role the state may play in promoting economic growth has not occurred.[56] Others, on the other hand, view a more active role for the state as instrumental in developing a country's economy. Given the enormity of the task confronting developing states in attempting to compete economically and to produce high levels of sustainable growth, it is argued that the state needs to intervene actively in the economy in order to ensure the success of national industries. It would be impossible for these embryonic industries to compete on a level playing field with the technologically advanced industrialized countries. Active intervention by the state is needed, it is argued, in order to ameliorate the otherwise overly harsh economic competition that they would face. Such intervention, though, is a complex affair often requiring different policies for different sectors of the economy:

> Countries with low productivity require low interest rates to stimulate investment, and high interest rates to induce people to save. They need undervalued exchange rates to boost exports, and overvalued exchange rates to minimize the cost of foreign debt repayment and of imports ... They must protect their new industries from foreign competition, but they require free trade to meet their import needs. They crave stability to grow, to keep their capital at home, and to direct their investment toward long-term ventures. Yet the prerequisite of stability is growth.[57]

Until the economic crisis of 1997, the growth of East Asia had far outstripped that of any other region of the world for several decades. Indeed, for a quarter of a century (1965–90) the eight high-performing economies (Japan, Hong Kong, South Korea, Singapore, Taiwan, Indonesia, Malaysia and Thailand) sustained double the growth of any other region, including the OECD countries.[58] As we saw in the last chapter, East Asia's growth is in large part due to its success in capturing a significant portion of the world market in both the secondary and tertiary sectors. On the other hand, African exports of manufactured goods constitute 30 per cent of its overall merchandise exports, representing an increase of 20 per cent over 40 years. But the emphasis remains mainly on primary commodities, particularly fuel (because of the oil crisis and the resulting increase in prices). In comparison, Asia's merchandise export profile changed radically between 1960 when manufactured goods constituted just under 19 per cent of exports and 2001 when they constituted over 69 per cent of exports.[59] The data also show that, in the same period, the developing world has increased its share in the production of electronic manufactures from 14 per cent to 34.2 per cent and that its share of textile manufactures remains high at approximately 49 per cent of world textile exports.[60] However, if this data is disaggregated by region, it becomes very apparent that the major share of exports in these sectors is highly limited to one major region, East Asia, which, as a result, increased its share of developing countries' manufactured exports from 56.9 per cent in 1985 to 69 per cent in 1998.[61] As we have seen, South Asia has also successfully re-oriented its industry so that labour-intensive manufacturing, such as textiles, now dominate their export sector. However, it still represents but a small proportion of the developing world's manufactured exports, for example its textiles still only constitute 12 per cent of the developing world's manufactured exports. By comparison, if one includes Taiwan, Singapore, Hong Kong and South Korea in the East Asian category, the region dominates the low- (70.2 per cent), medium- (63.8 per cent) and high- (85.5 per cent) technology exports from the developing world.[62]

How did these East Asian 'developmental states' successfully sustain high growth rates over such a long period and move into relatively high technology sectors that were able to compete with established industries?[63] Opinion is divided, with some emphasizing the fact that the four Asian Tigers and Japan benefited from boosts that the Korean and Vietnamese wars gave to their economies and also from the privileged access to Western economies for their exports as a result of their strategic importance during the Cold War.[64] But, in addition, analysts point to the fact that East Asia's economic policy has been based on export-orientated industrialization that involved the creation of a positive investment environment that included 'credit subsidies and tax incentives, educational policies, establishment of public enterprises, export inducements, duty-free access to inputs and capital goods and actual government coordination of investment plans'.[65] Generally speaking, these economies grew initially behind high tariffs and restrictions on capital movements. At the same time, the state provided a sound infrastructure, a well-educated work force (Taiwan, for example, 'trains 50% more engineers in proportion to its population than the United States'), credit and loans to industry and actively guided industrial planning.[66] Similarly, China and India are said to be new examples of this staged process; both grew in the 1980s but significant trade reform only began in the mid-nineties for the former and early nineties for the latter.[67] In addition, China's and India's trade restrictions 'remain among the highest in the world'.[68] This pattern of growth followed by tariff reductions would therefore appear to be the rule, rather than the exception, at least where East Asia and India are concerned.[69]

In other words, these states actively intervened in the running of the country's economy in order to protect fledgling industries both through subsidies and through tariffs on imports. The latter thus ensured that these companies were protected from more established overseas competition. The former ensured that the full start-up and running costs of operations were not borne by business alone, thus enabling them either to sell products at below market price or to make higher profits than would otherwise be possible. Similarly, the governments of Japan, South Korea, Taiwan and Singapore established R & D centres focused on new technologies and passed on their discoveries to 'private companies without transferring development costs'.[70] At least some of the cost of developing new technologies was thus defrayed by the state. In addition, these developmental states either created a conducive investment environment that ensured large inflows of long-term capital investments by providing healthy returns or introduced controls to ensure domestic private capital remained within the country (in the 1960s, South Korea, for example passed legislation concerning illegal transfers of capital above $1 million dollars that had a maximum penalty of death).[71]

These states, by supplying cheap credit, government-funded research developments, human capital and guaranteed market protection have been able to 'induce firms to engage in activities where the risk level would be so great as to deter firms acting alone'.[72] In addition, the state has taken on a strong coordinating role ensuring knowledge dissemination throughout the domestic industries concerned, organizing industrial amalgams thus ensuring a unified and orderly approach to development and providing access to financial resources for such industrial development. In addition to the usual regulatory and distributive (state as producer) roles of the state, it is argued that the success of East Asia lies in the state's high degree of 'embedded autonomy'. In other words, the state is embedded within society to a much higher degree compared to most other industrialized states – 'they are embedded in a concrete set of social ties that binds the state to society and provides institutionalized channels for the continual negotiation and re-negotiation of goals and policies'.[73]

Similarly, Linda Weiss argues that the form that state–society coordination has taken has been unique in East Asia. Rather than the state imposing certain industrial policies on the business community in a top-down manner, these countries have engaged in 'regular and extensive consultation, negotiation and coordination with the private sector'.[74] This has provided these states with very strong transformative capacities, i.e. 'the ability of a state to adapt to external shocks and pressures by generating ever-new means of governing the process of industrial change'.[75] This is in contrast to both liberal and corporatist states: liberal states have traditionally viewed 'interventions that must perforce be carried out from time to time, as something to be tolerated, however momentarily, rather than improved and perfected' while the corporatist state encompassed 'representation of organized interests (labour and capital)'.[76] The latter represents a compromise in which state policies took account of the interests of both organized labour and business in return for help in implementing such policies. Unlike the developmental states of East Asia which established cooperative collaboration with industry, the corporatist state thus compromises with organized interests to ensure the successful implementation of its policies – a bargaining process as opposed to a collaborative process.

Weiss' view of the East Asian state also differs from Pete Evens' notion of 'embedded autonomy'. As she rightly points out, the latter still depicts a top-down form of state management so that 'the state can have transformative capacity only while capital remains in a relatively dependent-subordinate relationship to the state'.[77] This leads Evans to the conclusion that these states will eventually experience a metamorphosis because they will become victims of their own success. The industrial and labour groupings that these states have nurtured will eventually challenge the foundations of the state itself, 'if state and society are mutually constitutive, having changed society the developmental state itself must change. The question is what form the state's own transformation will take'.[78] The state as midwife of industrial development produces its own grave diggers. Whereas for Weiss, the transformative capacity of these states is of a rather different form, producing a condition of 'governed interdependence', one in which 'public and private participants maintain their autonomy, yet which is nevertheless governed by broader goals set and monitored by the state'. The fact that both state and industry remain relatively autonomous means that the latter can be 'linked into the policy-making framework via a robust negotiating relationship'. In opposition to Peter Evans' argument, even when these industrial groupings have become significantly stronger, the state continues to play an autonomous role influencing the direction of the economy.[79]

That said, although there are common elements to the East Asian 'miracle', undoubtedly each country followed an economic course that was a somewhat individual combination of the above policies. One of the biggest differences was that South Korea sustained very high levels of public debt borrowed from abroad, whereas Hong Kong, Singapore and Taiwan did not borrow heavily from abroad in order to promote growth. Interestingly, Indonesia, Malaysia and Thailand also borrowed heavily from abroad, all of which were the worst hit when the Asian crisis of 1997 unravelled.[80] Other differences between the four Asian tigers plus Japan are also apparent: Singapore concentrated on attracting foreign direct investment while South Korea concentrated on attracting foreign capital in the form of loans and Japan intentionally limited FDI.[81] Hong Kong, on the other hand, adopted a 'hands off' approach to investment, probably because it had already benefited from large amounts of investment in the 1950s, particularly from investors looking to move their money out of mainland China after the communist revolution.[82] Although most of these states provided cheap credit, in South Korea, credit was extended to business 'at negative real interest rates' and price controls were established for a raft of basic commodities.[83] Hong Kong achieved a similar outcome by creating 'cartels to contain the price of basic foodstuffs', but had an open economy.[84] In the case of Taiwan, the 'most important direct subsidies ...

came in the form of tax incentives'.[85] For both South Korea and Taiwan, export subsidies were provided.[86] In addition, Singapore and Hong Kong have 'provided the world's largest public housing systems...which have served to subsidize wages.'[87] Taiwan was the first to establish an Export Processing Zone[88] and in the

Box 4.4 The East Asian Developmental State

How did these East Asian 'developmental states' successfully sustain high growth rates over such a long period and move into relatively high technology sectors that were able to compete with established industries?

Opinion is divided, with some emphasizing the fact that the four Asian Tigers and Japan benefited from boosts that the Korean and Vietnamese wars gave to their economies and also from the privileged access to Western economies for their exports as a result of their strategic importance during the Cold War[1] But in addition, analysts point to the fact that East Asia's economic policy has been based on export orientated industrialization that initially grew behind high tariffs and restrictions on capital movements. At the same time, the state provided a sound infrastructure and invested heavily in human capital generating a well educated and highly skilled work force.

These states actively intervened in the running of the country's economy in order to protect fledgling industries both through subsidies and through tariffs on imports. The latter thus ensured that these companies were protected from more established overseas competition. The former ensured that the full start-up and running costs of operations were not borne by business alone, thus enabling them either to sell products at below market price or to make higher profits than would otherwise be possible. Similarly, the governments of Japan, South Korea, Taiwan and Singapore established R & D centres focused on new technologies and passed on their discoveries to 'private companies without transferring development costs'[2] At least some of the cost of developing new technologies was thus defrayed by the state. In addition, these developmental states either created a conducive investment environment that ensured large inflows of long-term capital investments by providing healthy returns or introduced controls to ensure domestic private capital remained within the country.

Rather than concentrating on invention or innovation, these countries' form of industrialization was based on acquiring the technical know-how to establish a similar manufacturing base to that of the North. Once they had acquired this knowledge, the strategy seems to have been to produce higher quality goods at competitive prices which they were able to do through a combination of improved productivity and low wages.

1 S. Gill, 'The geopolitics of the Asian crisis', *Monthly Review*, vol. 50:10, March 1999, p. 4.
2 R. Appelbaum and J. Henderson (eds), *States and Development*, 1992, p. 22.

case of Japan, South Korea and Taiwan, the state has controlled credit availability and regulated licenses in such a way as to steer industry into the higher value-added sector.[89] China, Taiwan, Hong Kong and Malaysia have all benefited from investment from overseas Chinese.[90]

It should also be noted that protecting industries from international competition should not be taken to imply also that domestic competition was somehow stymied. Many of these developmental states have encouraged domestic competition in certain sectors of the economy, actively supporting successful enterprises while exposing poor performers to the full force of the market. In Japan and South Korea, for example, those firms that excelled were given further subsidies and licenses to expand their production activities whereas poor performers had to fend for themselves.[91] Similarly, China's policy has been described as one that is not based on ' "only winners should be picked" (an impossible task) but that "losers should be let go" '.[92] As pointed out earlier, India's initial reforms were designed to 'get industry "used" to competition internally, only then to expose it to the rigours of free external competition'.[93]

The developmental state as emulator

Some argue it was not only the case in East Asia that the state played an instrumental role in supporting embryonic industries, but also that the form of industrialization differed to what had gone before. For example, Alice Amsden uses Schumpeter's analysis of industrialization to distinguish between a first period of industrialization around the end of the eighteen century led by Britain based on scientific invention, and a second period at the end of the nineteen century led by Germany and the United States based on innovation (adopting scientific knowledge to new areas for commercial gain). The creation of these innovatory products ensured higher than average returns for the companies concerned because of the absence of competitors (given the novelty of the product).[94] The success of these second phase developers, it is argued, can be understood in terms of Schumpeterian rents. Rent is said to describe 'a situation where the parties who control a particular set of resources are able to gain from scarcity by insulating themselves from competition. This is achieved by taking advantage of or by creating barriers to the entry of competitors'.[95] Schumpeter viewed innovation as enabling entrepreneurs to receive higher than average returns because of the demand for their product (presuming it was successful) and the fact that, initially, no one else is making or is able to provide exactly the same commodity (until the know-how diffuses). Innovation is thus extremely profitable for a time, because the quantity of the product available is limited and competitors are confronted with a knowledge barrier – they lack the know-how to produce an identical product.[96] Entrepreneurs thus endeavour to maintain such rents using intellectual property rights to prevent competitors from entering the market and thus lowering profits that they would otherwise make on their products. In cases where such barriers do not exist, market prices spiral downwards as each producer endeavours to acquire a share of the market.

But this is only one of many ways in which to benefit from such rents, which may be endogenous or exogenous to the value chain. Raphael Kaplinsky has recently provided a useful classification of such rents. Endogenous rents are said to include: technology (the technology of the product and the associated manufacturing process); human resource (technical skill of the workforce); organizational (organization of the production system); marketing and design (branding); and relational rents (arising from '*relatively* unusual synergies between firms'). Exogenous rents, on the other hand, are said to include: resources (being resource rich relative to other countries); policy rents ('differential access resulting from government policies'); infrastructural rents (enabling firms to assemble, communicate, produce, transport etc. better and at lower cost than firms from another country); and financial rents (access to cheap long-term finance).[97]

Are the developmental states of the third wave of industrialization Schumpeterian innovators? Alice Amsden suggests that in several of the developmental states neither invention nor innovation was the driving force behind their success. Rather the defining aspect of industrial development was learning – 'borrowing, adapting and improving upon foreign designs'.[98] In the case of Korea this was primarily through the purchasing of foreign licences and the contracting in of foreign consultants rather than 'depending on foreigners to run Korean plants'.[99] As we saw earlier, China has required many foreign investors to set up joint ventures with Chinese companies and also stipulated a high level of domestic content in the final product thus ensuring the diffusion of the technical knowledge required to improve their own products and compete effectively. But if Germany and the United States were able to grow as a result of the high returns associated with innovatory products, how could production based on learning provide high growth levels? After all, if industries in the developmental state were making products of a similar kind to those already available in the market, unlike the innovators of the second phase of industrialization, they would not attract higher than average returns. Amsden argues that state subsidies based on productivity plus low wages were the key to success; they competed on the 'combined basis of low wages, state subsidies (broadly construed to include a wide range of governmental supports), and incremental productivity and quality improvements related to existing products'.[100]

It thus appears that this third phase of industrialization possessed its own unique characteristics. Instead of achieving rents through innovation, these countries' form of industrialization was based on acquiring the technical know-how to establish a similar manufacturing base to that of the North. Once they had acquired this knowledge, the strategy seems to have been to produce higher quality goods at competitive prices which they were able to do through a combination of improved productivity and low wages. However, some of the other rents listed above were in operation to ensure the profitability of business activity within these developmental states. As we have seen, these included exogenous forms, such as policy rents via government licensing and financial rents in terms of loans at below market cost. In terms of endogenous rents, companies within the developmental state have benefited from highly skilled workforces but they have also concentrated on improving the organization of the production system in order to improve productivity. One of the best examples of this is the Just in Time production system first introduced in Japan which created an ultra-lean production process as outlined in the introduction. This resulted in cost-savings by reducing the following: the amount of storage capacity required; the amount of wastage; and circulation time (time to market), thereby ensuring a quicker return on the capital outlaid.[101]

Conclusion

For the last quarter of a century the World Bank and IMF have vigorously promoted a policy of liberalization in the South, by making their loans conditional upon the acceptance by these states of very similar structural adjustment programmes. This has proved to be extremely controversial. Advocates of liberalization have argued that this is the best way in which to attract investors and to stimulate growth. Others, however, criticized the way in which World Bank/IMF analysts have linked increased trade liberalization with domestic economic growth. In practice it is very difficult to discern the direction of causality; it could equally be the case that because of domestic economic growth, these countries have ended up trading more. Critics also point to the fact that some of the most economically successful developing states have some of the highest trade tariffs in the world.

What can we conclude from this? It is not that countries should not adopt an export-orientated approach, but that this should be carried out in stages and should be implemented as part of a wider set of measures aimed at boosting economic growth. It is important to note the difference between this approach and the World Bank's. To produce sustained economic development export-orientated growth, it is argued, is rarely sufficient on its own. Indeed, the link between increased levels of exports and higher growth rates is questioned because although 'countries that grow fast tend to experience rising export-GDP ratios, the reverse is not true in general'.[102] The East Asian experience would seem to indicate that a successful export-orientated strategy involves initial protection of domestic industries through selective tariffs, the use of subsidies/cheap credit and attracting high levels of long term investment.

The World Bank agrees that economic growth in East Asia has been remarkable, '[F]rom 1965 to 1990 the twenty-three economies of East Asia grew faster than all other regions of the World' and that they have managed to do this in a more equitable fashion than have other developing countries, 'The HPAEs (Eight High Performing Asian Economies) are the only economies that have high growth *and* declining inequality. Moreover, the fastest growing East Asian economies, Japan and the Four Tigers, are the most equal'.[103] However, it questions several aspects of the policies associated with the East Asian 'Developmental State'. The World Bank argues that the main reasons for these states' spectacular growth are export-orientated growth and a 'superior accumulation of physical and human capital'.[104] According to its report, *The East Asian Miracle*, East Asia has been successful because it got the fundamentals of macro-economic policy right. These included:

a low rate of inflation by avoiding 'inflationary financing of budget deficits'; high levels of domestic savings that 'sustained the HPAEs high investment levels'; export-driven growth 'was predicated on competitive real exchange rates'; ensuring 'generally positive real interest rates on deposits and the creation of secure bank-based financial systems' compared to many developing countries where high inflation has often led to negative real interest rates which in turn has led to low levels of domestic savings; developing a 'relative abundance of educated workers'; absorbing foreign technology; and, finally, investment in agriculture remained and the adoption of new agricultural methods were widespread.[105]

Many of the writers examined above would not necessarily disagree with many of these findings. However, the report goes on to say that 'promoting specific industries did not work', and when 'interest rate subsidies were large, or export performance criteria were not imposed, direct credit often went to inefficient ventures'.[106] But it is less important that certain specific industries failed, as long as the general industrial policy worked (which it did). Furthermore, the latter point would seem to imply that the policies of these states sometimes failed because they did not pursue the 'developmental model' strongly enough, i.e. that performance conditions should always be applied when cheap loans are made available to businesses. The World Bank concludes that such a policy is no longer feasible, because 'these governments were able during the early stages of rapid growth to close their financial markets to the outside world. Few developing economies today have the institutional resources to impose performance-based criteria for credit allocation consistently. Moreover, the capital markets of all economies are becoming more and more integrated. Thus, successful repression of interest rates and contest-based allocation may only be possible for the very few developing economies with strong institutions and then only to a very limited degree'.[107] Rather than argue for greater government control of domestic and foreign capital and performance-related cheap credit for embryonic industries, the World Bank concludes that sound macro-economic policy together with an increased emphasis on exports on their own will ensure long term economic growth. But given the history of development in the last few decades, this is highly questionable at the very least.

As Robert Wade points out, there is of course a risk when using East Asia as a possible model to follow that we fall into a Darwinian fallacy, i.e. that 'because something exists it must be vital to the survival of the organism or society in which it exists'. In other words, because these countries adopted the policies outlined in the above chapter, these must be the keys to economic success. But as he rightly counter-argues, the Ptolemaic fallacy, i.e. 'the assumption that only those features of economic policy consistent with neoclassical prescriptions could have contributed to superior economic performance, so that everything else can be safely ignored', may prove to be even more harmful.[108]

The 'developmental state' model has also fallen out of vogue as a result of the East Asian crisis in 1997, which would seem to undermine the argument that their economic policies should be emulated. However, a closer examination would suggest otherwise. First, development in Thailand, Malaysia and Indonesia has differed substantially from the early NICs with far less state coordination of investment with 'a substantial proportion of domestic and foreign finance... allocated to speculative projects' for example, property development.[109] In the case of South Korea, the transformative capacity of the state had diminished considerably by the time of the crisis for three reasons: US trained economists have gradually replaced the earlier generation of planners and have pushed for less state intervention; the Economic Planning Board has been dismantled; and the *chaebol* have become more independent. The result has been that the *chaebol* have borrowed heavily from abroad and the lack of coordination in long term industrial planning has led to over production as a result of each of the *chaebols* encroaching upon each other's traditional domains.[110]

The 'developmental state' model is not therefore fundamentally undermined by the East Asian Crisis. However, the use of protective tariffs may be difficult to impose if developing states wish to become members (or remain active participants) in the WTO. Reform at the international level is therefore also needed. It has been suggested that one possible way around this problem would be that instead of developing states agreeing to bounded tariffs on a particular class of goods or services, they would be allowed to choose which sectors of the economy to apply tariffs to 'subject to the overall constraint of an average bound tariff, such an approach would balance multilateral discipline with policy flexibility'.[111] For example, there is little reason for developing countries to apply high tariffs in the medium- or high-technology sectors if their economies are not yet producing such goods. They could thus lower duties on such imported goods, while, say, maintaining relatively high protective duties on resource-based, labour-intensive and low-technology goods. Indeed, high tariffs on investment and intermediate goods, for example plant machinery or specialized intermediate inputs, will only increase the costs for embryonic industries.[112] The tariffs could then be shifted to other sectors such as medium- and high-technology goods once a country has embarked upon this form of production.

At the same time, the importance of investment cannot be understated. Dani Rodrik for example argues that the 'evidence from the experience of the last two decades is clear: the countries whose economies have grown most rapidly since the mid-1970s are those that have invested a large share of GDP and maintained macro-economic stability'.[113] In addition, government aid and protection for inchoate industries did not imply that uncompetitive firms were given unconditional aid, support was withdrawn for the least successful companies. As we will see in the next chapter, many developing states have been burdened with large debts as a result of borrowing 'petro-dollars' in the 1970s, placing a stranglehold over the economy. The announcement of large scale debt cancellation for many of the heavily indebted poor countries at the Gleneagles Summit in 2005 may provide a fresh start for many of these countries. However, what is required is a source of long term investment. One source for this should be the recent increase in many primary product prices as a result of the global economic upturn and China's insatiable appetite for raw materials. The tax returns on these exports, combined with the willingness of companies and financiers to invest in these industries as a result of this boom, offers some opportunity. However, it also requires reform in the international financial sector to ensure finance is made available at reasonable interest rates with less stringent conditions attached than has hitherto been the case.

5   Globalization and the reconfiguration of the state

A spectre is haunting the world's governments – the spectre of globalization. Some argue that predatory market forces make it impossible for benevolent governments to shield their populations from the beasts of prey that lurk beyond their borders. Others counter that benign market forces actually prevent predatory governments from fleecing their citizens. Although the two sides see different villains, they draw one common conclusion: omnipotent markets mean impotent politicians.[1]

There is much discussion in the globalization literature concerning the decline of state sovereignty in today's world. Such discussions are divided into two camps. There are those that examine global governance, the growth of international/regional institutions with powers to interpret and execute international laws or agreements. This debate hinges on whether this growth in global governance has changed the juridical status of the state and, if so, to what degree. There are others that focus on the *de facto* autonomy and capabilities of the state and whether or not globalization limits the range of feasible options available to policy makers and their ability to carry out certain tasks.[2] For these writers the focus is on the '"control gap" between the aspirations for control over an extended range of matters and the capability to achieve it'. In contradistinction to the first group the 'problem is not a loss of legal sovereignty but a loss of political and economic autonomy'.[3]

This chapter focuses on the impact of globalization on the political autonomy of states rather than the juridical aspect of sovereignty. In particular, this chapter examines the claim that economic globalization exerts certain pressures upon states in such a manner as to limit severely their autonomy and capability in core areas of policy making and implementation, that it 'exposes all economies ... to common pressures which, in turn, produce common outcomes'.[4] As a result of these common pressures, it is argued that there has been a general rolling back of the state with the privatization of core functions and a general reduction in welfare spending – 'pressure from global capital for reduced taxes and labour costs has driven many governments to cut back welfare programmes. In the cause of bolstering global competitiveness, governments across the planet have since 1980 rolled back social democracy ... Governments have generally implemented the greatest cuts in respect of sunk costs such as unemployment benefits, old-age pensions, and untied official development assistance ... almost no government today dares openly to pursue a programme of radical progressive redistribution of wealth'.[5]

In other words, economic globalization is viewed as leading to lower levels of corporate taxation and thus reductions in state expenditure resulting in, amongst other things, a decline in the provision of social welfare. This, in turn, produces a problem of legitimacy for both democracies and non-democracies alike. The democracies of the industrialized states may retain a high level of input legitimacy because the governments elected reflect the political choice of the citizens within their borders. However, states also rely upon a certain degree of output legitimacy, which means that they must 'effectively promote the welfare of the constituency in question'. However, if economic globalization does reduce the ability of the state to deliver a certain range of public goods, then there is a danger that the legitimacy of the state itself will suffer a major collapse.[6] Moreover, democracy may also be called into question if the elected government is unable to deliver the choices made by its citizens at the ballot box.

The chapter begins by examining four models that attempt to describe the restructuring of the contemporary state: the competition state; the compensatory state: the virtual state; and the catalytic state. It then proceeds to examine state expenditure in general and social welfare spending in particular of the core industrialized countries. The section concludes that these states are in the process of restructuring themselves, but in terms of the redistributive function of the state, it is difficult to discern whether this is as a result of globalization or as a result of a combination of internal factors, such as: demographic change, unemployment and rising costs to health care. The chapter therefore examines in greater detail the levels of government expenditure and, in particular, levels of welfare provision in these states. It finds that there is little evidence for the argument that a major retrenchment of the welfare state is occurring as a result of the pressures of economic globalization. Instead, states have adapted to contemporary pressures (both internal and external) in a variety of ways depending upon the constitution of their domestic institutions. Finally, the chapter turns to the developing states, arguing that the external pressures on these countries differ quite markedly to those that the industrialized states confront. Because of this, the chapter concludes that all three aspects of the so-called competition state model most accurately describe the changes occurring in this group of states.

The iron cage of globalization?

For those that believe states are facing increasing pressure to reduce their expenditures argue that, in one way or another, the nature of the external economic environment confronting states has substantially altered in recent times. The changes are such that they represent a fundamental shift in power away from the state in favour of various international economic actors. Globalists therefore argue that where 'states were once the masters of markets, now it is the markets which, on many crucial issues, are the masters over the governments of states. And the declining authority of states is reflected in a growing diffusion of authority to other institutions and associations'. The liberalization of capital accounts at the end of the seventies allowing the free movement of both short term and long term investments combined with the introduction of floating exchange rates has, it is argued, let the genie out of the bottle. Capital has become footloose and fancy-free. Multinational corporations and international financial institutions now choose which countries to invest in and lend money to, inevitably choosing those with the highest returns and best conditions (lowest risks). Some argue that these changes represent no less than a revolution in global affairs and that the 'last time that anything like this happened was in Europe when states based on a feudal system of agricultural production geared to local subsistence gave way to states based on a capitalist system of industrial production for the market'.[7]

The argument that the contemporary external economic environment imposes constraints on the autonomy and capability of the state has several elements to it. First, in relation to financial capital, it is argued that the increased mobility of finance increases the pressure on states to reduce their budget deficits. In today's world where the markets can pick and choose which states to lend to, international financial institutions will charge higher interest rates to those states that continually run large budget deficits. Financial globalization, it is argued, has therefore 'tended to put downward pressure on budget deficits because of the interest rate premiums the capital markets attach to them'.[8] The type of Keynesian state intervention to boost the economy during recessions is viewed as impossible in such circumstances. '[N]ational governments today can no longer implement the ambitious counter-cyclical policies that lifted their economies out of recession in the post-war peiod. Fiscal conservatism – the prudent management of government debt – is forced on them by world markets'.[9] In addition, the amount of money used in foreign exchange transactions on a daily basis now exceeds $1.8 trillion dollars Although in 1980 developed countries' reserves were more than the daily dealings on the various foreign exchanges, by the early nineties they did not even meet what was being exchanged every day on the FX markets. Even the most powerful economies in the world are therefore no longer in full control of their currencies. A loss in confidence in a country either because of an economic downturn or because its policies are perceived not to be market-friendly could therefore result in high volume selling of that currency resulting in a sharp devaluation. This in turn may trigger widespread exiting of short term investments and also lead to high levels of inflation.

Second, large scale interventions by government, whether it be to provide wide-ranging social welfare benefits to its population or to fund large scale infra-structural projects, have to be paid for through taxation in one form or another. It is argued that because multinational companies are now footloose and fancy-free, able to invest or disinvest wherever and whenever they please, any increase in corporate tax will either result in the exiting of these companies from the economy concerned or they will engage in transfer pricing, booking most of their profits in countries with low corporation tax. Worse, states themselves may begin to engage in competitive 'tax poaching' attracting investment by offering radically lowered tax rates.[10] Thus the very principles upon which the democratic interventionist state was based are being called into question, given that an underlying assumption has been that the provision of public goods would come from revenue extracted from all members of society – '[E]veryone agrees that they will benefit if public goods are produced. They resolve the classical problem of the public goods trap – freeloaders who seek to enjoy public goods without paying their way – by requiring everyone to contribute through taxation. This classic solution breaks down when taxation is not enforceable on mobile capital and corporations'.[11]

Two policies are said to result from this. In order to retain/attract multinational companies, state spending is reduced and a greater proportion of the tax burden is passed to its citizens either through consumption or income taxation. Confronted with mobile investors but a relatively immobile workforce the state, it is argued, opts for increasing the tax burden of the latter in order to ensure retention of the former. However, there is only so much tax that citizens are prepared to bear, even if much of it is in the form of indirect taxes. Democratic governments, mindful of their re-election chances therefore also limit or reduce their overall spending commitments.

Third, constraints are also said to arise from the increase in trade between nation-states. Once again, if a government increases corporation tax it is faced with a dilemma. Even if the country has a high proportion of firms that cannot or are unwilling to leave the country, it is argued, higher taxation would lead to a loss of competitive advantage and eventually a decline in exports. Any increase in corporation tax will be passed on to the consumer in the form of higher prices. If this were to happen companies would lose at least some of their export business to overseas rivals and this in turn would lead to a loss of revenue for the government concerned (as a result of the decline in company profits). Thus, because a company's tax burden is reflected in the price of goods 'welfare spending is inversely related to export competitiveness'.[12] In addition, an increase in imports would also be observed because, unburdened by the higher taxes, overseas companies would be able to undersell the products of domestic companies, thus leading to a balance of payments deficit.[13]

Finally, the regulatory function of the state has had to adapt to the new global environment. These changes are said to be occurring in two areas. The first concerns the regulation of foreign direct investment and finance. Many states have freed their capital accounts from most restrictions allowing the unimpeded flow of both short-term and long-term investments. But, in addition, there has been an easing of the regulatory conditions concerning loans and the plethora of financial instruments that have arisen in the last few decades. Similarly, previous conditions that had to be met when investing directly, such as domestic content rules and import–export balances no longer apply. State legislation concerning the pay and conditions of labour are also said to be affected. With regard to labour regulation, again the issue concerns the additional costs placed on businesses, but this time the costs derive from the regulations imposed by the state rather than the demand for higher taxation. Regulations, such as statutory limits on labour hours, health and safety, employment rights, overtime pay and maternity and sick pay add to the costs of running a business. Such costs could have two consequences. Either companies will exit from the state engaging in regulatory arbitrage seeking states with lax regulations. Or their products will become uncompetitive on world markets thus leading to the same scenario as outlined in the third point above. Therefore, the 'effect of competition from countries in which a regime of deregulation, low taxes and a shrinking welfare state has been imposed is to force downwards harmonization of policies on states which retain social market economies. Policies enforcing a deregulated labour market and cuts in welfare provision are adopted as defensive strategies in response to policies implemented in other countries'.[14]

As a result of the above pressures, it is argued that the state has become highly constrained in terms of the policies that it can pursue. Policies deemed not to be market friendly will result in currency instability and/or the exiting of capital investments. In response to such negative feedback, states are forced to revise their policies accordingly. However, such market-friendly policies will also usually entail a loss of revenue resulting from reductions in tax levels thereby reducing state capabilities in the long run. However, only the more extreme adherents to globalism would argue that this marks the end of the state. Most instead point to its metamorphosis, believing that these changes mean that 'it can no longer make the exceptional claims and demands that it once did'.[15]

Yet these changes impinge upon some of the core functions assumed by the state. It is therefore claimed that the state's infrastructural power, i.e. 'the capacity of the state actually to penetrate civil society, and to implement logistically political decisions throughout the realm' is severely affected.[16] If states can no longer fully control the value of their currencies, then they have lost one of their most fundamental capabilities given that a 'market economy cannot function without a stable medium of exchange, and it cannot grow unless savings are secure against depreciation'.[17] Second, it has been the traditional remit of the state, particularly since the Second World War, to choose the level of industrial nationalization, i.e. how much of the means of production is directly owned and controlled by the state.[18] Yet such enterprises, rightly or wrongly, are now viewed as less efficient compared to their privately owned counterparts and, it is argued, financial markets will react negatively to governments seeking greater control of the industries within their borders, thus crowding out private enterprise. As Philip Cerny comments, it is now assumed that the state and market have fundamentally different qualities, 'the *market*, which is seen as the only really dynamic wealth-creating mechanism in capitalist society (despite its susceptibility to "market failures"), on the one hand; and the *state*, which is seen as a hierarchical and essentially static mechanism, unable to impart a dynamic impetus to production and exchange'.[19]

Globalization is thus said to impinge upon the extractive and redistributive capacities of the state. These two core functions are strongly interrelated and concern the effectiveness of the state both in providing resources, such as the provision of education, state benefits etc., and acquiring resources from commercial activities, such as the collection of taxes. As we have seen, it is argued that the state's ability to raise extra revenue through higher corporation tax is now constrained as a result of the exit options available to firms. But also companies have become adept at using tax havens and reducing their tax burdens through 'secret bargaining between the firm and the two or more tax authorities claiming a share of its profits'.[20] The inability to raise revenue in this manner impinges upon the state's ability to provide a basic social safety net for its citizens. In addition, it also has redistributional consequences. Most liberal democratic states since the Second World War have operated under the assumption that free enterprise should be rewarded with reasonable returns on investment and hard work, but also that profits should be taxed in order to redistribute some of the benefits to the population in general. However, if the state's revenue-making abilities are constrained by the forces of globalization, then this will also have consequences for wealth redistribution within a society. Combined with the pressures of labour deregulation described earlier, it is argued that yet another function of the state – that of welfare provision and protection – has become restricted.

Four models of the contemporary state

The competition state

As a result of these pressures arising from globalization, Philip Cerny concludes that, in all three traditional areas of state intervention, regulatory, distributive and redistributive, its activities are now highly circumscribed. In terms of taxing, regulating and establishing the macroeconomic conditions for the country (regulatory), governments now concern themselves with ensuring non-inflationary growth and a business-friendly regulatory framework.[21] In terms of direct government ownership of production (i.e. control of the production and distribution of goods), states have relinquished or are relinquishing direct ownership of production, concentrating instead on improving infrastructure.[22] As a result, government functions have been reconfigured and geared towards attracting capital. Redistributive functions do remain, but in a restricted form. Moreover, the focus of such expenditure is upon developing human capital, ensuring a healthy, well-educated, skilled workforce. The state has undertaken this restructuring in order to become pro-business in orientation, thus competing with other states for finance and investment from around the world.

For Cerny, states are thus reconstituting themselves as providers of business-friendly environments by promoting 'enterprise, innovation and profitability in both private and public sectors'.[23] Rather than operating on the basis of comparative advantage, Philip Cerny argues that states have reacted to globalization by supporting businesses in their efforts to gain a competitive advantage in international markets. The state has thus moved away from its previous control and sometimes ownership of production towards a facilitating role for capital in its varied forms – '[T]he outer limits of effective action by the state in this environment are usually seen to comprise its capacity to promote a relatively favourable investment climate for transnational capital – i.e., by providing an increasingly circumscribed range of goods that retain a national-scale (or subnational-scale) public character or of a particular type of still-specific assets described as immobile factors of capital'. The state as business facilitator is said to involve providing a highly skilled, well-educated workforce (human capital); high quality reliable infrastructure such as roads, fibre-optic networks, mobile communications; research and development sites (e.g. universities); and a favourable investment climate.[24]

But this reorientation also involves a new market-friendly regulatory framework such that a 'new and potentially undemocratic role is emerging for the state as the enforcer of decisions and/or outcomes which emerge from world markets, transnational "private interest governments", and international quango-like regimes.[25] The decline of the state may therefore paradoxically involve the strengthening of the state with regard to labour relations, passing and policing legislation further circumscribing the powers and activities of organized labour, so that '[I]n most of the advanced industrial countries, albeit with variations, labour legislation covering trade union rights and union security, recognition, and financing has seen the introduction of numerous restrictions. Similarly, the broad category of employment standards, including holidays, length of work week, minimum age, grounds for dismissal, redundancy regulations, and retirement age has suffered increasing restriction or contraction in most of the industrial countries'.[26] The retrenchment of the welfare state is also said to be under way, 'citizens will probably have to live more and more without the kind of public services and many of the redistributive arrangements characteristic of the national welfare states. The "new public management" seeks not only to reorganize the state along the lines of private industry, but also to replace public provision with private provision (pension, prisons, etc.) and to replace direct payments for unemployment compensation, income support for the poor, etc. with time-limited, increasingly means-tested or work-related measures (or none at all)'.[27] At the same time, the provision of such public goods is increasingly being contracted out to the private sector. Although the state still retains responsibility for the provision of such goods, the actual supply has shifted to the private sector.

The virtual state

Proponents of this model argue that, in order to provide welfare for its citizens without increasing overall government expenditure, states are exhibiting behaviour that is somewhat analogous to that of MNCs. Rather than carry out what were previously considered to be core functions of the state, governments are increasingly outsourcing these tasks to suppliers that can provide the same quality of service for a lower cost. With regard to the state's distributive functions, the last few decades have witnessed large-scale denationalization of key industries such as transportation, energy, water supplies and telecommunications. Moreover, many states have also privatized core functions of the state itself, with the privatizations of refuse collection, health services and even prison and security services.

Box 5.1 Four models of the contemporary state

Competition state

The state's activities in three of its traditional spheres of intervention regulation, distribution and redistribution are now highly circumscribed. In terms of taxing, regulating and establishing the macroeconomic conditions for the country (regulatory), governments now concern themselves with ensuring non-inflationary growth and a business friendly regulatory framework. In terms of direct government ownership of production (control of the production and distribution of goods), states have relinquished or are relinquishing direct ownership of production, concentrating instead on improving infrastructure. Redistributive functions do remain, but in a restricted form.

Virtual state

In order to provide welfare for its citizens without increasing overall government expenditure, states are exhibiting behaviour that is somewhat analogous to that of MNCs. Rather than carry out what were previously considered to be core functions of the state, governments are increasingly outsourcing these tasks to suppliers that can provide the same quality of service for a lower cost.

Compensatory state

The cost of trade openness to the state is that it needs to compensate those citizens that are adversely affected by the associated economic displacement through unemployment benefits and retraining. A high level of state spending is necessary to counter the negative effects of greater openness to trade. Companies and investors may be willing to pay the taxes for such state intervention if they also benefit from the collective goods provided by the government, such as high quality infrastructure and a healthy, well-educated workforce.

Catalytic state

These states have actually actively engaged in promoting globalization. These so-called catalytic states have sought to encourage the expansion of their domestic companies' overseas operations in order to take advantage of lower production costs and to lower their own trade imbalances with certain key economies. This promotion has occurred on a variety of levels, including: linking overseas development aid to infrastructure projects that benefit national companies; financial support for joint ventures with foreign companies; helping plan and set up free-trade zones in foreign countries; providing assistance to those companies seeking to relocate overseas.

With regard to the industrialized states, the selling off of these companies has been pursued most vigorously by the US, the UK and New Zealand. For example: the French companies Vivendi and Ondeo operate water services in the US; Thames Water is owned by the German company RWE, which also bought npower and Yorkshire Power; France's Veolia owns three water companies in south-eastern England; Associated British Ports has recently (2006) been sold to a foreign consortium (it was initially privatized by the UK government in 1983); the British Airports Authority has also been taken over by the Spanish group Ferrovial (initially privatized in 1997) and London Electricity is owned by France's EDF (Électricité de France); while some of New Zealand's strategic energy resources are controlled by Shell.[28] At least in the case of the US and UK, it would seem that Adam Smith's assertion that defence of the realm is more important than opulence may no longer apply. The British Ministry of Defence has in recent years turned to the private sector to provide not only the renewal of its infrastructure, but even to train its soldiers.[29] Much of this is old news in the United States, where the estimated $100 billion industry has led to private security companies becoming the 'second largest military contingent' in Iraq.[30] There are also signs that more and more government services will be globally outsourced, for example, governments are currently (2006) considering outsourcing X-ray and mammography diagnoses.[31]

Thus it is argued that just as the communications revolution has had a profound effect on the production process giving rise to the 'virtual corporation', 'an entity which performs headquarters functions – research and development, product design, financing, marketing, insurance and transport – but which does not actually manufacture products', a similar transformation is occurring to the state.[32] This transformation is leading to the emergence of what Richard Rosecrance calls 'virtual states' which carry out 'headquarters or "head" functions and which produce their goods through reliable contracts with production or "body" nations somewhere else'.[33] As a result, the market is said to act 'as a direct provider of services, and the state contracts its role in the market'.[34] This model has much in common with Cerny's arguments concerning the decline of the distributive and redistributive functions of the state. But, in the case of the latter, it may not necessarily imply that welfare provision actually declines (although Rosecrance does presume this). It is equally plausible that states engage in this activity in order to either lower or cap government expenditure, whilst at the same time continuing to provide the same level of services as before.

However, this penchant for privatization and outsourcing does not necessarily apply to all of the other industrialized countries. A recent (January 2007) takeover bid for Portugal Telecom by the consortium Sonae led to the Portuguese government warning that it would use its 'golden share' if 'the national interest is at stake'.[35] Similarly, the possibility of PepsiCo launching a takeover bid for the French yogurt company Danone led the French government establishing 11 commercial sectors that are protected from foreign takeovers. The French government also stepped in to block the Italian company Enel launching a takeover of the waste water company Suez.[36] Governments that have not pursued neo-liberalism wholesale have therefore either retained certain core functions under direct state control, or if they have privatized these companies they have attempted to ensure that the majority ownership remains national. These states may therefore contract out certain functions, but the provision of such services continues to be sourced from inside the state's borders rather than sourced globally.

The compensatory state

Rather than evolving simply into a competition state, authors such as Geoffrey Garrett and Dani Rodrik argue that the state's compensatory function may in fact be becoming more, not less, important as a result of globalization. Building upon earlier work that identified a strong correlation between open economies and higher levels of state spending, they argue that 'societies (rich and poor alike) have demanded and received a larger government role as the price of exposing themselves to greater amounts of external risk'.[37] They therefore view the high levels of state spending as necessary to counter the negative effects of greater openness to trade. Evidence indicates that 'governments have expanded fastest in the most open economies'.[38]

It may well be, therefore, that the globalization argument needs to be turned on its head and that in fact '[G]lobalization may well require big, not small, government'.[39] According to the Heckscher–Ohlin model, trading patterns will reflect the relative factor endowments (land, labour, capital) of the countries concerned, i.e. the relative scarcity and abundance of the factors of production determine a country's comparative advantage. For example, those countries that have a relative abundance of capital will concentrate on those industries that are capital intensive (because capital will be relatively cheaper). Those countries, on the other hand, that have a relative abundance of labour will concentrate on labour-intensive production because they can produce these goods relatively more cheaply than others. As a result, when highly industrialized countries open their markets to lower wage economies, it is predicted that low-skill jobs will shift from the high-wage countries to those with lower wages. In high-wage countries this would then lead to greater unemployment in the low-wage sectors. Those workers would need to be retrained in order to be re-employed in a higher skilled sector. The cost of trade openness to the state is that it needs to compensate those citizens that are adversely affected by the associated economic displacement through unemployment benefits and retraining.[40]

If the state does behave in this manner, then it may need to increase its expenditure in this area, which will either require an increase in taxation or a reduction in spending elsewhere. Several authors have conducted detailed statistical analyses of the OECD countries examining whether or not globalization has affected the state as much as is claimed by those above.[41] Concerning capital taxation, Geoffrey Garrett argues that a more accurate picture is obtained if a distinction is made between marginal taxation, standard taxation and effective taxation. By so doing, it can be seen that in the last 15 years (prior to 1998) there has been a reduction in the higher levels of taxation.[42] However, it is also argued that governments have been active in closing tax loopholes and curtailing various investment incentive schemes etc., so that since the 1970s total effective tax rates on labour consumption and capital initially increased and have since stabilized. Others have concluded that 'there is no evidence for the period from the 1960s through the mid-1990s that the economic and political pressures associated with international capital mobility have dramatically shifted tax burdens from capital to other factors of production or substantially undercut the general fiscal capacity of governments to raise revenues'.[43] In particular, taxation on capital (corporate profits, capital gains, financial transactions and property holdings) has actually increased from around 30 per cent since the 1970s to around 40 per cent today.[44] In addition, such taxation is not associated with capital flight indicating that governments do have the option of increasing expenditure (within limits) without necessarily suffering a loss of investment. However, several authors do find evidence that financial institutions place a certain level of pressure upon the state by increasing the costs of borrowing for those states that run relatively high budget deficits in order to pay for their spending.[45]

Second, if convergence is occurring, there is little sign of it concerning OECD total government spending levels and annual budget deficits. If one takes current spending levels, then large differences in spending policies persist so that, for example Swedish public expenditure as a percentage of GDP is still twice that of Switzerland's. Moreover, from 1960 to 1994 there is no discernible trend toward a downward spiral in spending, and spending patterns have diverged significantly. For example, between 1985 and 1994, 'spending grew six times as much in Spain as in the United Kingdom' (although this comparison takes two countries whose spending rates have differed greatly during the chosen period).[46] Third, Garrett's work corroborates other findings that in fact greater trade openness is associated with higher, not lower, government spending.[47]

Elsewhere, Garrett has also found that these higher levels of spending may be dependent upon the type of government in power so that, 'the relationship between left-labor power and fiscal expansion has strengthened with greater internationalization'.[48] While Gary Teeple claims that left-of-centre parties are now social democratic only in name, Garrett finds that these parties increase spending in reaction to greater trade and capital mobility. He also found that they had a better record in relation to growth and employment than right-wing parties, although the price for this was higher inflation rates.[49] However, the data do suggest that the financial markets react negatively to large budget deficits. Yet, this concern does not stretch to actual levels of government spending – on this subject investors appear to be neutral. What does concern investors is the possibility of governments inflating their economies thereby reducing their debts in real terms. As one would expect, investors thus place an interest rate premium to cover for such a risk on loans to those governments that fund their spending through increased borrowing rather than from raising revenue internally. But even in these cases, it is found that the interest rates charged are not prohibitively higher; for example, despite Italy's continuing high levels of pubic debt the markets attach a relatively low premium (three to four per cent compared to Germany) on such prolificacy.[50]

In other words, these authors find that openness 'increases economic insecurity among broad cross sections of society, strengthening political incentives for governments to redistribute market allocations of risk and wealth'.[51] However, companies and investors may be willing to pay the taxes for such state intervention if they also benefit from the collective goods provided by the government. Echoing at least some aspects of the competition state, Garrett argues that investment logic is not necessarily dictated by the search for the lowest tax locations. Rather, productivity, stability, human capital, infrastructure and market access are also factored in and weighed against the taxation costs, 'firms must weigh cost and benefits of helping finance the provision of collective goods from which they benefit in one country versus paying lower taxes but receiving fewer benefits in another'.[52] The state needs to be mindful that it provides the collective goods required by businesses to prevent large scale exit. One of the major changes is that the state has become compensatory, providing those sections of society economically dislocated by increasing trade openness with the requisite reskilling and social safety net needed. Revenue not only provides a basic safety net for those negatively affected by market dislocations, but also provides certain attributes that firms and investors depend upon.

Harold Wilensky in his comprehensive examination of the industrialized welfare state also sees little pressure arising from foreign direct investment. Although the author accepts that these entities have become 'increasingly important in employment, sales and investment', this does not necessarily imply that states now have to compete with each other by conceding to the demands of the MNCs.[53] At least in these states, Wilensky finds that MNCs adapt to local conditions concerning welfare rights rather than trying to use their economic wherewithal to induce changes in various national practices. Rather than external pressures the overwhelming reason for any welfare reforms arises from internal reasons within these states – 'the external pressures that are labeled "globalization" have little or no effect in explaining social policies or system outputs – such non-trivial outcomes as economic performance, political legitimacy, equality, poverty reduction, safety, and real health'.[54]

Such claims are supported by additional evidence that has indicated that the behaviour of American MNCs is contrary to that depicted earlier. The research indicates that, where the industrialized states are concerned, rather than searching for the cheapest form of labour, the primary concern of these companies is to acquire a highly skilled workforce. So much so that 'countries need not encourage (and may not benefit from) wage restraint, since high hourly compensation costs do not reduce FDI, provided those costs are matched by higher skills and productivity'. Moreover, those countries that adopt ILO conventions would appear to attract greater levels of FDI (at least in the case of American FDI) and another study found 'investment significantly increasing with union density'.[55] These findings thus run counter to the argument that states have had to engage in the deregulation of labour practices.

The catalytic state

On the other hand, Linda Weiss presents the possibility that some countries are actually actively promoting globalization. As we saw in the last chapter, several East Asian states (Japan, Taiwan, Korea and Singapore) are said to have established a unique collaborative coordinating role with their domestic businesses. Weiss, on the other hand, emphasizes the transformative capacity of the state, concentrating upon the successful cooperative collaboration between government and business in East Asia. Using this transformative capacity, Weiss argues that they have actually actively engaged in promoting globalization. These so-called catalytic states have sought to encourage the expansion of their domestic companies' overseas operations in order to take advantage of lower production costs and to lower their own trade imbalances, particularly with the United States (the MNC's exports from an overseas base will be registered as exports from the other country). This promotion has occurred on a variety of levels, including: linking overseas development aid to infrastructure projects that benefit national companies; financial support for joint ventures with foreign companies; helping plan and set up free-trade zones in foreign countries; providing assistance to those companies seeking to relocate overseas.[56] Moreover, these states are actively engaged and playing a dominant role in coalitions either with other states or businesses. However, this is not the usual argument that states are pooling their sovereignty at the regional and global level in order to control cooperatively the economic environment in which they find themselves. Rather, catalytic states retain their independence while at the same time steering these coalitions in order to address problems that they are confronted with, 'this kind of state is one that seeks to be *indispensable* to the success or direction of particular strategic coalitions while remaining substantially *independent* from the other elements of the coalition'.[57]

Summary

Although at the far end of the spectrum, some dispute that these pressures from globalization are strong enough to adversely affect the performance of the industrialized states, others believe that it is altering the state's ability to either (or both) extract revenue from the population/companies within its borders or attract finance at a reasonable cost from the international markets. For these writers, these changes in the extractive capabilities of the state have ramifications for several of its other capabilities (regulatory, distributive, redistributive and transformative) that have been viewed as the normal remit of the modern state, at least in its post-Second World War form. What the state is actually evolving into depends upon which capability is chosen or emphasized. For Garrett, the two main pressures on the state arise from those sections of the population that are adversely affected by greater trade openness and by the financial markets attaching an additional interest premium for those states that persistently fail to balance their books. As long as the state provides the collective goods that industry requires (e.g. good infrastructure), companies will by and large remain, although of course they continually re-evaluate the costs and benefits of such a decision. This new condition is best described as the compensatory state, i.e. the main focus is upon the redistributive capabilities of the state, but specifically much of the redistribution is directed towards compensation to those workers adversely affected by greater economic openness.

In contradistinction, Cerny argues that the regulatory, distributive and redistributive capabilities have all been altered because of external pressures and are now highly pro-business in orientation, thus leading to the creation of the competition state. The pressures upon the state arising from the reduction of revenue may even lead to the state *qua* virtual state taking advantage of global outsourcing in order to continue providing the population with high levels of social welfare at a reduced cost. Linda Weiss, on the other hand, emphasizes the transformative capacity of the state, concentrating upon the successful cooperative collaboration between government and business in East Asia. In so doing, she turns the debate concerning the decline of the state on its head, arguing that state *qua* catalytic state has in several ways acted as the midwife of globalization, thus turning the globalization and the decline of the state argument on its head. It would seem, therefore, that the first two functions of the competition state may accurately depict the manner in which many (but not all) of the industrialized states have adapted. However, the supposed change in their redistributive function is highly contested. The next section therefore provides a closer examination of government expenditure and welfare provision of these states.

A race to the bottom?

The regulatory and distributive functions of the state may have changed for many of the industrialized states, but to what degree the redistributive function has altered remains open to question. How restrictive is this purported iron cage of globalization that states are said to be trapped in? Opinion varies widely. For those who believe that global investors and producers are now critical in limiting the economic policies that states can pursue, it is argued that:

> In a global pincer movement, the new international of capital is turning whole countries and social orders upside down. On one front it threatens to pull out altogether according to the circumstances of the hour, thus forcing massive tax reductions as well as subsidies running into billions of marks or the provision of cost free infra-structure. If that doesn't work, tax-planning in the grand style can often help out: profits are revealed only in countries where the rate of taxation is really low. All around the world, the owners of capital and wealth are contributing less and less to the financing of public expenditure.[58]

Sweden in the mid-nineties is seen as a classic example of what happens when states continue along a path deemed unacceptable by the financial markets and MNCs. For some years, the budget deficit had been spiralling upward, until in 1994 some domestic industrialists threatened to pull their companies out of the country unless the situation was rectified, then the head of a major insurance company 'called for a boycott of Swedish bonds, which had so far been traded at the average European rate of interest'.[59] As a result, '[A]lmost immediately, major international purchasers of its bonds went on strike, announcing that they would buy no more. Long-term interest rates soared into double figures, rising a full four percentage points that year ... though Sweden had elected a conservative government determined to scale back its celebrated welfare state, the annual deficit was still above 10 per cent of GDP and the government's accumulated debt had grown explosively, from 44 per cent of GDP in 1990 to 95 per cent in 1995. To quell the bondholder's boycott, Sweden's central bank was compelled to tighten credit still further and the prime minister quickly announced plans for further spending cuts. Yet Sweden's economy ... was already deeply depressed, with unemployment around 16 per cent'.[60]

These pressures have not been solely confined to finance, but are said also to include pressures from firms. Even strong states are said to have succumbed; Germany, for example, is said to have 'acceded to every major demand of industry and the banks for a recasting of the tax system. Twice recently it has cut the rate of tax on the profits of big corporations, and it has also reduced the top rate of income tax by 5 per cent'.[61] Yet, notwithstanding these inducements, companies are continuing to engage in reducing their tax burdens through transfer pricing. As a result of Ireland's 10 per cent corporation tax, hundreds of companies have established essentially non-functioning subsidiaries or offices in the country. A classic example of this accounting method is BMW, which in 1988 posted profits in Germany of '545 million marks', yet 5 years later, 'despite rising total profits and unchanged dividends, BMW actually declared losses on its domestic operations and got a refund'.[62] As a result of this cross-border tax competition aimed at attracting finance, or the production facilities/HQ of multinational companies, it is argued that it 'is no longer democratically elected governments which decide the level of taxes; rather, the people who direct the flow of capital and goods themselves establish what contribution they wish to make to state expenditure'[63] Greater financial openness is thus seen as marking a

> transition between two eras, from a world of national capitals and nation-states to a world of internationalized capital and supranational organizations, commissions, and agencies. They represent the coming transformation of long-established social and political institutions in the industrial nation-states. They embody a shift *from* the expansion of social reforms, rising national wealth, and limited political alternatives *to* the dismantling of reforms, the supersession of national economies, and political reaction ... Here, largely unfettered by political considerations, is a tyranny unfolding – an economic regime of unaccountable rulers, a totalitarianism not of the political sphere but of the economic.[64]

According to this view, financiers and firms are now firmly in the driving seat, not only setting levels of taxation that they deem acceptable by virtue of their ability to put their capital wherever they choose, but also demanding regulatory frameworks and infrastructure to improve both the functioning and profits of their enterprises. As a result, the prognosis for the state makes for grim reading indeed. Hans-Peter Martin and Harald Schumann argue that, '[I]n Washington, for example, the majority of schools are fit only for demolition ... Schools can carry on meaningful business only if volunteers lend a helping hand, while the police force has to carry out repairs at its own expense if it is to go on functioning. In Britain too ... Every third child there grows up in poverty, and 1.5 million children under the age of sixteen have to work because of the lack of social support ... Already a fifth of all twenty-one-year-olds – according to a representative sample – are unable to do simple sums in their head, and a seventh can neither read nor write.[65]

Regardless of the type of government in power, it is thought that all will have to respond eventually to the fact that they are confronted with a rapidly dwindling tax base and a global financial market that has become the judge and final arbiter of what constitutes sound economic policy: 'social democracy has lost much of its credibility as a party representing the working population, and hypocrisy has become its hallmark. Since social democracy can no longer promote or expand social reforms but must introduce neo-liberal reforms, by whatever name, working people in effect lose what limited representation they had in liberal democracies... Social democracy as we have known it has no future, because the conditions that gave rise to it are being transformed and because its policies and programs – the reforms of the nation-state era – were nothing more than what these conditions allowed or even demanded'.[66]

However, others have questioned the degree to which the external economic environment constricts the internal policies of states, even in the milder form described above. At one end of this spectrum, there are those, such as Hirst and Thompson, who agree that the nature of the Welfare State is changing. However, they see the pressures for this change arising from internal dynamics within the state itself, rather than from changes in the external economic environment:

> Welfare states are coming under intense pressure on costs and types of service for a variety of reasons – ageing population, high rates of family break-up, rising costs and complexity of health care, and increasing diversification and professionalization of services – and of these openness of the national economy to external shocks is neither the principal reason nor a new factor. Pressures to welfare reform should not be identified with globalization, although reforms may help to reduce the impact of external competitive pressures and economic shocks.[67]

They see Sweden as a rather exceptional case of a conjunctural crisis brought on by several factors coalescing at the same time, including: high unemployment; high level of government expenditure (66 per cent of GDP in 1995); the European recession at the time; the attempt to maintain currency parity with the Deutschmark; movement of Swedish capital to other European countries in preparation for European Union.[68] The Swedish case is thus seen as the exception rather than the rule and in fact the crisis has since subsided with the country continuing to maintain one of the highest levels of taxation within Europe.

It may be, therefore, that states have greater room to manoeuvre than these writers depict. Vito Tanzi, for example, examines the range of tax instruments at a state's disposal and concludes that 'the effect of globalization and tax competition on *total* tax revenue has been limited. However, the impact on *tax structures* is more evident'.[69] In other words, states are responding to globalization by changing their tax levels on a sectoral basis, decreasing the rate on more mobile agents and increasing the rate on the less mobile. For example, within the OECD, consumption taxes have increased in most countries and social security contributions have also increased both for employer and employee. Although the evidence is mixed on corporate tax, Tanzi concludes that this is likely to reduce in the future, being offset by the above and direct taxation on personal income.[70]

Others concur; finding that levels of government expenditure may well have fallen slightly since their peaks in the early- to mid-nineties, but that the data do not support the belief that we are witnessing a dramatic decline of state intervention (Table 5.1). Indeed, the current period may be a rather minor correction after unprecedented levels of spending, after all 'the much-vaunted era of globalization, has witnessed the development of the largest states the world has ever seen and there is little evidence of this trend being reversed'.[71] For several of the European states, government spending grew from around 30 per cent to 50 per cent of GDP between 1950 and 1996, while America's grew from around 21 per cent to 33 per cent and Japan's increased from 20 per cent to 36 per cent. Although much of this expenditure was absorbed by government consumption (19.6 per cent of GDP for a basket of European countries in 1994), a larger amount was directed towards ensuring the welfare of the population (social transfers totalled 23.6 per cent).[72]

Not only that. Increases in taxation were not commensurate with the increases in government spending, leading to consecutive budget deficits and an accumulation of public debt.[73] Rather than some actual existing pressure from globalization, Hay argues that it is equally plausible that the actual idea of globalization may be having an independent causal effect upon the behaviour of decision makers, 'if governments believe the thesis to be true, or find it to their advantage to present it as true, they will act in a manner consistent with its predictions, thereby contributing to an aggregate depreciation in corporate taxation – whether they are right to do so or not'.[74]

Concentrating on overall spending only provides information on whether or not the general level of welfare spending has altered and may therefore mask important changes within the welfare regime itself. For example, Italy uses 50 per cent of its welfare budget on pensions compared to 25 per cent in Ireland; Germany spends 30 per cent of its welfare budget on health care compared to Denmark's 18.5 per cent.[75] In addition, the funds each social sector receives (e.g. pensions, family allowances, education, health) have varied over time so that, for example, the changing structure of the population, such as an ageing society, will lead to greater spending on pensions and health at the expense of, say, education. For the OECD, many of these countries have witnessed a substantial increase in social

Table 5.1 The growth of government expenditure (as a percentage of GDP)

	circa 1913*	circa 1920*	circa 1937*	1961	1965	1970	1975	1980	1985	1990	1995	2000	2006
Austria	–	14.7	15.2	32.3	37.9	39.2	46.1	48.7	51.1	51.5	56.0	51.4	48.6
Belgium	–	–	21.8	29.8	32.3	36.5	44.5	51.6	61.9	52.2	51.9	49.1	50.1
Canada	–	13.3	18.6	30.0	29.1	35.7	40.8	40.8	47.1	48.8	48.5	41.1	38.9
France	17.0	27.6	29.0	35.7	38.4	38.9	43.5	46.4	52.2	49.3	54.4	51.6	54.5
Germany	14.8	25.0	42.4	33.8	36.7	38.7	49.0	48.3	47.6	44.5	48.3	45.1	46.1
Italy	11.1	22.5	24.5	29.4	34.3	34.2	43.2	46.0	51.6	53.5	52.5	46.1	47.8
Japan	8.3	14.8	25.4	17.4	20.0	19.4	27.2	33.1	32.3	31.8	36.5	39.2	36.7
Netherlands	9.0	13.5	19.0	35.4	38.7	46.0	56.6	59.7	60.7	53.1	49.7	43.7	46.5
Norway	8.3	13.7	–	29.7	34.2	41.0	46.6	49.1	42.9	54.0	51.5	42.7	41.8
Spain	8.3	9.3	18.4	13.0	19.6	22.2	24.7	32.6	42.2	42.6	44.2	39.0	38.2
Sweden	6.3	8.1	10.4	31.0	36.1	43.7	49.0	62.0	64.9	61.3	67.1	56.8	56.7
Switzerland	2.7	4.6	6.1	18.0	19.7	21.3	28.7	29.3	31.0	30.0	34.5	33.9	36.1
United Kingdom	12.7	26.2	30.0	33.4	36.4	39.3	46.9	45.6	46.0	42.2	45.0	37.5	45.6
United States	1.8	7.0	8.6	29.0	27.9	32.3	35.5	34.9	36.0	37.1	37.0	34.2	36.6

Source: *All figures prior to the Second World War taken from Tanzi, V. and L. Schuknecht, 'The growth of government and the reform of the state', 1995, Table 1. Post-Second World War figures, OECD Economic Outlook, 2006, 1983.[1]

Note
1   Figures after the Second World War are general government total outlays as a percentage of nominal GDP. Refer to OECD Economic Outlook, vol. 79, June 2006, Table 25, p. 189 and OECD Economic Outlook, vol. 33, July 1983, Table R8, p. 165.

security payments as rates of unemployment have increased (by 1996 the average unemployment rate for 16 European countries was 10.2 per cent).[76] Although it would be tempting to blame this rise in unemployment on trade openness, and evidence suggests that some unemployment may be for this reason; however, a far greater cause has been the extremely high increases in productivity and the lack of a commensurate increase in demand.[77]

In addition the demographics of the industrialized nations have changed significantly. Most notably, the age structure of society; for example in 1994, 'the male labour force was only 80.4 per cent of the population aged 15 to 64, whereas in the 1950s, the proportion was near to 95 per cent'.[78] In addition, a greater level of spending is dedicated to the servicing of interest on state debt; for the core OECD countries, this has tripled since 1970 (1.6 per cent of GDP to 4.6 per cent GDP in 1992).[79] It is therefore argued that the actual expenditure required to maintain the previous levels of service in some areas has proportionally diminished and is less than sufficient. In Europe, for example, since 1960 Health and Pension expenditure has risen at a far faster rate than has spending on education.[80] It is estimated, for instance, that for the OECD countries approximately half of all health spending will be on the retired. Although overall expenditure may not have diminished, greater amounts are now going to pensions, health and unemployment at the expense of other areas of state provision (Table 5.3).[81] This is seen most clearly in the increases in levels of social transfers during periods of high unemployment. For example, after reunification German unemployment climbed to 9.2 per cent in 1997, and has remained high ever since (9.5 per cent in 2004). Similarly, French unemployment rates were already high by 1985 (9.7 per cent) and have continued to register relatively high levels (in 2000 they were 11.7 per cent). In Britain

Table 5.2 Social spending for seventeen industrialized countries (as a percentage of GNP)

	1960	1980	1990	1995	2001
Austria	15.9	23.8	24.1	26.6	26.0
Germany	18.1	20.3	22.8	27.5	27.4
Belgium	13.8	24.2	25.4	25.8	24.7
France	13.4	22.7	26.6	29.2	28.5
Netherlands	11.7	27.3	27.7	25.6	21.8
Italy	13.1	18.4	23.3	23.0	24.5
Sweden	10.8	29.0	30.8	33.2	29.8
Denmark	10.6	29.1	29.3	32.4	29.2
United Kingdom	10.2	18.2	19.6	23.0	21.8
Finland	8.8	18.5	24.8	31.1	24.8
Norway	7.8	18.6	24.7	26.0	23.9
New Zealand	10.4	19.2	21.9	18.9	18.5
Switzerland	4.9	15.2	17.9	23.9	25.4
Canada	9.1	13.3	16.6	19.6	17.3
Australia	7.4	11.3	14.2	17.8	15.7
United States	7.3	13.1	13.4	15.4	14.7
Japan	4.1	10.1	11.2	13.5	16.9

Source: F. Castles, *The Future of the Welfare State*, 2004, Table 2.1 and *OECD Factbook*, 2006.

Table 5.3 Social security transfers (as a percentage of GDP)

	1960	1970	1985	1990	1995	2000
Austria	12.9	15.4	20.1	17.8	19.5	18.8
Belgium	11.5	11.7	24.9	16.1	16.6	15.3
Canada	7.9	6.6	12.2	11.6	13.1	12.4[a]
France	13.5	14.8	22.1	16.9	18.5	18.0
Germany	12.0	12.7	16.2	15.2	18.1	18.8
Italy	9.8	12.4	17.2	15.5	16.7	16.7
Japan	3.8	4.6	10.9	7.4	8.6	10.0
Netherlands	–	16.8	26.2	25.8	15.3	11.9
Norway	7.6	12.2	11.8	15.9	15.8	13.9
Spain	2.3	15.9	16.0	15.9	13.9	12.3
Sweden	8.0	11.0	18.2	19.5	21.3	18.3
Switzerland	5.7	8.2	13.7	8.4	11.2	11.9[b]
United Kingdom	6.8	8.8	13.5	11.8	15.3	13.2
United States	5.1	7.6	10.8	11.1	13.0	12.6[c]

Source: *OECD Historical Statistics 1970–2000*, Table 6.3 and *OECD Historical Statistics 1960– 1995*, Table 6.3. Social Security transfers include social security benefits for sickness, old age, family allowances, social assistance grants and unfunded employee welfare benefits. [a]1998 [b]1999 [c]1997.

unemployment rates were 11.2 per cent in1985 and remained so until around 1997 when they began to fall rapidly (in 2004 the rate was just 4.4 per cent). However, these patterns of spending are not solely explained by unemployment rates. For example Britain has managed to keep its social transfers at a relatively low level through a mixture of policies, including more stringent conditions for various social benefits and the delinking of pensions from general earnings (1980).[82]

Trying to identify whether or not there has been a general retrenchment of the welfare state is complicated by both the apparent national variations in resource allocation and the different methods of social transfers, i.e. cash benefits or delivery of services. In addition, policies may reflect the type of institutions within a state a recent study has indicated that the '*social welfare effects of international capital mobility are significantly shaped by domestic institutions*'.[83] The type of domestic institutions within a state will influence the effectiveness of opposition to policies pursued by government, facilitating or impeding their representation. Because of the structure of decision-making and the type of welfare institutions in social democratic and corporatist conservative welfare states the purported effects of globalization are not evident. For example, because electoral representation in the Nordic social democratic states is highly inclusive, any major reform by the right requires negotiation with the centre and left parties. For the corporatist conservative states, 'the nature of the occupationally based model of social insurance cultivates broad political coalitions of working- and middle-class beneficiaries, as well as public sector employees; it also tends to promote high levels of "cross-class solidarity", trust, and confidence in the system'.[84] As a result, there is a 'natural' defensive bulwark against any major reforms that would eventually lead to a reduction in social welfare. In regard to the liberal welfare states, Duane Swank finds that there is in fact evidence that 'embedded liberalism has begun to unravel', possibly as a result of several factors

Box 5.2 One size does not fit all?

Rather than all of the industrialized states conforming to one or other of the models described in the text, it is more likely that the effects of economic globalization vary according to the type of state in question.

Gøsta Esping-Andersen has identified three dominant models:

The Scandinavian social democratic model

Traditionally based on very high levels of services and benefits plus full employment. In reaction to internal and external pressures these states have engaged in greater regulation in order to ensure employment and training for younger generations (Sweden and Denmark). Emphasis has been on retraining and life-long learning but also targeting youth unemployment by guaranteeing jobs with training for those unemployed for more than a year.

The neo-liberal Anglo-Saxon model

Traditionally based on modest means-tested benefits and a permissive attitude towards temporary and part-time employment. These states (e.g. America, the UK, New Zealand) closely mirrored Cerny's argument that globalization was leading to the deregulation of labour practices such as the curtailment of trade union rights and the abolition of the minimum wage. Unemployment benefits have also been made conditional upon evidence of active job-seeking activities

The continental conservative corporatist model

Based on 'status differentiating' and family bias welfare programmes. The continental model, on the other hand, relies heavily upon the compensatory capabilities of the state, encouraging the exit of an older generation of workers by providing generous retirement benefits (Italy and France).

It is also quite possible that the state pursues a course of deregulation in one sphere of competence (e.g. lifting restrictions on capital movement) while strengthening regulation in another (e.g. labour conditions). This means that a country such as Sweden has reduced unemployment benefits and extended pension contribution years (altered its redistributive policies) but has also introduced a workfare style programme ensuring employment and training for its youth (altered its regulatory policies).[1]

1 G. Esping-Andersen, 'After the Golden Age?', pp. 13–14.

that have made it easier to implement reforms, such as: the majoritarian electoral systems preventing effective opposition; the selective welfare system previously in place (that involved targeting, means testing and the existence of private/public provision); plus the existence of pluralist interest group representation.[85]

The state, therefore, may well be adapting to both internal and external pressures. The manner in which it adapts may also be highly dependent upon the type of state and its domestic institutions. Following his earlier work *Three Worlds of Welfare Capitalism,* Gøsta Esping-Andersen identifies three dominant models of adaptation: the Scandinavian social democratic model based on very high levels of services and benefits plus full employment; the neo-liberal Anglo-Saxon model of modest means-tested benefits and a permissive attitude towards temporary and part-time employment; and the continental conservative corporatist model with its 'status differentiating' and family bias welfare programmes which, for example, does not include housewives in the social insurance scheme.[86] The Scandinavian social democratic model has dealt with such pressures by placing emphasis on retraining and life-long learning but also targeting youth unemployment by guaranteeing jobs with training for those unemployed for more than a year. For example, Denmark spends almost 2 per cent of its GDP and the Netherlands almost 1.5 per cent on training and job-search programmes for the unemployed, whereas the United States dedicates just 0.16 per cent.[87] The neo-liberal approach, on the other hand, has *a la* Cerny positively pursued a policy of deregulation of labour practices such as the curtailment of trade union rights and the abolition of the minimum wage and making the receipt of benefits conditional upon evidence of active job-seeking activities. Such deregulation, it is argued, has led to wage reductions, which in turn has helped these countries compete against low wage production overseas. The continental model differs from the other two through its emphasis on labour reduction, encouraging the exit of an older generation of workers by providing generous retirement benefits.[88]

The lack of change in overall state expenditure therefore hides as much as it reveals. Some sectors have not experienced commensurate increases in their budgets while others have done so, due to the changing structure of society. In particular, it hides the rise in health costs, unemployment benefits, pensions and interest repayments as a result of higher levels of state debt. In relation to the rise in unemployment rates, states have adopted quite different solutions, with countries such as the United States, United Kingdom and New Zealand following a neo-liberal approach of deregulation, but others have not chosen to do so. The adoption of such policies may simply reflect their historical predisposition towards neo-liberal solutions rather than pressures arising from economic globalization.

Welfare spending in less-developed countries

Do the same sorts of dynamics operate in the case of the developing states? Evidence suggests that both the external and internal environments are somewhat different. Historically, the levels of state spending and, in particular, levels of welfare spending have been much lower in these countries. Compared to Europe which spent on average 24.8 per cent of its GDP on social security (1990–6), for the same period Asian countries spent 6.4 per cent and Africa spent a mere 4.3 per cent; social security expenditure was slightly higher in Latin America and the Caribbean at 8.8 per cent.[89] Moreover, the level of welfare spending has actually declined in the last few decades.[90] It may also be that the positive benefits of welfare spending, such as poverty alleviation and lessening inequality may not actually be felt as much in the developing world because such social transfers may be used for 'purposes of political control and patronage instead of redistribution'; for example 'appointing teachers, health, and social workers in exchange for political support' and benefits have also been extended to 'more privileged workers (i.e. urban, salaried, formal sector workers) to contain labor militancy and gain their cooperation'.[91]

Explanations as to why welfare spending is both low and declining focus upon both external and internal dynamics. In terms of international finance, less developed countries confront far more stringent conditions than do their more industrialized counterparts and therefore find that such pressures constrain domestic economic policies. In the industrialized countries such constraints are said to be 'strong but narrow' compared to those in developing countries where the constraints are said to be 'strong and broad'.[92] That is, for the former, investors focus upon a narrow range of economic indicators, such as inflation, budget deficits, and occasionally exchange rates plus overall government debt: governments have to pay a premium to investors if any of these go above what are deemed acceptable limits. For the developing countries, on the other hand, the financial markets are far more occupied with the possibility of loan default. Investment in the North and the South are essentially driven by different dynamics. Investment in the former is viewed as stable and relatively risk free albeit with relatively low returns, while investment in the latter is 'driven by efforts at portfolio diversification and at high risk-adjusted returns'.[93]

As a result, investors not only examine and judge these countries on the criteria that they use for industrialized states; they also assess them using 'microindicators (e.g. the breakdown of government spending across areas and the structure of tax systems). They also analyze the political climate, for example, the type of governmental coalition expected after a general election'.[94] Because of the greater likelihood of political and economic instability combined with the possibility of countries defaulting on loans, it is argued that, unlike the case of industrialized countries, investors use a far greater level of information for their risk assessment. Thus, not only do less developed countries find it more difficult to attract investment, often having to issue dollar denominated bonds in order to protect investors from inflation (65 per cent of all international bond issues) and often have to resort to short-term debt issues, but their levels of taxation and expenditure are also closely scrutinized.[95] Less developed countries pay higher interest rates than the industrialized countries even if they have got the economic fundamentals right, but they are also judged upon how much they are spending and whether such spending is productive.[96] Despite the much lower levels of state expenditure in the South, these countries' policies are therefore far more constrained by the international financial markets than their northern counterparts.

This chimes with other findings indicating that many of the MNCs based in developing states work on different operating principles to those based mainly in the industrialized countries. Those based in the latter depend upon a highly skilled workforce and are willing to pay for such skills, however, in the former 'the results suggest that across low-skill-low-wage countries US MNCs invest more in locations with the lowest levels of education'.[97] For those companies using production techniques that do not require high levels of education, presumably the most important factors are low levels of taxation and low wages. If either of these become too high, companies will relocate to cheaper locations, '[I]n their efforts to locate in low-wage countries while matching low-skill-content operations with low-skill work-forces, US MNCs can be expected to search for lower low-skill-low-wage work-forces in alternative, more newly developing countries'.[98]

As we have seen above, Garrett argues that in the OECD countries, capital taxation has actually risen in the last few decades without a mass exodus of companies. It is believed that this is because most companies also gain from public goods, such as a modern infrastructure and a healthy well-educated workforce. However, the same may not therefore hold true for developing countries if the priority of MNCs is to obtain the cheapest form of labour. If this is indeed the case, companies would be less concerned that revenue collected by the government will be spent upon worthwhile projects developing infrastructure and investing in human capital. Because this is less important for labour intensive, low-skill industries, it is more likely that they will view corporation tax as an unnecessary burden.

This has long-term ramifications not only for the ability of less-developed states to collect higher revenues and increase state expenditure, but also for the possibility of the population mobilizing and petitioning the state for greater welfare cover. One possible internal factor affecting the welfare spending levels is the low degree of labour power in these countries. On average, surplus labour constitutes approximately 20 per cent of the working population and the majority of employment is in the low-skill sector concentrating on primary production, natural intensive manufacturing and labour intensive manufacturing.[99] As a result, union power in these countries will be low because such workers are easily replaced and are less likely to be able to place political pressure upon their governments. In addition, for much of the population the main concern is finding or maintaining employment, social welfare improvements are a lower priority. Thus, it is argued that globalization 'leads to lower social-welfare spending in labor-rich LDCs because low-skilled workers have limited political leverage'.[100] This mirrors similar arguments concerning the weakening of trade union bargaining power in the industrialized countries,[101] although the difference is that the power of trade unions in the South has never been strong.

As we have seen, the amount of FDI flowing to these countries is quite limited. In fact, the overall pattern of total investment for the South is highly concentrated with 20 countries accounting for 83 per cent of all investment flows to developing countries, with only one African country appearing in this group (South Africa with just over 1 per cent of total investment flows to developing states).[102] Indeed, as we have seen in earlier chapters, despite many of these countries endeavouring to attract investment, they have found it extremely difficult to do so (particularly in the case of Africa):

> Since 1984, however, many African countries have undertaken significant measures to liberalise their economies in their efforts to attract investment. Many countries have established export processing zones and have developed new investment codes. Unfortunately, the response of external investors to Africa's overtures has been very disappointing. Investor confidence is lacking since the general perception is that many aspects of the African economic crisis are unlikely to disappear in the near future...Given its decaying infrastructure, manpower shortage and the lack of political will to succeed, the chances that Africa will be able to attract a large column of foreign investment in the foreseeable future is virtually nil.[103]

Table 5.4 Debt servicing and government expenditure

		Percentage of central government expenditure	
	Year(s)	Basic social services	Debt service
Africa			
Tanzania*	1994–95	15	46
Kenya	1995	13	40
Malawi	1997	8	40
Zambia	1997	7	40
Côte d'Ivoire	1994–96	11	35
Niger	1995	20	33
Uganda	1994–95	21	9
South Africa	1996–97	14	8
Namibia	1996–97	19	3
Asia			
Philippines	1992	8	31**
Sri Lanka	1996	13	22
Nepal	1997	14	15
Thailand	1997	15	1**
Latin America and Caribbean			
Jamaica	1996	10	31
El Salvador	1996	13	27
Honduras	1992	13	21
Brazil	1995	9	20
Bolivia	1997	17	10**
Dominican Republic	1997	9	10
Colombia	1997	17	8**

Source: UNICEF, *The Progress of Nations,* 1999, p. 32.
*Excluding Zanzibar. **International Monetary Fund, *Government Finance Statistics Yearbook*, 1996, data for the same or latest available year. Cited in R. O'Brian and M. Williams, *Global Political Economy: Evolution and Dynamics*, p. 239.

The competition for any form of investment is thus extremely fierce and so developing states may therefore be more willing to adjust their tax policies in order to attract companies and investors to their country.

All of these aspects of globalization are likely to limit the levels of state expenditure in the South. International financial markets examine the tax and spend policies of those countries that they choose to invest in and judge them accordingly. Unlike in the North, multinational corporations have a greater number of exit options and their main objective is to seek out low tax, low wage territories in which to base their production facilities thus limiting a government's ability to extract greater revenue from such operations. In addition, the lack of organized labour opposition means that governments in the South rarely come under strong pressure to increase expenditure in the welfare sector (when one takes into account the very low levels of welfare in many of these countries).

Another factor explaining the low and declining levels of welfare spending is the extremely high debt burden. Table 5.4 illustrates the central difficulty that many of these countries face: much of their expenditure is dedicated to servicing their debts, with several countries having to dedicate well over a third of their budgets to do so. In the case of Tanzania, Kenya, Malawi and Zambia, the total amounts to 40 per cent or more. This essentially means that these countries have to dedicate well over a third of their budget to interest payments and repayments. It should be noted that not all countries with high levels of debt service are indicated in the table; for example, in 1997 Cameroon was also having to dedicate a large section of its budget to debt servicing (36 per cent). One of the main pressures on welfare spending in the South is therefore debt, rather than globalization *per se*. The recently announced debt cancellation for the heavily indebted poor countries (HIPC) at the G8 Gleneagles Summit in 2005 will therefore hopefully have a significant impact on the welfare of these populations.

In addition to their debt burden, the structural adjustment policies many of these countries have had to implement as a condition for further IMF loans has also led to a reduction in state/welfare expenditure. As was explained in the previous chapter, under structural adjustment, reducing inflation to reasonable levels is regarded as the top priority. Several policies are therefore recommended in order to reduce the money supply: a reduction in government spending (which would also lower budget deficits); high interest rates; the establishment of floating or pegged exchange rates signalling an abstention from competitive devaluation.[104] In the last two decades of the twentieth century, such structural adjustment policies were extremely widespread throughout the developing world; for example, in Sub-Saharan Africa 'thirty-eight out of forty-three countries, or 88 per cent, have entered an agreement with the IMF. Of the twenty-nine countries for which a classification of strong or weak reform effort is available, twenty-one (or 72 per cent) are strong reformers. Given this pervasive influence on development in SSA, it is all the more surprising that its effects have not been noted to any great extent in the globalization literature'.[105]

Evidence indicates that such structural adjustment policies have had a strong impact upon welfare spending with countries moving away from general state provision 'towards pay-as-you-go social services'.[106] It is estimated that as a result of these changes there has been a decline in overall government expenditure during the 1980s for 'two-thirds of the African countries for which data are available'. For some countries, this reduction has been severe with per capita expenditure cut by 50 per cent in Tanzania, 60 per cent in Zambia and a staggering 70 per cent in Sierra Leone and Zaire.[107] In addition to this overall decline, the amount of social expenditure as a proportion of total government spending 'fell in 12 out of 17 countries for which data are available' during the 1980s. In particular, education spending as a proportion of the overall budget 'fell from 15.4 to 12.8 per cent'.[108] This is not limited to Africa alone, with Latin America and much of the former Soviet bloc experiencing a similar decline. Table 5.5 maps social service expenditure as a percentage of overall government spending since 1980 for those states where data were available (as indicated above, some states have been affected far more severely, unfortunately data for the two decades were not available). Although many developing states are now endeavouring to increase the amount they spend on the general welfare of their populations, there was a significant decrease during the period when structural adjustment policies were being adopted (1980–90).

The second phase of structural adjustment involves the retreat of the state from direct ownership of productive enterprises: the selling to private interests of previously nationalized industries and the closure of inefficient enterprises;

Table 5.5 Central government expenditure 1980–1998

	Government expenditure* (percentage of GDP)		Social service expenditure (percentage of overall expenditure)		
	1980	*1998*	*1980*	*1990*	*1998*
Kenya	19.4	25.6	36.0	28.5	29.6
Lesotho	33.3	40.6	31.4	34.3	35.7
Botswana	23.1	28.5	41.5	33.9	42.7
Tunisia	22.1	25.9	53.7	36.9	46.6
Chile	25.3	18.0	65.3	63.9	71.3
Egypt	36.6	23.3	32.1	32.1	23.6
Indonesia	11.7	12.2	23.7	13.2	26.2
Philippines	9.9	16.3	25.4	22.5	26.5
Malaysia	19.2	15.2	31.0	35.6	42.5
Thailand	14.4	11.7	37.8	32.2	38.3
Sri Lanka	24.7	19.7	40.5	27.5	30.0
Turkey	15.5	26.5	33.0	26.3	25.7
Dominican Republic	11.4	11.6	53.0	44.0	44.2
Uruguay	20.1	31.6	67.6	61.6	75.8
Brazil	18.6	46.1[a]	43.5	33.0	34.5[b]
Costa Rica	21.3	27.2	73.9	58.7	59.6
Colombia	10.4	12.8	58.5	32.1	45.2

Source: World Development Reports 1997 and 2000/2001. Table 14.
a   1990.
b   1995.
*   Excluding capital expenditure.

Table 5.6 Infrastructure privatizations in developing countries 1988–95

Industry	Foreign investment (US$ millions)	Foreign investment as % of total revenues
Utilities (total)	3,994	35.9
Telecommunications	14,253	66.9
Transport (total)	2,178	29.0
Airlines	1,739	28.5
Railroads	99	21.8
Road Transportation	64	14.8
Ports and Shipping	276	52.3
Total	20,425	51.1

Source: C. Thomas, *Global Governance*, 2000, Table 5.2.

the cancelling/reduction of subsidies to both private and nationalized industries; abstention of price intervention by the government. Table 5.6 indicates the extent of privatization in the developing states in the last few decades, with over half of investment originating from private foreign sources. Thus, for those countries that have followed the prescriptions of the IMF, 'the public provision of basic services, such as water and electricity, at frequently subsidised prices, has been replaced by privatised provision at "economic" prices; industrial interventionism and labour protection have given way to laissez-faire; and from tax systems whose major purpose was to correct inequalities have been transformed into systems mainly intended to promote incentives and economic efficiency'.[109]

In contradistinction to the North, the restructuring of developing states in the last few decades is most accurately described by both the competition and virtual state models. Overall, government expenditure is much less than that of the industrialized countries. Moreover, social security spending is far lower varying from 4 to 8 per cent of GDP depending upon the region. Despite this, many of these states have experienced further reductions in their spending, particularly in the eighties, thus mirroring Cerny's description of the competition state and its paring back of welfare provision (its redistributive function). Second, these countries have also experienced large scale privatisation of public services and the denationalization of their key industries, i.e. their distributive capabilities have been greatly diminished. Moreover, much of this privatization has involved overseas investors and companies so that key functions are now outsourced to private operators, thus mirroring the restructuring depicted by the virtual state model.

Conclusion

The chapter began by outlining four types of state responses to the pressures of globalization: the competition state; the compensatory state; the catalytic state; and the virtual state. For the industrialized countries, some of the aspects outlined by the competition state model accurately depict the ongoing process of restructuring implemented by these states. In particular, these states now concern themselves with ensuring non-inflationary growth and a business-friendly regulatory framework, involving deregulation in both the financial and labour spheres. With regard to the state's distributive functions, the last few decades have witnessed large scale denationalization of key industries such as the energy, water supplies, transportation and telecommunications. Moreover, many states have also privatized core functions of the state itself, with the privatizations of refuse collection, health services and even prison and security services. The take-over of these companies by global competitors has thus far been most pronounced in the United States, the United Kingdom and New Zealand, but this may change in the near future.

However, in terms of the redistributive function of the state it was found that rumours of the Welfare State's demise have been greatly exaggerated and that the compensatory model of the state was the most applicable. Advocates of this model argue that as a result of globalization, states are placing ever greater emphasis upon their redistributive functions, directing their resources towards compensating those workers adversely affected by greater economic openness. Evidence for this can even be found in those labeled as neo-liberal states. The United States, for example, actually provides unemployment assistance for much longer periods (four times longer) to those identified as having been adversely affected by trade.[110] Certainly, from the data presented there is little evidence that the industrialized states are engaging in some wholesale reduction in general government expenditure or indeed in their welfare spending commitments. Indeed, the data would suggest that the current slight decline in welfare provision may be a rather minor correction after unprecedented levels of spending. However, what is also clear is that the industrialized states are coming under pressure from several internal factors, such as: demographic change (ageing population); rising health costs; and unemployment (although some of this may be as a result of globalization). The image that emerges is thus far more complex than one of states simply buckling under the pressures of economic globalization.

How each state copes with these challenges would appear to depend on the type of state concerned. For each state function (regulatory, distributive, redistributive), the specific type of policy adopted may therefore differ from state to state. For example, three different types of model were identified earlier: the Scandinavian; the neo-liberal; and the continental model. The first two, it was argued, registered changes to the regulatory function of the state. However, while the second model (e.g. America, the UK, New Zealand) mirrored Cerny's argument that globalization was leading to deregulation, the first model involves greater regulation by the state in order to ensure employment and training for younger generations (Sweden and Denmark) with an emphasis also on retraining and life-long learning. The continental model, on the other hand, relies heavily upon the compensatory capabilities of the state (Italy and France). However, these models should not be seen as mutually exclusive; it is quite possible, for example, that the state pursues a course of deregulation in one sphere (e.g. lifting restrictions on capital movement) while strengthening regulation in another (e.g. labour conditions). So that a country such as Sweden has reduced unemployment benefits and extended pension contribution years (altered its redistributive policies) but has also introduced a workfare style programme ensuring employment and training for its youth (altered its regulatory policies).[111]

For the developing states the last few decades are most accurately described by Cerny's competition model. But unlike the industrialized states, the restructuring is most apparent in their distributive and redistributive capabilities. In terms of deregulation, these states have never developed the same degree of labour regulation as the industrialized North, although in terms of finance these states have experienced further deregulation. Historically, government expenditure has always been much less than that of the industrialized countries. Despite this low point, many of these states have experienced further reductions in their spending, particularly in the eighties, thus mirroring Cerny's description of the competition state and its paring back of welfare provision (its redistributive function). The compensatory model is not applicable because these countries lack the economic wherewithal to provide but the most basic of welfare functions, let alone compensate and reskill those workers that lose their jobs as a result of overseas competition. Second, these countries have also experienced large scale privatization of public services and the denationalisation of their key industries, i.e. their distributive capabilities have been greatly diminished. Moreover, much of this privatization has involved overseas investors and companies so that key functions are now outsourced to private operators, thus mirroring the restructuring depicted by the virtual state model.

Many of the differences that arise when comparing state restructuring in the North and the South stem from the fact that their starting positions differ significantly. Over the last 30 years, the North has increased overall state expenditure and much of this increase has been on ensuring the welfare of the population. The South's level of welfare spending, on the other hand, has never been that high, particularly with regards to African states where it hovers at around 4 per cent. Second, the external pressures on these states differ sharply. Although economic globalization also acts as a force for change, much of the pressure on developing states has arisen as a result of their need to service their debt and from the conditions applied by the IMF to its loans. The fear of multinational or domestic companies exiting from their economies is certainly present, but it is the policies of the international financial institutions that have exerted the most pressure for policy change upon these states.

6   Patterns of global poverty and inequality

> It was the best of times, it was the worst of times, it was the age of wisdom, it was the age of foolishness, it was the epoch of belief, it was the epoch of incredulity, it was the season of Light, it was the season of Darkness, it was the spring of hope, it was the winter of despair, we had everything before us, we had nothing before us, we were all going direct to Heaven, we were all going direct the other way.[1]

Although Dickens was referring to 'the year one thousand seven hundred and seventy-five', his comments could be equally applied to the world today. With 20 per cent of the world 'accounting for 86 per cent of consumption' it would be more accurate to say that a few are already in heaven and the majority has already gone the other way. The disparities are indeed enormous with 225 people having a combined wealth ($1 trillion) – equal to that of the poorest 47 per cent (2.5 billion people). According to the UNDP, just 4 per cent of their wealth would provide universal access to education and health care, enough food, clean water and sanitation for those in need.[2] One can only marvel at how such a system continues to function without being fundamentally challenged.

It was argued in Chapter Four that those promoting trade and capital liberalization do so because they believe that this results in higher national growth (in comparison to a relatively closed economy). Many of these protagonists conclude not only that this will alleviate poverty but it may do so without necessarily increasing inequality. As Raphael Kaplinsky points out, this perspective views poverty in a globalizing economy as *residual* – as liberalization deepens 'the poor will be mopped up' without leading to inequality because 'the expansion of labour-intensive exports leads to greater equality'. At the far end of the spectrum are those that view poverty and inequality as being *relational* to globalization – that trade and capital liberalization are part of the problem rather than the solution.[3]

This chapter therefore examines both the changing patterns of global inequality and poverty in the last few decades and the possible reasons for such changes. However, much controversy actually surrounds the evidence concerning these patterns with many disputing both the definitions and data sets used in the official publications of the World Bank and United Nations. The chapter therefore also introduces to the reader the debates surrounding the various ways of measuring poverty and inequality and the disagreements that arise because of this. Despite these difficulties, the chapter argues that many of these studies do identify similar patterns. These are: the decline of poverty and inequality in much of South and East Asia, large increases in poverty in Sub-Saharan Africa; and the stagnation/increase in poverty in Central and Latin America.

The chapter then identifies several alternative explanations for these emerging patterns. These range from domestic factors, such as population growth, behavioural norms and land ownership through to the debt burdens of these countries. The final section examines the effects of trade and foreign direct investment on poverty and inequality, concluding that the effects of liberalization are more complex than are often portrayed. Blaming the current state of affairs all on globalization exaggerates its effects; this is equally true of those perspectives that praise globalization for all of the positive economic improvements in the last few decades. A more accurate depiction is of globalization having a differential impact across the world. Trade liberalization will affect countries very differently depending upon a host of factors, including type and level of state intervention, relative scarcity/abundance of factors of production, and supply and demand of exports. Finally, the chapter points to recent studies that indicate that the outcome of globalization may also very much depend on the level of development and income of the country concerned. Middle- and lower-income countries find it difficult to compete with those concentrating in services and high technology. Those low-income countries that do venture into the labour-intensive export market have found some success, but those that continue to concentrate on primary commodities are confronted by declining terms of trade. The middle-income countries are caught between competing with new, cheaper entrants utilizing the wide availability of low- and medium-level technology and being unable to compete in the high technology sector.

The measuring debate

This section examines the global patterns of both poverty and inequality that have emerged in recent decades. Much controversy surrounds both the definitions and methodologies used for both of these topics. The two concepts, poverty and inequality, should be kept analytically distinct, one referring to the relative economic wherewithal of an individual or group (inequality) and the other to some absolute measure below which an individual or group can manage to survive (in their society). The latter is thus concerned with '*absolute levels of living* – how many people cannot attain certain predetermined consumption needs' whereas the former is concerned with '*disparities in levels of living*'.[4] In terms of inequality we can therefore say that it refers to 'the differential appropriation of wealth (income and assets) by different individuals and social groups, relative to each other'.[5]

However, even if we are able to come up with reasonable definitions that most would agree with, how to actually measure inequality and poverty has courted much controversy. Should we use the Gini coefficient (which ranges from 1 indicating complete inequality to 0 indicating complete equality), a comparison of the top 10 per cent to the poorest 10 per cent (or 20 per cent), incomes rather than expenditure, etc.? There is also the issue of what exactly is being compared. Should we be comparing inequality across countries – thereby allocating equal weighting to each country, inequality across the population of the world – thereby allocating equal weighting to individuals, or should we be more concerned with inequality within countries or indeed comparing various social groups based on class, ethnicity or gender?[6]

It is no more straightforward when considering poverty as a concept. For example, the explanation above stated that poverty refers to some absolute measure below which an individual or group can manage to survive (in their society). The reason for the additional statement in parentheses is that one can view poverty as some economic level below which society deems an individual or group to be in a state of poverty or one can define it in terms of an absolute level below which human beings are said to be in poverty. For example Manuel Castells defines poverty as 'an institutionally defined norm concerning a level of resource below which it is not possible to reach the living standards considered to be the minimum norm in a given society at a given time'.[7] One such example of this type of approach is the EU's definition of relative poverty as an income below 60 per cent of the national median. However, this definition is one that is based upon the standard of living of the country concerned. If the standard of living is high in a country, then the minimum income/expenditure for someone to participate fully within that society will be higher. An alternative at the other end of the spectrum is to calculate how much an individual needs to survive, in terms of nutrition and shelter and calculate an absolute subsistence below which it is impossible to live. However, this is the very minimum of poverty lines and normally other aspects are included that most would regard as necessary in order to achieve even a rudimentary standard of living, such as education and access to health services. This approach, which sits in the middle of the two previous definitions, is often referred to as absolute poverty and involves establishing a common poverty line based upon the cost of an established basket of goods below which it is agreed that a person should be deemed to be in poverty.[8]

Inequality

One of the most potent symbols of the economic chasm that exists in the contemporary world is the 'champagne glass' of inequality graphically illustrating the huge gap between rich and poor.[9] This champagne glass image provides a stark snapshot of the distribution of world GDP divided into quintiles of the population. From this we can see that in 1989 the richest fifth of the world's population received 59 times the income of the poorest fifth. But what is also striking is that the third and fourth quintiles are also incredibly low, receiving only 2.3 per cent and 1.9 per cent of world income respectively. Moreover, the historical tendency has been for this to progressively worsen year on year. According to the UNDP, the income gap between the richest and poorest fifth of the world's population was 30:1 in 1960 and 60:1 in 1990. This trend would appear to be accelerating

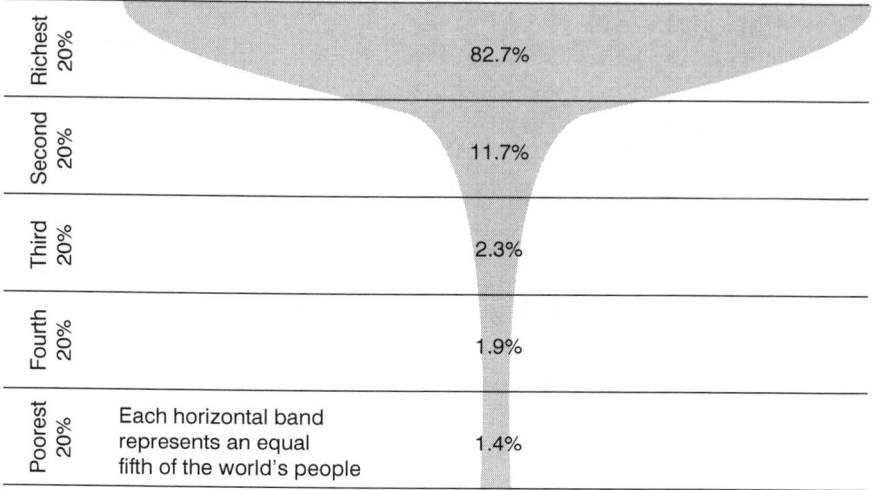

Figure 6.1 Quintiles of population ranked by income (Source: R. Wade, 'The rising
inequality of world income distribution', *Finance & Development*, 2001, vol.
38:4, Figure 1. © UMF 2001. Reprinted with the permission of the IMF)

with a reported widening of the ratio from 60:1 in 1990 to 74:1 in 1997, a space
of merely 7 years.[10]

It is worth pointing out what these data do not tell us as well as what they
do reveal. Intra-state data are not indicated and, although there is much dispute
concerning the wealth distribution within countries, in many cases the economic
divide in terms of class, gender and urban/rural cleavages continue or have
actually worsened. It is estimated that between 'the 1980s and the mid- to late
1990s inequality increased in 42 of 73 countries with complete and comparable
data'.[11] This also applies to inter-state comparisons; the champagne glass
division of the world hides the fact that some of the 'super-rich' reside in the less
developed countries (a small proportion, granted). But inter-state comparisons
also demonstrate a wide and widening gap between the industrialized and less
industrialized countries, from a GDP per capita income ratio of 1:5 in 1860 to
1:13 in 1970, increasing to 1:18 in 1989.[12] This is corroborated by data measuring
the gap (GDP per capita) between the richest and poorest country which has
grown from '3 to 1 in 1820, 11 to 1 in 1913, 35 to 1 in 1950, 44 to 1 in 1973 and
72 to 1 in 1992'.[13]

These figures and the method of comparison are not undisputed. For example,
the UNDP data are based on market exchange rates rather than on converting
currencies using measures of purchasing power parities. Using the latter method,
the gap between the richest fifth and poorest fifth narrows yielding a ratio of 11:
1 in 1960 and 15:1 in 1997, rather than 30:1 and 74:1 obtained using market
exchange rates.[14] So although the tendency for inequality to increase over time
is confirmed, this measurement yields a far smaller gap than that given by the
UNDP. Others have argued that a more accurate way of measuring inequality is to
calculate the average per capita income in the world and then to calculate the mean

Box 6.1 Poverty and inequality in a global age

Inter-state inequality

This has increased from a GDP per capita income ratio of 1:5 in 1860 to 1:13 in 1970, increasing to 1:18 in 1989.

Intra-state inequality

The 1980s and the mid- to late 1990s saw inequality increase in 42 of 73 countries with complete and comparable data. However, several countries in South Asia experienced lessening of inequality.

Global inequality

It is very difficult to discern whether inequality has increased or decreased overall on a global scale. Certainly, if the richest and poorest of the world are compared, then the disparity is increasing (the gap between the richest fifth and poorest fifth increased from 11:1 in 1960 to 15:1 in 1997). However, analyses of whether inequality generally increased or not vary. Branko Milanovic, in a recent survey of changes in inequality between 1988 and 1993, found that the Gini coefficient of world inequality had increased from 63 to 66. Steve Dowrick and Muhammad Akmal have found, using exchange rates, that the global Gini coefficient increased from 77.9 (1980) to 82.4 just 13 years later. Others have found more positive signs of globalization's effects. Xavier Sala-i-Martin finds a strong reduction in the global Gini coefficient from 64.2 in 1978 to 60.9 in 1998. This claim is supported by the research of Surjit Bhalla who examined the much longer period from 1950 to 2000 and found that in 1973 the Gini coefficient was 69.3 but then declined to 65.1 by 2000.[1]

Poverty

The World Bank argues that since 1980 there has been a clearly identifiable trend of declining numbers in poverty; in 1981 the number of people living on less than one dollar a day was 1.451 billion compared to today's 1.1 billion. This means that there are now 350 million fewer people in extreme poverty than two decades ago. However, once again this is very much disputed with researchers achieving very different results. Much of this is due to the different data sets employed and methods used to establish a common poverty line.

However, the reports do agree that there has been a significant reduction in poverty in East and South Asia, a substantial increase in Sub-Saharan Africa and either stagnation or an increase in Latin and Central America.

1   S. Bhalla, *Imagine There's No Country: Poverty, Inequality, and Growth in the Era of Globalization*, Washington, D.C.: Institute For International Economics, 2002, pp. 174-5.

log deviation, which measures the gap between a person chosen at random and this average. Such calculations indicate that the tendency for inequality to rise has recently been reversed. Although since 1820 inequality steadily increased, using this method the 1970s represented a watershed after which inequality began to decrease. In the 1970s the gap between a typical individual and the world average was 88.1 per cent (so if the average world income was $5,000 a typical individual would have earned $595), whereas in 1995 the difference had declined to 77.7 per cent (so if the average world income remained at $5,000 a typical individual would have earned $1,115).[15]

Needless to say, such claims have not gone unchallenged with critics pointing out that this method hides the fact that world income is not smoothly distributed (if it were, this method would be more applicable) but is instead highly polarized between the rich and poor.[16] In addition, Robert Huntley Wade has applied eight methods of measuring equality derived from the fact that methods vary according to '(1) the measure of inequality (a coefficient like the Gini, or quintile or decile [tenth] ratios, (2) the unit of inequality (countries weighted equally, or individuals weighted equally and countries weighted by population), and (3) the method of converting incomes in different countries to a common numeraire (current market exchange rates or purchasing power parity exchange rates)'. In doing so, Wade claims that in all but one method of measurement the result is the same – they indicate that world inequality is increasing. Furthermore, he argues that the one that differs, the Gini coefficient, gives greater weight to middle-income countries and not enough to incomes at the extreme (i.e. it does not give enough weight to what is happening to the extremely poor or, for that matter, to the extremely rich).[17]

However, if we examine inequality across regions comparing per capita incomes with the average income in OECD countries a more positive image presents itself, although with much regional variation. Over the last three decades East Asia and the Pacific have improved their per capita income relative to the high income OECD countries, rising from under one-tenth to approximately one-sixth of the income received in those OECD countries. The position of South Asia is the same now as it was in the sixties, but it has recovered from a relative decline that occurred in the sixties and seventies. However, much of the increase in inequality relative to high-income countries is explained by the decline in income of the least developed countries, most of which are located in Sub-Saharan Africa. As the report is careful to point out, although there was a recovery in South Asia in the eighties and nineties and a significant improvement of the relative position of East Asia and the Pacific, this is of course a relative measure. In absolute terms the UNDP estimates that the difference between the high income OECD countries and the region of East Asia and the Pacific 'widened from about $6,000 in 1960 to more than $13,000 in 1998'.[18]

The academic community is therefore divided over the issue of inequality; this is particularly the case when measuring inequality across the population of the world. Branko Milanovic, in a recent survey of changes in inequality between 1988 and 1993, found that the Gini coefficient of world inequality had increased from 63 to 66. The level of inequality was thus already very high but has increased at a rate 'faster than the increase experienced by the United States and the United Kingdom in the decade of the 1980s'.[19] During the same period world real per capita income rose by 5.7 per cent. However, the possibility of real income increases across the board including the most poor is ruled out by the finding that 'income of the bottom 75% of people was less in real terms in 1993 than in 1988'. In addition, whereas the 'poorest 5% have lost almost ¼ of their real income, the top quintile has gained 12%'.[20] However, the research has been criticised because of its short time span and the fact that the period chosen includes the time of the Tiananmen Square incident (a time of slower growth) and the Indian economic crisis of 1991.[21] But others have also found significant increases. Using exchange rates to convert incomes from 46 countries, Steve Dowrick and Muhammad Akmal have found, using exchange rates, that the global Gini coefficient increased from 77.9 (1980) to 82.4 just 13 years later.[22]

Others have found more positive signs of globalization's effects. Xavier Sala-i-Martin, for example, finds a strong reduction in the global Gini coefficient from 64.2 in 1978 to 60.9 in 1998.[23] This claim is supported by the research of Surjit Bhalla who examines the much longer period from 1950 to 2000. It corroborates other research that indicates that after a period of increasing inequality, some time in the seventies a turning point was reached and after that inequality started to decline – and at quite a rate. He calculates that in 1973 the Gini coefficient was 69.3 but then declined to 65.1 by 2000.[24] How can such differences arise? A full discussion of this will be left until the section on poverty, but much depends upon the data sets and methods of converting local currencies. This is the difficulty associated with endeavouring to establish economic patterns at the global level. Very different results arise if exchange rates are used rather than purchasing power parity rates, for example, or if household survey data is used rather than national account surveys.

Intra-state inequality

The industrialized countries

The trends of inequality within countries in the last few decades have been rather mixed. In the industrialized countries, most countries experienced increases in wage inequality. But this varied quite widely across countries with the largest increases experienced in the leading supporters of neo-liberalism, the UK and the US with the Nordic (with the exception of Sweden) countries registering the smallest increases. For example, during the 1980s in the United States the 'real minimum wage fell by 44 percent' and there has been a concomitant rise in inequality. The United Kingdom also experienced a 30 per cent rise in its Gini coefficient between 1978 and 1991.[25] Others, such as Germany and Italy, did not experience an increase in wage inequality. Household income inequality, based on income after direct taxation and transfers are taken into account, also increased during the 1980s and early 1990s but not to such a great extent as wage

Table 6.1 Income inequality in the industrialized nations, 2000

Country	Lowest 20% share of income	Top 20% share of income	Gini coefficient
Finland	9.6	36.7	26.9
Sweden	9.1	36.6	25.0
Belgium (1996)	8.3	37.3	25.0
Norway	9.6	37.2	25.8
Denmark (1997)	8.3	35.8	24.7
Austria (1997)	8.1	38.5	30.0
Germany	8.5	36.9	28.3
The Netherlands (1994)	7.3	40.1	32.6
Italy	6.5	42.0	36.0
Switzerland (1992)	6.9	40.3	33.1
France (1995)	7.2	40.2	32.7
Canada (1998)	7.0	40.4	33.1
Spain (1990)	7.5	40.3	32.5
Ireland (1996)	7.1	43.3	35.9
Australia (1994)	5.9	41.3	35.2
Japan (1993)	10.6	35.7	24.9
UK (1999)	6.1	44.0	36.0
United States	5.4	45.8	40.8

Source: World Bank, *World Development Report*, 2005, Table 2.

inequality.[26] Having said that, the income disparities of the population are still relatively low compared to those of most developing countries (refer to the tables in this chapter). Taking income figures between 1990 and 2000, Japan and the Nordic countries continued to register the lowest inequalities. In comparison, the United States saw the top 20 per cent receive a household income 8 times that of the poorest 20 per cent (Table 6.1). It is also apparent that there is wide variation within the industrialized grouping – 'Scandinavia, Austria and the Benelux countries have the least inequality followed by central Europe, then the Commonwealth countries … and southern Europe, with the United States, the United Kingdom, and Ireland at the bottom'.[27]

Latin and Central America

In Latin and Central America, using household income measurements, there is evidence of a sharp reversal during the eighties in the fortunes of the poor in comparison to the rich in these countries. Although for the region as a whole the 'income gap between the richest 20% of the population and the poorest 20% fell from 25 to 1 to 18 to 1' from 1970 to 1982, the situation deteriorated during the high period of structural adjustment in the eighties with the richest 10 per cent increasing its share of income by 10 per cent while the poorest decile experienced a decline of 15 per cent. According to the World Bank at the time, '[N]owhere in the developing world are the contrasts between poverty and national wealth more striking'.[28] The situation stabilized in the nineties, but for some countries, for example Honduras and Jamaica, the gap continued to widen.[29] The level of

Table 6.2 Income inequality in Latin and Central America 2000

Country	Poorest 20%	Richest 20%	Gini coefficient
Panama	2.4	60.3	56.4
Nicaragua (2001)	3.6	59.7	55.1
Uruguay	4.8	50.1	44.6
Costa Rica	4.2	51.5	46.5
Peru	2.9	53.2	49.8
Ecuador (1999)	3.3	58.0	43.7
Brazil (1998)	2.0	64.4	59.1
Paraguay (1999)	2.2	60.2	56.8

Source: World Bank, *World Development* Report, 2005, Table 2.

inequality is generally the highest in the world with the richest 20 per cent in countries such as Brazil and Paraguay receiving over 60 per cent of income. Unsurprisingly, the Gini coefficients are also extremely high, with many countries registering 50 or above (Table 6.2). The actual investment required to raise the region's poor out of poverty has been estimated at just '0.7 percent of regional GDP – the approximate equivalent of a 2 percent income tax on the wealthiest fifth of the population'.[30]

The former Soviet Union and Eastern Europe

In the former Soviet bloc, the rapid liberalization of these economies resulted in huge increases in poverty. Taking a poverty line of 120 dollars per month, the poverty level increased from around 14 million in 1987/88 to 147 million in 1993–5. Although this poverty line is far higher than the one the World Bank most often uses, the increases are still surprising. Concomitant with this increase in poverty, there has been a marked upward shift in inequality with a rise in the Gini coefficient from around 0.25–0.28 to 0.35–0.38 in just 10 years (since 1987). According to the UNDP, this represented 'the fastest ever recorded' change in inequality within states.[31] The actual increases were far steeper in the former Soviet Union than in Eastern Europe (with the exception of Bulgaria) as Table 6.3 indicates, with Russia, the Caucasus and Central Asia registering the highest levels of inequality, with some countries experiencing a 20 point increase or over. During the transition (1988–95) in every former Soviet bloc country with only one exception (Slovak Republic) the income of the richest 10 per cent increased while the income of the poorest 10 per cent decreased. Some of the greatest disparities of income were experienced: in Russia where the poorest decile received just 1.64 per cent of the nation's income and the richest 39.52 per cent; in Kyrgyzstan where the ratio was 0.8 per cent to 39.18 per cent; and Ukraine with 1.51 per cent to 32.74 per cent.[32] If one looks at the inequality between people in the region as a whole, the Gini coefficient has increased from 0.26 to 0.46 (from 1988 to 1993). The region has thus radically altered from being one of the most equal regions to one having a regional inequality similar to that of Africa.[33]

Table 6.3 Income inequality in the former Soviet Union and Eastern Europe

Country	Gini coefficient 1987–90	Gini coefficient 1996–99
Central Europe		
Czech Republic	0.19	0.25
Hungary	0.21	0.25
Slovenia	0.22	0.25
Poland	0.28	0.33
South Eastern Europe		
Albania	–	0.27[a]
Bulgaria (1997)	0.23	0.41
Croatia	0.36	0.36
Macedonia FYR	–	0.37
Romania	0.23	0.30[a]
Baltics		
Lithuania	0.23	0.34
Latvia	0.24	0.32
Estonia	0.24	0.37
Slavic countries		
Russian Federation	0.26	0.47
Ukraine	0.24	0.33[a]
Moldova	0.27	0.42
Belarus	0.23	0.28[a]
Caucasus and Central Asia		
Armenia	0.27	0.59
Georgia	0.29	0.43
Kyrgyz Republic	0.31	0.47
Kazakhstan	0.30	0.35[a]
Tajikistan	0.28	0.47
Turkmenistan	0.28	0.45[a]

Source: C. Jones and A. Revenga, *Making Transition Work for Everyone*, 2000, Table 4.1. [a]Based on consumption.

Asia

In Asia, most of the countries experienced an improvement both in terms of a reduction in poverty and in income distribution in the 1980s and early 1990s. China was the obvious exception, but also countries such as Thailand experienced an increase in inequality between 1975 and 1992.[34] Towards the end of the nineties there were some set-backs in the improvements in income distribution for some of the countries in Asia. For example, Bangladesh, Indonesia, Malaysia and Sri Lanka witnessed increases in inequality. However, inequality did not return to the much higher levels of the 1970s and, it should be added that Sri Lanka's figures have varied considerably from survey to survey. India, South Korea, the Philippines and Pakistan have continued to improve the income share for the poorest fifth of their populations.[35] However, the East Asian crisis of 1997 had a major impact upon the well-being of the population of those countries affected. In Indonesia, an extra 20 per cent of the population were pushed into poverty (40 million). For South Korea and Thailand the increase has been estimated at 12 per cent of the population (5.5 and 6.7 million respectively).[36]

Table 6.4 Expenditure inequality in Asia (selected countries), 2000

Country	Poorest 20%	Richest 20%	Gini coefficient
Bangladesh	9.0	41.3	31.8
India	8.9	41.6	32.5
Indonesia (2002)	8.4	43.3	34.3
Malaysia (1997 income)	4.4	54.3	49.2
Pakistan (1998/9)	8.8	42.3	33.0
Philippines	5.4	52.3	46.1
Sri Lanka (1995)	8.0	42.8	34.4
Thailand	6.1	50.0	43.2
China (2001)	4.7	50.0	44.7

Source: World Bank, *World Development Report*, 2005, Table 2.

Africa

For Africa, the eighties represented the lost decade in which living conditions deteriorated rapidly and economic growth failed to keep pace with population growth, so that, for example, between 1980 and 1985 'income per person declined more than 25% for the region as a whole'.[37] Figures for the 1980s indicate large disparities in income. Using real GDP per capita and comparing the richest 20 per cent with the poorest 20 per cent, the inequality ratios of some countries were incredibly high, rivalling those of Latin America (e.g. South Africa, Zimbabwe and Guinea-Bissau). However, the difficulty in using GDP as an indicator is that it fails to measure non-market production; a more accurate method is to examine household consumption.[38] Yet, even if one uses consumption measures the inequality ratios are still extremely high. The second and third sections of Table 6.5 indicate that this inequality continued into the nineties and into the new millennium. So the experience of Sub-Saharan Africa in the last few decades has been one of large increases in poverty and a continuation of very high levels of inequality within these countries. In terms of inequality between people in the region as a whole, the Gini coefficient has increased from 0.42 to 0.49 (from 1988 to 1993).[39]

To sum up, this section has examined three main methods of assessing global inequality. The first using an inter-state comparison finds that this form of inequality has increased over the longue durée. There has been a widening gap between the industrialized and less industrialized countries, from a GDP per capita income ratio of 1:5 in 1860 to 1:13 in 1970, increasing to 1:18 in 1989.[40] In addition, it is clear from the above that there continue to be large degrees of inequality within developing countries, and in many regions this has worsened over the last few decades. However, one should not automatically assume from these two assertions that inequality amongst the global population is therefore increasing. This last method is population weighted and the results can potentially be very different to the first method using the per capita GDP of a country. Second, it is also possible that intra-state inequality is increasing at the same time as global inequality is decreasing as both are relative measures – but of different subjects. The evidence concerning this measure of inequality is in fact rather mixed, with

Table 6.5 Inequality in Africa

Country	Real GDP per capita PPP$		Survey year	Richest 10% to poorest 10%	Richest 20% to poorest 20%	Gini coefficient	Survey year	Gini coefficient
	Poorest 20% 1980–94	Richest 20% 1980–94						
Tunisia	1,460	11,459	1995	13.8	8.5	0.42	2000	0.40
Algeria	1,922	12,839	1995	9.6	6.1	0.35		
South Africa	516	9,897	1993–4	42.5	22.6	0.59	2000	0.58
Zimbabwe	420	6,542	1990–1	26.1	15.6	0.57	1995	0.57
Ghana	790	4,220	1998	12.3	7.8	0.40	1999	0.41
Lesotho	137	2,945	1986–7	48.2	21.5	0.56	1995	0.63
Kenya	238	4,347	1994	19.3	10.0	0.45	1997	0.44
Madagascar	203	1,750	1997	17.2	9.6	0.46	2001	0.46
Nigeria	308	3,796	1996–7	24.9	12.8	0.51	2003	0.41
Mauritania	290	3,743	1995	11.2	6.9	0.37	2000	0.38
Tanzania	217	1,430	1993	10.8	6.7	0.38	2001	0.35
Uganda	309	2,189	1996	9.3	6.4	0.37		
Zambia	216	2,797	1998	36.6	17.3	0.53		
Côte d'Ivoire	551	3,572	1995	9.4	6.2	0.37	2002	0.45
Senegal	299	5,010	1995	12.8	7.5	0.41		
Guinea	270	4,518	1994	12.3	7.3	0.40	2003	0.39
Rwanda	359	1,447	1983–5	5.8	4.0	0.29		
Guinea-Bissau	90	2,533	1991	84.8	28.0	0.56	1993	0.40
Niger	296	1,742	1995	46.0	20.7	0.51		

Source: UNDP, 2001, Table 12; UNDP 1997, Table A2.1, WDR 2005, Table 2 and WDR 2006, Table A2. Final four columns based on consumption.

some researchers claiming that there has been a significant decline since the late seventies and others seeing a continuing increase in inequality over time.

Poverty

Things would appear to be better where poverty is concerned. The World Bank has claimed that between 1990 and 2001 the proportion of people within low- and middle-income countries living on less than $1 a day declined from 29 per cent in 1990 to 23 per cent of the population in 1998.[41] This represents a reduction from 1.219 billion people in extreme poverty to 1.1 billion. In other words, the World Bank claims that there are now just over 100 million fewer in extreme poverty than there were a decade ago; this is despite a 15 per cent increase in the population of these countries during this period. The World Bank argues that this is part of a long-term trend, citing the fact that in 1981 the number of people living on less than one dollar a day was 1.451 billion. This would mean that there are now 350 million fewer people in extreme poverty than there were two decades ago.[42]

However, even without questioning actual World Bank data, there are several reasons to contain one's optimism. First, if one excludes China from these figures, then the number in extreme poverty has risen in the last two decades from 845

Table 6.6 People living on less than $1 a day (millions)

Region	1981	1984	1987	1990	1993	1996	2001
East Asia and Pacific	767	558	424	472	416	287	284
China	606	421	308	377	336	212	212
Europe and Central Asia	1	1	2	2	17	20	18
Latin America/Caribbean	36	46	45	49	52	52	50
Middle East and N. Africa	9	8	7	6	4	5	7
South Asia	475	460	473	462	476	441	428
Sub-Saharan Africa	164	198	219	227	241	269	314
Total	1,451	1,272	1,169	1,219	1,206	1,075	1,101
Excluding China	845	850	861	841	870	863	888

Source: World Bank, *World Development Indicators,* 2004, Table 1d, p.3.

million (1981) to 888 million in 2001. The statistics are most telling in Sub-Saharan Africa where numbers almost doubled in the last 20 years from 164 million to 314 million people, but also Latin America and the Caribbean experienced an increase of 14 million, and Europe and Central Asia (as a result of the collapse of the Soviet Union) witnessed an increase from one million to 18 million people in extreme poverty. In addition, if one were to take a threshold of less than $2 a day as a definition of extreme poverty, then the positive trend described previously is reversed. Since 1981, the number of people living on less than $2 a day has increased by 314 million from 2.419 billion to 2.733 billion.[43]

As with the case surrounding the measurement of inequality, so too is there much debate surrounding the above claims on the reduction of poverty made by the World Bank. First, a question of internal consistency arises. The *World Development Report 2000/2001: Attacking Poverty* claimed that from 1987 to 1998 the number in extreme poverty (less than $1 a day) increased by 16 million; yet another report, *Globalization, Growth, and Poverty: Building an Inclusive World Economy*, indicated that from 1980 to 1998 there has been a decline in the number living in extreme poverty by 200 million.[44] In part, this discrepancy can be explained by the different data sets used for India in the two reports. A full survey carried out in India between 1999 and 2000 was not available to the authors of *Attacking Poverty* who could only rely on smaller surveys. The matter was further complicated by the fact that the design for the new full survey was different to those previously carried out by the Indian government and as a result 'measured poverty was lower than it would have been with the previous design'.[45] This is particularly unfortunate not only because over a quarter of the world's poor reside within the Indian population, but also India is one of the states that has liberalized its economy quite recently and would therefore be an extremely important case study. But there is also a problem with the way in which the information for *Globalization, Growth, and Poverty* was compiled. The estimate is calculated using two quite different data sets (one for 1980–92 and another for beyond 1992) so that the result is based on 'methodologically inconsistent estimates from two studies'.[46] One major difficulty is that the World Bank has actually changed its poverty line of $1 per day (1985) to one based on $1.08 per day (1993). Although

Table 6.7 People living on less than $2 a day (millions)

Region	1981	1984	1987	1990	1993	1996	2001
East Asia and Pacific	1,151	1,104	1,024	1,117	1,080	922	868
China	858	809	732	830	807	650	596
Europe and Central Asia	8	9	8	58	78	97	93
Latin America/Caribbean	99	119	115	125	136	117	128
Middle East and N. Africa	52	50	53	51	52	61	70
South Asia	821	859	911	958	1,005	1,022	1,059
Sub-Saharan Africa	288	326	355	382	409	445	514
Total	2,419	2,466	2,466	2,689	2,759	2,665	2,733
Excluding China	1,561	1,657	1,734	1,858	1,952	2,015	2,137

Source: World Bank, *World Development Indicators*, 2004, Table 1f.

this does not seem to be a significant difference, it actually leads to very large swings in the poverty count.[47]

This discrepancy is not limited to the overall global figure, but is also apparent when examining regional trends. For example, *Attacking Poverty* finds evidence for a dramatic improvement in East Asia and the Pacific and a reasonable improvement in the Middle East and North Africa. But the report also indicated a worsening situation elsewhere, particularly in Sub-Saharan Africa and South Asia where there was a recorded increase in the numbers in extreme poverty of 73 million and 47 million respectively between 1987 and 1998. Whereas the World Development Indicators in Table 6.6 show a decrease in poverty for South Asia of 47 million between 1981 and 2001.

Furthermore, other researchers have come up with estimates that actually vary quite considerably from these reports. For example, Shaohua Chen and Martin Ravallion have provided estimates through the 1980s and 1990s using an internally consistent data set. Compared to the World Bank's *Globalization, Growth, and Poverty* which estimates that 200 million people were raised above the $1 PPP per day threshold over the two decades, they actually find that the decrease in the number in extreme poverty is even greater (390 million). They also find that there was a huge decrease in poverty levels in China (a 400 million decrease) and also the number in extreme poverty in South Asia declined from '475 million in 1981 to 430 million in 2001'.[48] However, they find large increases in poverty in the former Soviet bloc, Latin America and the Caribbean and particularly in Sub-Saharan Africa.

However, certain overall trends outlined in *Attacking Poverty* are confirmed by the more recent figures given by the World Bank in their 2004 *World Development Indicators*. The two reports agree that poverty has: dramatically decreased in East Asia and the Pacific – this is despite the fact that it currently has the fastest population growth in the world; has also decreased in the Middle East and North Africa; but has increased in Europe and Central Asia, Latin America and the Caribbean; and drastically increased in Sub-Saharan Africa. The two reports differ with respect to South Asia with the first report stating that there has been an increase from 474 million to 522 million in overall poverty within the region between 1987 and 1998, while the second report notes a decline from 473 million in 1987 to 428 million in 2001.[49]

In fact, even without the issues surrounding these World Bank data sets, there are many reports that dispute such findings. As previously mentioned, Chen and Ravallion find that the number of people living below the minimum poverty level ($1 a day) has decreased from 1.481 billion in 1981 to 1.092 billion in 2001.[50] Sala-i-Martin also finds a decline from 514 million in 1980 to just 352 million in 1998.[51] Surjit Bhalla claims even more extreme improvements concerning the number in poverty, arguing that the numbers in poverty fell from over 1.4 billion in 1980 to 647 million in 2000 (but using $1.50 per day).[52] How can such variation come about? Several generic problems confront those endeavouring to estimate regional and global poverty trends.

First of all, the time lines chosen can have a significant effect on the outcomes. As was argued earlier, the fact that Branko Milanovic's research on inequality was based on a short time period and that this was a period of economic turmoil for the two most important countries in the data sets, India and China, may have skewed the results. Second, the time line of the population surveys themselves have a non-negligible effect. For example, something as simple as the recall duration can significantly affect the outcome when estimating consumption patterns, with those surveys asking participants to recall their consumption for longer periods generally generating lower estimates.

In order to compare across countries, each nation's currency has to be converted into a common currency – in this case dollars, but very different results are obtained from those that use purchasing power parity and those that use international exchange rates. Moreover, even if researchers all adopt one method, let's say purchasing power parity, difficulties remain. One of the reasons that Surjit Bhalla manages to arrive at such different estimates to the World Bank's is because he uses the published annual PPP exchange rates and the World Bank uses its own internal consumption PPP exchange rate.[53] Similar problems arise because some groups use household surveys and others national accounts. The variation between the two is probably because the rich are less likely to return the household surveys (or state their true wealth) and some types of consumption are not covered in the same manner. For example, in South Asia, 'between 1987 and 1998 the proportion of the consumption shown in national accounts covered by the household surveys fell from 73 per cent to only 56 per cent'. A combination of these differences therefore leads to wide fluctuations in the findings.[54]

There are also problems regarding the way in which purchasing power parity is currently calculated. The World Bank defines extreme poverty as those people living on less than $1 a day. This is calculated by taking a sample of developing countries' poverty lines. The calculation just happens to come to approximately $1 a day. However, one has to then calculate this benchmark poverty line into the domestic currencies of the various countries taking into account the cost of living (if, for example, the cost of living is less in a poorer country, then it will require fewer dollars to purchase the same amount of goods and services as in a richer country). Exchange rates could be used but are actually rather poor indicators of the differences in the cost of living between countries for a variety of reasons, for example, because of exchange rate instability and manipulation of a currency's value by the national government. In order to translate the poverty line of $1 a day across countries, purchasing power parity rates are therefore used. In order to establish the purchasing power parity of a currency in comparison to one dollar, it is necessary to calculate how much of a national currency is required to purchase a certain basket of goods – i.e. the purchasing power of the particular currency concerned.

At first glance, it would seem that the World Bank's adoption of the $1 a day extreme poverty line is based on the principle of absolute poverty, i.e. a subsistence level below which it is impossible to survive. However, as was pointed out earlier most measures are actually not based on absolute poverty *qua* minimal subsistence, but also include additional goods deemed necessary for an individual to achieve even a rudimentary standard of living. As a result, the basket of goods used to calculate a national currency's purchasing power parity includes a variety of goods including various services. Some therefore argue that by including such things in the equation, poverty is underestimated. Because services are generally much cheaper in poorer countries relative to the price of foodstuffs, the purchasing power of a currency may appear greater than it really is where the poorest are concerned. But it is unlikely that the poorest will be concerned with buying services which are generally very cheap in less industrialized countries and far more concerned with buying foodstuffs to live. [55] If an alternative basket of goods were used based on breads and cereals, for example, it has been estimated that 'national poverty lines of poor countries would be some 30 to 40 percent higher on average' and in some cases this 'entailed increases in poverty headcounts of a similar magnitude.[56]

These debates focus solely on income inequality and poverty, so it is worth noting various other factors that should not be overlooked. Life expectancy across the world varies widely so that someone born in Sierra Leone can expect to live for just 37 years compared to that of 77 years for a US citizen. For Sub-Saharan Africa, someone born 'between 1975 and 1979 has only 5.4 years of schooling' compared to 13.4 years for OECD countries.[57] In terms of capital investment and trade, for example, by 'the late 1990s the fifth of the world's population living in the highest-income countries' received '68% of foreign direct investment – the bottom fifth just 1%'. In terms of the OECD countries, they had '71% of global trade in goods and services, 58% of foreign direct investment'. In terms of infrastructure, the OECD countries accounted for '91% of all internet users' and the fifth of the population in the most well-off countries accounted for '74% of world telephone lines' compared to the bottom fifth who account for just 1.5%'.[58]

In terms of human development, in 1997, the richest 20 per cent consumed 16 times that of the poorest 20 per cent and 840 million people were malnourished, this includes 160 million children. In addition, 30,000 children under the age of five die each day from preventable diseases and 880 million people had no access to health services.[59] However, there were also certain positive signs with infant mortality decreasing between 1990 and 1997 from '76 per 1,000 live births to 58' and 'the share of the population with access to safe water nearly doubled'. Adult literacy also increased from '64% to 76%', although more than 850 million adults remain illiterate.[60]

Given such pressing concerns, one can therefore understand why one writer has referred to the above discussions as 'That Silly Inequality Debate'.[61] However, there are several reasons why we should take such 'people counting' seriously. First, it is important for an international institution like the World Bank to provide coherent and consistent inequality and poverty data. As was pointed out earlier, because of differences in data and measuring techniques there was a large discrepancy between some of its own reports. Such differences must be reconciled, particularly if the public institution concerned argues that '[G]lobalization generally reduces poverty because more integrated economies tend to grow faster and this growth is usually widely diffused' or that it is 'a force for poverty reduction, and has helped some large poor countries to narrow the gap with rich countries'.[62] Second, we need to discover the real impact of globalization so that we can assess whether it is having a positive or negative effect upon the welfare of the world's poorest. Finally, the methods of measuring poverty and inequality and the resulting different estimates partially explain the continuing disagreements between globalization theorists and why they have produced such varying explanatory accounts of the phenomenon, which we now turn to.

Given such diverging opinions and uses of the data, we are in danger of not seeing the wood for the trees. However, there are several patterns that can be drawn out from these various findings (albeit with some caveats). First, it would seem that world inter-state and intra-state inequality is increasing. Second, the numbers in extreme poverty have decreased quite dramatically in certain regions. Again the numbers are disputed, but there is a noticeable trend of poverty reduction in China and the rest of East Asia even if we use the more pessimistic figures of *Attacking Poverty*. The greatest debate surrounds India where the figures diverge in opposite directions, one indicating a decrease in poverty and the other an increase. However, most other reports support the conclusion that poverty has declined quite significantly in South Asia. We may therefore conclude that in East Asia and the Pacific plus South Asia there has been a significant reduction in poverty. However, most of the reports cited above also conclude that the poverty headcount in Sub-Saharan Africa has increased dramatically and that in Latin and Central America it has either not declined or has in fact increased.

Explaining the patterns of poverty and inequality

Explanations for the scale of poverty and inequality abound. Not all of these explanations are associated with globalization. For example, an alternative multi-causal explanation has been put forward by Robert Wade. Several factors are identified: differential population growth; the debt trap; technological change; and the decline in the terms of trade against primary commodities in favour of secondary and tertiary products.[63] One can clearly see the significance of the first factor by glancing at Figure 6.2: Africa, Latin America and the Caribbean, and

Asia have all experienced large increases in their population in the last 50 years and this trend looks set to continue for the next few decades. It is estimated that in 1950 the population of East Asia was 958 million; South Asia 471 million; Latin America 166 million; and Sub-Saharan Africa 177 million. By 2000 the numbers had reached 1.8 billion in East Asia; 1.3 billion in South Asia; 519 million in Latin America; and 662 million in Sub-Saharan Africa.[64]

However, using recent growth rates, it is apparent that East Asia's population increases have slowed significantly since the high levels of earlier decades. For example, between 1965 and 1975 the annual growth rate was around 2.7 per cent, whereas by the nineties this had slowed to just 1.5 per cent. South Asia's growth rate has remained relatively steady at around 2.4 per cent. Sub-Saharan Africa, on the other hand, increased from a rate of 2.6 per cent to 3.2 per cent – double that of East Asia.[65] Population increases may therefore be one aspect of the growth in poverty and inequality as these economies struggle to absorb a new and larger generation. But it cannot be the only explanation given the experience of East Asia and the Pacific, which has also witnessed a sharp increase in its population but has not suffered from a concomitant rise in poverty levels. China's population alone now stands at approximately 1.2 billion and yet, as we have seen, there has been a dramatic decline in poverty within that country.[66]

The second cause identified by Wade is the debt trap whereby countries borrowed money to invest in their economies, but once higher interest rates were levied at the beginning of the 1980s, they found themselves allocating substantial portions of state revenue to debt servicing. For example, in 1999, Guinea-Bissau had a debt that was equivalent to 366 per cent of its GNP; Somalia 307 per cent; Nicaragua 306 per cent. For those countries that are most heavily indebted these debts act as an iron cage, preventing them from providing even the most basic of welfare provision (Table 6.8). For instance, in 1995, 46 per cent of Tanzania's

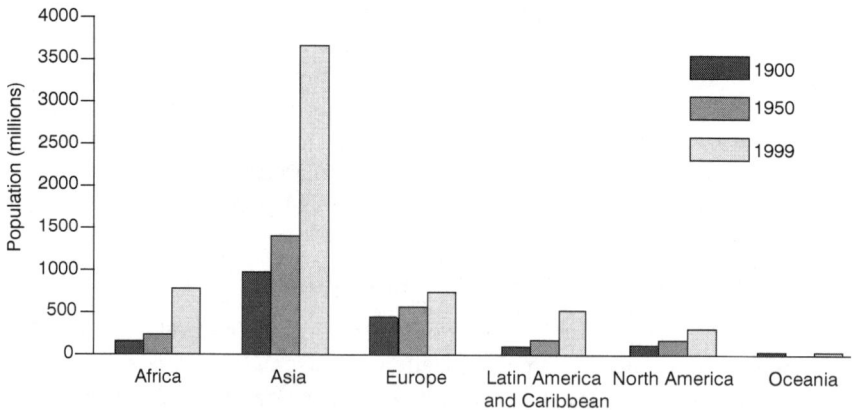

Figure 6.2 World population, past, present and future (Source: UNDIESA: *The World at Six Billion*, 1999, Table 2, p. 6. © UN 1999. Reprinted with permission of the United Nations).

state budget was spent in debt servicing; for Kenya it was 40 per cent; and for Jamaica it was 31 per cent. Figure 6.3 shows the levels of debt to GNP by region. The region with the highest level of debt, Sub-Saharan Africa, which in 1997 had more than double the amount of debt to GNP as compared to the other regions, is also the region with the highest increases in poverty. South-East Asia and Pacific which has been, of late, the most economically successful region also has the lowest debt.

As we saw in the previous chapter, the debt issue has had many implications for developing countries with most having to adopt structural adjustment policies in order to qualify for IMF loans. However, structural adjustment has not only involved trade liberalization but also a 'shift from state-provided welfare "from cradle to grave" towards pay-as-you-go social services. At the same time the public provision of basic services, such as water and electricity, at frequently subsidised prices, has been replaced by privatised provision at "economic" prices; industrial interventionism and labour protection have given way to laissez-faire; and from tax systems whose major purpose was to correct inequalities have been transformed into systems mainly intended to promote incentives and economic efficiency'.[67] Some writers have therefore attempted to provide a composite analysis incorporating changes in: government taxation; welfare spending; economic liberalization; and changes in various states' production bases to explain such shifts. In so doing, they distinguish between *primary incomes*, of which wages constitute the main element and *secondary incomes*, either money extracted from citizens through taxation or benefits provided by the state, such as pensions, health care, education, family credits, etc. ('public goods').

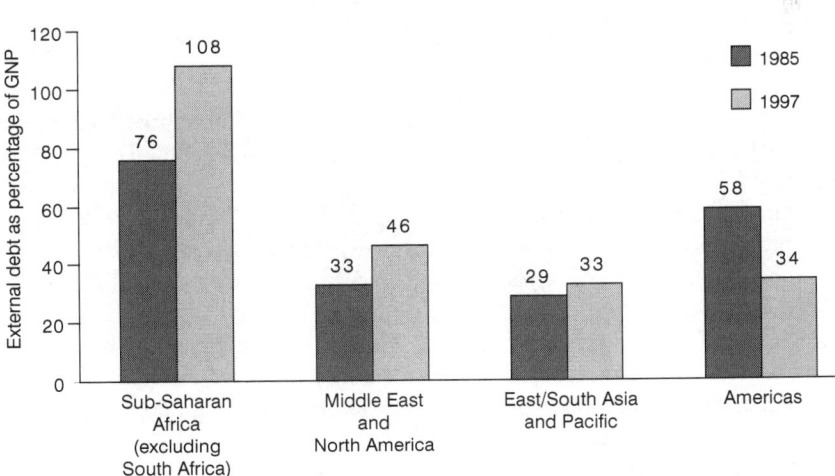

Figure 6.3 External debt as a percentage of GNP 1985 and 1997 (Source: UNICEF, *The Progress of Nations*, 1999, p. 31. © UN 1999. Reprinted with permission of the United Nations).

Table 6.8 Debt servicing and government expenditure: where the money goes

		Percentage of central government expenditure	
	Year(s)	*Basic social services*	*Debt service*
Africa			
Tanzania*	1994–95	15	46
Kenya	1995	13	40
Malawi	1997	8	40
Zambia	1997	7	40
Côte d'Ivoire	1994–96	11	35
Niger	1995	20	33
Uganda	1994–95	21	9
South Africa	1996–97	14	8
Namibia	1996–97	19	3
Asia			
Philippines	1992	8	31**
Sri Lanka	1996	13	22
Nepal	1997	14	15
Thailand	1997	15	1**
Latin America and Caribbean			
Jamaica	1996	10	31
El Salvador	1996	13	27
Honduras	1992	13	21
Brazil	1995	9	20
Bolivia	1997	17	10**
Dominican Republic	1997	9	10
Colombia	1997	17	8**

Source: UNICEF, *The Progress of Nations,* New York: UNICEF, 1999, p. 32.
*Excluding Zanzibar. **International Monetary Fund, Government Finance Statistics Yearbook, 1996, data for the same or latest available year. Cited in R. O'Brian and M. Williams, *Global Political Economy: Evalution and Dynamics*, p. 239.

After surveying both developed and less developed countries' economies in the 1980s these writers reach the following broad conclusions. First, inequality increased in the majority of industrialized countries as a combined result of increasing wage differentials, and the fact that '[M]ost direct tax systems became less progressive' (in other words, they have become less effective in redistributing wealth from the better off to the less well off).[68] In Latin America, in the cases of Argentina, Colombia, the Dominican Republic, Ecuador, Mexico and Uruguay, structural adjustment has led to: a shift of emphasis away from direct tax towards the less progressive indirect taxation; a decrease in public expenditure on health and education; and an increase in wage differentials. The authors thus conclude that the evidence 'points strongly at the policy package as a possible source of increasing inequality'.[69]

Others have been more damning, stating that 'poorly planned trade-liberalization measures have exposed local industries to extreme competition. Contrary to World Bank and IMF claims, the position of the poor and most vulnerable sections of society have all too often been undermined by the deregulation of labour markets and erosion of social welfare provisions, and by declining expenditures on health and education'.[70] For example, in Africa, where 29 countries agreed to adopt adjustment policies (although not all actually carried out such reforms fully), 'average real wages declined in 26 out of 28 African countries, while the real minimum wage fell in 22 out of the 29 countries for which figures are available'.[71] In terms of secondary incomes, the story is similar to other adjusting countries. For all countries there was a general shift from direct to indirect taxation, but this has been more so in those countries that have adopted adjustment policies. There was also a decline in overall government expenditure for 'two-thirds of the African countries for which data are available', and, in addition to this overall decline, the ratio of health and education spending to total government spending 'fell in 12 out of 17 countries for which data are available'.[72]

The final aspect, technological change, has also been highlighted by other writers. Wade argues that those industries requiring the latest technology (which are also high-value-added activities) tend to cluster together. Why this is so is not altogether clear; Wade points to 'the continuing economic value of tacit knowledge and "handshake" relationships in high-value-added activities'.[73] The need to have a very advanced infrastructure combined with close-at-hand state of the art suppliers may also be part of the reason. This clustering of technology in the North may be a part of a larger pattern of global activity in which high-value-added activities have remained within the more industrialized North. Labour-intensive aspects of production at the bottom end of the supply chain have lower yields of value-added ('value added consists of the wages, interest, and profit components added to the output by a firm or industry'[74]) compared to high-tech products and those activities at the top end of the supply chain such as sales, marketing and customer service – 'bulk or volume production which is concentrated at the lower end of the chain yields lower value-added than specialised, high-tech products which are concentrated at the higher end of the value chain'.[75]

Several reasons as to why this is so present themselves. First, high-value-added activities usually require a highly skilled work force of which the North has the greatest abundance. Second, those consumers most able to afford such products are based in these countries so it makes sense to at least have the final assembly point plus the marketing and service activities in the industrialized North. Finally, the establishment of a major production site will attract smaller suppliers to the region. This in turn will attract other major producers thereby generating an industrial cluster. This may not hold true for low-value activities where the trend has been towards ever-increasing amounts of outsourcing to other countries. But it may still hold true for those activities that require a highly skilled workforce.

Others have pointed to the internal characteristics of countries. Nancy Birdsall, for instance, views poverty and inequality as a result of a combination of factors including some of the above. However, she also includes: unequal land distribution; behavioural patterns; economic policy; and democracy.[76] In terms of unequal land distribution in less industrialized countries where agriculture and house husbandry are important resources the figures are quite staggering. The percentage of agricultural households that were landless or near landless between

Box 6.2 Explaining poverty and inequality

Population growth

It is estimated that in 1950 the population of East Asia was 958 million; South Asia 471 million; Latin America 166 million; and Sub-Saharan Africa 177 million. By 2000 the numbers had reached 1.8 billion in East Asia; 1.3 billion in South Asia; 519 million in Latin America; and 662 million in Sub-Saharan Africa.

External debt

In 1999, Guinea-Bissau had a debt that was equivalent to 366% of its GNP; Somalia 307%; Nicaragua 306%. For those countries that are most heavily indebted these debts act as an iron cage, preventing them from providing even the most basic of welfare provision. For instance, in 1995, 46% of Tanzania's state budget was spent in debt servicing; for Kenya it was 40%; and for Jamaica it was 31%.

Structural adjustment

In Latin America, in the cases of Argentina, Colombia, the Dominican Republic, Ecuador, Mexico, and Uruguay, structural adjustment has led to: a shift of emphasis away from direct tax towards the less progressive indirect taxation; a decrease in public expenditure on health and education; and an increase in wage differentials. In Africa average real wages declined in 26 out of 28 African countries, while the real minimum wage fell in 22 out of the 29 countries for which figures are available.

Unequal land distribution

In many developing countries the pattern of land distribution may be a major cause of poverty and inequality. For example, the percentage of agricultural households that were landless or near landless between the mid-1970s to mid-1980s in the Dominican Republic was 92%; in Ecuador and Peru, 75%; in Brazil, 70%. For the whole of Africa the figures are better, registering an average level of 40%, but this still indicates a high level of wealth disparity.

Institutional racism

This may induce self-reinforcing behavioural patterns, for example, because of racial discrimination in the labour market those marginalized ethnic groups see little reason to invest in education and skills for jobs that they are unlikely to gain.

Education

Education is viewed as a positive factor promoting growth in developing countries; for example, it has been estimated that a '10 percentage point increase in primary school enrolments in 1970 (among a sample of 98 developing countries) would have increased average annual growth in real per capita GDP between 1980 and 1985 by 0.21 percentage point; a 10 percentage point increase in secondary enrolments would have increased the growth rate by 0.33 percentage point'.[1]

Democracy

Some authors also point to the fact that Western democracies have generated equalizing economic growth – but the claim that democracy is somehow linked to greater equality is hotly disputed.

1 N. Birdsall and R. Sabot, *Virtuous Circles: Human Capital, Growth, and Equity in East* Asia, Washington, DC: World Bank, 1993, p. 96. Also refer to J. Campos and H. Root, *The Key to the Asian Miracle: Making Shared Growth Credible*, Washington, DC: The Brookings Institution, 1996, pp. 56–8.

the mid-1970s to mid-1980s in the Dominican Republic was 92 per cent; in Ecuador and Peru, 75 per cent; in Brazil, 70 per cent. For the whole of Africa the figures are better, registering an average level of 40 per cent, but this still indicates a high level of wealth disparity.[77]

Education is viewed as a positive factor promoting growth in developing countries; for example, it has been estimated that a '10 percentage point increase in primary school enrolments in 1970 (among a sample of 98 developing countries) would have increased average annual growth in real per capita GDP between 1980 and 1985 by .21 percentage point; a 10 percentage point increase in secondary enrolments would have increased the growth rate by .33 percentage point'.[78] But equally significant is the role that education can play in helping to ameliorate inequality. Those with higher skills are usually able to attract a substantial wage premium as a result of their extra years of education. This premium has tended to increase over time in many of the industrialized countries; for example, 'in 1979 the hourly earnings of recent college graduates were 23 percent higher than the earnings of recent high school graduates. By 1989 the college premium in wage rates for this group had increased to 43 percent'.[79] In countries with low educational levels, those that are more skilled usually receive a relatively higher wage than they would elsewhere as a result of benefiting from scarcity rents. For example, as a result of South Korea's investment in public education, it has experienced a large drop in wage differentials between those with high school education and those with only primary education, 'in 1976 workers with high school education earned 47 percent more than primary school graduates; by 1986 that premium had declined to 30 percent ... the net effect of educational expansion was to reduce substantially, by 22 percent, inequality of pay over the decade ... *By contrast, over the same period in Brazil* the wage premium earned by university leavers was 159 percent in 1976 and 151 percent in 1985'.[80]

Birdsall also points to self-reinforcing behavioural patterns, for example, because of racial discrimination in the labour market those marginalized ethnic groups see little reason to invest in education and skills for jobs that they are unlikely to gain. A recent study by the World Bank focusing on the continuing inequality in Latin America gives much credence to this argument. The report found that social and political discrimination present since the colonial period continues to pervade these countries, that '[D]espite the immense political, social, and economic changes of the past century, these historically-formed sources of inequality persisted until the present time, albeit in shifting institutional forms'. This inequality limits 'access to education, health and public services; access to land and other assets; the functioning of credit and formal labor markets; and attainment of political voice and influence' for those marginalised groups.[81] Even if these groups do attain a better level of education, institutionalized forms of exclusion may therefore 'prevent poor people from becoming upwardly mobile'.[82] But it should also be added that this inequality also serves to exclude the marginalized from education in the first place, as the report observes, 'higher education remains largely the preserve of the children of the rich, with…increases in inequality of enrolment in the past decade'.[83]

The third factor Birdsall cites is bad economic policy – large public sector borrowing to fund public programmes can lead to inflation or high interest rates. As we have already seen, such borrowing can also lead to unmanageable debts with large parts of the budget taken up by debt servicing. There is no doubt that the increase in borrowing in the seventies as a result of the abundance of 'petro-dollars' has severely affected the majority of Southern states. However, whether the severe structural readjustment policies recommended by the IMF is the right path to follow is a hotly debated issue, one that we will return to later.

The fourth factor is open to debate. Birdsall argues that Western democracies have 'generated sustained and equalizing economic growth'. It is interesting that the claim is made for Western democracies, rather than democracies as a whole. Taking a wider range, leads to a less certain picture. For example the United Nations Development Programme relatively recently examined the link between democracy and growth pointing out that 'the correlation between democracy and income weakens or disappears when only low-income countries are considered'.[84] Once again, there is a difficulty surrounding the direction of causation – do growth and subsequent improvements in the standard of living provide the conditions for democracy to flourish, or does democracy itself foster growth? The UNDP concluded that 'studies of sources of economic growth find no strong evidence that democracy is an explanatory factor'.[85] Similarly, the proposition that democracy has generated equalizing economic growth is not as clear-cut as it first seems. Once again the UNDP Report of 2002, dedicated to the issue of democracy, points out that in the last 20 years most of the OECD countries have experienced 'rising income inequality'.[86] This is not to say that democracy should not be pursued. Democracy in itself has intrinsic worth. However, the propositions that democracy helps promote growth and/or greater equality are not as straightforward as portrayed by Birdsall.

Trade and foreign direct investment

Trade liberalization

One of the reasons that the above debate on poverty and inequality is so important is that there are currently strong claims and counter-claims as to the effect globalization (in this case, greater trade openness) is having upon both inequality and poverty. For example, the former president of the World Bank, James Wolfensohn, has argued that 'these policies have contributed to more rapid growth in developing countries' per capita incomes than at any point since the mid-1970s. And faster growth has meant poverty reduction: the proportion of people worldwide living in absolute poverty has dropped steadily in recent decades, from 29% in 1980 to a record low of 23% in 1998'.[87] However, as was argued above, these estimates should not be taken as indisputable facts because some researchers argue that there has been an increase in the incidence of poverty over the same period, while others argue that there has been an even greater reduction. As a result of this uncertainty, claims over the positive or negative effects of trade on poverty and inequality remain hotly disputed.

Certainly standard trade theory predicts that trade liberalization should be beneficial for developing countries. As was explained in Chapter Five, the Heckscher–Ohlin model indicates that trading patterns will reflect the relative factor endowments (land, labour, capital) of the countries concerned, i.e. the relative scarcity and abundance of the factors of production determine a country's comparative advantage. As a result, when highly industrialized countries open their markets to lower wage economies, it is predicted that low-skill jobs will shift from the high-wage countries to those with lower wages. In high wage countries this would then lead to greater unemployment in the low-wage sectors.[88]

However, the effects of trade liberalization are very much dependent upon the structure of the domestic economy concerned and the effects of technology transfer that may occur. For example, if trade liberalization leads to the transfer of technology providing efficiency gains in labour-intensive industries then it is highly likely that wage levels will decline rather than rise in these sectors. On the other hand, if a country successfully competes internationally in the agricultural sector, it may lead to greater demand and thus raise wage levels for the least well off. The effects of integration into the world economy and the dislocations this will create are thus complex and varied.[89] Finally, one of the key assumptions of the model is that perfect competition exists whereas in the real world states more often than not directly and indirectly subsidize industry. Developing countries often find their domestic markets swamped by cheap imports, thus damaging their industries even in those sectors where they have a clear competitive advantage.

Furthermore, complications arise when attempting to observe this phenomenon because of other significant factors associated with industrialization that impact upon the income distribution of a nation's population. An example of this is the well known Kuznet's curve indicating that industrializing countries exhibit an increase in inequality in the initial phases with a succeeding phase in which inequality declines. The reasons for this continue to be disputed, but a possible explanation is that industrialization initially provides the opportunity of higher wage-higher productivity work compared to the agricultural sector. Once all the surplus labour is absorbed and the industrial revolution spreads to the agricultural sector also, wages between the two sectors become more even.[90] Others have argued that the effects of globalization are such that it leads to a similar type of curve because 'at a very low income level, it is the rich who benefit from openness. As income level rises…the situation changes and the relative income of the poor and middle classes rises compared to the rich'.[91] This may reflect the initial education levels in these countries, with higher wages accruing to those with some basic education. Once education levels of the poor improve it would seem that they too benefit from trade openness. There are therefore other factors at work associated with the general process of modernization that may affect the outcome of greater trade integration between countries.

What evidence is there to support the argument that trade liberalization has a positive effect on poverty and inequality? As Chapter Four indicated, a recent World Bank report has made strong claims concerning the benefits of trade in the last few decades arguing that we are currently experiencing a third wave of globalization, one that is affecting both industrialized and developing countries. These authors argue that the pattern of production and trade in the South has dramatically changed, that in this third wave, those countries that have globalized (those that 'have doubled their ratio of trade to income over the past two decades') have seen their per capita growth rate expand steadily from '1 percent in the 1960s, to 3 percent in the 1970s, 4 percent in the 1980s, and 5 percent in the 1990s' thereby outstripping growth in the OECD countries.[92] However, the remaining two-thirds of developing states experienced a decline in their trade to GDP ratios and overall also experienced a decline in their GDP per capita growth rate. The report concludes that, as a result of these globalizing economies, *poverty is declining* in these countries and *inequality has stopped increasing* – '[T]his third wave of globalization may mark the turning point at which participation has widened sufficiently for it to reduce poverty and inequality'.[93] The main argument of the report is therefore that greater trade has acted as a source of stimulation for the economy, resulting in growth for those countries that have embarked upon liberalization – '[G]lobalization generally reduces poverty because more integrated economies tend to grow faster and this growth is usually widely diffused'.[94] The report concludes that there is 'some evidence' that this growth has had a positive impact upon these populations by increasing their income levels and that increased trade raises 'not only the level of real income, but also its rate of growth'. The report also notes that trade on its own 'is certainly not sufficient for growth'.[95]

However, Dollar and Kraay in a series of publications have been far more sanguine about the benefits of globalization. In an economic two-step, they have argued that openness to trade and investment is associated with above average growth (i.e. when compared to 'non-globalizers') and that this openness 'has actually promoted economic equality and reduced poverty'.[96] The patterns of inequality that we are currently witnessing are said to be associated less with globalization *per se* and 'stem more from domestic education, taxes, and social policies'.[97] In another paper, the authors also examined the relationship between economic growth and incomes this time using 92 countries, concluding that 'openness to trade on average increases the income of the poor to the same extent that it increases the income of the other households in society'.[98] It is important to understand the ramifications of such a conclusion. As the authors point out, this does not imply that there is a 'trickle down' effect, i.e. wherein the rich initially benefit from such growth and some of these benefits finally trickle down to the poor. Rather, they claim that as the economy grows so too do the incomes of the poor and in such a way that the proportional increase in income is the same as for other economic classes within the country concerned, i.e. '[T]here is a one-to-one relationship between the growth rate of income of the poor and the growth rate of per capita income'.[99]

Needless to say, there have been many objections to the above analysis. First, the critics point out that the way in which the data are presented is quite misleading, for example, Dollar and Kraay argue that trade increases the income of the poor to the same extent as it does for other households: they fail to point out that what this actually means is that if their income is but one-hundredth that of the richest group, then they only gain 'one-hundredth of the rich person's gain'.[100] It should be pointed out that those who dispute Dollar and Kraay's conclusions do not necessarily dispute that trade can act as an engine of growth (under the right circumstances). But they do take exception to the manner in which the findings are presented. Some of these differences arise because of differing interpretations of changes in inequality. For example, one can view inequality either in absolute or in relative terms. To understand the difference consider the following example:

> ... two households, one with an income of $1,000 and the other with an income of $10,000. Distribution-neutral growth in the economy of 100% would double both incomes, and leave the Gini coefficient unchanged. However, the poorer household now has $2,000 and the richer $20,000. This means that the richer household gained ten times as much as the poor household. Many would not consider this a fair outcome, and would probably describe it as an example of increased inequality, despite the fact that *relative* inequality is unchanged.[101]

In the example above, one can either focus on the fact that the ratio of the two incomes has remained unchanged, i.e. 10:1, or one can emphasise the fact that absolute inequality has increased by $9,000 to $18,000. In other words, Dollar and Kraay are less concerned with the fact that absolute inequality may have increased and instead focus on their finding that the 'poor and the rich gain one-for-one from openness'.[102]

However, there are also substantive objections to the above analysis. As we have seen in Chapter Four, the manner in which countries have been categorized as globalizers and non-globalizers is questionable. Critics argue that this selection involves a process of ' "weeding" of the "bad" from the "good" '. In fact there were many other countries that pursued liberalizing policies but experienced reductions in the value of trade in their primary products as a result of the overall decline in terms of trade of these commodities, and/or balance of payment difficulties led to these states to contract their economies.[103] It was shown in the last chapter that the countries labelled as globalizers actually have maintained higher tariff rates than the so-called non-globalizers. In addition, if one compares the two periods, 1960–78 and 1978–98, generally higher rates of growth were obtained in the former period when many countries were pursuing import substitution rather than trade liberalization.[104]

A recent United Nations report concluded that increasing levels of trade do not automatically lead to increased growth; for example, 'GDP per capita declined or stagnated in 8 of the 22 least developed countries with increasing export orientation between 1987 and 1999'.[105] There is therefore no cast-iron guarantee that trade liberalization will lead to poverty reduction – in 10 of the 22 least developed countries poverty increased in the same period. Their experience also varied depending on the main exports of the country so that the highest poverty was witnessed in those countries concentrating on primary product exports, with 'more than 80 per cent of the people in mineral exporting countries living on less than $1 a day ... compared with 43 per cent in service exporters and 25 per cent in manufactured goods exporters (excluding Bangladesh)'. The report concluded that 'unless accompanied by sustained growth, greater export orientation was not associated with reduced poverty'. It therefore concludes that '[T]here is little correlation between trade liberalization and poverty reduction: poverty appears to be increasing unambiguously in the least developed countries with the most open and the most closed regimes. But between those extremes poverty is also increasing in countries that have liberalized trade more. While these findings do not prove liberalization increases poverty, they do show that liberalization does not automatically reduce poverty.'[106]

Trade liberalization is likely to affect countries very differently depending upon a host of factors, including: type and level of state intervention; relative scarcity/abundance of factors of production; supply and demand of exports. A recent study, for example, indicated that the outcome of globalization may also very much depend on the level of development and income of the country concerned. Middle- and lower-income countries find it difficult to compete with those concentrating in services and high technology. Those low-income countries that do venture into the labour-intensive export market have found some success, but those that continue to concentrate on primary commodities are confronted by declining terms of trade.[107] The middle-income countries, on the other hand, are caught between competing with new, cheaper entrants utilizing the wide availability of low- and medium-level technology and being unable to compete in the high-technology sector. Thus they 'have been unable to compete in high-value-added markets dominated by wealthy economies because their work forces are not sufficiently skilled and their legal and banking systems are not sophisticated enough. As a result, they have had little choice but to try to compete with China and other low-income economies in markets for standardized products made with widely available and relatively old technologies'.[108]

South Asia provides some evidence for this thesis. This region experienced an improvement both in terms of a reduction in poverty and in income distribution in the 1980s and early 1990s. During this period many of the countries in South and South-East Asia experienced a rapid increase in the percentage of textiles and clothing exported as a proportion of total exports. For example, Pakistan increased its textiles and clothing exports from 41 per cent to 69 per cent in just over 10 years. Similarly Sri Lanka's increased from 16 per cent to 52 per cent.[109] Concomitantly, most of these countries experienced an improvement both in terms of a reduction in poverty and in income distribution during this period. As Francis Stewart and Albert Berry report, at the end of the nineties there were some set-backs in the improvements in income distribution for some of the countries in Asia (Bangladesh, Indonesia, Malaysia and Sri Lanka witnessed increases in inequality). However, inequality has not returned to the much higher levels of the 1970s and, it should be added, Sri Lanka's figures have varied considerably from survey to survey. India, Korea, Pakistan and the Philippines, have continued to improve the income share for the poorest fifth of their populations.[110]

For many countries in Asia the emphasis on labour-intensive export-orientated production has continued apace; between 1990 and 1999, for example, 'increased exports of garments resulted in the export/GDP ratio in Cambodia increasing by a factor of six (to more than one-third); in Bangladesh the corresponding ratio doubled'.[111] The World Bank estimates that this has enabled approximately two million Bangladeshi families to escape poverty – 'about 13 per cent of the country's poor households'.[112] This shift of emphasis towards labour-intensive manufacturing would appear to have had a positive effect on poverty and inequality, boosting growth while at the same time absorbing large pools of labour. However, one needs to be cautious of being overly sanguine concerning the benefits of labour-intensive manufacturing. On the positive side, it absorbs large pools of relatively unskilled labour. On the negative side, such forms of production tend to be low-value-added activities, the terms of trade for textiles and garments 'are falling at around two per cent a year' and they are vulnerable to competition from other countries.[113]

Such difficulties are presently reflected in the replacement of the Multi-Fibre Arrangement (1974–1994) by the Agreement on Textiles and Clothing. The MFA was set up outside of GATT (hence the term 'arrangement') and was essentially an arrangement between developing and industrialized countries whereby the former would voluntarily limit their exports in textiles and garments and the latter would set annual import quotas for each developing country seeking to export to them. The Agreement on Textiles and Clothing established during the Uruguay Round of GATT talks sets out a phased withdrawal of such quotas over a ten-year period, ending in January 2005. As a result, many developing countries are suffering from the consequences of having to compete with even cheaper producers, such as those from China and India. Muhammad Yunus, founder of Bangladesh's Grameen Bank, recently summed up the chronic vulnerability associated with this sector.

Referring to the textile and garment industry he stated, '[I]f that industry gets threatened, then our society gets threatened'.[114]

Having said that, it would seem that these trading patterns, in part, explain the relatively positive changes that these countries have experienced in terms of their levels of poverty and inequality. This is in contradistinction to Sub-Saharan Africa which has, in the main, continued to concentrate on primary commodities. Such findings are supported by recent analyses concerning trade liberalization, type of exports and economic growth. Virtually all countries exporting manufactured goods and high technology experienced positive GDP per capita growth, with the former registering an average growth of 1.7 per cent and the latter 2.7 per cent growth over 18 years. In contrast, only 2 out of 13 fuel exporters experienced positive growth and overall as a group their GDP per capita declined by minus 1.5 per cent a year. Those mainly exporting non-fuel commodities also fared badly with less than half experiencing positive growth, and overall as a group these countries per capita GDP shrank by 0.1 per cent a year between 1980 and 1998 (Table 6.9).[115]

Foreign direct investment

Another possible source of the increasing levels of poverty and inequality that is often cited is the increasing amount of investment by MNCs across the world. Indeed, the recent growth of foreign direct investment in absolute terms has been staggering. In 1992 the *United Nations World Investment Report*, reflecting on the fact that by 1990 FDI flows amounted to $225 billion, stated that in the latter half of the 1980s there had been 'a massive outpouring of foreign direct investment'.[116] Yet this figure was to be dwarfed by the six-fold increase that was to occur in the nineties, with FDI inflows reaching a total of $1.3 trillion at the end of the millennium, although since then it has declined to $560 billion.[117] The cumulative effect of this investment has been that by the year 2000 the total value of FDI stock reached $6 trillion. The fact that '[O]ver 60,000 TNCs now own more than 820,000 affiliates abroad' and that the 'ratio of foreign affiliates' sales to global GDP was almost 50 per cent' gives grist to the Globalists' argument that a truly global network of production has developed.[118] Has this been a positive development for the world's poor, or a negative development?

Table 6.9 Economic growth rates by country group 1980–1998

Group	Countries that grew in GDP per capita	Average annual growth in GSP per capita (%)
Technology innovators	18 out of 18	1.7
Transition countries	4 out of 12	−1.7
Fuel exporters	2 out of 13	−1.5
Manufacturing exporters	23 out of 24	2.7
Commodity (non-fuel) exporters	29 out of 61	−0.1

Source: UNDP, *Human Development Report 2003*, Table 1. © UN 2003. Reprinted with the permission of the United Nations.

There are two main mechanisms by which FDI might either exacerbate or ameliorate poverty and inequality: wage levels and investment patterns. Certainly, cheaper labour in the developing world is one of the main factors for FDI, enabling companies to keep costs low and profits high. But if one compares the wages paid by TNCs within the developing world and the local wages paid by other companies, '[I]n some, but by no means all, cases, pay and conditions are comparable with domestic firms'.[119] In addition, this form of investment is more stable and long term than some other forms of finance, such as commercial bank loans and portfolio investments.[120] For example, although FDI remained relatively stable during the East Asian economic crisis in 1996, the withdrawal of other forms of investment 'were equivalent to more than ten per cent of GDP for some countries'.[121] If this is the case, then it is possible that MNCs may have a positive impact upon overall poverty levels in developing countries. However, recent research also indicates that, if one takes into account the characteristics of a production plant, e.g. size, age, productivity, then MNC subsidiaries are 20 per cent more likely to close down than are domestic factories.[122] Thus the higher wages may reflect the higher job insecurity associated with employment by MNCs.

In the previous chapter, it was pointed out that for those MNCs investing in developing countries using production techniques that do not require high levels of education, presumably the most important factors are low levels of taxation and low wages. If either of these become too high, companies will relocate to cheaper locations: '[I]n their efforts to locate in low-wage countries while matching low-skill-content operations with low-skill work-forces, US MNCs can be expected to search for lower low-skill-low-wage work-forces in alternative, more newly developing countries'.[123] This is not necessarily contradictory. Multinationals may locate to the cheapest sources of unskilled labour, yet pay the going rate or even a premium to attract the right quality of workers and to compensate for the temporary nature of their investment. But the overall effect may be to suppress wages in the developing world because of their ability to relocate to wherever labour costs are the lowest.

However, it also needs to be borne in mind that these companies accrue many benefits from the plethora of special economic zones within the developing world that offer tax breaks and subsidies and, in some cases, the more lax labour and environmental regulations that are in place. There is a body of work regarding MNCs assessing their impact upon the economies of developing countries in comparison to local capital investment, i.e. whether foreign investment is less beneficial over the long run when compared to investment from domestic sources. Some have found that domestic capital generally outperforms foreign investment, but that generally 'foreign investment benefits LDCs (Less Developed Countries)'.[124] However, this claim is based upon a relatively short period of time from 1967 to 1973. Others have used data over a longer period (52 years) going back to 1938 and have found that 'peripheral countries with relatively high dependence on foreign capital exhibit slower economic growth than those less dependent peripheral countries'.[125] If this is true, it might offer a partial explanation of the increasing inter-state inequality identified in the first section.

Two other points are worth noting here. This form of investment is more beneficial than the increasingly popular practice of out-sourcing where the recipient company (of the goods produced) has no direct managerial control at the workplace and therefore has difficulty ensuring that ethical labour practices are adhered to.[126] Second, the rate of profit repatriation of MNCs does vary considerably from region to region. On average, '[F]or every $1 transferred to developing countries in the form of FDI, around $0.30 leaves in the form of repatriated earnings'. But in the case of Sub-Saharan Africa the rate is far higher, repatriated profits standing at 75 per cent of the FDI that flows into the region.[127] This may be a factor in explaining the poor economic performance of these states; money that could have been employed domestically to further economic growth is instead taken out of the country.

The focus on MNCs and their effect upon patterns of inequality and poverty continues to be debated. Within countries it may be that MNCs provide reasonable wages (in local terms) in order to both attract the best labour and to compensate for the fact that the term of employment is relatively shorter than in domestic firms. This is not to say that all MNCs pay higher wages; as recent reports of the more egregious offenders indicate, many MNCs do engage in highly exploitative employment practices. Domestic capital would appear to be better than FDI at stimulating growth. However, whether over the long term FDI leads to slower growth compared to those countries less dependent upon foreign capital is still hotly debated. If it does, it may partly explain the increasing levels of inter-country inequality. It may be that the role of MNCs actually varies by region and by the type of production that they are engaged in. If that is the case more research is needed in order to compare regions and the production processes in which MNCs participate.

Conclusion

Significant changes in the patterns of global inequality and poverty have occurred in the last few decades. According to the World Bank, at one end of the spectrum we have the reductions in poverty experienced in East Asia, and to a lesser extent, in South Asia. At the other end of the spectrum, we have large increases in poverty in Sub-Saharan Africa. However, as this chapter has demonstrated, these figures are not unquestionable and may overestimate or underestimate poverty levels across the world. However, this chapter has identified some main trends. These are: the decline of poverty and inequality in much of South and East Asia; large increases in poverty in Sub-Saharan Africa; and the stagnation/increase in poverty in Central and Latin America. The chapter has also indicated that in fact there are many competing explanations of these patterns. By so doing, the variety of causes may alert us to the possibility that the explanation may be far more complex than it first appears and that factors other than globalization may also, at least in part, explain these emerging patterns. These range from domestic factors, such as population growth, behavioural norms and land ownership through to the Kuznet effect associated with industrialization. High levels of debt as a result of borrowing heavily in the 1970s have forced governments to allocate a large proportion of their revenues in servicing such debt, but it has also led to these governments having to adopt severe structural adjustment policies that, amongst other things, have led to large reductions in welfare spending. The debt cancellation announced at the Gleneagles Summit in 2005 should therefore significantly improve poverty alleviation programmes within these countries.

Other writers focus on a wider interpretation of globalization and examine the political and economic developments of the last few decades, particularly the Washington consensus involving 'the recognition of the importance of macroeconomic discipline, trade liberalization rather than import substitution and industrialization, and development of the market economy rather than the leading role of the state'.[128] In addition, an analysis examining the internal effects of structural adjustment policies on both primary and secondary incomes indicated that these policies have had an overall negative impact upon levels of inequality and poverty. This situation has been exacerbated by population growth and high levels of foreign debt initially accumulated in the 1970s. These writers thus help to provide a more sophisticated picture of what is affecting poverty and inequality in the world. Yet, by so doing, they alert us to the possibility that the explanation may be far more complex than it first appears and also that factors other than globalization may also, at least in part, explain these emerging patterns.

The literature concerning trade, growth and their relation to poverty indicated that there is still much disagreement as to whether trade liberalization is the best policy for stimulating economic growth in developing countries. There are those that view the above average growth of those countries that they have identified as globalizers as evidence that poverty should be regarded as *residual* – as countries become ever more integrated into the global economy, poverty levels will reduce and without necessarily paying the price through increases in inequality. The chapter has indicated that there are good reasons for questioning such claims, but that does not mean that trade and capital liberalization should be viewed in an entirely negative light. A more accurate depiction is of globalization having a differential impact across the world. Trade liberalization will affect countries very differently depending upon a host of factors, including: type and level of state intervention; relative scarcity/abundance of factors of production; supply and demand of exports.

In much of this analysis the importance of the state's role in steering the process of liberalization, ameliorating its worst excesses through redistribution and ensuring protection for key sectors of the economy is absent. Some research indicates that 'income distribution tends to be much more sensitive to trade flows in developing countries than it is in the more industrialized nations. The results indicate that increasing amounts of trade worsen income distribution in the developing world *if* the government does not engage in certain types of social spending to alleviate it'.[129] Previous chapters have already made reference to the key role that states made in East Asia – engaging in highly selective trade while at the same time providing the right economic conditions to nurture their embryonic industries. But these states also sought to ensure a reduction in poverty and to keep levels of inequality within certain limits. Indeed the World Bank acknowledges that an important factor often missed is that the leaders of these states 'established the principle of shared growth promising that as the economy expanded all groups would benefit'.[130]

Does all of this mean that no firm conclusions can be drawn about the effects of globalization? Much is still disputed, but recent work would suggest that the outcome of globalization may depend on the level of development and income of the country concerned. Middle- and lower-income countries find it difficult to compete with those concentrating in services and high technology. Those low-income countries that do venture into the labour-intensive export market have found some success, but those that continue to concentrate on primary commodities are confronted by declining terms of trade. At the same time, it would seem that a certain level of development is first required in order to take advantage of the benefits of economic globalization. In other words, to shift to labour intensive may not be enough on its own. For countries to attract FDI and to compete effectively they also require to reach a certain qualitative threshold in terms of 'human capital, physical infrastructure and political institutions'.[131] The middle-income countries are caught between competing with new, cheaper entrants utilizing the wide availability of low- and medium-level technology and being unable to compete in the high-technology sector.

7 Global governance: is more better?

States can no longer be sovereign in the traditional sense of the word. For both physical and ideational reasons, a state cannot in cotemporary globalizing circumstances exercise ultimate, comprehensive, absolute and singular rule over a country and its foreign relations. State sovereignty depends on territorialism where all events occur at fixed locations: either within territorial jurisdictions; or at designated points across tightly patrolled borders. The end of territorialism has therefore brought the end of sovereignty.[1]

As can be seen from the above quote, one of the central claims of globalization theorists is that state sovereignty is rapidly becoming an anachronism in today's world, ill-suited to the processes of globalization occurring around us. Because of the increasing scope and intensity of economic and social activities criss-crossing borders on an unprecedented scale, states, it is argued, are unable to monitor and manage such activities on their own, leading to both a decline in effectiveness and thus legitimacy: 'the more that the scale of goods and assets produced, exchanged, and/or used in a particular economic sector or activity diverges from the structural scale of the national state – both from above (global scale) and from below (the local scale) – and the more that those divergences feed back into each other in complex ways, then the more that the authority, legitimacy, policy-implementing effectiveness of states will be challenged from both without and within'.[2] In order to manage these cross-border activities states have responded by establishing a plethora of international arrangements in order to do so. As a result, it is argued that a 'reconceptualization of sovereignty is necessary, timely and possible'.[3] Although the most forcible predictions were made shortly after the end of the Cold War, such claims are still commonplace today.[4] For example, David Held has recently argued that, the 'classic regime of sovereignty has been recast by changing processes and structures of regional and global order. States are locked into diverse, overlapping, political and legal domains – that can be thought of as an emerging multilayered political system. National sovereignty and autonomy are now embedded within broader frameworks of governance and law in which states are increasingly but one site for the exercise of political power and authority'.[5]

Thus at the core of much of the literature on global governance and the decline of state sovereignty there is a growing recognition that the economic and political spheres are no longer coterminous. Rather, the image is one of a multitude of economic activities by private agents spanning the globe, criss-crossing frontiers seemingly at will, producing many morbid symptoms, if not in fact rendering the state moribund. Globalization has reached such a level that the state, so the argument goes, is unable to monitor and control such activities adequately. Moreover, the state is involved in a lose–lose situation. If it tries to impose higher taxes on capital, money will flow to more welcoming shores and domestic industry will become uncompetitive. If it endeavours to levy additional tariffs on imported goods, then other states will reply in kind. The image is thus one of a modern state caught between the Scylla of inter-state economic competition in which trade is based upon mutual tariff agreements and the Charybdis of a global market economy in which capital flows to the lands providing the greatest profit and opportunity.

However, there are several reasons to question such an image. First, the disjuncture between the state's control of a delimited finite territory and the unfettered nature of capital is not a new one, although there are disagreements as to whether its origins coincide with the evolution of the capitalist mode of production or earlier.[6] Of course, few would dispute that in certain spheres the world is witnessing unprecedented levels of economic activity, nor the novelty of some of these activities. However, in a few decades' time we may come to describe this movement as 'back to the future', viewing contemporary globalization as a return to a previous state of affairs interrupted by, amongst other things, three major wars – two that happened and one that never quite did.[7] The economic turmoil of the inter-war years combined with the economic demands of those who had suffered but survived the unspeakable horror of the Second World War produced a general consensus in favour of far greater state intervention in the economy than had been hitherto seen. At the same time, Cold War competition was not limited solely to the military, but encompassed the political, economic, cultural and ideological spheres as well. As such, each side engaged in welfare provision for their populations on an unprecedented scale. In today's post-Cold War world and with the general consensus in favour of comprehensive state interventionism fast fading, it is unlikely that we will return to a world of 'embedded liberalism', in which states place priority on social policies even if this requires greater controls on capital.[8]

Yet we have seen that the contemporary world economy differs in several ways from the economies of previous periods. In terms of trade, the major industrialized countries are currently at the point of surpassing previous levels of trade – even those recorded during the *belle époque*. At the same time, we have also witnessed the appearance of so called 'supertrader states' whose economies are critically dependent upon their integration in the world economy. We have seen that current levels of foreign investment and international financial activity are unprecedented. The sheer volume of foreign exchange transactions has reached a bewildering level, to the extent that the daily transactions on the world's foreign exchange markets exceed that of most countries' annual GDP. There have also been significant qualitative changes with the creation of innovatory financial instruments, such as hedge funds, options and swaps. Not only has this heralded a new level of complexity in the financial sphere, but the concomitant improvement in technology means that millions of these transactions can be executed at speeds previously unheard of.

However, it would be wrong to conclude that this has ushered in a completely new economic order, particularly one that involves the irreversible decline of the state. Certainly, there are fewer controls on capital, but this does not necessarily mean that states, or at least those in the northern core, are being forced into a race to the bottom as a result of tax arbitrage by multinational companies or via trade competition. The vast majority of foreign direct investment remains concentrated in just a small group of states. These companies take into account an array of factors when deciding where to locate, ranging from taxation, labour costs and market access through to infrastructure, skill levels and the existence of industrial R & D clustering. The level of state intervention has certainly changed in the last few decades. This can be seen most emphatically in the denationalization of key sectors of the economy, a clear reversal of post-Second World War policies when the state controlled the means of production in a host of sectors.

For writers such as Philip Cerny the state has also retreated from its regulatory and redistributive roles. It is argued that these state functions have been reconfigured and geared towards attracting capital. Redistributive functions do remain, but in a restricted form. Moreover, the focus of such expenditure is upon developing human capital, ensuring a healthy, well-educated, skilled workforce. In terms of its regulatory function, it is said that the state has shifted emphasis away from the protection of labour towards promoting a more business-friendly regulatory framework. Yet, this picture of a state in full retreat as a result of globalization is called into question by evidence suggesting that, in some cases, the state itself has promoted globalization. In addition, rather than reducing levels of taxation, it would appear that many states have taken on an active compensatory role as a result of the new circumstances they find themselves in. There is also strong evidence to suggest that much of the pressure on states to reduce their levels of welfare spending originate from within rather than without. Confronted with mounting costs in areas such as unemployment benefits, pensions and health care, the state has had to steal from Peter in order to pay Paul – selectively reducing expenditure in certain areas in order to meet rising demands in others.

Although many of the established capabilities and activities therefore remain, northern states have also been active in constructing new governance structures at the international level. This has led to an 'unbundling of sovereignty' resulting in a plethora of functions parcelled out to various international/regional institutions or groups such as the WTO, APEC, EU, ASEAN and BCBS.[9] However, although the number of such arrangements is unprecedented their creation is not novel, preceded by the likes of the IMF, World Bank and the G7 (now the G8). Indeed, one can argue that one of the underlying principles of such arrangements was also evident in the Cold War military alliances, such as the Warsaw Pact and NATO.

In essence, such arrangements developed in order for states to aggregate their capabilities in the military realm. In today's world, states increasingly have to aggregate a different set of capabilities in order to extend their strategic reach and control at the economic level.[10] Such multilateralism is said to emerge 'because governments see it as a way to share and pool resources, reducing transaction costs and enabling a concentration of the expertise and capacity necessary to achieve particular kinds of international policy'.[11] Without such cooperation this would not be possible, in other words, states are increasingly involved in cooperative action because such objectives 'would otherwise be difficult or impossible to attain'.[12]

This rapid growth in the number of international and regional arrangements has led to much talk of states pooling their sovereignty and the demise of the state. But it is worth noting some points concerning such claims. First, such arguments are not as new as they seem. Hedley Bull famously wrote 30 years ago that, if 'modern states were to come to share authority over their citizens, and their ability to command their loyalties, on the one hand with regional and world authorities, and on the other hand with sub-state or sub-national authorities, to such an extent that the concept of sovereignty ceased to be applicable, then a neo-mediaeval form of universal political order might be said to have emerged'.[13] But maybe more importantly, there exists a long history of state interference in the affairs of other states and of states having to compromise their autonomy to a certain degree in order to obtain certain desired objectives. Sovereignty therefore might best be regarded as a form of 'organized hypocrisy' because '[B]reaches of the Westphalian model have been an enduring characteristic of the international environment because there is nothing to prevent them … There has never been some golden age of the Westphalian state.'[14]

Second, in order to understand more clearly the effects of globalization upon sovereignty we need to break it down into its constitutive elements. Sovereignty has both a domestic and international dimension. The internal domestic aspect is founded upon the 'idea that there is a final and absolute political authority in the political community…and no final and absolute authority exists elsewhere'.[15] The external aspect involves the recognition of a state as sovereign by other member states of the international community. In Chris Brown's felicitous phrase, state rulers 'were sovereign in so far as they accepted no internal, "domestic" equals; on the other hand, they were sovereign in so far as they accepted no external "international superiors"'[16] We thus have two elements, the legal equality of states or what Stephen Krasner labels 'international legal sovereignty and Westphalian sovereignty based on territoriality and the exclusion of external actors from domestic authority structures'.[17]

A distinction also needs to be made between juridical sovereignty and state autonomy. The former refers to 'the political authority within a community which has the undisputed right to determine the framework of rules, regulations and policies within a given territory and to govern accordingly'.[18] As was explained in Chapter Two, many writers compare the economic wherewithal of multinational corporations to that of states, with some arguing that globalization heralds the end of the nation-state. Two points are worthy of consideration. First, the power and influence of MNCs in today's world is not unprecedented. Indeed, it could be argued that they are not as influential as their predecessors. For example, in Charles II's reign, the East India Company had its own private force which was allowed to 'make peace or war with any Prince or People (that are not Christians) in any place of their trade, as shall be most for the advantage and benefit of the said Governor and Company: also to erect and garrison fortifications at any of their settlements'.[19] Second, to compare the economic wherewithal of companies with that of states fails to distinguish between juridical sovereignty and state autonomy; as Kal Holsti asks, do 'TNCs have the authority and thus the right to establish productive facilities wherever they wish without the consent of states? Or to make and apply law within a state's territory? Authority is a particular type of relationship that presumes a right to rule, to make law and to enforce it. It is not the same as influence or power'.[20]

Juridical sovereignty therefore has an absolute quality to it, i.e. 'states either are, or are not, legally sovereign'.[21] An exception to this general rule may be the European Union which may eventually develop into a truly supranational entity. State autonomy, on the other hand, refers to a state's possession of certain capabilities which enable it to perform various tasks, such as monitoring and controlling activities within its borders or providing and extracting resources from the population. The degree of autonomy that the state possesses therefore depends upon the range of tasks it is capable of performing, i.e. the scope of tasks.[22] The difference is best illustrated with regard to the developing world and the existence of what Robert Jackson has labelled 'quasi-states'. Despite the fact that many of these states lack the economic wherewithal to provide for their populations and are not militarily strong enough to defend themselves if they were to be attacked, they are supported from the outside by international society through the acknowledgement of their legal sovereignty and the principle of territorial inviolability that attends such recognition.[23]

Globalization has affected these various elements of sovereignty very differently. Stephen Krasner has produced a useful typology, arguing that sovereignty has been compromised through conventions, contracts, coercion and imposition. Although coercion ('when rulers in one state threaten to impose sanctions') may yield little light on the current topic, it is noteworthy that the use of economic sanctions has been rendered more difficult by globalization, yet also more costly to the target state if the sanctions can be effectively applied.[24] Imposition is said to occur when 'the target is so weak that it has no choice but to accept the demands of the more powerful'.[25] This may rarely occur between the stronger states within the international system, but is highly relevant in relation to the developing world. In essence, in order to receive funds in order to carry out the daily tasks of the state, Westphalian sovereignty has been compromised by these countries accepting the Structural Adjustment Programmes set out by the IMF as part of the conditions for loans being made available. Conventions, on the other hand, 'are voluntary agreements in which rulers make commitments to follow certain kinds of practices involving relations between rulers and ruled within their own borders; commitments that are not contingent on the extent to which other signatories honor the same accord', for example, the European Human Rights regime.[26] However, it is the final aspect, contracts, i.e. 'agreements between two or more rulers, or a ruler and another international actor, such as an international financial institution, that is mutually acceptable, Pareto-improving, and contingent', which is of most concern here.[27]

As stated earlier, globalization has made it increasingly difficult for states to monitor, influence or directly control a whole host of cross-border activities so that states increasingly have to aggregate a different set of capabilities (often through the creation of international institutions) in order to extend their strategic reach and control at the international level. But states have also created institutions and signed up to agreements because they have perceived it to be in their interest to do so, ranging from environmental agreements such as the Kyoto Protocol, regional political and economic arrangements such as the European Union or international trade agreements under the WTO's umbrella. Such arrangements are seen as mutually advantageous by states thus promoting cooperation, although in certain cases they may turn out only to improve conditions for some and not all (i.e. Pareto-improving).

Although it is states themselves (particularly the most powerful states) that have created most of these institutions and agreements, they have become caught in a web of their own making. In earlier chapters, it was explained how the OECD actively promoted the liberalization of capital controls amongst its members. As a result, it has become increasingly difficult for any individual state within this grouping to unilaterally re-impose significant controls on the movement of capital across its borders. Similarly, the core industrialized states have been central to the development of GATT and its successor the WTO, yet even the most economically powerful states feel the need to comply with the rulings of its dispute settlement body. However, substantive or effective sovereignty should not be confused with legal sovereignty and the juridical status of states. States still retain the legal right to withdraw their consent from agreement and participation in institutions, although it is becoming increasingly costly to do so. Thus, the above does not imply that the growth of global governance is not significant nor does it mean that such growth has not had a significant impact upon states' substantive authority. In order to carry out a whole array of tasks, ranging from monitoring international finance, setting standards, to preventing transnational criminal activity, states have bestowed authority upon various organizations. States have the right to rescind such authority, but in today's world that would mean that they would be unable to carry out a multitude of tasks upon which they rely. As some of those writing on the decline of state sovereignty recognize, in principle states retain legal sovereignty but in reality the political costs of extracting themselves individually from such agreements and institutions is far too high.[28]

Several points concerning these arrangements are worth noting. First, the architecture of these international arrangements differs considerably. The exclusive G8 summits where the élite of the most powerful countries in the world meet, is obviously very different to that of the more inclusive forum found in the WTO. Mathias Koenig-Archibugi has outlined a three-fold classification that is useful in helping to understand the diversity of these arrangements: publicness (the type of participant – government or private, e.g. NGO): delegation (legislative, executive and/or judicial delegation of state functions to international organizations); and inclusiveness (the degree to which those affected by organizational policies are included in the decision-making process).[29] Using this schema, the G8 summits score highly in the first category – but low in the other two categories. This is because the key members of each state's executive branch normally attend, but there is no delegation and despite the fact that the effects of their decisions are extremely wide-ranging, having an impact well beyond their domestic constituencies, those involved in the decision-making process are limited to the higher echelons of the member states. On the other hand, the WTO is said to score highly in all three categories. This is because membership consists of the states themselves, therefore the level of 'publicness' is high. Moreover, inclusiveness is also high because each member state has a vote, although, for example, in cases that are brought to the Dispute Settlement Body, panel reports are adopted through a process of negative consensus, i.e. for a panel report to be rejected there must be a consensus amongst member states not to adopt the report.[30] Finally, because of the WTO's compulsory dispute settlement mechanism in which independent experts adjudicate and states then vote whether to adopt such decisions, the organization also exhibits a high degree of delegation.[31]

Can states, by pooling their sovereignty at the international level, exert control over finance and investment? Although this book has argued that in the last few decades we have witnessed an increase in the levels of trade, financial transactions and investment at the international level, this does not automatically imply that states have completely lost influence and control over such matters, although it has certainly become more difficult. It remains the case that coordinated and concerted efforts by the most economically powerful states would be successful in regulating capital. However, apart from interventions aimed at influencing exchange rates such as the Plaza Accord of 1985 there are few examples of any long-term collaboration by states in the field of economic regulation. Rather, in the last few decades such political will has been absent. Indeed, it has been more a case of the leading industrialized nations facilitating the world-wide free movement of capital and goods, even though at times the effects have been pernicious – at least for developing countries. Through institutions such as the OECD and the IMF, the major economic powers have pushed for ever greater economic liberalization leading to the relaxation of capital controls.

Thus far, there is little reason why the industrialized countries would seek to change an environment which has worked, by and large, in their favour. As we have seen, their share of world merchandise trade has remained largely unaffected and some stand to gain from increases in trade in services as well as new investment opportunities provided by the liberalization process in the rest of the world. At the same time, fears of a tidal wave of jobs landing on the shores of the South have, to date, proved to be exaggerated.[32] As a result, a major upsurge of domestic political discontent pressurizing the industrialized countries into an about-turn in economic policy has therefore been largely absent. The anti-globalization protests at the end of the millennium were mainly (but not entirely) directed towards development issues and would appear to have been relatively short-lived. For the time being at least, the debt cancellation initiatives and the promise of a development trade round aimed at helping developing countries has diminished the political pressures on these states. Rather than a major overhaul, tweaking the current economic system as and when required seems to be the most that can currently be expected. Concerted efforts at controlling capital would more than likely be successful, but the political will is just not there.

One possible example of states successfully imposing regulations in the financial sphere is the creation of the Basel Committee on Banking Supervision (BCBS) by the G10 in 1975 and the subsequent negotiations that have led to the Basel Capital Accords (Basel I in 1988 and Basel II in 2004). With the increase of international banking activity and the use of ever more complex financial instruments, the Basel I (1988) accord attempted to ensure that these institutions retain an adequate level of reserves thus protecting themselves from any unforeseen losses (8 per cent if the risk level is assessed to be 100 per cent).[33] The accords thus endeavoured to bring some degree of stability to a more complex world of finance by providing an agreed-upon standard of capital adequacy. It also established an important principle of home country control. Although financial institutions now operate in a plethora of foreign markets and have established themselves in these host countries, it was agreed that the key roles would be with the home country, so that 'home country supervision of financial institutions came to dominate that of host country supervision'.[34]

Basel II has endeavoured to improve upon its predecessor by more accurately reflecting the risk exposure of financial institutions, particularly with regard to the transfer of credit risk through the use of derivatives and securities. The accord thus includes in its calculations not only credit risk, but also market and operational risk as well. Another objective of the new accord was to address the issue of short-term loans. Because the first accord placed a lower risk rating on short-term loans (20 per cent) compared to long-term loan risk ratings to developing countries (100 per cent), it inadvertently encouraged short-term lending to developing countries. This produced a more volatile financial system; developing countries experiencing an economic downturn suddenly found themselves unable to secure international loans just when they needed them most. Basel II seeks to overcome this by doing away with the rather overly simplistic dichotomy in the first accord between OECD and non-OECD countries. Under Basel I, sovereign lending to OECD countries was assigned a risk weighting of zero per cent while all other countries were assigned a risk weighting of 100 per cent.[35] The second accord does away with this by assigning separate sovereign ratings to each country. In addition, short-term lending will now be reduced from 12 months (Basel I) to 3 months. For those countries with good sovereign credit ratings, such as East Asia, the change in risk assessment is a positive development because international banks will look upon them more favourably (as an 8 per cent reserve will not be required).[36] However, for those countries with less positive risk assessments, there is concern that they will find it even more difficult to attract loans and will be forced into very short-term lending agreements thereby producing more, not less, volatility in these markets.

Although the BCBS's creation of the Basel Accords and the creation of a Financial Stability Forum by the G7 monitoring and supervizing international financial institutions can be cited as evidence of states asserting their control over international finance, such a conclusion needs to be qualified.[37] As Hirst and Thompson point out, with the plethora of financial instruments that are now at the disposal of international financial institutions and the ever-greater use of information technology enabling the storage and transmission of vast volumes of data, there has been a 'sense of organizational "loss of control" experienced by both central bankers and the managers of financial institutions'.[38] There is thus a confluence of interest of both states and international financial institutions in attempting to bring greater stability to the financial system by establishing an agreed-upon set of basic principles. Such institutions were directly involved in the construction of the accords and thus had a voice in the final outcome. Second, such cooperation between the industrialized countries should not be overstated. There are currently questions over whether Basel II will in fact be implemented as it now stands (2006) with the United States seeking to introduce an additional simpler form of risk measurement.[39]

We saw in Chapter Two that very little of the huge turnover in the foreign exchange markets is to do with businesses buying currencies for actual use and more to do with currency speculation (e.g. buying a currency in the expectation that its value relative to other currencies will increase) and even more so currency arbitrage (profiting from differences in the value of a currency in two or more currency markets by buying in one market while simultaneously selling in another). With regard to currency arbitrage, the actual difference in exchange rates between financial centres is usually very small. Therefore, if significant amounts are to be made by such activity, vast amounts of the requisite currencies need to be bought and sold as rapidly as possible. Moreover, as soon as one transaction cycle is complete, for example buying dollars in Frankfurt while selling in New York, then another transaction cycle is initiated. These iterations continue until the dollar exchange rate in both financial centres equalizes.

In order to dampen such activity, at the end of the 1970s James Tobin suggested placing a small tax on each foreign exchange transaction. The tax would be low enough so that it would not impede those who required foreign currencies for business purposes. Hirst and Thompson are quite right to point out that such a tax would not reduce speculative activity, particularly during volatile periods.[40] However, because the tax would be levied on each transaction it would mean that the current high levels of turnover for arbitrage purposes would be rendered unprofitable unless the differences became significant. In addition, implementation of this proposal could bring social benefits to the developing world if the money generated were used for public investment in these countries.[41] Unfortunately, some of the major economies, such as the United States and the United Kingdom have dismissed the idea.[42] In other quarters it has received a warmer welcome, for example, the EU presidency recently suggested that it could be used to fund some of the costs of EU activities.[43] The requisite collaborative, coordinated action is therefore lacking and even if it were present, there appears to be a difference of opinion concerning how best to use the proceeds.

A similar argument surrounds the other major aspect of what has been called 'casino capitalism', the enormous growth of securities and derivatives.[44] Concerning derivatives, it was argued in Chapter Two that these instruments provide the buyer assurance that they can hedge against possible future fluctuations in the market for a vast range of commodities through the use of, for example, futures and options. However, because the capital outlay on such instruments is but a fraction of the final purchase price this has allowed international financial institutions to multiply their speculative activity, effectively continually 'betting' on market trends. Of course derivatives provide a useful economic function, providing protection against price fluctuations, therefore 'derivatives could be restricted to the genuine market-hedging needs of multinational commerce by requiring that the issuing banks post capital reserves to back up these contracts'.[45] This would not commit them in any way to the completion of the contract but it would prevent the speculative activity that has brought so much volatility to the financial markets. A counter argument to these suggestions might be that such transactions are now impossible to monitor and therefore impossible to either tax or regulate. But, although the electronic age has increased the speed, volume and complexity of financial transaction, this does not necessarily mean that such activity is impossible to monitor and control. As William Greider points out: '[A]stute traders, as we saw earlier, share their own informal intelligence system on the daily capital flow – who is buying what from whom, hour by hour, around the world – and there is no reason government regulators could not easily duplicate this surveillance in a more systematic manner'.[46]

Finally, governments of the industrialized countries do face a major problem from the vast increase in intra-firm trade. Multinationals can and do engage in transfer pricing activity, artificially reducing profits in high taxation countries and increasing them in countries that offer lower tax rates. But, it is quite possible to audit these companies and calculate the real prices of goods that are being traded internally within such MNCs. The fear is that if governments were to do so, maybe these companies would withdraw and invest elsewhere. However, we have seen that such fears would appear to be greatly exaggerated when it comes to the industrialized countries and if countries do not do something they are in danger over the long term of eroding their tax base. As an aside, it is also possible to overcome the taxation laxity problem with regard to money being deposited in banks based in overseas tax havens. This could be done by governments preventing their own domestic banks from transferring funds to such places.[47]

All of the above are possible but not probable. As we shall see, there may be an argument in favour of less rather than more governance when it comes to developing countries, but where industrialized countries are concerned there are strong arguments for coordinated action to monitor and control both the financial markets and multinational companies. But the political will is currently not there and such cooperation is highly unlikely because, as Greider put it, these 'regimes are all closely allied with the interests of global finance and enthralled by its conservative orthodoxy'.[48]

Governance and the South

Although one would assume that as a result of reductions in tariffs and capital controls a relatively greater proportion of investment would flow towards the South and there would be relatively greater proportions of exports from these countries, this book has called this picture into question. Chapter Three demonstrated that, with the exception of a few countries, the South's relative share of world trade has declined sharply. A similar pattern holds for relative shares of service exports. With regard to FDI, Africa's level is down to just 2 per cent of the total of world investment stocks. The South's share of investment has stabilized at approximately 30 per cent of world FDI, but although other regions of the South would appear to have fared better, in actual fact two-thirds of this investment is directed to just ten countries.

Theories abound as to why after so many decades so few countries of the South have succeeded in taking off economically. Many point to the structural adjustment policies of the IMF which resulted in a sharp decline in the influence of the state in a wide range of activities. The denationalization of industries, the abolition of price controls and market boards, reductions in state spending, the cancellation or reduction of subsidies, etc. reduced the scope of state involvement in the economies of these countries. This approach has been criticized for its negative effects on the most poor and vulnerable in these societies and, in the vast majority of cases, has not led to the growth rates promised. Views differ widely as to the efficacy of export-led growth. At one end of the spectrum there are those who argue that this policy is actually having a pernicious effect upon many of these countries. It is argued that the concentration on primary commodities has led to market saturation and a sharp deterioration in the terms of trade for such exports.[49] This is supported by evidence comparing the growth rates of the decades in which states pursued a policy of import substitution and the period since 1978 after which states began to switch to export-led growth.[50] At the other end of the spectrum are those who see the emphasis on exports as the best way to sustain growth in the developing economies. Moreover, such policies are also viewed as having a positive impact upon real economies throughout the societies concerned.[51]

Others do not take issue with the benefits of export-led growth, but argue that historically such policies have been executed in combination with high import tariffs in order to protect embryonic industrial development. As pointed out earlier, the growth of the East Asian 'miracle economies' has been markedly stronger than the world average and higher than those of any other region. The general trend in East Asia has been one of export-orientated industrialization that involved the creation of a positive investment environment that included 'credit subsidies and tax incentives, educational policies, establishment of public enterprises, export inducements, duty-free access to inputs and capital goods and actual government coordination of investment plans'.[52] From this perspective, export-orientated growth is not enough on its own. The state is actively involved in establishing the supportive infrastructure within which companies can flourish, but also steers the economy by providing an array of incentives encouraging companies to diversify into key sectors of the global market. At the same time, high levels of domestic investment are required to help such enterprises to take off. From this perspective, it is no coincidence that those states that grew 'most rapidly since the mid-1970s are those that have invested a large share of GDP and maintained macro-economic stability'.[53]

At the same time, many question the IMF's policy of encouraging a move towards a pegged or floating exchange rate, and the freeing up of capital flows thereby effectively limiting the range of macro-economic policies that the state can pursue. Indeed, after the Asian financial crisis of 1997, even some within the IMF and World Bank agree that there is a need for some type of state control on capital flows. As a result of the economic slowdown in the region the short-term capital that had been used to help fuel the growth of these countries stampeded out of the region. Although the amount of money borrowed by these countries in the years before the crash meant that at some point there would be a need for some type of correction (between '1994 and 1996 net private inflows into Indonesia, Korea, Malaysia, Thailand and the Philippines grew from US$48 billion to US$93 billion'[54]), the financial investors overreacted precipitating a meltdown.[55] But because these countries had earlier liberalized their capital accounts there were no mechanisms in place to prevent or slow down the financial exodus.[56] As Jagdish Bhagwati has commented, 'it is hardly plausible that the miracle would have vanished precipitously. As capital accumulated relative to labor, the future return to capital would decline only slowly, except in the most singular circumstances. But what happened in reality was that the economies *crashed*'.[57]

The volatility that can accompany capital account liberalization may not just be limited to the Asian crisis. A recent large-scale survey by Geoffrey Garrett examined the varying effects of tariff reductions and capital liberalization upon high-, middle- and low-income countries. It was found that capital account liberalization had a negative impact upon economic growth for medium- and low-income countries because 'financial liberalization in the absence of the kind of developed domestic capital markets and prudential regulations that only exist in the advanced industrial democracies is a recipe for volatility, unpredictability, and boom and bust cycles in capital flows'.[58] In addition, a recent report by the IMF found that 'there is evidence that international investors do engage in herding and momentum trading in emerging markets, more so than in developed countries. Recent research also suggests the presence of contagion in international financial markets … countries that are in the early stages of financial integration have been exposed to significant risks in terms of higher volatility of both output and consumption'.[59]

Although with each round of GATT/WTO talks we have witnessed the further reduction of trade barriers it appears that '[T]hose who shout loudest about free trade do not actually practise it'.[60] It has been estimated that the reluctance of the

Box 7.1 The legitimacy of international institutions

Input legitimacy

The policies of these international institutions are legitimate if and because they reflect the will of their member states. In the case of the IMF, the number of votes a state has is determined by its quota which is itself based on the size of a country's economy. Because of their high quota allocation, the G7 plus the rest of the European Union possess a majority of the voting rights and the United States also possesses a veto on key issues because an 85% vote is required for major decisions (the US currently holds 17.1% of the voting rights). Although the issue of voting rights was supposed to be addressed at the Annual General Meeting in Singapore in 2006, the reforms were quite minor with four countries gaining greater influence, but the North's majority and the United States' veto remained. The hope is that phase two of these reforms will be agreed by the next annual meeting and will produce far more significant changes.

Output legitimacy

Governance for the benefit of all member states: policies are deemed legitimate if and because they effectively promote the welfare of all member states' constituencies.[1] For many developing countries, the experience of structural adjustment has not been a happy one and therefore the output legitimacy of the IMF has suffered accordingly with many questioning its future. At the same time, the IMF is currently confronting certain challenges because of the changing international financial environment. As a result of Argentina ($10bn) and Brazil ($15bn) paying back their loans early, the amount of outstanding loans has fallen dramatically. After 25 years of lending relatively large amounts, new loans have fallen dramatically to levels not seen since the 1970s and amounted to a mere $2.5 billion for 2005. This not only raises the question of the IMF's future role, but also how it will continue to function given that it relies on the interest payments it receives to fund its activities.

Procedural fairness

Procedural fairness 'focuses on the openness and transparency of the negotiation process'. It seeks to address the issues of the 'asymmetry of power and the asymmetry of information' associated with negotiations. In the previous Uruguay Round, many countries were excluded from important discussions because of the so-called 'Green Room' process whereby a select group of states, chosen by the director-general or chairperson, would meet and achieve consensus on important policy issues and then present them

(continued)

Box 7.1 Continued

to other states. Rather like the ripples from a pebble dropped in a pond, the consensus would be carried forward by the momentum of more and more states agreeing to the proposals and a critical point would be reached where those that disagreed finally realized that they had lost the battle. This process has now been abandoned, but asymmetries in the number of trade specialists each country can staff and the information at their disposal still remain.

1　The definition is derived from F. W. Scharpf, *Governing in Europe: Effective and Democratic?*, New York: Oxford University Press, 1999, p. 6. See also F. W. Scharpf, 'Economic Integration, Democracy and the Welfare State, *Journal of European Public Policy*, vol. 4:1, March 1997, pp. 18–36.

industrialized countries to implement trade liberalization combined with extant inequitable trade barriers has resulted in the developing countries losing '$2.9bn a day in 1999.'[61] A situation in which the subsidy per cow under the European Union is 'higher than the income of more than half the world's population' cannot be construed as free and fair trade, nor can the United States' cotton subsidy which reached $2 billion in 2001, leading to a doubling of its share of world exports in just five years.[62] Although the Uruguay Round ended with assurances by the OECD that subsidies would be reduced by 2005, 'support for producers rose from $275 billion in 1988 to $362 billion in 1999'.[63] But it is not only that GATT/ WTO has failed to deal effectively with the issue of subsidies, the talks thus far have concentrated on the manufacturing and service sectors. For many developing countries, these are of secondary importance because their economies are geared towards primary production. The outcome of this emphasis on manufactured goods and services is that the United States 'imposes tariffs of between 0–1% on major imports from Britain, France, Japan, and Germany, but taxes of 14 or 15% on produce from Bangladesh, Cambodia and Nepal.[64] This remains an issue in the Doha Round where there are demands that the developing countries open their service sector to international competition for reductions in agricultural tariffs in the North. This, it is argued, ignores 'the egregious unfairness of the world trade system, which over 50 years has reduced tariffs on goods of export interest to the rich countries and protected goods that should be exported by the poor countries'.[65]

Somewhat separate from the issues of which economic policies developing states should pursue is the issue of debt. The last chapter indicated that the causes of poverty and inequality are in fact manifold, but one of the major factors is the high level of debt that many of these countries have accumulated since the seventies. This has effectively shackled the spending power of these states, with very large proportions of government expenditure dedicated to servicing their debt, thus reducing their ability to implement poverty-reduction programmes, health strategies etc. The problem began with the availability of cheap loans as a result of the flooding of financial markets with petrodollars from oil-producing countries. However, a combination of higher international interest rates and poor state management of funds have left many countries unable to pay back what they borrowed. It is often assumed that this has been exacerbated by the fact that private financial institutions lent much of the money during this period and as a result higher interest rates were incurred. This was certainly true in the 1970s when the real interest rates charged by official creditors was much lower, but by the mid-1980s 'the terms on official loans were hard to distinguish from those on private loans', thus calling into question the role of the richer nations.[66]

Finally, the dire economic situation of these countries has been exacerbated by a historical reduction in aid from the North, which is only now being addressed. For the richest 21 countries, overseas development aid as a percentage of GNP declined from 0.33 per cent in 1990 to 0.22 per cent in 1997 and for the G7 countries there was a 30 per cent decline in aid. Although the richest countries obviously donate the most in absolute terms with Japan giving $9.4 billion, the US $6.9 billion and Germany $5.9 billion (1997 figures), as a percentage of GNP their contribution is much less than that of many other countries (0.22 per cent, 0.09 per cent and 0.28 per cent respectively).[67] This stands in stark contrast to the agricultural subsidies mentioned earlier that prevent these countries competing on a level playing field with the North. To put such contributions into perspective, in 2002, the United States spent almost 7 times more on agricultural subsidies than on aid, Japan 6 times more and the European Union 3.7 times more.[68]

The future of the international financial and trade institutions

If the overriding aims of international institutions are 'the management of power, the promotion of common interest, and the mediation of difference', how successful have the IMF, World Bank and the WTO been at meeting these objectives?[69] For the industrialized countries, since the end of the Second World War to the present, these institutions (i.e. including GATT prior to the creation of the WTO) have successfully managed the re-industrialization of both Europe and Japan and integrated these economies back into a thriving international financial and trading system. Any differences have not spilled over into an overt challenge to the general principles concerning the management of the international economic system. The major exception to this came in 1971 with the United States' decision to no longer peg the dollar to gold and the move away from a fixed exchange system to a floating exchange.

This is not to say that these institutions have not changed considerably since their creation over half a century ago. In fact, initially 'the IMF was created to defend and manage a fixed exchange-rate system that is now regarded as economically inappropriate and practically unworkable'. While the World Bank after its inception 'emphasized national plans for government-managed industrial development … Now the consensus of professional economists and international agencies calls for the opposite policies: flexible exchange rates, market-determined economic development, and free trade'.[70] But these changes have been incremental and even the establishment of the WTO can be seen as a natural evolution given the increasing membership and complexity of agreements under GATT.

From a northern perspective these institutions have successfully nurtured a common interest amongst these states to the extent that the institutions and their policies are seen, at least by the political elite, as legitimate. It is worth elaborating a little further on this for a later comparison with the developing countries' perspective. Although, in general, the industrialized states have continued to support such institutions because it is in their own self-interest to do so, this does not mean that the policies adopted manage to satisfy the self-interest of all members all of the time. A critical distinction therefore needs to be made between interest and self-interest – '[A]ctors who are interested act rationally to pursue goals, but we know nothing a priori about what those goals are. Assuming *self*-interest involves adding a presumption about the egoistic attitude of the self toward others or to the rules'. With regard to states' behaviour towards international institutions, if they only acted purely in terms of self-interest it would result in states engaging in 'a continuous reassessment of every rule and relationship from an instrumental point of view'. If this were the case, such international arrangements would be inherently unstable, often resulting in the complete breakdown of previous agreements. However, if states act merely in an interested manner, then it is possible that states will perceive that a policy of maintaining an institution and abiding by its policies should be followed even if some of those policies are not in its self-interest in the stricter sense.[71] However, such behaviour still depends upon states benefiting in general from such arrangements. Earlier chapters have demonstrated that northern states have maintained their economic dominance in the areas of trade, finance and investment and therefore view the various agreements and institutions at the international level as broadly in their interest.

Of course legitimacy is not solely derived from policy outcomes, but also from representation in the deliberative formulation of these policies. In the case of the WTO, each member has equal representation in the formal sense concerning the adoption of trade round decisions. In the case of the IMF, the number of votes a state has is determined by its quota which is itself based on the size of a country's economy. Because of their high quota allocation, the G7 plus the rest of the European Union possess a majority of the voting rights and the United States also possesses a veto on key issues because an 85 per cent vote is required for such changes (the US currently holds 17.1 per cent of the voting rights). As others have pointed out, the United States' unique position means that it can wield great influence, using its veto 'in effecting a predetermined outcome in the form of a "consensus"'.[72] Although the issue of voting rights was supposed to be addressed at the Annual General Meeting in Singapore in 2006, the reforms were quite minor with four countries gaining greater influence, but the North's majority and the United States' veto remained.[73] The hope is that phase two of these reforms will be agreed by the next annual meeting and will produce far more significant changes.

Can the same be said for the developing countries' perspective? Although some countries, such as East Asia, have definitely gained from their integration into the international financial and trading system, the experience and form of integration of the majority of other developing countries has not been similar. The situation is best described as one involving structural dependence and compellance rather than involving common interest and the mediation of difference. In relation to the international financial institutions, many argue that the large amount of debt owed by much of the developing world has allowed the IMF with assistance from the World Bank to impose strict conditions upon these countries that they would otherwise not have adopted (compellance). Some even argue that, structural adjustment policies have amounted to 'a situation very similar to the colonial period where a scaled-down form of "indirect rule" is being used to bolster an imperialist project'.[74]

For many countries, the experience of structural adjustment has not been a positive one. Structural adjustment has left much of the population of these countries far worse off having experienced a decline in many social welfare benefits ranging from direct social transfers through to food subsidies, free education and health care. In addition, greater liberalization of trade has not produced a condition of fair trade. Most of these countries cannot compete with the better quality manufactured products of industrialized countries, and yet at the same time they have found themselves competing against subsidized agricultural products. As a result of these policies, the developing countries have experienced a decline in primary product trade as a proportion of overall world trade in such items, a situation that is hard to comprehend yet nonetheless true. At the same time, until very recently they have also experienced a general decline in the terms of trade of primary commodities *vis-a-vis* manufactured goods and services.

The IMF is thus confronting a crisis both in terms of input-orientated legitimacy and output-orientated legitimacy. The former is usually defined in terms of 'government *by the people*'. '[P]olitical choices are legitimate if and because they reflect the "will of the people"', whereas the latter is defined in terms of 'government *for the people*', where '[P]olitical choices are legitimate if and because they effectively promote the welfare of the constituency in question'.[75] In the case of the IMF the referent objects are states rather than people (the working assumption is that states, in one way or another, represent their citizens although obviously this is not always the case). Because representation in the IMF is based on quota allocations (how much), there is a question concerning representational justice. At the moment, the major economic powers retain the majority of votes, thus guaranteeing their continuing dominance. However, there is not always consensus amongst the major powers concerning IMF's policies. For example, as early as 1991, Japan argued in favour of providing protection to embryonic industries 'for a certain period of time in order to allow a viable export industry to develop'. Second, it argued in favour of a certain degree of state intervention because 'It is impossible to achieve optimum allocation of resources solely through market principle, regardless of the level of development...Where market interest rate cannot handle some problem, the introduction of subsidized interest rate becomes indispensable'(sic). Finally it added that 'Most developing countries have had bitter experience with colonialism. The idea of transferring the basic industries to foreign capital is a serious political and social issue in view of their history. Moreover, even from an economic standpoint, we must also consider that monopoly of foreign capital will lead to the repatriation of rents' (sic).[76]

Although continual consensus between the major powers should not be assumed, it is still true that they dominate in terms of voting power and that the IMF suffers from a lack of input legitimacy as a result of under-representation by the developing countries. Moreover, as a result of loan conditionality, where developing states and the former socialist countries are concerned, decision-making power by the international financial institutions has increased at the expense of state autonomy. Thus some have described the 'political regulation in this emerging (dis)order as a twofold division between local *responsibility without power* and the supra-national exercise of *power without responsibility*.'[77]

It was argued earlier that for the majority of developing countries, the experience of structural adjustment has not been a happy one and therefore the output legitimacy of the IMF has suffered accordingly with many questioning its future. At the same time, the IMF is currently confronting certain challenges because of the changing international financial environment. As a result of Argentina ($10bn) and Brazil ($15bn) paying back their loans early, the amount of outstanding loans has fallen dramatically. After 25 years of lending relatively large amounts, new loans have fallen to levels not seen since the 1970s and amounted to a mere $2.5 billion for 2005. This not only raises the question of the IMF's future role, but also how it will continue to function given that it relies on the interest payments it receives to fund its activities.[78] Martin Wolf has recently argued that the IMF will remain relevant in the future because it provides several categories of public goods: 'information; analysis; advice to individual governments; advice on coordination of policies; management of defaults; and emergency lending'.[79] However, it is precisely because of its poor performance concerning economic outcomes that its advice and analysis are currently being called into question.

In relation to the World Trade Organization, a rather different relationship obtains. Developing countries are confronted with unfair competition from the industrialized countries but because of their dire need for access to markets and in the hope of influencing future trade initiatives, these countries actively participate in the WTO. The situation is therefore more accurately described as one of structural dependence rather than compellance. The previous section indicated that issues of inequality continue to surround the trading arrangements that have thus far been agreed, particularly concerning the bias towards manufactured goods and services and the fact that northern agribusiness continues to be heavily subsidized. The WTO therefore also suffers from a lack of output legitimacy.

However, because of the more equitable representative basis of this institution (each member state has a vote and recourse to the Dispute Settlements Body) it has the potential of possessing greater input-legitimacy than many other international institutions. However, although the WTO has provided some opportunities for developing countries to challenge certain decisions by the industrialized countries many hurdles remain. First, there is an issue of procedural justice. Although in principle any member state can bring a case to the Dispute Settlements Body, in practice many developing countries are reluctant to do so because of the legal costs involved. Injustices surrounding unfair trade practices or intellectual property rights may abound, but these may go unchallenged by developing states simply because of the costs involved. For example, the 'EC, Japan and the US were complainants in almost half (143 of 305) of all bilateral disputes in the WTO Dispute Settlement system between 1995 and 2002. By contrast the 49 members classified by the UN as Less Developed Countries did not bring a single challenge in that period'.[80] There is thus a strong case for the WTO to provide public legal assistance, the costs to be borne by all member states. The mechanism should also be redistributive with contributions based on some measure of the member states' wealth, such as GDP.

Second, greater transparency during trade negotiations is critical. In the previous Uruguay Round, many countries were excluded from important discussions because of the so-called 'Green Room' process whereby a select group of states, chosen by the director-general or chairperson, would meet and achieve consensus on important policy issues and then present them to other states. Rather like the ripples from a pebble dropped in a pond, the consensus would be carried forward by the momentum of more and more states agreeing to the proposals and a critical point would be reached where those that disagreed finally realized that they had lost the battle.[81] This process has now been abandoned, but asymmetries in the number of trade specialists each country can staff and the information at their disposal still remain. Some of these problems could be overcome by providing impact assessments of potential trade agreements to all member states.[82]

Third, there is an issue of enforcement powers that states possess through the WTO. If a country takes a case to the settlement body and is successful, the country is then given the right to impose additional tariffs on exports from the offending country. However, even if a developing country were to impose such sanctions, the effects on a major economic power would be minor. The converse does not hold true. Thus, '[I]n practice, the WTO system has no effective way of enforcing penalties against an unfair trade action whose main impact is on small developing countries'.[83] Although these categories are best classified under procedural justice, they eventually lead to unequal or unfair outcomes and thus impact upon the institution's output legitimacy.

The South is also aware that the single undertaking mandate of the WTO 'compels governments to accept agreements as a complete package rather than on an individual basis' thus confronting them with an all or nothing option.[84] For these reasons it is more difficult to mediate political differences amongst its members because the North can no longer compel the South to adopt policies that favour the former. Given the current stalled status of the Doha Round it would seem that it remains extremely difficult to reconcile such differences. The Doha Declaration of November 2001 stated that there is a need 'for all our peoples to benefit from the increased opportunities and welfare gains that the multilateral trading system generates'.[85] The future legitimacy of the WTO depends heavily upon the outcome of the Doha Round, the delivery of such promises and the creation of a more equitable trade regime.

One author has argued that the current process at the international level represents coercive socialization in which 'interaction within a highly unequal international system leads to the adoption and incorporation of external ideas, norms and practices. As part of the process of internalization, historically embedded conceptions of interest shift, actors reevaluate their political options, organizational structures are revised, and a changing institutional context provides the framework for an evolving set of bargains between state and society'.[86] However, there is scant evidence that this is occurring within North–South relations. Rather, many developing countries feel that they are compelled to adopt the adjustment programmes recommended by the IMF. Concerning the world trade system, they feel that they are structurally dependent upon trade with the North and although GATT and the WTO have not served their interests well, for now it is better to be a member and attempt to improve the situation through trade reform.

Practicable policy prescriptions

Since the turn of the millennium several important milestones have been reached concerning the crisis in the South. The Conference on Financing for Development of March 2002 established some basic principles and objectives that became known as the Monterrey Consensus (after the site of the conference). The consensus entailed a compact between the industrialized and developing states wherein the former would increase their overseas development assistance and the latter would commit to good government plus social and economic reforms. However, these commitments were, by and large, non-binding, although the USA and the EU did declare that they would 'increase their aid by US $12bn per annum from 2006'. But what was particularly significant was the acceptance by both sides of certain responsibilities and the need for change.[87]

Following on from this understanding, concrete commitments by the industrialized countries were finally undertaken at the G8 meeting that took place in the United Kingdom at Gleneagles in July 2005. The obligations agreed mark a major move towards debt cancellation and increased aid to developing countries. The increase in aid to around $50 billion over the next five years with $25 billion promised specifically for Africa in addition to the 100 per cent debt cancellation, including debt stock, for 18 HIPC countries with a possible nine more to be included at a later stage represents a significant step forward, albeit a rather tardy one.[88] Despite the package not meeting the expectations of many, it will have a positive and relatively quick impact on those countries that have been granted debt cancellation. The plan is for the immediate cancellation of debt totalling $40 billion for the first 18 countries and then a further 9 countries once they are eligible under the HIPC programme's conditions. If all 38 countries finally qualify, the total package will amount to $55 billion.[89] Moreover, the debt cancellation should not come at the expense of the usual aid contributions via official development assistance, although questions over whether countries really will honour such an agreement have already been raised.[90]

As we saw in Chapter Five, by 1998 African total external debt had reached $324 billion (108 per cent of GNP) whilst Latin American external debt had risen to $786 billion (58 per cent of GNP) with Africa being $55 billion in arrears.[91] For particular countries the situation was even more dire, for example, in 1999, Guinea-Bissau had a debt that was equivalent to 366 per cent of its GNP; Somalia 307 per cent; Nicaragua 306 per cent. For those countries that are most heavily indebted these debts act as an iron cage, preventing them from providing even the most basic of welfare provision. For instance, in 1995, 46 per cent of Tanzania's central government expenditure was spent in debt servicing and only 15 per cent on basic social services; for Zambia it was 40 per cent and only 7 per cent on basic social services; and for Niger it was 33 per cent and 11 per cent respectively. The region with the highest level of debt, Sub-Saharan Africa, had more than double the amount of debt to GNP compared to any other region.[92] It is also the region with the highest increases in poverty in the last two decades, almost doubling from 164 million living on less than $1 PPP a day in 1981 to 314 million in 2001.[93]

The package of debt cancellation will thus provide much-needed relief to these countries, allowing them to allocate more of their resources to the welfare needs of their populations. However, at the same time as announcing these aid and debt programmes, some leaders have also argued that the long-term solution to these countries' problems lies in trade reform. In particular, they have singled out the agriculture subsidies of the industrialized countries, which amount to approximately a billion dollars a day.[94] The elimination of such subsidies would have a significant impact upon economic growth for less developed countries.[95] However, such reforms have to go much further to have a long-term impact upon the growth prospects of these countries. The reforms suggested would appear still to be based upon the principles of unfettered free trade, which, it is thought, will eventually benefit less-developed countries. This chapter questions the evidence upon which this assumption is based and puts forward an alternative approach; one which would help nurture embryonic industrialization within the less developed countries.

The removal of agricultural subsidies has thus become a priority of the first order. Under the Doha or 'Development Round' of talks, it would appear that the elimination of export subsidies could go ahead, but domestic farm subsidies remains unresolved. Developing countries continue to suspect that the industrialized countries will simply redefine or create new subsidies and shift them into different categories. Indeed, recent negotiations suggest that some industrialized countries are endeavouring to shift some of their subsidies to categories with less stringent restrictions attached thereby avoiding fundamental reforms.[96] But if industrialized countries are sincere in their stated wish to see an improvement in the economies of developing countries, then both export and domestic subsidy support must be radically reduced. Clearly, this will run into entrenched opposition from various interested parties in the US, Japan and Europe.

There is also a need to provide support for the developing countries' transition to more open economies. In order to compete internationally, products from these countries have to be on par with similar products from around the world. They also need the managerial skills, technology and general infrastructure in order to successfully integrate into the world economy – '[W]ithout assistance to overcome gaps in infrastructure, boost product quality and connect to international supply chains, tariff cuts have little effect on trade from the poorest countries.'[97] To that end, industrialized countries could provide much-needed technical assistance and investment specifically earmarked for such transitions. Indeed, as part of the Doha Round, Japan has pledged $10 billion in order to improve production and increase trade from developing countries by providing 'technical cooperation for projects such as improving ports, customs facilities and training'.[98] Hopefully, others will follow its lead.

However, in addition to the elimination or radical reduction of such subsidies, the trade arrangements for special and differential treatment for less developed and least developed countries should be enhanced. A large variety of non-reciprocal tariff arrangements currently exist, including those that provide for reductions on MFN duty rates under the Generalized System of Preferences (GSP). There are also non-reciprocal tariff arrangements with least developed countries that involve duty free and quota free access to the recipient country's domestic market. These include: Canada's Least Developed Country Tariff; ACP–EU partnership (African, Caribbean, Pacific) and the Everything But Guns (EBG) initiative for least developed countries; Japan's special treatment for Least Developed Countries; and the United States' African Growth and Opportunity Act (AGOA). While such moves have had some impact, several improvements can be made. Given that the least developed countries' share of world exports has declined from 3.06 per cent in 1954 to just 0.42 per cent in 1998, further initiatives are needed.[99] These include the expansion of countries included; for example, AGOA covers only 37 countries at the moment and although originally an initiative focused solely on Africa it could be modified to include all least developed countries. The arrangements should be modified to grant full duty free and quota free treatment (DFQFT) for the least developed countries. At the moment these various arrangements cover differing arrays of goods; the situation would be much improved if a uniform approach was adopted and the range of goods increased to cover all products from these countries *a la* the European Union's 'Everything But Arms' initiative.

The recent Gleneagles Communiqué lent support to the further intensification of South–South trade.[100] One way of attaining this is for the rules of origin applied to DFQFT to be changed permitting global cumulation allowing for inputs not only from other Least Developed Countries but also from other GSP countries (although a certain minimum input from Least Developed Countries should be retained thus ensuring that they remain the main beneficiaries).[101] For the Least Developed Countries, non-reciprocal unilateral preferences should be given to services from these countries. This may seem controversial given the recent concerns that have been raised with regard to job losses in the industrialized world arising from the out-sourcing of services, but one needs to bear in mind that the Least Developed Countries currently capture only 0.4 per cent of world exports of commercial services. It is estimated that such reforms could lead to exports gains of $6.4 billion annual increase in Least Developed Countries' exports and a targeted services package could lead to anywhere between $10 to $20 billion a year extra.[102]

Although such gains will bring significant benefits, it is also vital that the proposed form of tariff reductions currently proposed under the Doha Round by

Box 7.2 Trade reform

Agricultural subsidies

Agricultural subsidies of the industrialized countries currently amount to approximately a billion dollars a day. A situation in which the subsidy per cow in the European Union is 'higher than the income of more than half the world's population' cannot be construed as free and fair trade.[1] The removal of agricultural subsidies is thus of paramount importance. Under the Doha or 'Development Round' of talks, this issue has come to the fore, but is as yet unresolved.

An alternative Development Round Trade Agreement

Alternatives to the current trade proposals abound, two are presented here:

Flexible but bounded tariffs

One suggested alternative is to allow developing states the freedom to choose which sectors of the economy to apply tariffs to: 'subject to the overall constraint of an average bound tariff, such an approach would balance multilateral discipline with policy flexibility'.[2] For example, there is little reason for developing countries to apply high tariffs in the medium- or high-technology sectors if their economies are not yet producing such goods. They could thus lower duties on such imported goods, while, say, maintaining relatively high protective duties on resource-based, labour-intensive and low-technology goods. The tariffs could then be shifted to other sectors such as medium- and high-technology goods once a country has embarked upon this form of production.

Market access proposal

Another proposal is for all countries to provide free market access to 'all developing countries poorer and smaller than themselves'.[3] A relatively rich country would, under such a proposal, have an obligation to open up its markets to poorer countries. However, those poorer countries would not have to reciprocate in kind, but would have to open their markets to countries poorer than themselves. The Market Access Proposal (MAP) would thus promote free trade and bring great benefits for the poorest

---

(continued)

Box 7.2 Continued

countries of the world. Middle income countries would go along with such an agreement because they would then benefit from market access to the richest countries, such as Europe, Japan and the United States. The proposal continues to promote general free trade through adhering to Most Favoured Nation (MFN) tariffs already agreed and does not exclude the possibility of further agreements on an MFN basis.[4]

1 L. Elliot, 'Stop treating debtors as poor cows', *The Guardian*, 23 September 2002 and *The Economist*, 'Unpicking cotton subsidies', 30 April–6 May 2005.
2 Y. Akyüz, *The WTO Negotiations on Industrial Tariffs: what is at stake for developing countries*, Geneva: Third World Network, 2005. Online. Available http://www.twnside.org (accessed 3 August 2005), p. 28.
3 J. Stiglitz and A. Charlton, *Fair Trade For All*, p. 94.
4 Ibid., pp. 94–102.

the industrialized countries are not the ones finally agreed upon. What is required is a mechanism through which nascent industries in the South are somehow protected whilst also integrating these countries further into the world economy. In short, the policies of the international financial institutions and the trading practices between these states and the industrialized countries should return to some of the principles of 'embedded liberalism' that guided the post-Second World War international economy for three decades.[103] In the current climate although a return to all of the principles that underpinned 'embedded liberalism' is unlikely, it would appear that the G8 now regard development of the South as a primary objective. But, in addition, if the Doha Round of trade talks is to live up to its name as the 'development round', then positive evidence is required that this latest round does 'place their needs and interests at the heart of the Work Programme'.[104]

One suggested way forward is to allow developing states to be 'free to choose their applied tariffs for individual industries/products subject to the overall constraint of an average bound tariff, such an approach would balance multilateral discipline with policy flexibility'.[105] This has the merit of avoiding line-by-line tariff reductions and instead allows developing countries the freedom to choose to which sectors of the economy such tariffs should be applied. For example, there is little reason for developing countries to apply high tariffs in the medium- or high-technology sectors if their economies are not yet producing such goods (although of course they would lose some fiscal income). They could thus lower duties on such imported goods, while, say, maintaining relatively high protective duties on resource-based, labour-intensive and low-technology goods. The tariffs could then be shifted to other sectors such as medium- and high-technology goods once a country has embarked upon this form of production.

Another possibility put forward by Joseph Stiglitz and Andrew Charlton is for all countries to provide free market access to 'all developing countries poorer and smaller than themselves'.[106] A relatively rich country would, under such a proposal, have an obligation to open up its markets to poorer countries. However, those poorer countries would not have to reciprocate in kind, but would have to open their markets to countries poorer than themselves. Such countries could be easily identified by their GDP and GDP per capita. The Market Access Proposal (MAP) would thus promote free trade and bring great benefits for the poorest countries of the world. Middle-income countries would go along with such an agreement because they would then benefit from market access to the richest countries, such as those in Europe and Japan and the United States. The proposal continues to promote general free trade through adhering to Most Favoured Nation (MFN) tariffs already agreed and does not exclude the possibility of further agreements on an MFN basis.[107] The main weakness of this approach is that there is very little in it for the richest nations. However, if they are serious about promoting a fairer trading regime this should not necessarily prevent them from supporting such a move.

There are thus several feasible ways forward under the auspices of the Doha Round of trade talks that could secure a fairer trade regime for the developing world. The new round of trade talks began promisingly with what appeared to be a fresh determination to address the issues of the South with the possibility of significant reductions in tariffs or even in the elimination of tariffs 'in particular on products of export interest to developing countries'[108] However, although the Doha Round's emphasis was supposed to be on development, the talks have evolved into an agriculture for manufacturing and services deals and are currently (2006) mired in a tough bargaining process with little tangible progress.[109] As the Indian trade minister put it, the Doha Round now lies 'between intensive care and the crematorium'. Whether it can be rescued and still live up to its declared objective of development for the South, only time will tell.[110]

Less rather than more governance?

Although the aid and debt relief outlined at the beginning is to be welcomed, the debt write-off is conditional. It requires the countries concerned to follow IMF PRGF (Poverty Reduction and Growth Facility) programmes. These were introduced in 1999 by the IMF as an alternative to their Structural Adjustment Programs and as a result of the failure of their initial debt reduction initiative (the Heavily Indebted Poor Countries initiative began in 1996, but by 1999 only three countries had become eligible). Lending is now subject to approval of national Poverty Reduction Strategy Papers (PRSPs). With the launch of the World Bank's Comprehensive Development Framework, it would thus seem that the emphasis has shifted towards poverty reduction and a set of policy prescriptions arrived at through collaboration between the World Bank, IMF and recipient states. This is an improvement upon previous procedures because the country requesting the loan is given the responsibility of drawing up long-term plans for economic growth and poverty reduction, but it still requires final approval by the IMF and thus tends to conform to the macro-economic policies favoured by that institution. The fact that the debt relief is conditional upon countries following PRGF programmes thus ensures that these countries remain 'caught in a complex of IMF and World Bank eligibility conditions'.[111]

Critics have pointed out that these programmes more often than not result in the privatization of key sectors of the economy often leading to higher costs for services and the reduction of subsidies for the most vulnerable. In addition, it is argued, it remains the case that *'export-led growth as the route to development is not held up for scrutiny, but rather assumed as common sense'*.[112] Historically, IMF policies have often resulted in these countries relying on their primary commodity sector for foreign currency earnings. As we have seen, despite many countries following structural adjustment policies since 1979, the per capita GDP growth in Latin America was only 0.8 per cent between 1978 and 1998; for Africa per capita growth was virtually non-existent at 0.1 per cent. In addition, the UNDP has asserted that '[N]o fewer than 100 countries – all developing or in transition have experienced serious economic decline over the past three decades. As a result per capita income in these 100 countries is lower than it was 10, 20, even 30 years ago.[113] Given that this was during a period of increased activity in the developing world by the IMF and World Bank, their policies have been questionable at the very least. Many therefore argue that debt write-offs should be de-linked from these countries adhering to IMF PGRFs; instead it should be based solely upon submission and approval of a Poverty Reduction Strategy Paper, preferably not under IMF auspices but through some new independent body composed of representatives both from states and from civil society.[114]

Therefore, it is not only that these institutions need to address certain issues of representational justice, but they also need to allow greater state autonomy in relation to their economic policies. Critics point out that the policies prescribed by the World Bank and the IMF are not the ones that were followed by the industrialized states themselves during their early stages of economic development: '[I]n reality, the relationship between trade openness and growth is likely to be contingent on a host of internal and external factors. That nearly all of today's industrial countries embarked on their growth behind tariff barriers, and reduced protection only subsequently, surely offers a clue…it is also true that no country has developed simply by opening itself to foreign trade and investment. The trick has been to combine the opportunities offered by global markets with strategies for domestic investment and institution building, to stimulate domestic entrepreneurs.'[115] What is good for the goose should be good for the gander.

The frequent example of success often cited is the developmental state model of East Asia. Although there are many differences in the economic policies of each of these countries and some aspects of their policies have been criticized, until the economic crisis of 1997 the growth of East Asia had far outstripped any other region of the world for several decades. Indeed, for a quarter of a century (1965–90) the eight high-performing economies (Japan, Hong Kong, South Korea, Singapore, Taiwan, Indonesia, Malaysia and Thailand) sustained double the growth of any other region, including the OECD countries.[116] As we saw in Chapter Three, Asia's growth is in large part due to its success in capturing a significant portion of the world market in both the secondary and tertiary sectors. In terms of the latter, it has already been pointed out that Asia's share of world trade in services has increased dramatically in the last two decades and now stands at 16.8 per cent. In addition, placing greater emphasis on secondary production has had positive economic benefits for the countries of Asia.

As a result of East Asia's success, many view a more active role for the state as instrumental in developing a country's economy. '[T]he awesome paradox of free-market capitalism in this revolutionary era is that the poorer nations that have succeeded most spectacularly during the last three decades are ones that exercised stringent controls over capital. They restricted the cross border flows of foreign capital and their own domestic wealth by quantity or quality. They purposefully steered capital to selected domestic industries and away from other sectors closed to outsiders. On the whole it worked. At least, the fastest-rising economies in the world all followed variations on this basic economic strategy'.[117] Given the enormity of the task confronting developing states in attempting to compete economically and to produce high levels of sustainable growth, it is argued that the state needs to intervene actively in the economy in order to ensure the success of national industries. It would be impossible for these embryonic industries to compete on a level playing field with the technologically advanced industrialized countries. Active intervention by the state is needed, it is argued, in order to ameliorate the otherwise overly harsh economic competition that they would face. Such intervention, though, is a complex affair often requiring different policies for different sectors of the economy.[118]

Arguments for greater state autonomy should not be confused with calls for autarky. East Asia would not have developed as rapidly as it did without integration into the world economy (although there were of course several other external factors, such as US support during the Cold War). Trade and FDI can, if managed correctly, act as conveyor belts of knowledge. Once an embryonic industry has successfully established itself, the gradual opening of a state's borders permitting some international competition can provide critical market feedback and stimulate further improvements in production. Similarly, FDI, particularly in the form of joint ventures, can be an important source of both technical and managerial knowledge. Whether liberalization is successful will, however, depend very much on the active participation of the state. The state can actively promote the dissemination of this knowledge by encouraging joint ventures, but also by helping to establish domestic competitors to the MNCs through the provision of subsidies and tax breaks. Attracting at least some of those who have worked in such joint ventures to newly established domestic industries will ensure that best practice in managerial techniques and information concerning industrial processing will be emulated. Similarly, the state can serve a critical role concerning trade. By ensuring these industries are protected in the first instance and by providing subsidies and/or tax incentives, states can nurture the green shoots of domestic industries. However, government intervention should not just be limited to so-called 'selective policies'.

Developing states also need to ensure there is the requisite level of technical skill amongst the workforce. This will involve identifying key technical skills required by industry and providing the requisite training. Such 'horizontal policies' also require investment in R & D facilities providing the technical inputs required by industry.[119]

As Dani Rodrik points out, all of this requires high levels of domestic investment.[120] Debt cancellation or reduction combined with increases in ODA will enable many countries to channel vital resources into some of these activities. As was indicated earlier, previously extremely high levels of government expenditure had to be earmarked for debt servicing. This is an extremely important first step, but even more money is needed for investment. Some of this may come from the increases in primary product prices that have occurred in the last few years as a result of the general global economic upswing, but mainly from China's insatiable demand for raw materials. In addition, various ways of providing such investment funds have been put forward, such as a Tobin Tax on currency exchange and an international aviation fuel tax.[121] But a new Basel Accord specifically addressing the needs of developing states would also be an important step forward. At the moment, the high sovereign risk weighting of developing states means that the international financial institutions are reluctant to invest and when they do, a high interest rate is charged to reflect this risk. An important first step would be a new requirement that a certain percentage of international bank lending be dedicated to developing states.

Will such policies ensure economic success? The most obvious weakness with such strategies is that, as we have seen, if the market becomes saturated, then prices and profits will decline. The only protection against such a possibility is diversification and innovation. As was explained earlier, innovatory products can attract higher profits because of the initial absence of competition. In a global market, it is therefore insufficient merely to tread water; rather, firms have to establish continually either innovatory industrial processes (involving either cost-saving techniques or improvements in product quality) or innovatory products.

The weakness of the above approach is that such policies are geared towards stimulating growth, but this does not guarantee a reduction in poverty nor greater equality. As Chapter Five demonstrated, the oft-cited corollary of the Heckscher–Ohlin model that inequality should decline as a country opens itself to trade may not apply in all cases. Once again, it is argued that the original 'Asian Tigers' were quite successful in this regard – '[B]roadly similar historical circumstances led each regime to pursue shared growth as a strategy for legitimating its rule … The leaders recognized the importance to their survival of improving the living standards of the less well-off'.[122] The state, it is argued, directly intervened 'to persuade the elites to share the benefits of growth with the middle class and the poor. Finally, to win the cooperation of the middle class and the poor, the leaders had to show them that they would indeed benefit from the future growth'.[123] At the international level, the IMF has made an important step in the right direction by recognizing the importance of ensuring that economic growth also benefits the worse off in society through its promotion of pro-poor growth strategies.

Conclusion

Through collective action and the aggregation of their capabilities, northern states possess the wherewithal to monitor and control the plethora of economic activities that have blossomed at the international level in the last few decades. Chapter Two demonstrated that international trade, foreign direct investment and international financial activity are at a post-Second World War high, but this does not necessarily imply that the industrialized states now find themselves in a strait-jacket incapable of constraining the worst excesses of the international economy. Indeed, there is good evidence that these states have actively promoted economic globalization, at least in some aspects, in a very similar manner to those states labelled by Linda Weiss as 'catalytic states'. Many of the industrialized states have played an astute political game of double standards. Through international or regional bodies (for example, the IMF, World Bank, OECD), they have actively promoted economic liberalization, yet blamed the very forces that they have chosen to unleash for the economic woes within their borders. Some of these woes may be as a result of globalization, but as was demonstrated in Chapter Five many of the difficulties these countries face concerning welfare spending are to do with internal demographics rather than external economic pressures from without.

Politicians have been more than willing to sidestep their responsibilities and shift the blame onto the faceless forces of globalization thereby depoliticizing many critical (and very political) decisions concerning the economy. Thus far, the industrialized states have been able to maintain both their share of international trade and of foreign direct investment. Although many northern countries have suffered from economic dislocation, these states possess the economic wherewithal to compensate their workforces and re-orientate their economies to these challenges. By and large, opposition to liberalization has not thus far been of sufficient strength to force a reversal of such policies. Despite there being good arguments for greater control of the economic sphere and for some form of redistributive taxation (redistributed to the developing nations) to be applied to the super-profits accrued by international financial institutions, this is unlikely to happen in the near future. But if globalization were to impact significantly on the economic well-being of large sections of the population in the North, then it may well be that we will witness a roll back of the economic liberalization that we have seen in the last few decades and for a far greater level of control to be imposed on such activities. Concerning the industrialized states, more governance may be better, but is unlikely in the near future.

With regard to the developing states of the South, this chapter has indicated that the main international financial institutions need to address the issues of representational justice, procedural justice and the consequences of their policies (output legitimacy). Currently, there are moves to increase the voting power of several developing states in both the IMF and World Bank, but, as we have seen, this is unlikely to alter dramatically the voting power of the most powerful states. Although the constitutional basis of the WTO is such that all states are represented, reforms are required to ensure greater procedural justice. Full and free access to impact assessment information concerning proposed trade agreements to all member-states should be made compulsory. In addition, the transaction costs involved in bringing a case to the Dispute Settlement Body are clearly unaffordable for most of the developing states. The creation of a legal advice council providing public legal assistance with the running costs paid by all members on an ability to pay basis would go a long way in the right direction.[124] In the long term, improved input legitimacy and procedural fairness will produce fairer outcomes and improve the output legitimacy of these institutions.

Some of the proposals suggested above may appear unrealisable at the moment, but in recent years there has been a noticeable shift towards greater international support for these states. Concerning trade reform, the proposals chime with the overall intentions of the Doha Declarations which stated that the talks would 'make positive efforts designed to ensure that developing countries, and especially the least-developed among them, secure a share in the growth of world trade commensurate with the needs of their economic development'.[125] Similarly, the more recent Gleneagles Summit urged a conclusion to the Doha Round, which the G8 regarded as having 'the potential to help lift millions out of poverty'.[126] The historical analysis of the changing patterns of trade given earlier would suggest that if this is to happen, much needs to be done to change the current situation and the sooner the better.

The World Bank and IMF have often been criticized for their 'one size fits all' remedy for the economic problems confronting most of the developing world. Rather than applying general economic policies albeit with some recognition of local conditions, it would be better for states to have a much greater say in their own development. In other words, 'both of these public financial powers have to develop greater respect for the indigenous strategies for growth, promoting a more patient development of domestic economic foundations instead of simply enforcing the financial imperatives of the global system'.[127] It is hoped that greater national autonomy will also lead to greater economic diversity, a move away from the production of highly similar products and therefore towards a less saturated international market. Where the South is concerned, less, rather than more, governance may therefore be better.

The IMF has endeavoured to reply to such criticism by moving away from the imposition of Structural Adjustment Policies to the countries concerned to follow IMF PRGF programmes. However, loans under the PRGF are still subject to IMF scrutiny and must adhere to certain macro-economic policies set out by the Fund. Thus it is argued that the 'core mandate of the Fund remains unchanged, even if it may appear softer around the edges'.[128] However, individual industrialized countries may be moving away from this decades-old approach. A recent Department for International Development paper (March 2005) would seem to suggest that the UK, at least, is willing to contemplate a radical redrawing of policy. The paper stated that '[W]e will not force trade liberalization on developing countries either through trade negotiations or aid conditionality'.[129] At the same time, others, such as Japan, have recognized the crucial importance of investment in both human capital and infrastructure in enabling developing states to take-off economically.

Some have also seen the reforms at the IMF and World Bank not merely as an exercise in 'paradigm maintenance' but as a true paradigm shift; it has been argued that 'by retaining the idea of prudential macro-economic management, yet rejecting the notion of "neutral" or "intervention-free" trade regimes, and embracing the idea of state effectiveness, neoclassical thinking can be seen to share common ground with the institutional analysis of the so-called "new political economy"'.[130] But athough there appears to be a new consensus forming at the World Bank and IMF that they need to be more sensitive to the economic effects of their policies on the poor, a fundamental reassessment of the positive role the state may play in promoting economic growth has not yet occurred.[131] An over-emphasis on free trade and the diminution of the state's intervention in the economy still remains, despite its lack of success. New policies need to be introduced; ones that produce a more favourable investment and trade environment for developing states and a less top-down approach that provides these states with a greater degree of autonomy.

8   Conclusion

This book began by arguing that globalization encapsulates both changes and continuities and has been driven by a combination of underlying and proximate causes. Capitalism was identified as a central dynamic behind the process of globalization. The pressure to reduce costs has driven companies to look farther afield for cheaper material inputs and labour. At the same time, it is imperative that circulation time be reduced as much as is feasibly possible. There is therefore a strong incentive to invest in new forms of transport that will shorten the time between producing a product and selling it in its designated market. Because of the inevitability of market saturation, capitalism also produces an expansionary dynamic, establishing new markets for commodities wherever they can be found. However, the current epoch is marked by important new developments in technology and the promotion of neo-liberal economic policies across the globe.

The advent of these new technologies has produced significant innovations in both retailing and production. The development of EDI and EPOS have provided the means through which retailers can minimize their inventory, relying instead upon daily sales feedback and deliveries that reflect the changing demands of the consumer. At the production end, technology has enabled manufacturers to move to flexible production techniques that allow for far greater variety and far less wasteful stockpiling of materials through the application of the 'Just in Time' philosophy. The development of ultra-efficient supply chains has led companies to move away from the idea of the vertically integrated organization encompassing all of the activities relating to a product. Increasingly, companies prefer to outsource much of the production activity to external suppliers – 'organizations are now focusing on their "core business" – in other words the things they do really well and where they have a differential advantage.'[1] Product Life-cycle Management software allows such companies not only to design and manage their products, but also to coordinate tasks across the globe.

The impact of such technological innovations and industrial restructuring were clearly evidenced by the increases in vertical specialization that countries across the globe are now engaged in. Chapter Three indicated that measuring the degree of vertical specialization, i.e. the level of country involvement in just one or two sections of a larger production process, is rather difficult. But several studies have tried to capture how common this is by measuring the number of imported goods entering a country that are used as inputs for products that are then exported to other countries. By doing so, it was estimated that this form of production can constitute up to 30 per cent of overall trade (for example, in the cases of South Korea, Ireland and Taiwan). This global integration of the production process was also very much apparent between countries of the South as well as between the North and South. South–South trade now accounts for 43 per cent of their total trade. East Asia accounts for the majority of this, reflecting the enmeshment of this region in the international manufacturing trade network and its countries' increasing involvement in vertical specialization.

However, technology may have enabled increases in trade and finance between countries and the integration of production processes, but in the last half-century this has been spurred on by America's promotion (with the cooperation of others) of neo-liberal economics with its strong emphasis on trade and capital liberalization. Several international organizations, such as the OECD, IMF and World Bank, have been central to the promotion of such policies. It has been a central theme of this book that the debt accumulated by the developing world during the 1970s and the ensuing debt crisis were used primarily by the United States as leverage to get these countries to adopt neo-liberal economic policies. The IMF's decision in 1979 to make lending to developing states conditional upon their adoption of structural adjustment policies marked a watershed both in terms of its relationship with these countries and in the spread of neo-liberal economics. Its influence became all the greater with the collapse of the Berlin Wall in 1989 and the final dissolution of the Soviet Union at the end of 1991. Although the actual degree of implementation of these policies varied, the objective was global in nature, because the IMF sought to promote neo-liberalism throughout the transition countries and developing world.

At the same time, other international institutions have been critical to the development of common standards across the world. Such standard setting is not always necessary when particular practices or devices prove to be popular world-wide. An obvious case is the common architecture adopted for personal computers as a result of the success of IBM's personal computer range in the 1980s. However, in many circumstances these international institutions have helped establish financial, legal and technical standards across the world. This has facilitated, to name but a few aspects: the integration of supply chains; the integration of companies on a global scale; communications between people, businesses and systems; the creation of global products (by complying with common health and safety standards); and the creation of global markets through agreements concerning common intellectual property rights. For example, common accounting procedures have provided confidence to those seeking to pursue investment, merger and acquisition opportunities. Without the enormous amount of computer protocols, the seamless electronic systems that business relies upon would not be possible.

Chapter Four described the economic arguments and evidence behind this pursuit of greater trade and capital liberalization. These policies are said to produce strong rates of growth, which in turn will lift large numbers of the population out of poverty. As we have seen, some go further and argue that such growth may even be possible without further increasing the levels of inequality within these states. However, there are many reasons to question such assertions. Others have questioned the manner in which the 'globalizers' (those states that have pursued economic liberalization strongly) were chosen for these studies. In contrast, their research indicates that the liberalization–solid growth link is highly questionable. Indeed, very recently, the World Bank established an academic panel to examine its research projects. They concluded that the Bank often took 'new and untested results as hard evidence that its preferred policies work' and, moreover, used this research to 'proselytise on behalf of bank policy'.[2]

Critics of this over-reliance on liberalization compare the GDP per capita growth rates in the period before neo-liberal economic reforms were implemented with the period after. In contradistinction to the above finding, which claims that greater benefits have accrued to those states that have liberalized their economies, they find that the GDP growth rate per capita was significantly higher in previous less liberalized periods. Chapter Three of this book also indicated that the last few decades have registered extremely disappointing results for the developing world concerning their share of relative trade and foreign direct investment. It was established that, with the exception of East and South-East Asia, the developing world's share of world trade has declined significantly. In terms of merchandise exports, since the fifties Latin America's share of world trade has halved. Africa's share has also more than halved since the fifties and has the lowest share of world exports at some 2.4 per cent. If one takes the developing world as a whole, then in terms of the proportion of world inward FDI stock, stasis best describes the last few decades of economic activity.

Although much of this can be explained by the worsening terms of trade and the failure of these countries to move up the value chain into higher technology products and services, other factors are also involved in these shifting patterns. First, it should be pointed out that the relative share of world trade and investment accruing to the developing world as a whole has remained quite stable. However, East Asia's (and to a lesser extent South-East Asia's) share has increased to such a degree that it now takes up a much larger portion than any other region. Second, important qualitative changes are also occurring within the northern bloc. Two main aspects were identified: the increasing levels of regional intra-industrial trade and vertical specialization. It was found that intra-regional trade has increased both as a result of further product differentiation leading to high levels of intra-industrial trade, but also more recently because of the relocation of production sites and out-sourcing within the regional bloc taking advantage of cheaper labour outside the major economic powerhouses of the region concerned. The last few decades have thus witnessed further economic integration within regional blocs and an intensification of trade between East Asia and the core industrialized states.

It was also found that a clear triadization of FDI had occurred, with the North as a whole maintaining their high levels of FDI from other counties. Various reasons were put forward to explain this. Some of these overseas production sites may be aimed at replacing trade and overcoming significant non-tariff barriers. However, companies not only engage in marketing and distribution but also produce goods within the other two legs of the triad. FDI may also occur within the triad to take advantage of research clusters or to have production sites close to markets. In other words, the reasons for investment very much depend on the type of production companies are engaged in. For example, it is more likely that companies involved in heavy industry will set up production sites in the country concerned than will companies involved in information technology where the components/finished product can be transported long distances relatively cheaply.

The intensification of intra-industry trade and vertical specialization within regions explains many of the trading patterns that are emerging. Similarly the patterns of FDI investment can also be partially explained by the internal dynamics both within and between the areas of the triad. However, such dynamics do not explain why the greatest increases in North–South trade and investment can be found in East and South-East Asia. Although this region continues to supply large volumes of basic commodities, such as textiles, they have also managed to become embedded in the supply chain for higher value-added manufactured goods in the low-, medium- and high-technology sectors, and this is reflected in their shares of world exports, supplying both intermediate and final products to the northern industrialized core. East Asian trading activity accounts for two-thirds of this South–South trade mainly as a result of vertical specialization with countries providing intermediate products within a larger production process. These countries are therefore not only involved in producing final products for exporting abroad, but have become embedded within complex global production chains. Given that there has been a shift in favour of higher technology exports world-wide and a move towards increasing levels of vertical specialization, it is likely that we will see a further marginalization of those countries that do not, or cannot, engage in such activity.

Paradoxically, it was found that much of the success of East Asia was as a result of the direct intervention of the state in the running of the economy. As a regional grouping these countries stand out from other developing states by their success both in industrializing and capturing a significant segment of world trade. Chapter Four argued that this third phase of industrialization possessed its own unique characteristics. Instead of achieving rents through innovation, these countries' form of industrialization was based on acquiring the technical know-how to establish a similar manufacturing base to that of the North. Once they had acquired this knowledge, the strategy seems to have been to produce higher quality goods at competitive prices which they were able to do through a combination of improved productivity and low wages.

However, the state played a critical role in providing a conducive environment in which embryonic industries could flourish. These states engaged in highly selective trade policies protecting domestic industries by levying high tariffs on imports that would otherwise take most of the share of the domestic market. However, this did not mean that these states pursued a policy of high tariffs across the board. For example, tariffs on strategic products required to aid industrialization were deliberately lowered. At the same time as providing protection from external sources, these states actively intervened in the domestic economy via government licensing and financial rents in terms of loans at below market cost. As a result of these states providing their populations with a high standard of education, business could reap the benefits of having a highly skilled workforce readily available. This is not to say that these states did not adhere to sound business principles. If companies did not prove to be successful, they found it difficult for licences to be renewed and cheap loans were no longer made available.

This form of state intervention has been so successful in that region that some commentators have proposed that other developing states should follow their example. Robert Wade, for example, has outlined ten prescriptions for economic growth. First, '[U]se national policies to promote industrial investment within the national boundaries, and to channel more of this investment into industries whose growth is important for the economy's future growth'. Second, '[U]se protection to help create an internationally competitive set of industries'. Third, '[I]f the wider strategy calls for heavy reliance on trade, give high priority to export promotion policies'. Fourth, '[W]elcome multinational companies, but direct them toward exports'. Fifth, '[P]romote a bank-based financial system under close government control'. Sixth, '[C]arry out trade and financial liberalization gradually, in line with a certain sequence of steps'. Seventh, '[E]stablish a "pilot agency" or "economic general staff" within the central bureaucracy whose policy heartland is the industrial and trade profile of the economy and its future growth path'. Eighth, '[D]evelop effective institutions of political authority before the system is democratized'. Ninth, '[D]evelop corporatist institutions as or before the system is democratized'. Tenth, '[M]ake piecemeal reforms even in soft states so as to create an institutional configuration better able to support a modest industrial policy'.[3]

It may well be that others differ over the sequencing and importance of some of these prescriptions, but they are listed here because they neatly summarize most of the lessons to be drawn from the East Asian developmental experience. Can such policies be followed in the more globalized world we live in? Given the current trade regime, members of the WTO would find it difficult to follow such prescriptions concerning the protection of their domestic industries. But this is more an argument for changing the WTO and implementing reforms outlined in the last chapter, rather than an argument for not adopting such policies. With fewer controls on capital movement, today's world presents even greater obstacles to states that wish to place conditions on investment or companies seeking to borrow large sums to invest in new areas. However, imposing conditions that are not overly burdensome on capital is not impossible if the state provides a relatively stable environment for such investment and the possibility of earning relatively high returns.

The other major reason for arguing in favour of emulating the East Asian model is that it is far and above the most successful case of accelerated development since the end of the Second World War. In the absence of any other tried and tested highly successful model, it stands out as the obvious candidate to emulate. If the external economic environment is less conducive, then this is a strong argument for instigating reforms on capital controls rather than for abandoning the model (for example developing a Basel III Accord that sets targets for lending levels to developing countries). It may also be the case that investors do not view conditions placed on investments as the determining factor when investing in developing countries. As Chapter Four indicated, China has not been reticent in placing conditions on foreign direct investments (such as joint ventures and domestic content requirements), yet because of the overall positive economic environment combined with the possibility of receiving good returns, strong capital flows have continued. Chile throughout the nineties required foreign investors to place a percentage of portfolio investment in non-interest-bearing accounts at the national bank in order to dissuade highly speculative short-term capital flows from entering the country and destabilizing the economy.

However, there are certain domestic factors that may mean that similar growth patterns to those exhibited by East Asian countries are no longer possible. Earlier, it was pointed out that these states witnessed strong growth, but that this growth also benefited the poorer segments of society, keeping the levels of inequality within certain limits. The aftermath of the Second World War and the geopolitical circumstances that these states found themselves in may have created a level of solidarity that would be difficult to replicate elsewhere. This does not mean that growth *per se* is not possible elsewhere but it may mean that the high levels of equality will not be repeated. Second, many analysts of the so-called East Asian miracle refer to the critical role played by autonomous highly skilled bureaucratic cadres.[4] However, many developing countries suffer both from skill migration and 'state capture' by those governing who use the state for their own ends. The first difficulty might be overcome through incentives. The second is a far more difficult hurdle to overcome, but if the compact between developing and industrialized states that was made at Monterrey is to mean anything, then developing states must commit themselves to establishing independent bureaucracies and judiciaries.

Can the above patterns of trade and investment explain the patterns of global poverty and inequality? Chapter Six indicated that there are many other factors that also impact upon the levels of poverty and inequality in any one country. These range from domestic factors, such as educational levels, population growth, behavioural norms and land ownership through to the Kuznet's effect associated with industrialization. However, one of the most obvious factors is the debt trap that many of these countries have found themselves in. High levels of debt have forced governments to allocate a large proportion of their revenues in servicing such debt, but it has also led to these governments having to adopt severe structural adjustment policies that, amongst other things, have led to large reductions in welfare spending. Such reductions not only impact directly on the population's secondary incomes, i.e. benefits provided by the state, such as pensions, health care, education and family credits, but also contribute to the continuation of such poverty and inequality from generation to generation because of the reductions in state spending on education. The cancellation of debt for the HIPC is therefore to be warmly welcomed as a first stage in a programme of poverty reduction in the countries concerned.

Discussions concerning global patterns of poverty and inequality are thus complicated by the many factors that lie behind them. But Chapter Six also indicated that many differences concerning the actual figures for global poverty and inequality remain unresolved. Despite these difficulties, the chapter argued that many of these studies do identify similar patterns. These are: the decline of poverty and inequality in much of South Asia, large increases in poverty in Sub-Saharan Africa; and the stagnation/increase in poverty in Central and Latin America. One possible explanation put forward argued that these patterns can be partially explained by the type of production and exports that countries are involved in. The chapter cited recent evidence by the United Nations indicating that those developing countries involved in manufacturing and technology experienced strong growth. This evidence becomes all the more compelling when compared to those countries that continue to rely on primary products and have experienced negative GDP per capita growth over the last two decades. [5] In relation to exports the chapter highlighted recent work indicating that low-income countries that do venture into the labour-intensive export market have found some success, but those that continue to concentrate on primary commodities are confronted by declining terms of trade.[6] The middle-income countries, on the other hand, are caught between competing with new, cheaper entrants utilizing the wide availability of low- and medium-level technology and being unable to compete in the high technology sector. This would explain both the reduction of poverty in some countries in South and South-East Asia, but also has the merit of explaining the increases in poverty in Africa and the stagnation in Latin and Central America.

These pressures on welfare spending in the developing countries stand in stark contrast to the patterns of spending in the industrialized countries. Despite much talk of the terminal decline of the welfare state, it was found that rumours of its demise were greatly exaggerated. To be sure, there has been a decrease in the last decade, but this was preceded by a decade of significant increases. Greater changes have been witnessed in the regulatory and distributive functions of these states. But again, not all states have opted for wholesale deregulation and privatization. Chapter Five argued that the Scandinavian social democratic states and several so-called continental states have reacted quite differently to the pressures of globalization. The former emphasized retraining and life-long learning but also targeted youth unemployment by guaranteeing jobs with training for those unemployed for more than a year. The continental model has tended to emphasize labour reduction, encouraging the exit of an older generation of workers by providing generous retirement benefits. Similarly, although privatization of public assets has gone ahead in these countries, many governments have either opted to retain a controlling share or have intervened directly, blocking foreign takeovers of industries that they view as strategic.

One of the central themes of this book has been that the core industrialized states have played a key role in promoting globalization through the international financial and trade organizations. In most cases, their financial and industrial sectors have gained from the access to new markets and new investment opportunities that liberalization has offered them. At the same time, the threat of foreign competition has provided a useful tool for both politicians and employers in controlling labour demands which reached a peak in the mid- to late-seventies. As was pointed out in the last chapter, politicians have been more than willing to sidestep their responsibilities and shift the blame onto the faceless forces of globalization thereby depoliticizing many critical (and very political) decisions concerning the economy. However, although in those countries that have pursued neo-liberalism most vigorously labour movements may have been successfully neutered for the time being, there is an attendant risk (for politicians) that populations will view their governments as ineffective and turn to alternative forms of political expression.

Indeed, the protests in Seattle, Gothenburg, Genoa and elsewhere may herald the advent of a new variety of politics partly generated as a result of the failure of politicians to control the worst excesses of capitalism. These protests, together with the events of 9/11 and the continual pressure by various NGOs, finally resulted in the G7 recognizing that the only way to improve conditions for the world's poorest countries was to write off their debts. However, although this is a positive step forward it is only a temporary 'ameliorative and purgative policy'.[7] What is required is a much more fundamental reshaping of the international financial and trade regimes than has hitherto been attempted. The replacement of structural adjustment policies by Poverty Reduction and Growth Facility programmes signal some willingness by the international financial institutions to reform. Similarly, the declared intention of the new Doha Round of trade negotiations that the main focus should be development is to be welcomed.

As a result, many now refer to the current period as a 'post-Washington consensus'. This is true if it is meant to reflect the rather mild reforms that have been implemented thus far. But such a title should be questioned on four grounds. First, as the last chapter indicated, the new PRGF arrangements are such that the IMF still retains strong control over the direction of these countries' economies. Second, we have yet to see what the result of the Doha Round will be; thus far there are reasons to question whether it will deliver significant benefits for the developing world. Third, many of these states have already liberalized their economies because of the previous policies that these international institutions pursued. Finally, most developing countries have become integrated into the liberal trade regime governed by the WTO. As Grahame Thompson has pointed out, 'these countries are now members of various institutions of international economic governance that police the domestic policy regimes of developing countries'.[8] The less strident policies may merely reflect the fact that the mission of these institutions has generally been accomplished.

This book has argued that if the term 'post-Washington consensus' is to live up to its name, such reforms need to go much further. Although the book has argued in favour of the East Asian model, this can only be applied in a benign financial and trade environment. Changes at the domestic level will only work if they are matched by reforms at the international level. The developmental model requires, amongst other things, the ability of the state to pursue selective but flexible tariffs in order to protect industries deemed strategic for economic growth. At the same time, in order to benefit fully from foreign direct investment, these countries need to promote joint ownership projects and stipulate domestic content conditions. But in order to do this the WTO would be required to move towards a different form of trade regime, one that reflects these needs. In terms of tariff reductions, the developmental state would require the WTO to adopt either flexible but bounded tariffs or tariffs based on the Market Access Proposal (or some other viable alternative). At the same time, many of the requirements set out under the WTO's Trade Related Investment Measures (TRIMs) such as those prohibiting states from stipulating domestic content or technology transfer through joint ventures would need to be abandoned.

Although these reforms are feasible, they are possible but not probable mainly because there is a lack of will by the core industrialized countries. This book has argued that contrary to the usual portrayal of these states being helpless in the more globalized world that we now find ourselves in, cooperative collaboration between the major economic powers to alter the current economic environment is still possible. But in the absence of major political pressure from their populations the political leaders of these countries see little reason to instigate major reform. However, politicians do respond to pressure and therefore the future shape of the global economy will depend very much on the political circumstances in which it is embedded.

Notes

1 Introduction

1 G. Vidal, *The Judgement of Paris*, London: Heinemann, 1953, p.6.
2 J. A. Scholte, *Globalization: a Critical Introduction*, Basingstoke: Palgrave, 2000, p. 43.
3 K. Booth (ed.), *New Thinking About Strategy and International Security*, London: HarperCollins, 1991, p. 10.
4 A. Leyshon, 'Annihilating space? The speeding-up of communications', in J. Allen (ed.), *A Shrinking World?*, Oxford: Oxford University Press, 1995, p. 14.
5 B. Anderson, *Imagined Communities: Reflections on the Origin and Spread of Nationalism*, London: Verso, 1991.
6 M. Mcluhan, *The Gutenberg Galaxy: The Making of Typographic Man*, Toronto: Toronto University Press, 1962, p. 32.
7 On underlying and proximate causes refer to S. Van Evera, 'Hypotheses on Nationalism and War' in S. Lynn-Jones and S. Miller (eds), *Global Dangers: Changing Dimensions of International Security*, Cambridge, MA: MIT Press, 1995, pp. 0251–85.
8 J. Allen, 'Post-Industrialism and Post-Fordism', in S. Hall, D. Held and T. McGrew (eds), *Modernity and its Futures*, Oxford: Blackwell, 1999, pp. 170–203.
9 *The Economist*, 'Moore's Law at 40', 23 March – 1 April, 2005, p. 59
10 A. Leyshon, 'Annihilating space?', p. 28.
11 *Annual Report of the International Civil Aviation Council*, 2001, Montreal, International Civil Aviation Council, p. 2.
12 *The Economist*, 'The World in a Box', 18–24 March, 2006, pp. 77–8.
13 D. Held, A. McGrew, D. Goldblatt and J. Perraton, *Global Transformations: Politics, Economics and Culture*, Cambridge: Polity Press, 1999, p. 15.
14 The phrase is to be found in Marx's **Grundisse**; refer to D. Harvey, 'The geography of capitalist accumulation: a reconstruction of Marxism theory', 1975, *Antipode*, vol. 7, p. 12.
15 R. Keohane and J. Nye, 'Globalization: What's new? What's Nnot? (and so what?)', *Foreign Policy*, vol. 118, 2000, p.113.
16 R. Keohane and J. Nye, 'Power and interdependence in the information age', *Foreign Affairs*, vol. 77:5, 1998, p. 83.
17 The term 'imagined community' was first used to describe the feeling of belonging to the nation. Refer to B. Anderson, *Imagined Communities: Reflections on the Origin and Spread of Nationalism*, London: Verso, 1991, p. 6.
18 R. Keohane R. and J. Nye, *Transnational Relations and World Politics*, Cambridge, MA: Harvard University Press, 1970, p. xi.
19 A. Leyshon, 'Annihilating space?', p. 14.

20 Surgeons in New York used a remote controlled robot to operate on a patient in France in 2001. Refer to M. Henderson, 'Surgeons operate by remote control over the Atlantic', *The Guardian*, 20 September 2001, p. 20.

21 S. Barnes and B. Hunt, *E-Commerce and V-Business: Business Models for Global Success*, Oxford: Butterworth-Heinemann, 2001, p. ix.

22 S. Barnes and B. Hunt, *E-Commerce and V-Business*, p.2.

23 M. Christopher, *Logistics and Supply Chain Management*, p. 179.

24 M. Christopher, *Logistics and Supply Chain Management*, p. 209; J. L. Gattorna and D. W. Walters, *Managing the Supply Chain: A Strategic Perspective*, Basingstoke: Macmillan, 1996, p. 143.

25 M. Christopher, *Logistics and Supply Chain Management*, p. 15.

26 'value added consists of the wages, interest, and profit components added to the output by a firm or industry'. Refer to P. Samuelson and W. Nordhaus, *Economics: International Edition*, New York: McGraw-Hill, 1995, p. 764. Also A. Hoogvelt, *Globalisation and the Postcolonial World: The New Political Economy of Development*, Basingstoke: Macmillan, 1997, p. 145.

27 M. Castells, *The Information Age: Economy, Society and Culture, vol. 1: The Rise of the Network Society*, Oxford: Blackwell, 1996, p. 92.

28 A. Giddens, *The Nation-State and Violence: Volume Two of a Contemporary Critique of Historical Materialism*, Cambridge: Polity Press, 1985, pp.138–9.

29 M. Castells, *The Information Age: Economy, Society and Culture, vol. 1*, p. 17.

30 Ibid., p. 91.

31 Roland Robertson, *Social Theory and Global Culture*, London: Sage Publications, 1992, p.183.

32 A. Giddens, *The Nation-State And Violence*, pp. 137–41. I also follow Giddens' distinction between technology and industrialism – the latter is said to involve the organization of human relations.

33 K. Polanyi, *The Great Transformation: The Political and Economic Origins of our Time*, Boston, MA: Beacon Press, 1944, p. 57.

34 K. Marx, *Das Kapital Volume 1*. Quoted in D. Harvey, 'The Geography of Capitalist Accumulation: a reconstruction of Marxism theory', *Antipode*, 1975, vol. 7, p. 9.

35 K. Maguire, 'BT strike threat over Indian call centres', *The Guardian*, 03.07.2003, p. 9; G. Gibbs, 'Dyson, champion of British Industry, switches production to far east', *The Guardian*, 06 February.2002, p. 3; D. Gow, 'Dyson profits from Malaysian move', *The Guardian*, 08 November, 2003, p. 26.

36 K. Marx, *Grundisse,* quoted in D. Harvey, 'The geography of capitalist accumulation, p. 12.

37 Ibid., p. 15.

38 C. Krauthammer, 'The unipolar moment', *Foreign Affairs,* vol. 70:1, 1990, pp. 23–33; C. Layne, 'The unipolar illusion: why new great powers will arise', *International Security,* vol 17:4, 1993, pp. 5–51; W. Wohlforth, 'The stability of a unipolar world', *International Security*, vol. 24:1, 1999, pp. 5–41; M. Mastanduno, 'Preserving the unipolar moment: realist theories and US grand strategy', *International Security,* vol. 21:4, 1997, pp. 49–88.

39 H. Martin and H. Schumann, *The Global Trap: Globalization and the Assault on Democracy and Prosperity*, London: Zed Books, 1997, pp. 206–7.

40 Harold Laski quoted in N. Ferguson, *Colossus: The Price of America's Empire*, New York: The Penguin Press, 2004, p. 68.

41 J. G. Ruggie, *Building the World Polity: Essays on International Institutionalization*, London: Routledge, 1998, p. 112.

42 W. R. Mead, *Power, Terror, Peace, and War*, pp. 23–5. See also J. Nye, 'Soft Power', *Foreign Policy,* vol. 80, Fall 1990, pp. 153–71. Although great benefits accrued to the United States' closest allies, as will be shown later, this was not necessarily true for the majority of states in the international system.

43 I. Clark, *Globalization and Fragmentation: International Relations in the Twentieth Century*, Oxford: Oxford University Press, 1997, p. 132.

44 Ibid., p.122.

45 D. Farrell, 'The US trade deficit does not spell doom, *Financial Times Asia*, 10 February, 2005, p.13.

46 F. Halliday, *The Making of the Second Cold War*, London: Verso, 1986.

47 M. Shaw, *Theory of the Global State: Globality as an Unfinished Revolution*, Cambridge: Cambridge University Press, 2000, p. 119–20.

48 Uzbekistan and Turkmenistan would appear to have improved their GDP beyond the rates of 1989; however, their economic performance may not be as strong as it first appears. It should be noted that the manner in which the official state Consumer Price Index is calculated tends to underestimate price rises. This tends to exaggerate real GDP because the deflator employed is based on the (underestimated) CPI. Also, there is a large discrepancy between the figures given above for Turkmenistan and the figures generated by the EBRD which estimates that Turkmenistan's GDP in 2000 was running at 75% of output generated in 1989. Refer to *Republic of Uzbekistan: Recent Economic Developments: IMF Staff Country Report No. 00/36*, Washington DC: IMF, 2000, pp. 1–11; *Annual Report 2000 of the European Bank of Reconstruction and Development*, London: Ventura Litno Ltd., 2000, p. 16.

49 *Economic Survey of Europe 2002*, No. 1, Geneva: Economic Commission for Europe, 2002.

50 J. Falkingham, *Welfare in Transition: Trends in Poverty and Well-being in Central Asia*, London: Centre for Analysis of Social Exclusion, 1999. PPP refers to purchasing power parity, i.e. the amount of local currency required to purchase the equivalent of $1 worth of goods at international prices – refer to B. Milanovic, *Income, Inequality, and Poverty during the Transition from Planned to Market Economy*, Washington, DC: World Bank, 1988, p. 65.

51 *World Development Report 2000/20001*, Oxford: Oxford University Press, 2001, p. 282 and C. Jones and A. Revenga (eds), *Making Transition Work for Everyone: Poverty and Inequality in Europe and Central Asia*, Washington, DC: World Bank, 2000, p.35.

52 J. Kirsher, 'Keynes, capital mobility and the crisis of embedded liberalism', *Review of International Political Economy*, vol. 6:3, 1999, pp. 317–22.

53 R.W. Cox, *Production, Power and World Order: Social Forces in the Making of History*, New York: Columbia University Press, 1987, pp. 253–65.

54 K. Polanyi, *The Great Transformation*, p. 43.

55 G. Teeple, *Globalization and the Decline of Social Reform*, Toronto: Garamond Press, 1995, pp. 78–84.

56 P. Krugman, 'Dutch tulips and emerging markets', *Foreign Affairs*, vol. 74:4, 1995, p. 29.

57 C. Thomas, *Global Governance, Development and Human Security*, London: Pluto Press, 2000, p. 56. For a review of this process in the US, UK and New Zealand, refer to chapter two of John Gray's, *False Dawn: The Delusions of Global Capitalism*, London: Granta Books, 1999.

58 J. Gray, *False Dawn*, p. 25.

59 Near the beginning of their second term, Labour announced that government spending would increase by £93 billion by 2006. Refer to M. White and L. Elliott, 'Brown's Big Gamble', *The Guardian*, 16 July 2002, p.1

60 C. Hay, 'Globalization's impact on states', in Ravenhill, J. (ed.), *Global Political Economy*, Oxford: Oxford University Press, 2005, p. 247.

61 It has increased from just under 30% of GDP in 1960 to nearly 50% in 1995, refer to *United Nations Development Programme: Human Development Report 1999*, Oxford: OUP, 1999, p. 95.

62   Simon Eagle, 'Trade in context: approaches to globalization', in A. Taylor and C. Thomas (eds), *Global Trade and Global Social Issues*, London: Routledge, 1999, p. 21.
63   J. Gray, *False Dawn*, p. 26.
64   W. Hutton, *The State We're In*, London: Vintage, 1996, p. 55.
65   J. Ruggie, 'International regimes, transaction, and change', p. 418.
66   L. Andor and M. Summers, *Market Failure: A Guide to the East European 'Economic Miracle'*, London: Pluto Press, 1998, p. 2.
67   R. Hague, M. Harrop and S. Breslin, *Comparative Government and Politics: an Introduction*, Basingstoke: Macmillan, 1998, p. 52.
68   L. Elliott and V. Brittain, 'The rich and poor grow further apart', *The Guardian*, 9 September, 1998, p. 18.
69   A. Hoogvelt, *Globalisation and the Postcolonial World*, p. 138.
70   S. Milne, 'Billion jobless worldwide', *The Guardian*, 24 September, 1998, p. 27.
71   N. Mathiason, 'IMF's "one size" fits few', *The Observer*, 28 April, 2002, p. 3.
72   A.Giddens, *The Consequences of Modernity*, Cambridge: Polity Press, 1990, p. 19.
73   J. Saurin, 'Global environmental degradation', Caroline Thomas (ed.), *RIO: Unravelling the Consequences*, Essex, UK: Frank Cass, 1994, p. 48.
74   A. Giddens, *The Consequences of Modernity*, p.19.
75   Ibid, p. 21.
76   Ibid., p.21.
77   D. Prerau, *Saving the Daylight: Why we Put the Clocks Forward*, London: Granta Books, 2006, p. 28. The following paragraph is based on Chapter Two of this book.
78   A. Giddens, *The Consequences of Modernity*, p. 19. Although the French were initially unwilling to accept this and only agreed in 1911, but still insisted on calling it 'Paris Mean Time, retarded by 9 minutes and 21 seconds'. For a fascinating insight into the process refer to D. Prerau, *Saving The Daylight*, p. 24.
79   Ibid., p.22.
80   Ibid., p.27
81   Ibid., p.28.
82   Ibid., p.29
83   Ibid., p. 113.
84   Ibid., p. 33.
85   J. Rosenberg, *The Follies of Globalisation Theory: Polemical Essays*, London: Verso, 2000, p. 93.
86   Quoted in Ibid., p. 101.
87   J. A. Scholte, *Globalization: a Critical Introduction*, Basingstoke: Palgrave, 2000, p. 104.
88   C. Thomas, 'Introduction' in C. Thomas and P. Wilkin (eds), *Globalization, Human Security and the African Experience*, Boulder, CO: Lynne Rienner, 1999, p. 2.
89   John Burton, *World Society*, London : Cambridge University Press, 1972.
90   A. Giddens, *The Consequences of Modernity*, p. 21.
91   A. Giddens, *The Consequences of Modernity*, p. 64.
92   R. Robertson, *Globalization*, p. 183
93   M. Shaw, *Theory of the Global State*, p.11.
94   C. Thomas , 'Introduction' in C. Thomas and P. Wilkin (eds), *Globalization, Human Security and the African Experience*, p. 2.
95   R. Keohane and J. Nye, 'Globalization: What's New?', p.117.
96   C. Thomas , 'Introduction' in C. Thomas and P. Wilkin (eds), *Globalization, Human Security and the African Experience*, p. 2.
97   D. Held, A. McGrew, D. Goldblatt and J. Perraton, *Global Transformations*, p. 16.
98   J. A. Scholte, 'The Globalization of World Politics', in John Baylis and Steve Smith, *The Globalization of World Politics*, Oxford: Oxford University Press, 1997, p. 14.

99 P. Cerny, 'Paradoxes of the competition state: the dynamics of political globalization', *Government and Opposition*, vol. 32:2, 1997, p. 260. See also P. Cerny, *The Changing Architecture of Politics: Structure, Agency, and the Future of the State*, London: Sage Publications, 1990, especially Chapter 8.; P. Cerny, 'What next for the state', in E. Kofman and G. Youngs (eds), *Globalization: Theory and Practice*, London: Pinter, 1996, pp. 123–37.

100 P. Cerny, 'Globalization and the changing logic of collective action', *International Organization*, vol. 49:4, 1995, p. 611.

101 J. Stiglitz and A. Charlton, *Fair Trade for All: How Trade Can Promote Development*, Oxford: Oxford University Press, 2005, pp. 81–5.

2 Globalization: myth or reality?

1 T. Pelagidis and H. Papsotiriou, 'Globalization or regionalism? States, markets and the structure of international trade', *Review of International Studies*, vol. 28:5, 2002 p. 529.

2 A. McGrew, 'The globalization debate: putting the advanced captialist state in its place', *Global Society*, vol. 12:3, September 1998, p. 299–322.

3 Ibid., p. 302.

4 P. Dicken, *Global Shift: Transforming the World Economy*, 4th ed., London: Sage Publications, 2003, p. 9.

5 M. Castells, *The Information Age: Economy, Society and Culture, vol. 1: The Rise of the Network Society*, Oxford: Blackwell, 1996, p. 96.

6 P. Dicken, *Global Shift*, p. 29.

7 S. Anderson and J. Cavanaugh, *Field Guide to the Global Economy*, New York: New Press, 2005. Online. Available HTTP: <http://www.ips-dc.org> (accessed 17 December 2005).

8 P. Hirst and G. Thompson, *Globalization in Question*, Cambridge: Polity Press, 1999, 2nd ed., p. 270.

9 It should be pointed out that Angus Maddison does not take a particular stance with reference to this debate. Rather, his work is referred to by the globalists, transformationalists and sceptics. The export figures have been doubled to enable comparison with alternative total trade data given later.

10 K. Ohmae, 'Putting global logic first', *Harvard Business Review*, January–February 1995, p. 119.

11 K. Ohmae, *The Borderless World: Power and Strategy in the Global Marketplace*, London: HarperCollins, 1990, pp. 158–61.

12 J. Aart Scholte, *Globalization: a Critical Introduction*, 2nd ed., Basingstoke: Palgrave, 2005, p. 161.

13 H. Martin and H. Schumann, *The Global Trap: Globalization and the Assault on Democracy and Prosperity*, London: Zed Books, 1997, p. 48.

14 Anthony Giddens, *Runaway World: How Globalisation is Reshaping our Lives*, London: Profile Books, 1999, p.10.

15 H. Martin and H. Schumann, *The Global Trap*, p. 48.

16 J. Aart Scholte, *Globalization*, p. 166.

17 M. Castells, *The Information Age*, 1996, p. 93.

18 This included the UK (1979); Japan (1980); Australia (1983); New Zealand (1984); Netherlands (1986); Denmark (1988); and France (1989). S. Griffith-Jones, R. Gottschalk and X. Cirera, *The OECD Experience with Capital Account Liberalisation*, Sussex: Institute of Development Studies, 2000. Online. Available HTTP: <http://www.ids.ac.uk/ids> (accessed 17 December 2005), p. 12.

19 D. Held, A. McGrew, D. Goldblatt and J. Perraton, *Global Transformations: Politics, Economics and Culture*, Cambridge: Polity Press, 1999, p. 206.

20 M. Castells, *The Information Age*, 1996, p. 93

21 G. Arnold, *Corporate Financial Management*, Harlow: Prentice Hall, 1998, pp. 484–5.

22 A. Hoogvelt, *Globalization and the Postcolonial World*, p. 82.

23 G. Arnold, *Corporate Financial Management*, p. 909.

24 Ibid., p. 894.

25 Ibid., p. 921.

26 S. Griffith-Jones, R. Gottschalk and X. Cirera, *The OECD Experience With Capital Account Liberalisation*, p. 10. On the establishment of options trading, refer to D. Held, A. McGrew, D. Goldblatt and J. Perraton, *Global Transformations*, p. 208.

27 J. A. Scholte, 'Global trade and finance' in John Baylis and Steve Smith (eds), *The Globalization of World Politics*, Oxford: Oxford University Press, 2005, p. 612.

28 L. Mosely, *Global Capital and National Governments*, Cambridge: Cambridge University Press, 2003, p. 27.

29 Japan's outward FDI stocks (7.8% of GDP) reflecting its investments in other countries are more than three times the amount of FDI that it attracts. Refer to UNCTAD, *World Investment Report 2004: the Shift towards Services,* Annex Table B6.

30 P. Dicken, *Global Shift*, p. 14.

31 S. Palmisano, 'Multinationals have been superseded', *Financial Times*, 12 June, 2006, p. 15. Also see *Foreign Affairs* May–June

32 *The Economist*, 'Special Report: Better By Design', 17 September–23 September, 2005, pp. 21–3.

33 A. McGrew, 'The globalization debate, p. 303.

34 J. A. Scholte, 'The globalization of world politics', in John Baylis and Steve Smith (eds), *The Globalization of World Politics*, Oxford: Oxford University Press, 1997, p. 15 (bold typescript in the original) and Paul Hirst and Grahame Thompson, *Globalization in Question*, 1999, p. 8.

35 J. Allen, 'Crossing Borders: footloose multinationals?', in John Allen and Chris Hamnett (eds), *A Shrinking World?: Global Unevenness and Inequality*, Oxford: Oxford University Press, 1995, p.59.

36 United Nations, *World Investment Report 2002 Transnational Corporations and Competitiveness*, New York: United Nations Conference on Trade and Development, 2002, p. 153.

37 P. Hirst and G. Thompson, *Globalization in Question*, 1999, p. 11.

38 K. Ohmae, *The End of the Nation-state: The Rise of Regional Economies*, London: HarperCollins, 1995, p. 3.

39 M. Castells, *The Information Age*, 1996, p. 92.

40 K. Ohmae, *The End of the Nation-state*, pp.2–11.

41 R. Rosecrance, 'International security and the virtual state: states and firms in world politics', *Review of International Studies*, vol. 28:4, 2002, p. 447.

42 UNCTAD, *World Investment Report 1993: Transnational Corporations as Integrated International Production*, Geneva: UNCTAD, 1993, p. 143.

43 H. Wiig, 'How much globalization? Reassessing the growth of international trade and investments in the OECD', *Norsk Utenrikspolitisk Institutt*, Report No.241. February 1999, p. 22. Available online. http://www.nupi.no/IPS/filestore/ How_much_Globalisation.pdf. (accessed 01 January 2006).

44 M. Castells, *The Information Age*, 1996, pp. 163–4.

45 H. Wiig, 'How much globalization?', p. 22.

46 K. Ohmae, *The Borderless World*, p. xii.

47 K. Ohmae, 'Putting global logic first', p. 119.

48 K. Ohmae, *The Borderless World*, p. x.

49 M. Castells, *The Information Age*, 1996, p. 147.

50 M. Castells, *The Information Age: Economy, Society and Culture, vol. III: End of Millennium*, Oxford: Blackwell, 2000, 2nd ed., pp. 165.

51 F. Fox Piven, 'Is it global economics or neo-laissez-faire', *New Left Review*, vol. 213, 1995, p. 110.
52 P. Hirst and G. Thompson, *Globalization in Question*, 1999, pp. 1, 6.
53 S. Griffith-Jones, R. Gottschalk and X. Cirera, *The OECD Experience With Capital Account Liberalisation*, p. 12.
54 P. Hirst and G. Thompson, *Globalization in Question*, 1999, pp. 33–5.
55 G. Garrett, 'Capital mobility, trade, and the domestic politics of economic policy', *International Organization*, vol. 49:4, Autumn 1995, p. 669.
56 L. Weiss, 'Globalization and the myth of the powerless state', *New Left Review*, vol. 225, September–October, 1997, p. 21.
57 P. Hirst and G. Thompson, *Globalization in Question*, 1999, p. 9.
58 Ibid., pp. 10–13.
59 Ibid., pp.4, 8.
60 P. Hirst, 'The global economy – myths and realities', *International Affairs*, Vol. 73:3, p. 414.
61 The first cable was laid in 1858, but worked for just a short duration. M. Castells, *The Information Age*, 1996, p. 92 and P. Krugman, 'Growing world trade: causes and consequences', *Brookings Papers on Economic Activity*, 1995, p. 330 (this is not to imply that Krugman is a sceptic – but is the source of the preceding information).
62 P. Hirst and G. Thompson, *Globalization in Question*, 1999, pp. 2, 9, 11.
63 Ibid., p. 88.
64 Ibid., p. 2.
65 Ibid., p. 36.
66 L. Weiss, *The Myth of the Powerless State*, p. 178.
67 For a break down of the various definitions of perfect capital mobility, refer to J. Frankel, 'Measuring international capital mobility: a review', *The American Economic Review*, vol. 82:2, pp. 197–202.
68 Refer also to P. Hirst and G. Thompson, *Globalization in Question*, 1999, p. 36.
69 J. Frankel, 'Measuring international capital mobility', p. 201. Italics in the original.
70 M. Feldstein and C. Horioka, 'Domestic saving and international capital flows', *The Economic Journal*, vol. 90:358, June 1980, p. 315.
71 P. Hirst and G. Thompson, *Globalization in Question*, 1999, p. 39.
72 K. French and J. Poterba, 'Investor diversification and international equity markets', *The American Economic Review*, vol. 81:2, p. 222.
73 Ibid., p. 224.
74 M. Feldstein and C. Horioka, 'Domestic Saving and international capital flows', pp.324–9.
75 C. Hay, 'Globalization's impact on states', in J. Ravenhill (ed.), *Global Political Economy*, Oxford: Oxford University Press, 2005, p. 257.
76 C. Hay, 'Globalization's impact on states', p. 257.
77 P. Hirst and G. Thompson, *Globalization in Question*, 1999, pp. 42–5.
78 P. Hirst and G. Thompson, *Globalization in Question*, 1999, p. 47.
79 'In 1913 average tariff rates on imported manufactures were 13 percent in Germany, over 20 percent in France, 44 percent in the United states and 84 percent in Russia. In Britain they were zero'. Refer to N. Ferguson, *Colossus: the Price of America's Empire*, New York: The Penguin Press, 2004, p. 187.
80 Paul Hirst and Grahame Thompson, *Globalization in Question*, 1999, p. 62
81 A. Maddison, 'The nature and functioning of European capitalism: a historical and comparative perspective', *Banca Nazionale Del Lavoro Quarterly Review,* vol. L:203, 1997, pp.431–79. The same conclusion is made by H. Wiig in 'How much globalization?: Reassessing the growth of international trade and investments in the OECD', *Norsk Utenrikspolitisk Institutt*, Report No.241. February 1999. Available online. http://www.nupi.no/IPS/filestore/How_much_Globalisation.pdf. (accessed 01 January 2006).

82 Robert Gilpin, *The Challenge of Global Capitalism: the World Economy in the 21ˢᵗ Century*, Princeton, NJ: Princeton University Press, 2000, p. 169.

83 P. Hirst, 'The global economy-myths and realities', *International Affairs*, vol. 73:3, 1997, p. 415.

84 L. Weiss, 'Globalization and national governance: antinomy or interdependence?', *Review of International Studies*, vol. 25:5, 1999, pp. 59–88.

85 L. Weiss, 'Globalization and the myth of the powerless state', p. 8.

86 Although not all countries include retained earnings in their FDI figures. Refer also to P. Hirst and G. Thompson, *Globalization in Question*, 1999, p. 77.

87 M. Edelstein, *Overseas Investment in The Age of High Imperialism: the United Kingdom 1850–1914*, New York: Columbia University Press, 1982, p. 3.

88 M. Edelstein, *Overseas Investment*, p. 37.

89 W. Cooke and D. Noble, 'Industrial relations systems and US foreign direct investment abroad', *British Journal of Industrial Relations*, vol. 36:4, 1998, p. 596 and F. Traxler and B. Woiteach, 'Transnational investment and national labour market regimes: a case of "Regime Shopping"', *European Journal of Industrial Relations*, vol. 6:2, 2000, p. 149.

90 H. Wilensky, *Rich Democracies: Political Economy, Public Policy, and Performance*, Berkely, CA: University of California Press, 2002, p. 666–8.

91 P. Hirst, 'The global economy-myths and realities', pp. 415–9. Also refer to J. Allen and G. Thompson, 'Think global, then think again – economic globalization in context', *Area*, vol. 29:3, 1997, pp. 213–27.

92 J. Stopford, 'Multinational corporations', *Foreign Policy*, vol. 112, Winter 1998–99, p. 12.

93 L. Weiss, 'Globalization and the myth of the powerless state', p. 7.

94 J. Perraton, D. Goldblatt, D. Held and A. McGrew, 'The globalization of economic activity', *New Political Economy*, vol. 2:2, 1997, p. 274.

95 D. Held, A. McGrew, D. Goldblatt and J. Perraton, *Global Transformations*, p. 11.

96 D. Held, A. McGrew, D. Goldblatt and J. Perraton, *Global Transformations*, p. 185; J. Perraton, D. Goldblatt, D. Held and A. McGrew, 'The globalization of economic activity', *New Political Economy*, vol. 2:2, 1997, pp. 257–77.

97 J. Perraton, D. Goldblatt, D. Held and A. McGrew, 'The globalization of economic activity', p. 258.

98 D. Held, A. McGrew, D. Goldblatt and J. Perraton, *Global Transformations*, p. 11.

99 Personal correspondence with Grahame Thompson.

100 M. Wolf, 'Countries still rule the world: Tthe notion that corporations wield more power than governments rests on flawed calculations and conceptual confusion', *Financial Times*, 06 February, 2002, p.17.

101 G. Thompson, 'Globalization as the total commercialization of politics', *New Political Economy*, vol. 8:3, 2003, p. 402.

102 S. Anderson and J. Cavanaugh, *Field Guide To The Global Economy*.

103 UNCTAD, *World Investment Report 1995: Transnational Corporations and Competitiveness*, Geneva: UNCTAD, 1995, p. 4.

104 D. Held, A. McGrew, D. Goldblatt and J. Perraton, *Global Transformations*, p. 218.

105 Ibid., p. 217; see also Jonathan Perraton, 'The scope and implications of globalisation', in J. Michie (ed.), *The Handbook of Globalisation*, Cheltenham:: Edward Elgar, 2003, p. 52.

106 Ibid., p. 185; J. Perraton, D. Goldblatt, D. Held and A. McGrew, 'The globalization of economic activity', p. 267.

107 D. Held, A. McGrew, D. Goldblatt and J. Perraton, *Global Transformations*, 1999, p. 218.

108 Bank for International Settlements, *71st Annual Report*, Basle: BIS, 2001, p. 32.

109 D. Held, A. McGrew, D. Goldblatt amd J. Perraton, *Global Transformations*, p. 214.

110 Refer to P. Hirst and G. Thompson, *Globalization in Question*, 1999, p. 76.

111 J. Stopford, 'Multinational corporations', *Foreign Policy*, Winter 1998–9, p. 17 and Susan Strange, 'Globaloney?', *Review of International Political Economy*, vol. 5:4, 1998, pp. 704–10.

112 D. Held, A. McGrew, D. Goldblatt and J. Perraton, *Global Transformations*, 1999, p. 246.

113 M. Obstfeld and A. Taylor, *Global Capital Markets: Integration, Crisis and Growth*, Cambridge: Cambridge University Press, 2004, p. 55.

114 J. H. Dunning, 'The new geography of FDI', in Ngaire Woods (ed.), *The Political Economy of Globalization*, Basingstoke: Palgrave, 2000, pp. 20–53.

115 A. Hoogvelt, *Globalization and the Postcolonial World*, p. 127.

116 For more on this, refer to Martin Christopher, *Logistics and Supply Chain Management: Strategies for Reducing Cost and Improving Service*, Harlow: Prentice Hall, 1992, p. 15.

117 D. Held, A. McGrew, D. Goldblatt and J. Perraton, *Global Transformations*, p. 170.

118 This is something that the sceptics readily recognize. Refer to P. Hirst and G. Thompson, 'Globalization in one country? The peculiarities of the British', *Economy and Society*, vol. 29:3, August 2000, p. 338.

119 M. Bordo, B. Eichengreen and D. Irwin, 'Is globalization today really different than globalization a hundred years ago?', Available online. <http://emlab.berkeley.edu/users/eichengr/research/brooking.pdf.> (accessed 21 January 2006), p. 7.

120 Endeavouring to calculate private GDP is of course quite difficult in reality. The tranformationalists define it as GDP – general government expenditure (so it does not take into account transfer payments e.g. social security payments). Personal correspondence with Jonathan Perraton.

121 UNDP, *Human Development Report 1999: Globalization with a Human Face*, Oxford: Oxford University Press, 1999.

122 D. Held, A. McGrew, D. Goldblatt and J. Perraton, *Global Transformations*, p. 167.

123 P. Hirst and G. Thompson, 'The future of globalisation', in J. Michie (ed.), *The Handbook of Globalisation*, Cheltenham: Edward Elgar, 2003, p. 29.

124 R. Robertson, *Globalization: Social Theory and Global Culture*, London: Sage Publications, 1992, p. 183.

125 A. Hoogvelt, *Globalization and the Postcolonial World*, pp. 145–7.

126 UNCTAD, *World Investment Report 1995: Transnational Corporations and Competitiveness*, Geneva: UNCTAD, 1995, p. 4.

127 A. McGrew, 'The globalization debate', p. 30.

128 S. Lee, 'The political economy of the third way', in J. Michie (ed.), *The Handbook of Globalisation*, Cheltenham:: Edward Elgar, 2003, p. 340.

129 S. Lee, 'The Political Economy of the Third Way', p. 340.

130 D. Held and A. McGrew, *The Global Transformations Reader: an Introduction to the Globalization Debate*, Cambridge: Polity Press, 2000, p. 250.

131 A. McGrew, 'The globalization debate', p. 309.

132 D. Held, A. McGrew, D. Goldblatt and J. Perraton, *Global Transformations*, p. 9.

133 P. Hirst and G. Thompson, *Globalization in Question*, 1996, p. 15.

134 P. Dicken, *Global Shift*, pp. 20, 122.

135 K. Ohmae, *The Borderless World*, p. xii.

136 S. Strange, 'Globaloney?', pp. 704–10.

137 P. Krugman, 'Growing world trade', pp.332–7.

138 R. Feenstra, 'Integration of trade and disintegration of production in the global economy', *Journal of Economic Perspectives*, vol. 12:4, Autumn 1998, pp. 35–6 (pp. 31–50).

139 D. Hummels, J. Ishii and K. Yi, 'The nature and growth of vertical specialization in world trade', *Journal of International Economics*, vol. 54, 2001, pp. 85, 93. See D. Hummels, D. Rapoport and K. Yi, 'Vertical specialization and the changing nature of

world trade', *Federal Reserve Bank of New York Economic Policy Review*, June 1998, pp.79–99.

140   D. Hummels, J. Ishii and K. Yi, 'The nature and growth of vertical specialization', p. 93.

141   D. Hummels, D. Rapoport and K. Yi, 'Vertical Specialization and the Changing Nature of World Trade', p. 85, 88.

3   How global is globalization?

1   P. Krugman, 'Growing world trade: causes and consequences', *Brookings Papers on Economic Activity*, 1995, pp. 332–7.

2   J. A. Scholte, *Globalization: a Critical Introduction*, Basingstoke: Palgrave, 2000, p. 52.

3   Zygmunt Bauman, *Globalization: the Human Consequences*, Cambridge: Polity Press, 1998, p. 1.

4   UN-TCMD, *World Investment Report 1992: Transnational Corporations as Engines of Growth: an Executive Summary*, New York: United Nations Transnational Corporations and Management Division, 1992, p. 1.

5   The Economist, 'Footloose firms: are global companies too mobile for workers' good?', 27 March–1 April, 2004, p. 69; and United Nations, *World Investment Report 2004: The Shift towards Services*, New York: United Nations Conference on Trade and Development, 2004, p. 1

6   United Nations, *World Investment Report 2001: Promoting Linkages*, New York: United Nations Conference on Trade and Development, 2001, p. 9.

7   T. Pelagidis and H. Papsotiriou, 'Globalization or regionalism? States, markets and the structure of international trade', *Review of International Studies*, vol. 28:5, 2002, pp. 519–35; R. Väyrynen, 'Regionalism: Old and New', *International Studies Review*, vol. 5, 2003, pp. 25–51; P. Hirst and G. Thompson, *Globalization in Question*; A. Hoogvelt, *Globalization and the Postcolonial World: The New Political Economy of Development*, London: Macmillan, 2001; P. Hirst, 'The global economy – myths and realities'; P. Hirst, and G. Thompson, 'Globalization in one country?' P. Hirst and G. Thompson, 'The future of globalisation', in J. Michie (ed.), *The Handbook of Globalisation*, Cheltenham: Edward Elgar, 2003; D. Held, A. McGrew, D. Goldblatt and J. Perraton, *Global Transformations: Politics, Economics and Culture*, Cambridge: Polity Press, 1999; J. Perraton, D. Goldblatt, D. Held and A. McGrew, 'The globalization of economic activity', *New Political Economy*, vol. 2:2, 1997, pp. 257–77; J. Perraton, 'The scope and implications of globalisation', in J. Michie (ed.), *The Handbook of Globalisation*, Cheltenham: Edward Elgar, 2003, pp. 37–60; C. Hay, 'What's globalization got to do with it? Economic interdependence and the future of European Welfare States', *Government and Opposition*, vol. 41:1, 2006, pp. 1–22.

8   However, international and regional financial systems are not compared here; for more on this subject refer to G. Thompson, 'The supra-national regionalization of the international financial system: how far and with what prospects?' Presented at the GARNET Conference in Holland, September 2006. Online. Available http://wi-garnet.uni-muenster.de (accessed 19 October 2006).

9   J. Mittelman, 'The global restructuring of production and migration' in Y. Sakamoto (ed.), *Global Transformation: Challenges to the State System*, Tokyo: UNU Publications, 1994, pp. 276–98.

10   D. Gordon, 'The global economy: new edifice or crumbling foundations?', *New Left Review* vol. 168, 1988.

11   For a brief overview of this approach refer to D. Held and A. McGrew, *Globalization/ Anti-globalization*, Cambridge: Polity Press, 2002, pp. 84–7; A. Hoogvelt, *Globalization and the Postcolonial World*; P. Hirst and G. Thompson, *Globalization in*

Question; Oswaldo De Rivero, *The Myth of Development: the Non-viable Economies of the 21st century*, London: Zed Books, 2001; J. Petra and H. Veltmeyer, *Globalization Unmasked: Imperialism in the 21st Century*, London: Zed Books, 2001; J. Petra and H. Veltmeyer, 'Globalisation of Imperialism', *Cambridge Review of International Affairs*, XIV:1 2000, pp. 32–48 and 'Age of reverse aid: neo-liberalism as catalyst of regression', *Development and Change*, 33:2 2002, pp. 281–93; S. Amin, *Capitalism in the Age of Globalization: The Management of Contemporary Society*, London: Zed Books, 1997.

12 D. Held, A. McGrew, D. Goldblatt and J. Perraton, *Global Transformations*, p. 167; D. Held, *Global Covenant*, p. 30. T. Nierop, *Systems and Regions in Global Politics: An Empirical Study of Diplomacy, International Organization and Trade 1950–1991*, Chichester: John Wiley, 1994.

13 Hoogvelt, *Globalization and the Postcolonial World*, p.76.

14 Ibid., p.90.

15 Ibid., p.78.

16 Ibid., p. 264.

17 United Nations, *World Investment Report 2001*, p. 9; and UNCTAD, *Development and Globalization: Facts and Figures*, Geneva: UNCTAD, 2004, p. 33 (the figure of 26.8% is taken from this report).

18 Figures for 1960 and 1973 are taken from, D. Held, A. McGrew, D. Goldblatt and J. Perraton, *Global Transformations,* p. 249.

19 Hoogvelt, *Globalization and the Postcolonial World*, p. 78.

20 China, Hong Kong, Mexico, Singapore and Brazil were the top five recipients.

21 Percentages represent share of FDI of total received by developing economies. Russia and Poland were also some of the main recipients each receiving 2.3% of the developing countries' share.

22 In current prices, FDI to the developing world has increased seven-fold. UNCTAD, *World Investment Report 2004*, Table B.3, pp.376–80.

23 Ibid., Table B.6.

24 World Bank, *World Development Report 2005*, Washington DC: World Bank, 2005, Table 3, pp. 260–1.

25 ECE, *Economic Survey of Europe 2002, No. 1*, Geneva: Economic Commission for Europe, 2002, p. 230.

26 United Nations, *International Trade Statistics Yearbook*, New York: UN, 2003, p. 467.

27 The figures quoted are for exports compared to Hoogvelt's figures for total trade. Given that this book is interested in wealth creation for developing countries, world exports are chosen. However, if one uses total trade the trends described here are approximately the same. Refer to WTO, *International Trade Statistics: 2004*, Geneva: WTO, 2004.

28 The table refers to the Chinese mainland and excludes Hong Kong which is aggregated into the six East Asian Traders.

29 A. Hoogvelt, *Globalization and the Postcolonial World*; Manuel Castells, *End of Millennium: The Information Age: Economy, Society and Culture Volume III*, 2nd ed., Oxford: Blackwell, 2000.

30 Ankie Hoogvelt, *Globalization and the Postcolonial World*, p.73.

31 WTO, *Selected Long-term Trends*, Geneva: WTO, 2004, Tables III.4, p. 40.

32 WTO, *Selected Long-term Trends*, Geneva: WTO, 2005, Tables IV.26, p. 129.

33 On the reasons for the Asian crisis and its aftermath, refer to W. Bello and S. Rosenfeld, *Dragons in Distress: Asia's Miracle Economics in Crisis*, Harmondsworth: Penguin, 1990; W. Bello, 'The Asian economic implosion: causes, dynamics, prospects', *Race and Class*, vol. 40:2/3; S. Gill, 'The geopolitics of the Asian Crisis', *Monthly Review*, vol. 50:10, March 1999; W. Tabb, 'The East Asian financial crisis', *Monthly Review*, vol. 50:2, pp. 34–48; R. Higgott, 'The Asian economic crisis: a study in the politics

of resentment', *New Political Economy*, vol. 3:3, 1998, pp. 333–57; Figures are from the World Bank's *Thailand and Malaysia at a Glance*, Online. Available HTTP: http://devdata.worldbank.org/AAG/tha_aag.pdf accessed (02 May 2006).

34 All data taken from United Nations, *International Trade Statistics Yearbook*, New York: UN, 2003, p. 467 and United Nations, *International Trade Statistics Yearbook*, New York: UN, 1960, pp. 12–17.

35 Oxfam, *Rigged Rules and Double Standards: Trade, Globalization, and the Fight against Poverty*, London: Oxfam, 2002, p. 50.

36 A. Rugman, *The End of Globalization*, London: Random House Business Books, 2000, p. 1. On regionalism and regionalization refer to J. Ravenhill, 'Regionalism' in J. Ravenhill (ed.), *Global Political Economy*, Oxford: Oxford University Press, 2005, pp. 120–22; World Bank, *Global Economic Prospects: Trade, Regionalism and Development*, Washington, DC: World Bank, 2005; WTO, *World Trade Report 2003*, Geneva: WTO, 2003; S. Schrim, *Globalization and the New Regionalism*, Cambridge: Polity Press, 2002; Björn Hettne, 'The Double Movement: global market versus regionalism', in R. Cox, *The New Realism: Perspectives on Multilateralism and World Order*, Basingstoke: Macmillan, 1997.

37 K. Ohmae, *The Borderless World: Power and Strategy in the Global Marketplace*, London: HarperCollins, 1990, p. xii. Although Ohmae also argues that this integration will expand beyond the so-called inter-linked economy of the triad to 'encompass most East European countries, most of Asian newly industrialized economies (NIEs), and some Latin American countries'. On triadization refer also to C. Hay, 'Globalization's impact on states', in J. Ravenhill (ed.), *Global Political Economy*, Oxford: Oxford University Press, 2005, pp. 235–62 and P. Hirst and G. Thompson, *Globalization in Question*, 1996, pp. 63–7.

38 ASEAN (1967) initially consisted of Indonesia, Malaysia, Philippines, Singapore and Thailand. Brunei joined in 1984.

39 For an excellent outline of these agreements refer to J. Ravenhill, 'Regionalism' in J. Ravenhill (ed.), *Global Political Economy*, Oxford: Oxford University Press, 2005, pp. 120–2.

40 The above is a summary of the hierarchical classification in World Bank, *Global Economic Prospects: Trade, Regionalism and Development*, Washington, DC: World Bank, 2005, p. 28.

41 J. Ravenhill, 'Regionalism', pp. 120–2.

42 Ibid., p. 130.

43 World Bank, *Global Economic Prospects*, p. 135.

44 J. Ravenhill, 'Regionalism', p. 117.

45 B. Hettne, 'Globalization and the new regionalism: the second great transformation', in B. Hettne, A. Inotai and O. Sunkel (eds), *Globalism and the New Regionalism*, Basingstoke: Macmillan, 1999, p. 17.

46 A. Rugman, *The End of Globalization*, p. 110.

47 B. Hettne, 'Globalization and the New Regionalism', p. 1.

48 Ibid. p. 2.

49 Ibid., p. 9.

50 B. Hettne, 'The Double Movement: global market versus regionalism', in R. Cox (ed.) *The New Realism: Perspectives on Multilateralism and World Order*, Tokyo: United Nations University Press, 1997, p. 240.

51 C. Oman, 'Globalization, regionalization and inequality' in A. Hurrell and N. Woods, *Inequality, Globalization, and World Politics*, Oxford: Oxford University Press, 1999, p. 59.

52 J. Mittelman, 'Rethinking the "New Regionalism" in the context of globalization', in B. Hettne, A. Inotai and O. Sunkel (eds), *Globalism and the New Regionalism*, Basingstoke: Macmillan, 1999, p. 39.

53 P. Hirst and G. Thompson, 'The future of globalisation', in J. Michie, *The Handbook of Globalisation*, Cheltenham: Edward Elgar, 2003, pp. 28–9.

54 A. Rugman, *The End of Globalization*, p. 96 and WTO, *Selected Long-Term Trends*, Geneva: WTO, 2004, Tables III.15, p. 47.

55 WTO, *Selected Long-term Trends*, Geneva: WTO, 2004, Tables II.3, 4 and 5.

56 UNCTAD, *World Investment Report 2001: Promoting Linkages*, New York: UNCTAD, 2001, p. 13.

57 For example, in the case of Portugal investment flows increased from $2 billion in 1980 to $11 billion in 1990. Refer to S. Donnenfeld, 'Regional blocs and foreign direct investment', *Review of International Economics*, vol. 11:5, 2003, pp. 770–88.

58 G. Thompson, 'The supra-national regionalization of the international financial system: how far and with what prospects?'; A. Rugman, *The End of Globalization*; A. Rugman, 'Globalisation and Regional Production', in J. Ravenhill (ed.), *Global Political Economy*, Oxford: Oxford University Press, 2005, pp. 263–90; A. Rugman, 'Regional Multinationals and the Myth of Globalization', *CSGR Annual Conference*, October 2005, Available. Online http://www2.warwick.ac.uk/fac/soc/csgr/activitiesnews/conferences/2005_conferences/8_annual_conference/rugman.doc (accessed 20 October 2006); A. Rugman, 'Regional transnationals and triad strategy', *Transnational Corporations*, vol. 13:3, 2004, pp. 1–20; A. Rugman, *The Regional Multinationals: MNEs and 'Global' Strategic Management*, Cambridge: Cambridge University Press, 2005; P. Hirst and G. Thompson, *Globalization in Question*, 1999.

59 A. Rugman, 'From globalisation to regionalism: the foreign direct investment dimension of international finance', in K. Kaiser, J. Kirton and J. Daniels (eds), *Shaping a New Financial System: Challenges of Governance in a Globalizing World*, Aldershot: Ashgate Publishers, 2000, p. 195.

60 OECD, 'Intra-industry and intra-firm trade and the internationalisation of production', *OECD Economic* Outlook, vol. 71, Section 6, June 2002. Online, Available http://www.oecd.org/dataoecd/6/18/2752923.pdf (accessed 21 June 2003), pp. 163–4.

61 A. Rugman, 'From globalisation to regionalism', p. 187; P. Hirst and G. Thompson, 'The future of globalisation', p. 28.

62 The World Bank, *World Development Indicators 2004*, Section 6.1, 'Integration with the world economy'.

63 P. Krugman, 'Growing world trade', pp. 332–7

64 J. H. Dunning, 'The new geography of FDI', in Ngaire Woods (ed.), *The Political Economy of Globalization*, Basingstoke: Palgrave, 2000, pp. 20–53.

65 For more on this, refer to M. Christopher, *Logistics and Supply Chain Management: Strategies for Reducing Cost and Improving Service*, Harlow: Prentice Hall, 1992, p. 15.

66 P. Dicken, *Global Shift: Transforming the World Economy*, 4th ed., London: Sage Publications, 2003, p. 14.

67 OECD, 'Intra-industry and intra-firm trade and the internationalisation of production', *OECD Economic* Outlook, vol. 71, Section 6, June 2002. Available. Online http://www.oecd.org/dataoecd/6/18/2752923.pdf (accessed 21 June 2003).

68 A. Hoogvelt, *Globalization and the Postcolonial World*, pp.70–7.

69 OECD, 'Intra-industry and intra-firm trade and the internationalisation of production', p. 162.

70 P. Dicken, *Global Shift*, p. 14.

71 D. Hummels, J. Ishii and K. Yi, 'The nature and growth of vertical specialization in world trade', *Journal of International Economics*, vol. 54, 2001, pp. 85, 93. See also D. Hummels, D. Rapoport and K. Yi, 'Vertical specialization and the changing nature of world trade', *Federal Reserve Bank of New York Economic Policy Review*, June 1998, pp.79–99

72 D. Hummels, D. Rapoport and K. Yi, 'Vertical specialization and the changing nature of world trade', pp. 85, 88.
73 D. Hummels, J. Ishii and K. Yi, 'The nature and growth of vertical specialization', p. 93.
74 Ibid p. 93.
75 Oxfam, *Rigged Rules*, p. 76.
76 Ibid., p. 77.
77 D. Held, A. McGrew, D. Goldblatt and J. Perraton, *Global Transformations*, p. 172.
78 Oxfam, 'South-South Trade and GSTP', June 2004. Available. Online http://www.oxfam.org.uk/what_we_do/issues/trade/south_trade.htm (accessed 01 May 2006).
79 UNCTAD, *Trade And Development Report 2005: New Features Of Global Interdependence*, Geneva: UNCTAD, 2005, p.130.
80 Oxfam, *Rigged Rules*, p. 150.
81 Ibid., p.151.
82 UNCTAD, *Development and Globalization*, p. 61; UNCTAD, Trade and Development Report 2004, Geneva: UNCTAD, 2004, p. 55, Table 2.4.
83 A. Hoogvelt, *Globalization and the Postcolonial World*, p.172.
84 World Bank, *World development Indicators 2004*, pp. 198–200.
85 UNCTAD, *Development and Globalization*, p. 57.
86 Oxfam, *Rigged Rules*, p. 71.
87 All quotes and figures from S. Lall, 'The technological structure and performance of developing country manufactured exports, 1985–98', *Oxford Development Studies*, vol. 28:3, 2000, pp. 343–4.
88 Ibid., pp. 344.
89 Ibid., p. 345. Resource-based manufactures are said to include prepared foods, petroleum/rubber products, cement; low-technology manufactures include textiles, pottery, furniture, plastic products, toys etc.; medium technology manufactures include automotive products, synthetics, iron chemicals and paints, ships, industrial machinery; high technology manufactures include TVs, transistors, data processing and telecommunications equipment, pharmaceuticals. For a full list refer to above p. 341.
90 Ibid., Table 4, p. 347.
91 Ibid., p. 347.
92 Ibid., p. 344.
93 Ibid., Table A2, p. 367.
94 OECD, 'Intra-industry and intra-firm trade and the internationalisation of production', p. 163.
95 Ibid., pp. 163–4.
96 On the effect of state capture by élites and the impact this has on economic performance refer to Christine Jones and Ana Revenga, *Making Transition Work for Everyone: Poverty and Inequality in Europe and Central Asia*, Washington, DC: World Bank, 2000. On the internal factors affecting the economic performance of developing countries, particularly conflict, refer to United Nations, *Investing in Development: a Practical Plan to Achieve the Millennium Development Goals*, London: Earthscan, 2005, Chapter 14.

4 Trade liberalization and economic growth

1 World Bank, *Globalization, Growth, and Poverty: Building an Inclusive World Economy*, Washington, DC: World Bank, 2002, p. 9.
2 World Bank, *World Development Indicators 2004*, Washington DC: World Bank, 2004, p. 303 and WTO, *Selected Long-term Trends*, Geneva: WTO, 2004, p.191.
3 G. Garrett, 'The three worlds of globalization: market integration, economic growth and the distribution of income in high, middle and low-income countries'. Online.

Available HTTP: http//:www.international.ucla.edu/profile/ggarrett (accessed 11 June 2005), p. 6.

4   C. Thomas, *Global Governance, Development and Human Security*, London: Pluto Press, 2000, p. 55.

5   L. Andor and M. Summers, *Market Failure: a Guide to the East European 'Economic Miracle'*, London: Pluto Press, 1998, p. 2.

6   D. Rodrik, *The Global Governance of Trade: As if Trade Development Really Mattered*, New York: UNDP, 2001, p. 20.

7   C. Thomas, 'Globalization and development in the South', in J. Ravenhill (ed.), *Global Political Economy*, Oxford: Oxford University Press, 2005, pp. 328–9.

8   Thus avoiding another cause of inflation. Devaluing a currency may lead to an increase in exports, but it also leads to domestic inflation as internal prices increase to reflect world prices (domestic prices x exchange rate = world prices).

9   Although the details differ in my version, the three-fold classification is taken from C. Thomas, 'Globalization and development in the South', pp. 328–9.

10   For more on all three stimuli refer to J. Stiglitz and A. Charlton, *Fair Trade for All: How Trade Can Promote Development*, Oxford: Oxford University Press, 2005, p. 30.

11   D. Rodrik, *Comments on "Trade, Growth, and Poverty"*, October 2000. Online. Available http://ksghome.harvard.edu/~drodrik/Rodrik%20on%20Dollar-Kraay. PDF, (accessed 23 March 2006), p. 2 and B. Milanovic, 'The two faces of globalization: against globalization as we know it', *World Development*, 2003, vol. 31:4, pp. 674–5.

12   M. Castells, *The Information Age: Economy, Society and Culture, vol. III: End of Millennium*, Oxford: Blackwell, 2000, 2nd ed., p. 86.

13   Oxfam, *Rigged Rules and Double Standards: Trade, Globalisation, and the Fight against Poverty*, London: Oxfam, 2002, p. 150.

14   Ibid., p. 151.

15   UNCTAD, *Globalization and Development*, Geneva: UNCTAD, 2004, p. 61. Between 1980 and 2003 the decline in terms of trade was 1.3% per annum for the whole of the developing world. Refer to UNCTAD, *Trade and Development Report 2004*, Geneva: UNCTAD, 2004, p. 55, Table 2.4.

16   R. Kaplinsky, Globalization, *Poverty and Inequality: Between a Rock and a Hard Place,* Cambridge: Polity Press, 2005, pp. 161–2

17   *Globalization, Growth, and Poverty*, p. 28.

18   Ibid., p. 5.

19   Ibid., p. 5

20   D. Rodrik, *Comments on 'Trade, Growth, and Poverty'*, p. 2 and Branko Milanovic, 'The two faces of globalization', pp. 674–5.

21   Unweighted, the average tariffs reduced from 32.7% to 19.5% for the globalizers and 30.1% to 20.6% for the non-globalizers in the same period. D. Dollar and A. Kraay, 'Trade, Growth and Poverty', *World Bank Policy Research Department Working Paper No. 2615*, Washington: World Bank, 2001, pp.8, 28.

22   IMF, *World Economic Outlook,* Washington, DC: IMF, 1997. Quoted in F. Rodriguez and D. Rodrik, 'Trade policy and economic growth: a skeptic's guide to the cross-national evidence', *National Bureau of Economic Research Working Paper 7081*, April 1999, p. 1.

23   J. Sachs and A. Warner, 'Economic reform and the process of global integration', *Brookings Papers on Economic Activity*, vol. 1995:1, 1995, p. 22.

24   F. Rodriguez and D. Rodrik, 'Trade Policy and Economic Growth', p. 20.

25   Ibid., p. 39. Refer to D. Ben-David, 'Equalizing exchange: trade liberalization and income convergence', *The Quarterly Journal of Economics*, vol. 108:3, 1993, pp. 653–79; S. Edwards, 'Openness, productivity and growth: what do we really know?', *Economics Journal*, vol. 108, 1998, pp. 383–98; D. Dollar, 'Outward-oriented

developing economies really do grow more rapidly: evidence from 95 LDCs, 1976–85', *Economic Development and Cultural Change*, vol. 40, 1992, pp. 523–44.

26 J. Stiglitz and A. Charlton, *Fair Trade For All*, p. 35.

27 World Bank, *Globalization, Growth, and Poverty*, p. 37.

28 D. Dollar and A. Kraay, 'Trade, growth and poverty', *World Bank Research Report WPS2615*, Washington, DC: World Bank, June 2001, p.3. Online. Available http://wdsbeta.worldbank.org/external/default/WDSContentServer/IW3P/IB/2002/08/23/000094946_02082304142939/Rendered/PDF/multi0page.pdf (accessed 16 June 2006), p.1.

29 Branko Milanovic, 'The two faces of globalization', p. 673. WENAO stands for Western Europe and Northern America.

30 A. Sumner makes a similar point, but with slightly different definitions. Refer to A. Sumner, 'Why are we still arguing about globalization?', *Journal of International Development*, 2004, vol. 16, p. 1016.

31 D. Rodrik, *The Global Governance of Trade*, p. 22.

32 For example the World Bank includes both in its list of globalizers in its report, *Globalization, Growth, and Poverty*.

33 World Bank, *India at a Glance*. Online. Available http://devdata.worldbank.org/AAG/ind_aag.pdf (accessed 28 March 2006).

34 Refer to Jayati Ghosh, *Christian Aid Policy Discussion Paper: Is India a Success Story of Economic Liberalization?*, p. 4. Online. Available http://www.christian-aid.org.uk/indepth/505india/CA%20policy%20 discussion%2001.pdf (accessed 12 March 2006) and World Bank, *World Development Report 2005:*, Washington DC: World Bank, 2005, Table 3, pp. 260–1.

35 Richard McGregor, 'Beijing lifts economic growth estimates', *Financial Times*, 10.01.2006, p. 3. and World Bank, *China at Glance*. Online. Available http://www.worldbank.org.cn/English/Content/chn_aag02.pdf (accessed 28 March 2006).

36 J. Bhagwati, *In Defense of Globalization*, Oxford: Oxford University Press, 2004, p. 64.

37 World Bank, *Globalization, Growth, and Poverty*, p. ix.

38 D. Rodrik, *Comments on 'Trade, Growth, and Poverty'*, p. 2.

39 The current account deficit increased from '$2.8 billion in 1980–1 to $9.68 billion in 1990–91'. Refer to T. N. Srinivasan, 'Comments on Dani Rodrik and Arvind Subraimanian, "From Hindu Growth" to productivity surge: The mystery of the Indian growth transition'. Online. Available http://www.imf.org/ external/pubs/ft/staffp/2004/00–00/sriniv.pdf, (accessed 23 March 2006), p. 8 and Jagdish Bhagwati, *India in Transition: Freeing the Economy*, Oxford: Clarendon Paperbacks, 1993, p. 66.

40 J. Bhagwati, *India In Transition*, p. 86.

41 D. Rodrik and A. Subramanian, 'From "Hindu Growth" To productivity surge', p. 2.

42 Ibid., p. 20, fn. 26 and J. Bhagwati, *India In Transition*, p. 80.

43 Ibid., p. 19.

44 J. Bhagwati, *India In Transition*, p. 85.

45 B. Milanovic, 'The two faces of globalization', pp.674–5.

46 D. Rodrik, 'What's so Special about China's Exports?', 2006. Online. Available http://ksghome.harvard.edu/~drodrik/Chinaexports.pdf (accessed 23 March 2006), pp. 18, 22.

47 UNDP, *Making Global Trade Work for People*, Stirling, Virginia: Earthscan Publications, 2003, p. 31.

48 Ibid., p. 30.

49 Ibid., p. 28.

50 Ibid., p. 30.

51 W. Bello, 'The Asian economic implosion: causes, dynamics, prospects', *Race and Class*, vol. 40:2/3, p. 135.

52 Although in September 1998, Malaysia, against the wishes of the IMF, did put in place selective exchange controls. Refer to J. Bhagwati, *In Defense of Globalization*, p. 206.

53 J. Bhagwati, *In Defense of Globalization*, p. 201. See also, D. Held, *Global Covenant: The Social Democratic Alternative to the Washington Consensus*, Cambridge: Polity Press, 2004.

54 G. Garrett, 'The three worlds of globalization', p. 9.

55 E. Prasaad, K. Rogoff, S. Wei and M. Kose, 'Effects of financial globalization on developing countries: some empirical evidence', *IMF*, 17 March 2003. Available. Online at http://www.imf.org/external/np/res/docs/2003/031703.pdf, (accessed 3 April 2006), p. 10

56 Concerning this change in the IFI's stance refer to D. Held, *Global Covenant: The Social Democratic Alternative to the Washington Consensus*, Cambridge: Polity Press, 2004, p. 49 and J. Bhagwati, *In Defense of Globalization*, p. 207.

57 A. Amsden, *Asia's Next Giant: South Korea and Late Industrialisation*, Oxford: Oxford University Press, 1989, p.13.

58 World Bank, *The East Asian Miracle: Economic Growth and Public Policy*, Oxford: Oxford University Press, 1993, p. 1.

59 United Nations, *Globalization and Development*, Geneva: United Nations Conference on Trade and Development, 2004, p.57.

60 S. Lall, 'The technological structure and performance of developing country manufactured exports, 1985–98', p. 345. Resource-based manufactures are said to include prepared foods, petroleum/rubber products, cement; low-technology manufactures include textiles, pottery, furniture, plastic products, toys; medium-technology manufactures include automotive products, synthetics, iron chemicals and paints, ships, industrial machinery; high-technology manufactures include TVs, transistors, data processing and telecommunications equipment, pharmaceuticals. For a full list refer to above p. 341.

61 Ibid., Table 4, p. 347.

62 Ibid., p. 347.

63 C. Johnson, *MITI and The Japanese Miracle: the Gowth of Industrial Policy, 1925–1975*, Palo Alto, CA: Stanford University Press, 1982; M. Woo-Cumings, *The Developmental State*, Ithaca, NY: Cornell University Press, 1999; J. Woo, *Race to the Swift: State and Finance in Korean Industrialization*, New York: Columbia University Press, 1991; and R. Wade, *Governing the Market: Economic Theory and the Role of Government in East Asian Industrialization*, Princeton, NJ: Princeton University Press, 1990.

64 S. Gill, 'The geopolitics of the Asian crisis', *Monthly Review*, vol. 50:10, March 1999, p. 4.

65 D. Rodrik, *The Global Governance of Trade: as if Trade Development Really Mattered*, New York: UNDP, 2001, pp.18–19.

66 A. Amsden, 'The state and Taiwan's economic development', in P. Evans, D. Rueschmeyer and T. Skocpol, *Bringing the State Back In*, Cambridge: Cambridge University Press, 1985, p. 97.

67 Milanovic argues that China maintained its 40% average weighted tariff rate until 1996 when it was reduced to 26% and then further reduced to 26% and for India the rates were between 80 and 90% coming down to 40% between 1991 and 3. B. Milanovic, 'The two faces of globalization', pp. 676.

68 D. Rodrik, *The Global Governance of Trade*, p.24.

69 D. Rodrik outlines the similar cases of South Korea and Taiwan in D. Rodrik, *The Global Governance of Trade*, p. 6.

70 R. Appelbaum and J. Henderson (eds), *States and Development in the Asian Pacific Rim*, Newbury Park, CA: Sage Publications, 1992, p. 22.

71 A. Amsden, *Asia's Next Giant*, p.17.

72 L. Weiss, *The Myth of the Powerless State: Governing the Economy in a Global Era*, Cambridge: Polity Press, 1998, pp. 6, 48.

73 P. Evans, *Embedded Autonomy: States and Industrial Transformation*, Princeton, NJ: Princeton University Press, 1995, p.12.

74 L. Weiss, *The Myth of the Powerless State*, p. 48.

75 Ibid., p. 4.

76 Ibid., p. 24.

77 Ibid., p. 37.

78 P. Evans, *Embedded Autonomy: States and Industrial Transformation*, Princeton, NJ: Princeton University Press, 1995, p. 230.

79 L. Weiss, *The Myth of the Powerless State*, p. 38.

80 World Bank, *The East Asian Miracle*, p. 113.

81 M. Castells, 'Four Asian tigers with a dragon head: a comparative analysis of the state, economy, and society in the Asian Pacific Rim', in R. Appelbaum and J. Henderson (eds), *States and Development*; P. Evans, 'Transnational linkages and the role of the state', in P. Evans, D. Rueschmeyer and T. Skocpol (eds), *Bringing the State Back In*, Cambridge: CUP, 1985, p. 209

82 D. Rodrik, *The New Global Economy and Developing Countries: Making Openness Work*, Washington, DC: Overseas Development Council, 1999, p. 56.

83 A. Amsden, *Asia's Next Giant*, pp.17, 144; UNDP, *Making Global Trade Work for People*, Sterling, Virginia: Earthscan Publications, 2003, p. 39; Tabb, W., 'The East Asian financial crisis', *Monthly Review*, vol. 50:2, p. 31.

84 R. Appelbaum and J. Henderson (eds), *States and Development*, p. 22.

85 In 1960 the highest business tax was slashed from 32.5% to just 18%; refer to D. Rodrik, *The New Global Economy and Developing Countries*, p. 53.

86 UNDP, *Making Global Trade Work For People*, p. 39; Dani Rodrik outlines the similar cases of South Korea and Taiwan in D. Rodrik, *The Global Governance of Trade*, p. 2.

87 R. Appelbaum and J. Henderson, *States and Development*, p. 22.

88 M. Castells, 'Four Asian tigers with a dragon head', p. 43.

89 R. Appelbaum and J. Henderson (eds), *States and Development*, 1992, p. 21.

90 R. Appelbaum and J. Henderson (eds), *States and Development*, 1992, p. 12.

91 A. Amsden, *Asia's Next Giant*, p.14 and R. Appelbaum and J. Henderson (eds), *States and Development*, p. 22.

92 D. Rodrik, 'What's so Special about China's Exports?', 2006. Online. Available http://ksghome.harvard.edu/~drodrik/Chinaexports.pdf, (accessed 23 March 2006), p. 24.

93 J. Bhagwati, *India in Transition*, p. 85.

94 A. Amsden, *Asia's Next Giant*, Chapter One.

95 R. Kaplinsky, *Globalization, Poverty and Inequality: Between a Rock and a Hard Place*, Cambridge: Polity Press, 2005, p. 62.

96 J. A. Schumpeter, *The Theory of Economic Development: an Inquiry into Profits, Capital, Credit, Interest, and the Business Cycle*, Cambridge, MA: Harvard University Press, 1951, Chapter IV.

97 The above is a summary of Raphael's Kaplinsky classification in, *Globalization, Poverty and Inequality*, Chapter 3.

98 A. Amsden, *Asia's Next Giant*, p.141.

90 Ibid., p. 21.

100 Ibid., pp. 4, 5.

101 Refer to R. Kaplinsky, *Globalization, Poverty and Inequality*, Chapter 3.

102 D. Rodrik, *The New Global Economy and Developing Countries*, p. 33.

103 World Bank, *The East Asian Miracle*, pp. 2–4.

104 Ibid., p.5.

105 Ibid., pp. 5, 347–52.

106 Ibid., p. 356.
107 Ibid., p. 358.
108 R. Wade, *Governing the Market,* pp. 348–9.
109 L. Weiss, *The Myth of the Powerless State*, p. xiii.
110 L. Weiss, *The Myth of the Powerless State*, p. x.
111 Y. Akyüz, *The WTO Negotiations on Industrial Tariffs: What is at Stake for Developing Countries*, Geneva: Third World Network, 2005. Online. Available http://www.twnside.org (accessed 03 August 2005), p. 28.
112 D. Rodrik, *The New Global Economy and Developing Countries*, p. 137.
113 Ibid., p. 137.

5 Globalization and the reconfiguration of the state

1 M. Wolf, 'Will the nation-state survive globalization?', *Foreign Affairs*, vol. 80:1, 2001, p. 178.
2 For more on the differences between juridical and political sovereignty refer to C. Brown and K. Ainley, *Understanding International Relations*, Basingstoke: Palgrave Macmillan, 2005, 3rd ed., p.116.
3 R.O. Keohane and J. S. Nye, *Transnational Relations and World Politics*, Cambridge, MA: Harvard University Press, 1972, p. 393 – Quoted in G. Garrett, 'Global markets and national politics: collision course or virtuous circle', *International Organization*, vol. 52:4, 1998, p. 795.
4 C. Hay, 'Globalization's impact on states' in J. Ravenhill (ed.), *Global Political Economy*, Oxford: Oxford University Press, 2005, p. 242
5 J. A. Scholte, 'Global capitalism and the state', *International Affairs*, vol. 73:3, 1997, p. 448.
6 F. Scharpf, *Governing in Europe: Effective and Democratic?*, New York: Oxford University Press, 1996, p. 6; F. Scharpf, 'Economic integration, democracy and the Welfare State', *Journal of European Public Policy*, Vol. 4:1, 1997, p. 19.
7 S. Strange, *The Retreat of the State: the Diffusion of Power in the World Economy*, Cambridge: Cambridge University Press, 1996, pp.4, 87.
8 G. Garrett, 'Global markets and national politics: collision course or virtuous circle', *International Organization*, vol. 52:4, 1998, p. 788.
9 J. Gray, *False Dawn: the Delusions of Global Capitalism*, London: Granta Books, 1999, p. 79.
10 M. Obstfeld, 'The global capital market: benefactor or menace?' *The Journal of Economic Perspectives*, vol. 12:4, p. 19.
11 J. Gray, *False Dawn*, p. 89.
12 N. Rudra, 'Re-assessing the relationship between globalization and welfare: welfare spending and international competitiveness in less developed countries' in S. Chan and J. Scarritt (eds), *Coping with Globalization: Cross-national Patterns in Domestic Governance and Policy Performance*, London: Frank Cass, 2002, p. 146.
13 The above is a summary of the pressures that globalization bring to bear set out by Geoffrey Garrett in G. Garrett, 'Global markets and national politics', p. 788.
14 J. Gray, *False Dawn*, p. 88.
15 S. Strange, *The Retreat of the State*, p. 73.
16 M. Mann, 'The autonomous power of the state', in John Hall (ed.), *States in History*, Oxford: Blackwell, 1986, p. 113
17 S. Strange, *The Retreat of the State*, p. 73.
18 Ibid., p. 74.
19 P. Cerny, 'Paradoxes of the competition state: the dynamics of political globalization', *Government and Opposition*, vol. 32:2, 1997, p. 261.
20 S. Strange, *The Retreat of the State*, p. 77.

21 P. Cerny, 'Paradoxes of the competition state', p. 260; See also P. Cerny, *The Changing Architecture of Politics: Structure, Agency, and the Future of the State*, London: Age Publications, 1990, especially Chapter 8; P. Cerny, 'What next for the state?', in E. Kofman and G. Youngs (eds), *Globalization: Theory and Practice*, London: Pinter, 1996, pp. 123–37.

22 P. Cerny, 'Globalization and the changing logic of collective action', *International Organization*, vol. 49:4, 1995, p. 611.

23 P. Cerny, 'Paradoxes of the competition state', p. 260.

24 P. Cerny, 'Globalization and the changing logic of collective action', p. 611.

25 P. Cerny, 'Paradoxes of the competition state', p. 258.

26 G. Teeple, *Globalization and the Decline of social Reform*, Toronto: Garamond Press, 1995, p. 113.

27 P. Cerny, 'Paradoxes of the competition state', pp. 260–70.

28 BBC, 'Britain's asset sell-off', Online. Available HTTP: <http://news.bbc.co.uk/1/hi/business/5079148.stm> (accessed 10 January 2007); M. Melhuish, *Energy and Sustainable Development in New Zealand*, Wellington, New Zealand: Helio International, 2002. Online. Available http://www.helio-international.org/Helio/Reports/2002 /English/NewZealand/NZtot.pdf (accessed 10 January 2007).

29 *The Economist*, 'Under PFIre', 13–19 January 2007, p. 29.

30 *The Economist*, 'Blood and treasure: after the windfall of Iraq, where is the next fortune to be found?', 4–10 November 2006, p. 78.

31 S. Ranger, 'Offshoring an "Unstoppable Force" says NHS IT Chief', Online. Available http://www. services.silicon.com/offshoring.html (accessed 20 July 2006). Similar moves have been reported in the United States.

32 R. Rosecrance, 'International security and the virtual state: states and firms in world politics', *Review of International Studies*, vol.28:4 p. 447.

33 Ibid., p. 448.

34 Ibid., p. 449.

35 *The Economist*, 'Peninsular campaign: what the battle for Portugal Telecom says about business in Iberia', 13–19 2007, p. 60.

36 BBC, 'Patriotism and protectionism in the EU', Online. Available http://news.bbc.co.uk/1/hi/world/europe/4837150.stm (accessed 10 January 2007).

37 D. Rodrik, *Has Globalization Gone too Far?*, Washington, DC: Institute For International Economics, 1997, p. 64. See also P. Katzenstein, *Small States in World Markets: Industrial Policy in Europe*, Ithaca, NY: Cornell University Press, 1985 and D. Cameron, 'The expansion of the public economy: a comparative analysis', *American Political Science Review*, vol. 72:4, pp. 1243–61.

38 D. Rodrik, 'Why Do more open economies have bigger governments?', *NBER Working Paper Series 5537*, Cambridge, MA: National Bureau of Economic Research, April 1996, p. 26.

39 Ibid., p. 26.

40 Refer to E. Heckscher, 'The effect of foreign trade on the distribution of income' in The American Economic Association, *Readings in the Theory of International Trade*, London: Allen & Unwin, 1950, pp. 272–300; B. Ohlin, *Interregional and International Trade*, Cambridge, MA: Harvard University Press, 1933; J. L. Ford, *The Ohlin–Heckscher Theory of the Basis and Effects of Commodity Trade*, London: Asia Publishing House, 1965.

41 L. Mosely, *Global Capital and National Governments*, Cambridge: Cambridge University Press, 2003; D. Swank, *Global Capital, Political Institutions, and Policy Change in Developed Welfare States*, Cambridge: Cambridge University Press, 2002; G. Garrett, 'Global markets and national politics: collision course or virtuous circle', *International Organization*, vol. 52:4, 1998; pp. 787–824; Geoffrey Garrett, 'Shrinking states? Globalization and national autonomy in the OECD', *Oxford Development Studies*, vol. 26:1, 1998, pp. 71–98.   See also

P. Katzenstein, *Small States in World Markets: Industrial Policy in Europe*, Ithaca, NY: Cornell University Press, 1985 and D. Cameron, 'The expansion of the public economy: a comparative analysis', *American Political Science Review*, vol. 72:4, pp. 1243–61.

42 G. Garrett, 'Global markets and national politics, p. 814

43 D. Swank, *Global Capital*, , p. 256.

44 Ibid., p. 249 and G. Garrett, 'Global markets and national politics, p. 814. See also G. Garrett, 'Capital mobility, trade, and the domestic politics of economic policy', *International Organization*, vol. 49:4, 1995, pp. 657–87; L. Mosely, *Global Capital.*

45 D. Swank, *Global Capital*, pp. 277–8; G. Garrett, 'Global markets and national politics'.

46 G. Garrett, 'Global markets and national politics', p. 815.

47 D. Rodrik, *Has Globalization Gone Too Far?*, Washington, DC: Institute For International Economics, 1997, p. 64.

48 G. Garrett, 'Capital Mobility', p. 682.

49 G. Garrett, *Partisan Politics*, p. 133

50 G. Garrett, 'Global markets', p. 804. Layna Mosely finds that the premium is even less with a ten per cent deficit attracting on average only 0.5 per cent extra, although this seems rather low. Refer to L. Mosely, *Global Capital*, p. 85.

51 Ibid., p. 791.

52 Ibid., p. 801.

53 H. Wilensky, *Rich Democracies: Political Economy, Public Policy, and Performance*, Berkeley, CA: University of California Press, 2002, p. 654.

54 Ibid., p. 640.

55 W. Cooke and D. Noble, 'Industrial Relations', p. 596 and F. Traxler and B. Woiteach, 'Transnational investment and national labour market regimes: a case of "regime shopping"', *European Journal of Industrial Relations*, Vol. 6:2, p. 149.

56 L. Weiss, *The Myth of the Powerless State: Governing the Economy in a Global Era*, Cambridge: Polity Press, 1998, pp. 207–8. See also L. Weiss, 'Globalization and the myth of the powerless state', *New Left Review*, vol. 225, Sept-Oct. 1997, pp. 3–27.

57 M. Lind, 'The Catalytic State', *National Interest*, vol. 27, pp. 3–12. Quoted in L. Weiss, *The Myth of the Powerless State*, p. 209.

58 H. Martin and H. Schumann, *The Global Trap: Globalization and the Assault on Democracy and Prosperity*, London: Zed Books, 1997, p. 7.

59 Ibid., p.68

60 William Greider, *One World, Ready or Not: the Manic Logic of Global Capitalism*, New York: Simon & Schuster, 1996, p. 281 , quoted in J. Gray, *False Dawn*, p. 91.

61 H. Martin and H. Schumann, *The Global Trap*, p.68.

62 Ibid., pp. 198–201.

63 Ibid., p. 201.

64 G. Teeple, *Globalization*, pp. 150–1.

65 H. Martin and H. Schumann, *The Global Trap*, p. 206–7.

66 G. Teeple, *Globalization*, pp. 150–1.

67 P. Hirst. and G. Thompson, *Globalization in Question*, p. 188.

68 Ibid., p. 169.

69 V. Tanzi, 'Globalization, tax competition and the future of tax systems', *IMF Working Paper*, Washington, DC:IMF, 1996, p. 21.

70 Ibid., pp. 1–21.

71 C. Hay, 'Globalization's impact on states', in Ravenhill, J. (ed.), *Global Political Economy*, Oxford: Oxford University Press, 2005, p. 247.

72 A. Maddison, 'The nature and functioning of european capitalism: a historical and comparative perspective', *Banca Nazionale Del Lavoro Quarterly Review*, Vol. L: 203, pp. 431–79.

73 G. Garrett, *Partisan*, pp. 136–9.

74 C. Hay, 'Globalization's impact on states', p. 260.
75 F. Scharpf, 'Economic integration, democracy and the Welfare State', *Journal of European Public Policy*, Vol. 4:1, 1997, p. 26.
76 A. Maddison, 'The Nature and functioning of European capitalism', p. 457.
77 M. Wolf, *Why Globalization Works*, New Haven, CT: Yale Note Bene, 2005.
78 A. Maddison, 'The Nature and functioning of European capitalism', p. 438. Also V. Tanzi and L. Schuknecht, 'The Growth of Government and the Reform of the State in Industrial Countries': *Working Paper WP/95/130*, Washington, DC: IMF, December 1995, p. 12.
79 V. Tanzi and L. Schuknecht, 'The growth of government', pp. 1–39.
80 V. Tanzi, 'Globalization and the future of social protection', p. 9.
81 G. Esping-Andersen, 'Welfare states without work: the impasse of labour shedding and familialism in continental European social policy', in G. Esping-Andersen, *Welfare States in Transition: National Adaptations in Global Economies*, London: Sage Publications, 1996, p. 73.
82 *OECD Factbook 2006: Economic, Environmental and Social Statistics*, Paris: OECD, 2006.
83 D. Swank, *Global Capital*, p. 279.
84 Ibid., p. 280.
85 Ibid., p. 66.
86 M. Rhodes, 'The Welfare State: internal challenges, external constraints', in M. Rhodes, P. Heywood and V. Wright (eds), *Developments in West European Politics*, Basingstoke: Macmillan, 1997, p. 63; G. Esping-Andersen, 'After the Golden Age? welfare dilemmas in a global economy', in G. Esping-Andersen, *Welfare States in Transition: National Adaptations in Global Economies*, London: Sage Publications, 1996, pp. 1–31; G. Esping-Andersen, *The Three Worlds of Welfare Capitalism*, Princeton, NJ: Princeton University Press, 1990.
87 *The Economist*, 'In the Shadow of prosperity', 20–26 January 2007, pp. 28–30.
88 G. Esping-Andersen, 'After the Golden Age?', pp. 1–31.
89 ILO, World Labour Report 2000, ILO, Geneva, 2000, Statistical Annex, Table 14. Online. Available http://www-ilo-mirror.cornell.edu/public/english/ protection/ socsec/publ/wlrblurb.htm (accessed 23 July 2006).
90 N. Rudra, 'Globalization and the decline of the Welfare State in less-developed countries', *International Organization*, vol. 56:2, pp. 411–45.
91 N. Rudra, 'Openness, welfare spending, and inequality in the developing world', *International Studies Quarterly*, vol. 48, 2004, pp. 686, 699.
92 L. Mosely, *Global Capital*, p. 110.
93 Ibid., p. 111.
94 Ibid., p. 116.
95 Ibid,, pp. 114–5.
96 Ibid., pp. 128, 148.
97 W. Cooke and D. Noble, 'Industrial relations systems', p. 596.
98 Ibid., p. 603.
99 N. Rudra, 'Globalization and the decline of the Welfare State', p. 421 and J. Stiglitz and A. Charlton, *Fair Trade For All: How Trade Can Promote Development*, Oxford: Oxford University Press, 2005.
100 N. Rudra, 'Globalization and the Decline of the Welfare State', p. 420.
101 G. Teeple, *Globalization,* pp. 150–1.
102 L. Mosely, *Global Capital*, pp. 106–7.
103 F. Cheru, 'Global apartheid and the challenge to civil society: Africa in the transformation of world order', in R. Cox (ed.) *The New Realism: Perspectives on Multilateralism and World Order*, Tokyo: United Nations University Press, 1997, p. 213.

104 Thus avoiding another cause of inflation. Devaluing a currency may lead to an increase in exports, but it also leads to domestic inflation as internal prices increase to reflect world prices (domestic prices x exchange rate = world prices).

105 G. Mohan, 'Globalisation and governance: the paradoxes of adjustment in sub-Saharan Africa', in E. Kofman and G. Youngs (eds), *Globalization: Theory and Practice*, London: Pinter, 1996, p. 292.

106 Frances Stewart and Albert Berry, 'Globalization, liberalization, and inequality: expectations and experience', in A. Hurrell and N. Woods (eds), *Inequality, Globalization, and World Politics*, Oxford: Oxford University Press, 1999, pp. 150–1.

107 All quotes from F. Stewart and A. Berry, 'Globalization, liberalization', p.167.

108 Ibid., p.167.

109 Ibid., p.150–1.

110 *The Economist*, 'In the shadow of prosperity', 20–26 January 2007, pp. 28–30.

111 G. Esping-Andersen, 'After the Golden Age?', pp. 13–14.

6 Patterns of global poverty and inequality

1 C. Dickens, *A Tale of Two Cities*, London: Penguin Books, 2007, p. 1.

2 L. Elliott and V. Brittain, 'The rich and poor grow further apart', *The Guardian*, 09 September 1998, p. 18.

3 R. Kaplinsky., *Globalization, Poverty and Inequality: Between a Rock and a Hard Place*, Cambridge: Polity Press, 2005, p. 48.

4 M. Ravallion, 'The debate on globalization, poverty and inequality: why measurement matters', *International Affairs*, vol. 79:4, 2003, p. 740.

5 M. Castells, *The Information Age: Economy, Society and Culture, vol. III: End of Millennium*, Oxford: Blackwell, 2000, 2nd ed., p. 69.

6 UNDP, *Human Development Report 2003: Millennium Development Goals*, Oxford: Oxford University Press, 2003, p. 39.

7 Manuel Castells, *End of Millennium*, p. 69.

8 M. Ravallion, 'The debate on globalization', 2003, p. 740.

9 Robert Wade, 'The rising inequality of world income distribution' in Mitchell A. Seligson and John T. Passé-Smith (eds), *Devlelopment and Underdevelopment: The Political Economy of Global Inequality*, London: Lynne Rienner, 2003, pp. 33–9.

10 *Human Development Report 1999: Globalization with a Human Face*, Oxford: Oxford University Press, 1999, p. 3.

11 For an excellent overview of the current information, refer to R. Kaplinsky, *Globalization, Poverty and Inequality*, pp. 43–7; also *UNDP, Human Development Report 2003*, Oxford: Oxford University Press, 2003, Chapter 2, pp. 33–66.

12 These data refer to non-communist countries only. Refer to A. Hoogvelt, *Globalisation and the Postcolonial World: The New Political Economy of Development*, Basingstoke: Macmillan, 1997, p.85.

13 UNDP, *Human Development Report 1999*, p. 38.

14 'Convergence, Period' *The Economist*, 20–26 July 2002, p.68

15 D. Dollar and A. Kraay, 'Spreading the wealth', *Foreign Affairs*, vol. 81:1, January/February 2002, p.123.

16 R. Wade, 'Winners and losers', *The Economist*, 28 April–4 May, 2001, p.93; A. Wells-Dang, 'Having it both ways', *Foreign Affairs*, vol. 81:4, pp.180–2.

17 Robert Wade, 'The rising inequality of world income distribution', pp. 35–6.

18 Calculated on a 1985 PPP to US dollars. All data derived from United Nations, *UNDP Human Development Report 2001: Making New Technologies Work for Human Development*, Oxford: Oxford University Press, 2001, p. 16. The majority of least developed countries so defined by the report are in sub-Saharan Africa, for a full break down refer to p. 259 of the report.

19 B. Milanovic, 'True world income distribution, 1998 and 1993: First calculation based on household surveys alone', *The Economic Journal*, 112, 2002, p. 88.

20 Ibid., p. 74.

21 M. Wolf, *Why Globalization Works*, New Haven: Yale Note Bene, 2005.

22 S. Dowrick and M. Akmal, *Contradictory Trends in Global Income Inequality: a tale of Two Biases*, Helsinki: UNU/WIDER Conference, May 2003, pp. 1–23. Online. Available http://www.wider.unu.edu/conference/conference-2003, (accessed 25 March 2005), p. 19, Table 5.

23 X. Sala-i-Martin, *The Disturbing 'Rise' Of Global Income Inequality*, Cambridge, MA: NBER, April 2002, p. 60, Table 1.

24 S. Bhalla, *Imagine There's No Country*, pp. 174–5.

25 P. Gottschalk and T. Smeeding, 'Cross-national comparisons of earnings and income inequality', *Journal of Economic Literature*, vol. XXXB, June 1997, p. 646, 667.

26 UNDP, *Human Development Report 1999*, p. 39.

27 P. Gottschalk and T. Smeeding, 'Cross-national comparisons of earnings', p. 662.

28 World Bank, *World Development Report 1990: Poverty*, Washington DC: World Bank, 1990, p. 141.

29 UNDP, *Human Development Report 1999*, p. 39.

30 World Bank, *World Development Report 1990*, p. 141.

31 UNDP, *Human Development Report 1999*, p. 39.

af B. Milanovic, *Income, Inequality, and Poverty during the Transition from Planned to Market Economy*, Washington, DC: World Bank, 1988, Appendix 2.

33 B. Milanovic, 'True world income distribution', p. 66.

34 Frances Stewart and Albert Berry, 'Globalization, liberalization, and inequality', pp.175–6 in A. Hurrell and N. Woods (eds), *Inequality, Globalization, and World Politics*, Oxford: Oxford University Press, 1999.

35 This is a summary of figures from 1973 to 1992 in Frances Stewart and Albert Berry, 'Globalization, liberalization, and inequality', pp.175–6 and more recent figures given in World Bank, *World Development Report: a Better Investment Climate for Everyone*, Washington DC: World Bank, 2005, Table 2, pp. 258–9.

36 UNDP, *Human Development Report 1999*, p. 40.

37 UNDP, *Human Development Report 1990: Concept and Measurement of Human Development*, Oxford: Oxford University Press, 1990, p. 34.

38 Refer to C. Jones, 'On the evolution of the world income distribution', *The Journal of Economic Perspectives*, vol. 11:3, 1997, pp. 19–36.

39 B. Milanovic, 'True world income distribution', p. 66.

40 These data refer to non-communist countries only. Refer to A. Hoogvelt, *Globalisation and the Postcolonial World: the New Political Economy of Development*, Basingstoke: Macmillan, 1997, p.85.

41 T. Pogge, and S. Reddy, 'How *not* to count the poor', March 2003, Online. Available http://www.columbia.edu/~sr793/count.pdf. (accessed 6 June 2005), p. 3.

42 All data quoted in this paragraph are derived from *World Development Indicators 2004*, Washington DC: World Bank, 2004, pp. 2–3.

43 World Bank, *World Development Indicators 2004*, pp. 2–3.

44 World Bank, *World Development Report 2000/2001: Attacking Poverty*, Washington, DC: World Bank, 2001, p. 23; *Globalization, Growth, and Poverty: Building an Inclusive World Economy* (Washington, DC: World Bank, 2002), p. 7. For a discussion of this discrepancy, refer to Angus Deaton, 'Is world poverty falling?', *Finance and Development*, vol. 39:2, June 2002. Online. Available http://www.imf.org/external/pubs/ft/fandd/2002/06/deaton.htm (accessed 25 March 2005).

45 A. Deaton, 'Is world poverty falling?', p.2.

46 S. Chen and M. Ravallion, *How Have The World's Poorest Fared Since The Early 1980s?*, Washington DC: World Bank Development Research Group, 2000, p. 2.

47 T. Pogge and S. Reddy, 'How *not* to count the poor', p. 7. T. Pogge and S. Reddy, 'Unknown: The extent, distribution, and trend of global income poverty', – Web page of The Institute of Social Analysis and Columbia University. Online. Available http:// www.columbia.edu/~sr793/povpop.pdf, p.4.
48 S. Chen and M. Ravallion, *How Have the World's Poorest Fared*, p. 16.
49 Refer to *World Development Report 2000/2001: Attacking Poverty*, pp.23–5 and *World Development Indicators 2004*, pp. 2–3.
50 S. Chen and M. Ravallion, *How Have the World's Poorest Fared*, p. 29, Table 3. Using household surveys.
51 Sala-i-Martin, X., *The World Distribution of Income*, p. 34, Table 1. Using national accounts.
52 S. Bhalla, *Imagine There's No Country*, 2002, p. 148, Table 9.4. Using national accounts.
53 Ibid., p. 94.
54 Ibid., p. 161. For an excellent discussion on these problems of method, refer to Aisbett, E., 'Why are the critics so convinced that globalization is bad for the poor', *NBER Working Paper Series 11066*, January 2005. Online. Available http://www. nber.org/papers/w11066 (accessed 20 September 2005).
55 T. Pogge and A. Reddy, 'Unknown: the extent, distribution, and trend of global income poverty', pp. 1–9.
56 Ibid., p. 3.
57 World Bank, *World Development Report 2006: Equity and Development*, Washington DC: World Bank, 2006, p. 6.
58 All quotes are from *Human Development Report 1999*, p. 3.
59 D. Held, *Global Covenant: the Social Democratic Alternative to the Washington Consensus*, Cambridge, Polity Press, 2004, p. xiii.
60 Unless otherwise stated all figures are derived from the *Human Development Report 1999*, p. 22.
61 N. Birdsall, 'That silly inequality debate', *Foreign Policy*, May 2002, p. 92.
62 *Globalization, Growth, and Poverty*, pp. 1, 18. See also, R. Wade, 'The rising inequality of world income distribution', *Finance and Development*, vol. 38:4, December 2001. Online. Available http://www.imf.org/external/pubs/ ft/fandd/2001/12/wade.htm (accessed 25 March 2005).
63 R. Wade, 'The rising inequality of world income distribution', p. 4.
64 S. Bhalla, *Imagine There's No Country*, p.18.
65 World Bank, *World Development Report 1990*, p. 199.
66 And the population of India is now estimated to be one billion. Refer to UNDIESA (United Nations Department of International Economic and Social Affairs), *Long-range World Population Projections: Based on the 1998 Revision*, New York: United Nations, 1999, Table 2, p. 6.
67 Frances Stewart and Albert Berry, 'Globalization, liberalization, and inequality: expectations and experience', in A. Hurrell and N. Woods (eds), *Inequality, Globalization, and World Politics*, Oxford: Oxford University Press, 199, pp. 150–1.
68 Frances Stewart and Albert Berry, 'Globalization, liberalization, and inequality', p.159.
69 Frances Stewart and Albert Berry, 'Globalization, liberalization, and inequality', p.169.
70 K. Watkins, 'Debt relief for Africa', *Review of African Political Economy*, 1994, vol. 62, p. 126.
71 Frances Stewart and Albert Berry, 'Globalization, liberalization, and inequality', p.163. For the number of countries signing up to these adjustment policies refer to A. Hoogvelt, *Globalisation and the Postcolonial World*, p. 170.
72 Ibid., p.167.
73 R. Wade, 'The rising inequality of world income distribution', p. 4.

74 P. Samuelson and W. Nordhaus, *Economics: International Edition*, New York: McGraw-Hill, 1995, p. 764.

75 A. Hoogvelt, *Globalisation and the Postcolonial World*, p. 145.

76 N. Birdsall, 'Life is unfair: inequality in the world', *Foreign Policy*, vol. 111 (Summer 1998), pp. 76–93.

77 Caroline Thomas, 'Poverty, development, and hunger' in J. Baylis and Steve Smith (eds), *The Globalization of World Politics*, Oxford: Oxford University Press, 1997, pp. 449–67.

78 N. Birdsall and R. Sabot, *Virtuous Circles: Human Capital, Growth, and Equity in East Asia*, Washington, DC: World Bank, 1993, p. 96. Also refer to J. Campos and H. Root, *The Key to the Asian Miracle: Making Shared Growth Credible*, Washington, DC: The Brookings Institution, 1996, pp.56–8.

79 P. Gottschalk and T. Smeeding, 'Cross-national comparisons of earnings', p. 645.

80 N. Birdsall and R. Sabot, *Virtuous Circles*, pp. 106–7. Cited in J. Campos and H. Root, *The Key to the Asian Miracle: Making Shared Growth Credible*, Washington, DC: The Brookings Institution, 1996, pp. 56–8.

81 World Bank, *Inequality in Latin America and the Caribbean: Breaking with History?*, Washington DC: World Bank, 2004, Introduction, pp. 1–8.

82 Ibid., Chapter 4, p. 17.

83 Ibid., Introduction, p.11.

84 UNDP, *Human development Report 2002: Deepening Democracy in a Fragmented World*, Oxford: Oxford University Press, 2002, p. 56.

85 UNDP, *Human Development Report 2002*, p. 56.

86 Ibid., p. 20.

87 Quoted in Pogge, T. and Reddy, A., 'Unknown: the extent, distribution, and trend of global income poverty', p.1.

88 Refer to E. Heckscher, 'The effect of foreign trade on the distribution of income' in The American Economic Association, *Readings in the Theory of International Trade*, London: Allen & Unwin, 1950, pp. 272–300; B. Ohlin, *Interregional and International Trade*, Cambridge, MA: Harvard University Press, 1933; J. L. Ford, *The-Heckscher–Ohlin Model of the Basis and Effects of Commodity Trade*, London: Asia Publishing House, 1965.

89 J. Stiglitz and A. Charlton, *Fair Trade for All: How Trade Can Promote Development*, Oxford: Oxford University Press, 2005, pp. 194–203.

90 Refer to World Bank, *World Development Report 2006*, p. 44; S. Kuznets, 'Economic growth and income inequality', in M. Seligson and J. Passé-Smith, *Development and Underdevelopment: The Political Economy of Global Inequality*, Boulder, CO: Lynne Rienner Publishers, 2003, 3rd ed., pp. 61–76 and Branko Milanovic, 'Can we discern the effect of globalization on income distribution?', *World Bank Policy Research Working Paper 2876*, April 2002, pp. 1–22.

91 Branko Milanovic, 'Can we discern the effect of globalization on income distribution?', *World Bank Policy Research Working Paper 2876*, April 2002, p. 20.

92 *Globalization, Growth, and Poverty*, p. 5.

93 Ibid., p. 7.

94 Ibid., p.1.

95 Ibid., p.38. The preceding two paragraphs are a summary of the report's findings outlined in the report's 'Overview' and 'Chapter One: The New Wave of Globalisation and its Economic Effects'.

96 D. Dollar and A. Kraay, 'Spreading the Wealth', *Foreign Affairs*, vol. 81:1, January/February 2002, pp. 120–1.

97 Ibid., pp. 120–1.

98 Refer to 'Growth is good for the poor', *World Bank Policy Research Department Working Paper No. 2587 (March 2002 Version)*, Online. Available http://www.imf.org/external/pubs/ft/fandd/2001/09/dollar.htm (accessed 25 March 2005), p.27.

99 D. Dollar and A. Kraay, 'Trade, Growth and Poverty', *World Bank Research Report WPS2615*, Washington, DC: World Bank, June 2001, p.3. Available. Online at http:// wdsbeta.worldbank.org/external/default/WDSContentServer/IW3P/IB/2002/08/2 3/00 0094946_02082304142939/Rendered/PDF/multi0page.pdf (accessed 16 June 2005).

100 Branko Milanovic, 'The two faces of globalization: against globalization as we know it', *World Development*, 2003, vol. 31:4, p. 667.

101 E. Aisbett, 'Why are the critics so convinced that globalization is bad for the poor', p. 3

102 Branko Milanovic, 'The two faces of globalization, p. 667.

103 Ibid., pp.674–5.

104 Ibid., p. 672.

105 UNDP, *Human Development Report 2003*, Oxford: Oxford University Press, 2003. UNDP, *Making Global Trade Work for People*, Virginia: Earthscan Publications, 2003, p. 34.

106 UNDP, *Making Global Trade Work for People*, p. 34.

107 G. Garrett, 'Globalization's missing middle', *Foreign Affairs*, vol. 83:6, November/ December 2004, p. 84–96.

108 Ibid., p. 89.

109 F. Stewart and A. Berry, 'Globalization, liberalization, and inequality', p. 174.

110 This is a summary of figures from 1973 to 1992 in F. Stewart and A. Berry, pp.175–6 and more recent figures given in World Bank (2005) *World Development Report: a Better Investment Climate for Everyone*, Washington DC: World Bank, Table 2, pp. 258–9.

111 Oxfam, *Rigged Rules and Double Standards: Trade, Globalisation, and the Fight against Poverty*, London: Oxfam, 2002, p. 75

112 *Financial Times*, 'Fifteen poor states seek US garment preferences', 04 May 2005, p. 3.

113 Oxfam, *Rigged Rules*, pp. 70–1.

114 *Financial Times*, 'Fifteen poor states', p. 3.

115 UNDP, *Human Development Report 2003*. Also refer to S. Fukuda-Parr, 'The millennium development goals: the pledge of world leaders to end poverty will not be met with business as usual', *Journal of International Development* vol. 16, 2004, pp. 925–32.

116 United Nations, *World Investment Report 1992: Transnational Corporations as Engines of Growth (An Executive Summary)*, New York: United Nations Transnational Corporations and Management Division, 1992, p. 1.

117 *The Economist*, 'Footloose firms: are global companies too mobile for workers' good?', 27 March–01 April, 2004, p. 69; and United Nations, *World Investment Report 2004~The Shift towards Services*, New York: United Nations Conference on Trade and Development, 2004, p. 1

118 United Nations, *World Investment Report 2001: Promoting Linkages*, New York: United Nations Conference on Trade and Development, 2001, p. 9.

119 D. Held, T. McGrew, D. Goldblatt and J. Perraton, *Global Transformations: Politics, Economics and Culture*, Cambridge: Polity Press, 1999, p. 279.

120 'during the period 1992–1997, commercial bank loans displayed the highest volatility (0.71), as measured by the coefficient of variations, followed by total portfolio investment (4.3) and FDI (0.35). Refer to United Nations, *World Investment Report 1998: Trends and Determinants*, New York: United Nations Conference on Trade and Development, 1998, p.14.

121 Oxfam, *Rigged Rules*, p. 176.

122 A. Bernard and F. Sjöholm, 'Foreign Owners and Plant Survival', *NBER Working Paper Series*, October 2003, Working Paper No. 10039, p. 12. Online. Available http//: www.nber.org/papers/w10039 (accessed 10 May 2005). The paper focuses solely on

Indonesia, but similar conclusions are reached (albeit with a reduced probability of closure) in a study on TNCs in the United States, refer to A. Bernard and J. Jensen, 'Firm structure, multinationals, and manufacturing plant deaths', September 2003, Online. Available http//:www.mbatuck. Dartmouth.edu/pages/faculty/andrewbernard/ deaths.pdf (accessed 10 May 2005).

123 W. Cooke and D. Noble, 'Industrial relations systems and US foreign direct investment abroad', *British Journal of Industrial Relations*, vol. 36:4, 1998, p. 603.

124 G. Firebaugh, 'Growth effects of foreign and domestic investment', in M. Seligson and J. Passé-Smith, *Development and Underdevelopment: the Political Economy of Global Inequality*, Boulder, CO: Lynne Rienner Publishers, 2003, 3rd ed., p. 340.

125 J. Kentor, 'The long-term effects of foreign investment dependence on economic growth, 1940–1990', in M. Seligson and J. Passé-Smith, *Development and Underdevelopment: the Political Economy of Global Inequality*, Boulder, Colorado: Lynne Rienner Publishers, 2003, 3rd ed., p. 354.

126 For an example of the difficulties in ensuring labour standards, refer to the *Financial Times*, 'Chinese factories accused of faking records', 22 April.2005, pp. 1, 13.

127 Oxfam, *Rigged Rules*, p. 178.

128 Thus defined by the creator of the term, John Williamson. Quoted in G. Garrett, 'The three worlds of globalization', op. cit., p.53.

129 N. Rudra, 'Openness, welfare spending, and inequality in the developing world', *International Studies Quarterly*, vol. 48, 2004, p. 684.

130 World Bank, *The East Asian Miracle: Economic Growth and Public Policy*, Oxford: Oxford University Press, 1993, p. 13.

131 D. Held, *Global Covenant*, p. 48.

7   Global governance: is more better?

1   Scholte, J. A., *Globalization: A Critical Introduction*, Basingstoke: Palgrave, 2000, p. 136.

2   P. Cerny, 'Globalization and the changing logic of collective action', *International Organization*, vol. 49:4, 1995, p. 611.

3   J. Camilleri and J. Falk, *The End of Sovereignty? the Politics of a Shrinking and Fragmenting World*, Aldershot: Edward Elgar, 1992, p. 237.

4   K. Ohmae, 'Putting global logic first', *Harvard Business Review*, vol. 73:1, January–February 1995, pp. 119–25; K. Ohmae, *The Borderless World: Power and Strategy in the Global Marketplace*, London: HarperCollins, 1990; K. Ohmae, *The End of the Nation-state: the Rise of Regional Economies*, London: HarperCollins, 1995.

5   D. Held, 'Law of states, law of peoples: three models of sovereignty', *Legal Theory*, vol. 8:1, 2002, p. 17.

6   I. Wallerstein, *The Modern World System*, Vol. 1. New York: Academic Press, 1974; I. Wallerstein, *The Modern World System*, Vol. 2. New York: Academic Press, 1980; I. Wallerstein, *The Modern World System*, Vol. 3. New York: Academic Press, 1989; I. Wallerstein and A. Frank, 'Two views of world history', *Review*, vol. XV:4, 1992; D. Held, A. McGrew, D. Goldblatt and J. Perraton, *Global Transformations: Politics, Economics and Culture*, Cambridge: Polity Press, 1999.

7   Other influences include the efficient performance of the state managing the war economy. Refer to D. Thompson, *Europe Since Napoleon*, Harmondsworth: Penguin Books, 1985.

8   J. Kirsher, 'Keynes, capital mobility and the crisis of embedded liberalism', *Review of International Political Economy,* 1999, vol. 6:3, pp. 317–22. John Ruggie popularized the term in his 'International regimes, transactions, and change: embedded liberalism in the postwar economic order', *International Organization*, 1982, vol.36:2.

9   Or, as John Ruggie puts it, the 'unbundling of territoriality'. Refer to J. G. Ruggie, 'Territoriality and beyond: problematizing modernity in international relations', *International Organization*, vol. 47:1, 1993, p. 171.

10 S. G. Brooks and W. C. Wohlforth, 'Hard Times for Soft Balancing', *International Security*, vol. 30:1, 2005, pp. 76–7.

11 N. Woods, 'The role of institutions', in D. Held and A. McGrew (eds), *Governing Globalization: Power, Authority and Global Governance*, Cambridge: Polity Press, 2002, p. 29.

12 R. Keohane, *After Hegemony: Cooperation and Discord in the World Political Economy*, Princeton, NJ: Princeton University Press, 1984, p. 88.

13 H. Bull, *The Anarchical Society*, London: Macmillan, 1977, pp. 254–5.

14 S. Krasner, *Sovereignty: Organized Hypocrisy*, Princeton, NJ: Princeton University Press, 1999 and S. Krasner 'Compromising Westphalia', *International Security*, vol. 20:3, Winter 1995–6, p. 115.

15 F.H. Hinsley, *Sovereignty*, Cambridge: Cambridge University Press, 1986, 2nd ed., p. 26.

16 C. Brown, *Understanding International Relations*, London: Macmillan, 2005, Chapter 7, 'Global Governance', p. 116.

17 S. Krasner, *Sovereignty*, p. 20.

18 D. Held and A. McGrew, 'Globalization and the Liberal Democratic State', *Government and Opposition*, vol. 28:2, p. 265.

19 R. Moxham, *Tea: Addiction, Exploitation and Empire*, London: Constable and Robinson, 2003, p.20.

20 K. J. Holsti, *Taming the Sovereigns: Institutional Change in International Politics*, Cambridge: Cambridge University Press, 2004, p. 63.

21 C. Brown, *Understanding International Relations*, London: Macmillan, 2005, Chapter 7, 'Global Governance', p. 116.

22 M. Mann, 'The autonomous power of the state', in John Hall (ed.), *States in History*, Oxford: Basil Blackwell, 1986, pp. 113–39.

23 R. Jackson, *Quasi-states: Sovereignty, International Relations and the Third World*, Cambridge: Cambridge University Press, 1990.

24 S. Krasner, *Sovereignty: Organized Hypocrisy*, Princeton, NJ: Princeton University Press, 1999, p. 36.

25 Ibid., p. 37.

26 Ibid., p. 30.

27 Ibid., p. 33.

28 For instance, refer to D. Held, 'Law of states, law of peoples: three models of sovereignty', *Legal Theory*, vol. 8:1, 2002, p. 17. The possible exception to this argument is the European Union, but much will depend upon its future development.

29 M. Koenig-Archibugi, 'Mapping global governance', in D. Held and A. McGrew (eds), *Governing Globalization: Power, Authority and Global Governance*, Cambridge: Polity Press, 2002, pp.46–69.

30 This requires consensus rather than unanimity, in other words some states may abstain. Refer to G. Winham, 'The evolution of the global trade regime', in John Ravenhill (ed.), *Global Political Economy*, Oxford: Oxford University Press, 2005, pp. 87–117.

31 M. Koenig-Archibugi, 'Mapping global governance', pp.46–69. Quote is from p. 55.

32 The McKinsey Global Institute recently estimated that the offshoring of service jobs would amount to 1.2% of the demand for labour in the North by 2008. Refer to *The Economist*, 'Nightmare scenarios: Western worries about losing jobs and talent are only partly justified', Special Survey, 7–13 October, 2006, p. 12.

33   Online. Available http://www.banktrack.org/doc/File /BankTrack%20publications/ BankTrack%20fact%20sheets/What%20is%20basel%20II.pdf.   (accessed   20 November 2006).

_34 P. Hirst and G. Thompson, *Globalization in Question*, p. 206.

35   Online. Available http://www.deloitte.com/dtt/cda/doc/content/ru_en _FSUpdate_ Feb_March06(1).pdf. (accessed 20 November 2006).

36   Online. Available http://www.networkideas.org/featart/aug2006/Capital Accord.pdf (accessed 20 November 2006). Online. Available http:// www.microfinancegateway. org/files/26273_file_Basel_II_and_MF_April_2005.doc (accessed 20 November 2006).

37   J. A. Scholte, 'Governing Global Finance', in D. Held and A. McGrew (eds), *Governing Globalization: Power, Authority and Global Governance*, Cambridge: Polity Press, 2002, p. 194.

38   P. Hirst and G. Thompson, *Globalization in Question*, p. 205.

39   *The Economist*, 'Bank Regulations: A battle over Basel 2', 4–10 November 2006, p. 101.

40   P. Hirst and G. Thompson, *Globalization In Question*, p. 208.

41   C. Thomas, 'Where is the third world now', *Review of International Studies*, vol. 25:5, 1999, p. 241.

42   H. Stewart, 'Brown dismisses Tobin tax plan', *The Guardian*, 23 July 2002, p. 21.

43   W. Schussel, 'Speculators should face taxation: EU presidency', *Financial Times Asia*, 19 January 2006, p. 3.

44   S. Strange, *Casino Capitalism*, Oxford: Blackwell, 1986.

45   W. Greider, *One World , Ready Or Not: The Manic Logic of Global Capitalism*, New York: Simon & Schuster, 1997, p. 318.

46   Ibid., p. 319.

47   Ibid., p. 318.

48   Ibid., p. 319.

49   A. Hoogvelt, *Globalization and the Postcolonial World*, p.172: For an overview of current issues concerning this institution, refer to N. Woods, 'Special Issue: understanding pathways through financial crises and the impact of the IMF', *Global Governance*, vol. 12:4, October–December 2006.

50   B. Milanovic (2003) 'The two faces of development', *World Development*, 2003, vol. 31: 4, Table 3, p. 673. WENAO stands for Western Europe and Northern America.

51   UNCTAD (2004) *Globalization and Development*, Geneva: UNCTAD, p.38. The preceding two paragraphs are a summary of the report's findings outlined in the report's 'Overview' and 'Chapter One: The new wave of globalisation and its economic effects'.

52   D. Rodrik (2001) *The Global Governance of Trade: as if Trade Development Really Mattered*, New York: UNDP pp.18–19.

53   D. Rodrik, *The New Global Economy and Developing Countries: Making Openness Work*, Washington, DC: Overseas Development Council, 1999, p. 137.

54   R. Higgott, 'The Asian economic crisis: a study in the politics of resentment', *New Political Economy*, vol. 3:3, 1998, p. 339.

55   W. Bello, 'The Asian economic implosion: causes, dynamics, prospects', *Race and Class*, vol. 40:2/3, p. 135.

56   Although in September 1998, Malaysia against the wishes of the IMF did put in place selective exchange controls. Refer to J. Bhagwati, *In Defense of Globalization*, Oxford: Oxford University Press, 2004, p. 206.

57   D. Held, *Global Covenant: The Social Democratic Alternative to the Washington Consensus*, Cambridge: Polity Press, 2004.

58   G. Garrett, 'The three worlds of globalization: market integration, economic growth and the distribution of income in high, middle and low-income countries'. Online.

Available http//:www.international.ucla.edu/profile/ggarrett (accessed 11 June 2005), p. 9.

59 E. Prasaad, K. Rogoff, S. Wei and M. Kose, 'Effects of financial globalization on developing countries: some empirical evidence', *IMF*, 17 March 2003. Online. Available http://www.imf.org/external/np/res/docs/2003/031703.pdf, (accessed 3 April 2006), p. 10.

60 For example, in textile manufacturing, by June 2000, 'the US had lifted only 13 out of 750 restrictions acknowledged during Uruguay; the EU 14 out of 219; Canada 29 out of 295'. B. Gunnell, 'Trade: what we want', *New Statesman,* 22 October 2001, pp. 23–4.

61 B. Gunnell, 'Trade: what we want', p. 23.

62 L. Elliot, 'Stop treating debtors as poor cows', *The Guardian*, 23 September, 2002 and *The Economist*, 'Unpicking cotton subsidies', 30 April–6 May 2005.

63 B. Gunnell, 'Trade: what we want', *New Statesman,* 22.10.2001, pp. 23–4.

64 G. Monbiot, 'The worst of times', *The Guardian*, 03 September 2003, p. 21.

65 J. Stiglitz and A. Charlton, 'The Doha round is missing the point on helping poor countries', *Financial Times Asia*, 13 December 2005, p. 15.

66 P. Lindhert, 'Response to debt crisis: what is different about the 1980s' in B. Eichengreen and P. Lindhert (eds), *The International Debt Crisis in Historical Perspective*, Cambridge, MA: MIT Press, 1989, p. 242.

67 UNICEF, *The Progress of Nations 1999*, New York: United Nations International Children's Emergency Fund, 1999, p. 33.

68 WDR, *World Development Report 2006: Equity and Development*, Washington, DC: World Bank, 2006, p. 220.

69 A. Hurrell, 'Power, institutions, and the production of inequality', in M. Barnett and R. Duvall (eds), *Power in Global Governance*, Cambridge: Cambridge University Press, 2005, p. 35.

70 M. Feldstein, 'Refocusing the IMF', *Foreign Affairs*, vol. 2, March/April 1998, pp. 28–9.

71 I. Hurd, 'Legitimacy and authority in international politics', *International Organization* vol. 53:2, 1999, p. 386.

72 C. Thomas, 'Global governance, development and human security: exploring the links', *Third World Quarterly*, vol. 22:2, p. 172.

73 Similar dominance by these countries can be seen in the Board of Directors at the World Bank.

74 G. Mohan, 'Globalization and governance: the paradoxes of adjustment in sub-Saharan Africa', in E. Kofman and G. Youngs (eds), *Globalization: Theory and Practice*, London: Pinter, 1996, p. 296. See also H. Martin and H. Schumann, *The Global Trap: Globalization and the Assault on Democracy and Prosperity*, London: Zed Books, 1997, p. 48.

75 Refer to F. W. Scharpf, *Governing in Europe*, p. 6.

76 Japan's Overseas Economic Cooperation Fund issued a white paper, 'Issues related to the World Bank's approach to structural adjustment – proposal from a major partner', Tokyo: OECF, 1991. Refer to W. Greider, *One World*, p. 277.

77 G. Mohan, 'Globalisation and Governance', p. 290.

78 A. Balls, 'IMF dilemma as new loans start to decline', *Financial Times Asia*, 28.12.2005, p. 4.

79 M. Wolf, 'The world needs a tough and independent monetary fund', *Financial Times Asia*, 22.02.2006, p. 15.

80 J. Stiglitz and A. Charlton, *Fair Trade For All,* p. 83.

81 C. Thomas, 'Globalization and development in the South', in J. Ravenhill (ed.), *Global Political Economy*, Oxford: Oxford University Press, 2005, p. 336.

82 J. Stiglitz and A. Charlton, *Fair Trade For All*, p. 73.

83 Ibid., p. 77. All three points above are based on Chapter 5 of this book.

84 UNDP, *Making Global Trade Work for People*, Sterling, Virginia: Earthscan Publications, 2003, p. 5. However, previous rounds have included issue specific negotiations, for example, agriculture and services that were not included as part of the remit of the single undertaking.

85 WTO, *Doha Declarations*, Geneva: WTO, 2001, Ministerial Declaration (2), p. 2.

86 A. Hurrell, 'Power, institutions, and the production of inequality', p. 53.

87 D. Radke, 'The Monterrey Consensus: the conference on financing for development'. Available online at http://www.eldis.org/static/DOC1942.htm, (accessed 3 December 2006).

88 *The Gleneagles Communiqué*, (2005). Section on Africa, Article 28.

89 L. Elliott and A. Seager, '£30bn debts write-off agreed', *The Guardian*, 11 June 2005, p. 3.

90 Joint European NGO Report, *EU Aid: Genuine Leadership or Misleading Figures?* Available online at http://www.eurodad.org, (accessed 3 December 2006).

91 A. Maddison, *The World Economy: a Millennial Perspective*, Paris: Development Centre of the OECD, 2001, p.166.

92 All figures from UNICEF, *The Progress of Nations*, New York: UNICEF, 1999, p. 32.

93 World Bank (2004) *World Development Indicators: 2004*, Washington DC: World Bank, p.3.

94 I. Taylor, '"Advice is judged by results, not by intentions": why Gordon Brown is wrong about Africa', *International Affairs*, vol. 81:2, March 2005, p. 307.

95 For example, for Latin America and sub-Saharan Africa it is estimated that it would increase their GDP by up to 0.6%. Refer to Larry Elliott, 'Stop treating debtors as poor cows`, *The Guardian*, 23 September 2002.

96 Some countries are trying to shift some of their subsidies from the Amber Box with its minimal support allowance of 5 per cent of agricultural production for industrialized countries and 10 per cent for developing countries to the Blue or Green boxes, which do not have limits. M. Khor, 'Preliminary comments on the WTO's Geneva July decision', 2005, *Third World Network*. Online. Available http://www.twnside.org (accessed 03 August 2005), p. 6.

97 J. Stiglitz and A. Charlton, 'The Doha round is missing the point on helping poor countries', *Financial Times Asia*, 13 December 2005, p. 15.

98 M. Sanchanta, 'Japan pledges aid for trade', *Financial Times Asia*, 10 December, 2005, p. 1.

99 Bijit Bora, Lucian Cernat and Alessandro Turrini, *Duty Free and Quota-free Access for LDCs: Further Evidence from CGE Modeling*, Geneva: UNCTAD, 2002, p. 3.

100 *The Gleneagles Communiqué* (2005). Section on Africa, Article 22 (c).

101 L. Puri (2005) *Towards a New Trade 'Marshall Plan' for Least Developed Countries*, Geneva: UNCTAD, p. 27.

102 L. Puri, pp. iv, 30.

103 J. Kirsher (1999) 'Keynes, capital mobility and the crisis of embedded liberalism', *Review of International Political Economy*, vol. 6:3, pp. 317–22.

104 WTO (2001) *Doha Declarations*, Geneva: WTO. Ministerial Declaration (2), p. 2.

105 Y. Akyüz, p. 28.

106 J. Stiglitz and A. Charlton, *Fair Trade for All*, p. 94.

107 Ibid., pp. 94–102.

108 G. Monbiot, 'The worst of times', *The Guardian*, 03 September, 2003, p. 21.

109 J. Stiglitz and A. Charlton, The Doha round is missing the point on helping poor countries', p. 15.

110 Quoted in *The Economist*, 'In the twilight of Doha', 29 July–4 August 2006, p. 67.

111 F. Cheru, 'The Heavily Indebted Poor Countries (HIPC) initiative: old wine in a new bottle?' in A. McGrew and N. Poku (eds), *Globalization, Development and Human Security*, Cambridge: Polity Press, 2007, p. 75.

112 C. Thomas, 'Globalization and development in the South', pp. 335. Italics in original.

113 UNDP (1998) *Human Development Report 1998: Consumption for Human Development*, Oxford: Oxford University Press, p.37.

114 For more on the conditions applied refer to Oxfam, *Do the Deal*, London: Cafod, Action Aid UK and Oxfam, 2005.

115 UNDP, *Making Global Trade Work for People*, p. 30.

116 World Bank, *The East Asian Miracle: Economic Growth and Public Policy*, Oxford: Oxford University Press, 1993, p. 1.

117 W. Greider, *One World , Ready or Not:*, p. 264.

118 A. Amsden, *Asia's Next Giant: South Korea and Late Industrialization*, Oxford: Oxford University Press, 1989, p.13.

119 R. Kaplinsky, *Globalization, Poverty and Inequality*, p. 241.

120 D. Rodrik, *The New Global Economy and Devloping Countries: Making Openess Work*, Washington, DC: Overseas Development Council, 1999, p. 137.

121 For more on these proposals refer to WDR, *World Development Report 2006: Equity and Development*, Washington, DC: World Bank, 2006, p. 221.

122 J. Campos and H. Root, *The Key to the Asian Miracle: Making Shared Growth Credible*, Washington, DC: The Brookings Institution, 1996, p.3.

123 World Bank, *The East Asian Miracle*, p. 13; W. Greider, *One World*, p. 280.

124 J. Stiglitz and A. Charlton, *Fair Trade for All*, pp. 81–5.

125 WTO, *Doha Declarations*, Geneva: WTO, 2001, Ministerial Declaration (2), p. 2.

126 *The Gleneagles Communiqué* 2005. Conclusion, Section 35.

127 W. Greider, *One World*, p. 327.

128 C. Thomas, *Global Governance, Development and Human Security*, London: Pluto Press, 2000, p. 64.

129 DTI, *Economic Partnership Agreements: Making EPAs Deliver for Development*, March 2005, pp. 1, 3.

130 L. Weiss, *The Myth of the Powerless State: Governing the Economy in a Global Era*, Cambridge: Polity Press, 1998, p. 42.

131 Concerning this change in the World Bank and IMF's stance refer to D. Held, *Global Covenant*, p. 49 and J. Bhagwati, *In Defense of Globalization*, p. 207.

8 Conclusion

1 M. Christopher, *Logistics and Supply Chain Management: Strategies for Reducing Cost and Improving Service*, London: Pearson Education, 1992, p. 15.

2 *The Economist*, 'What the World Bank knows', 13–19 January 2007, p. 67. Full report, A. Banerjee, A. Deaton, N. Lustig, K. Rogoff and E. Hsu, *An Evaluation of World Bank Research, 1998–2005*, Washington DC: World Bank, 2006. Online. Available http://siteresources.worldbank.org/DEC/Resources/84797-1109362238001/726454-1164121166494/RESEARCH-EVALUATION-2006-Main-Report.pdf (accessed 02 February 2007).

3 R. Wade, *Governing The Market: Economic Theory and the Role of Government in East Asian Industrialization*, Princeton, NJ: Princeton University Press, 1990, pp. 350–77.

4 P. Evans, *Embedded Autonomy: States and Industrial Transformation*, Princeton, NJ: Princeton University Press, 1995, Chapter 2; R. Wade, *Governing The Market*, pp. 371–2; C. Johnson, *MITI and the Japanese Miracle: the Gowth of Industrial Policy*, 1925–75, Palo Alto, CA: Stanford University Press, 1982.

5 UNDP, *Human Development Report 2003: Millennium Development Goals*, Oxford: Oxford University Press, 2003. Also refer to S. Fukuda-Parr, 'The millennium development goals: the pledge of world leaders to end poverty will not be met with business as usual', *Journal of International Development* vol. 16, 2004, pp. 925–32.

6   G. Garrett, 'Globalization's missing middle', *Foreign Affairs*, vol. 83:6, November/ December 2004, p. 84–96.

7   G. Thompson 'Whither the "Washington Consensus", the "Developmental State", and the "Seattle Protests?": Can "managed free trade and investment" become an alternative developmental model?', *Problemas Del Desarrollo*, vol. 34:131, 2003, p. 235.

8   G. Thompson, 'Whither the "Washington Consensus"', p. 230.

Bibliography

Aisbett, E., 'Why are the critics so convinced that globalization is bad for the poor', *NBER Working Paper Series 11066*, January 2005. Online. Available http://www.nber.org/papers/w11066 (accessed 20 September.2005).

Akyüz, Y., *The WTO Negotiations on Industrial Tariffs: What is at Stake for Developing Countries*, Geneva: Third World Network, 2005. Online. Available http://www.twnside.org (accessed 03 August 2005).

Allen, J., 'Crossing Borders: footloose multinationals?', in J. Allen and C. Hamnett (eds), *A Shrinking World?: Global Uneveness and Inequality*, Oxford: Oxford University Press, 1995, pp. 55–102.

—— 'Post industrialism and post Fordism', in S. Hall, D. Held and T. McGrew (eds), *Modernity and its Futures*, Oxford: Blackwell, 1999, pp. 170–203.

Allen, J. and Hamnett, C., *A Shrinking World?: Global Uneveness and Inequality*, Oxford: Oxford University Press, 1995.

Allen, J. and Thompson, G., 'Think global, then think again – economic globalization in context', *Area*, vol. 29:3, 1997, pp. 213–27.

Amin, S., *Capitalism in the Age of Globalization: The Management of Contemporary Society*, London: Zed Books, 1997.

Amsden, A., 'The State and Taiwan's Economic Development', in P. Evans, D. Rueschmeyer and T. Skocpol (eds), *Bringing the State Back In*, Cambridge: Cambridge University Press, 1985, pp. 78–106.

—— *Asia's Next Giant: South Korea and Late Industrialisation*, Oxford: Oxford University Press, 1989.

Anderson, B., *Imagined Communities: Reflections on the Origin and Spread of Nationalism*, London: Verso, 1991.

Anderson, S. and Cavanaugh, J., *Field Guide To The Global Economy*, New York: New Press, 2005. Online. Available http://www.ips-dc.org (accessed 17 December 2005).

Andor, L. and Summers, M., *Market Failure: A Guide to the East European Economic Miracle*, London: Pluto Press, 1998.

Appelbaum, R. and Henderson, J. (eds), *States and Development in the Asian Pacific Rim*, Newbury Park, California: Sage Publications, 1992.

Arnold, G., *Corporate Financial Management*, Harlow: Prentice Hall, 1998.

Ayoob, M., 'Security in the Third World: the worm about to turn?', *International Affairs*, 1984, vol. 60:1, pp. 41–51.

Banerjee, A., Deaton, A. Lustig, N. Rogoff, K. and Hsu, E., *An Evaluation of World Bank Research, 1998–2005*, Washington D.C.: World Bank, 2006. Online. Available http://siteresources.worldbank.org/DEC/Resources/84797-1109362238001/726454-

1164121166494/RESEARCH-EVALUATION-2006-Main-Report.pdf (accessed 02 February 2007).

Bank for International Settlements, *71st Annual Report*, Basle: BIS, 2001.

Banz, R., Clough, S., 'Globalization reshaping world's financial markets', *Journal of Financial Planning*. Online. Available http://www.fpanet.org/journal /articles (accessed 17 January 2006).

Barnes, S. and B. Hunt, *E-Commerce and V-Business: Business Models for Global Success*, Oxford: Butterworth-Heinemann, 2001.

Barnett, M. and R. Duvall (eds), *Power in Global Governance*, Cambridge: Cambridge University Press, 2005.

Bauman, Z., *Globalization: The Human Consequences*, Cambridge: Polity Press, 1998.

Baylis, J. and Smith, S. (eds), *The Globalization of World Politics*, Oxford: Oxford University Press, 2005.

Bello, W., 'The Asian economic implosion: causes, dynamics, prospects', *Race and Class*, vol. 40:2/3, 1999, pp. 133–43.

Bello, W., and Rosenfeld, S., *Dragons in Distress: Asia's Miracle Economics in Crisis*, Harmondsworth: Penguin, 1990.

Ben-David, D., 'Equalizing exchange: trade liberalization and income convergence', *The Quarterly Journal of Economics*, vol. 108:3, 1993, pp. 653–79.

Bernard, A. and Jensen, J., *Firm Structure, Multinationals, and Manufacturing Plant Deaths*, September 2003. Online. Available http//:www.mbatuck. Dartmouth.edu/ pages/faculty/andrewbernard/deaths.pdf (accessed 10 May 2005).

Bernard, A. and Sjöholm, F., 'Foreign owners and plant survival', NBER Working Paper Series, October 2003, Working Paper No. 10039. Online. Available http//:www.nber. org/papers/w10039 (accessed 10 May 2005).

Bhagwati, J., *India In Transition: Freeing the Economy*, Oxford: Clarendon Paperbacks, 1993.

—— *In Defense of Globalization*, Oxford: Oxford University Press, 2004.

Bhalla, S., *Imagine There's No Country: Poverty, Inequality, and Growth in the Era of Globalization*, Washington, D.C.: Institute For International Economics, 2002.

Birdsall, N., 'Life is unfair: inequality in the world', *Foreign Policy*, vol. 111 (Summer 1998), pp. 76–93.

Birdsall, N. and Sabot, R., *Virtuous Circles: Human Capital, Growth, and Equity in East Asia*, Washington, D.C.: World Bank, 1993.

Booth, K. (ed.), *New Thinking About Strategy and International Security*, London: HarperCollins, 1991.

Bora, B., Cernat, L. and Turrini, A., *Duty Free and Quota-Free Access for LDCs: Further Evidence from CGE Modeling*, Geneva: United Nations Conference on Trade and Development, 2002.

Bordo, M., Eichengreen, B. and Irwin, D., *Is Globalization Today Really Different than Globalization a Hundred Years Ago?*, Online. Available http://emlab.berkeley.edu/ users/eichengr/research/brooking.pdf. (accessed 21 January 2006).

Brooks, S. G. and Wohlforth, W. C., 'Hard times for soft balancing', *International Security*, vol. 30:1, 2005, pp. 72–108.

Brown, C. and Ainley, K., *Understanding International Relations*, Basingstoke: Palgrave Macmillan, 2005, 3rd ed.

Bull, H., *The Anarchical Society*, London: Macmillan, 1977.

Burton, J., *World Society*, Cambridge: Cambridge University Press, 1972.

Camilleri, J. and Falk, J., *The End of Sovereignty? The Politics of a Shrinking and Fragmenting World*, Aldershot: Edward Elgar, 1992.

Cammack, P. , 'Attacking the Poor', *New Left Review*, vol. 13, 2002, pp. 125–34.

Campos, J. and Root, H., *The Key To The Asian Miracle: Making Shared Growth Credible*, Washington, DC: The Brookings Institution, 1996.

Castells, M., 'Four Asian tigers with a dragon head: a comparative analysis of the state, economy, and society in the Asian Pacific Rim', in R. Appelbaum and J. Henderson (eds), *States and Development in the Asian Pacific Rim*, Newbury Park, California: Sage Publications, 1992, pp. 33–70.

—— *The Information Age: Economy, Society and Culture, vol. 1: The Rise of the Network Society*, Oxford: Blackwell Publishers, 1996.

—— *The Information Age: Economy, Society and Culture, vol. III: End of Millennium*, Oxford: Blackwell Publishers, 2000, 2nd ed.

Cerny, P. , *The Changing Architecture of Politics: Structure, Agency, and the Future of the State*, London: Age Publications, 1990.

—— 'Globalization and the changing logic of collective action', *International Organization*, vol. 49:4, 1995, pp. 595–625.

—— 'What Next for the State', in E. Kofman and G. Youngs (eds), *Globalization: Theory and Practice*, London: Pinter, 1996, pp. 123–37.

—— 'Paradoxes of the competition state: the dynamics of political globalization', *Government and Opposition*, vol. 32:2, 1997, pp. 251–74.

Chan, S. and Scarritt, J. (eds) *Coping with Globalization: Cross-national Patterns in Domestic Governance and Policy Performance*, London: Frank Cass, 2002.

Chen, S. and Ravallion, M., *How Have the World's Poorest Fared since the Early 1980s?*, Washington DC: World Bank Development Research Group, 2000, pp. 1–39.

Cheru, F., 'Global apartheid and the challenge to civil society: Africa in the transformation of world order', in R. Cox (ed.) *The New Realism: Perspectives on Multilateralism and World Order*, Tokyo: United Nations University Press, 1997, pp. 205–22.

—— 'The Heavily Indebted Poor Countries (HIPC) Initiative: old wine in a new bottle?' in A. McGrew and N. Poku (eds), *Globalization, Development and Human Security*, Cambridge: Polity Press, 2007, pp. 66–82.

Christopher, M., *Logistics and Supply Chain Management: Strategies for Reducing Cost and Improving Service*, Harlow: Prentice Hall, 1992.

Clark, I., *Globalization and Fragmentation: International Relations in the Twentieth Century*, Oxford: Oxford University Press, 1997.

Cooke, W. and Noble, D., 'Industrial relations systems and US foreign direct investment abroad', *British Journal of Industrial Relations*, vol. 36:4, 1998, pp. 581–609.

Cox, R., *Production, Power and World Order: Social Forces in the Making of History*, New York: Columbia University Press, 1987.

—— (ed.), *The New Realism: Perspectives on Multilateralism and World Order*, Tokyo: United Nations University Press, 1997.

De Rivero, O., *The Myth of Development: The Non-viable Economies of the 21ˢᵗ Century*, London: Zed Books, 2001.

Deaton, A., 'Is world poverty falling', *Finance and Development*, vol. 39:2, June 2002. Online. Available http://www.imf.org/external/pubs/ft/fandd/2002/06/deaton.htm (accessed 25 March 2005), pp. 1–5.

Dicken, P. , *Global Shift: Transforming the World Economy*, London: Sage Publications, 2003, 4th ed.

Dollar, D., 'Outward-oriented developing economies really do grow more rapidly: evidence from 95 LDCs, 1976–85', *Economic Development and Cultural Change*, vol. 40, 1992, pp. 523–44.

Dollar, D. and Kraay, A., 'Trade, growth and poverty', *World Bank Policy Research Department Working Paper No. 2615*, Washington: World Bank, 2001, pp. 1–32. Online. Available http://www.imf.org/external/pubs/ft/fandd/2001/09/dollar.htm (accessed 25 March 2005).

—— 'Spreading the Wealth', *Foreign Affairs*, vol. 81:1, Jan/Feb 2002, pp. 120–33.

—— 'Growth is good for the poor', *World Bank Policy Research Department Working Paper No. 2587* (March 2002 Version). Online. Available http://www.imf.org/external/pubs/ft/fandd/2001/09/dollar.htm (accessed 25 March 2005).

Donnenfeld, S., 'Regional blocs and foreign direct investment', *Review of International Economics*, vol. 11:5, 2003, pp. 770–88.

Dowrick, S. and Akmal, M., *Contradictory Trends in Global Income Inequality: A Tale of Two Biases*, Helsinki: UNU/WIDER Conference, May 2003, pp. 1–23. Online. Available www.wider.unu.edu/conference/conference-2003 (accessed 25 March 2005).

Dunning, J. H., 'The new geography of FDI', in Ngaire Woods (ed.), *The Political Economy of Globalization*, Basingstoke: Palgrave, 2000, pp. 20–53.

Eagle, S., 'Trade in context: approaches to globalization', in A. Taylor and C. Thomas (eds), *Global Trade and Global Social Issues*, London: Routledge, 1999, pp. 14–30.

EBRD, *Annual Report 2000 of the European Bank of Reconstruction and Development*, London: Ventura Litno, 2000.

ECE, *Economic Survey of Europe 2002*, No. 1, Geneva: Economic Commission for Europe, 2002.

Edelstein, M., *Overseas Investment In The Age of High Imperialism: the United Kingdom 1850–1914*, New York: Columbia University Press, 1982.

Edwards, S., 'Openness, productivity and growth: what do we really know?', *Economics Journal*, vol. 108, 1998, pp. 383–98.

Eichengreen, B. and P. Lindhert (eds), *The International Debt Crisis in Historical Perspective*, Cambridge, MA: MIT Press, 1989, pp. 227–75.

Esping-Andersen, G., *Welfare States in Transition: National Adaptations in Global Economies*, London: Sage Publications, 1996.

—— 'After the Golden Age? Welfare dilemmas in a global economy', in G. Esping-Andersen, *Welfare States in Transition: National Adaptations in Global Economies*, London: Sage Publications, 1996, pp. 1–31.

—— 'Welfare states without work: the impasse of labour shedding and familialism in continental European social policy', in G. Esping-Andersen (ed.), *Welfare States in Transition: National Adaptations in Global Economies*, London: Sage Publications, 1996, pp. 66–87.

Evans, P. , 'Transnational linkages and the role of the state', in P. Evans, D. Rueschmeyer and T. Skocpol (eds), *Bringing the State Back In*, Cambridge: Cambridge University Press, 1985, pp. 46–83.

—— *Embedded Autonomy: States and Industrial Transformation*, Princeton, New Jersey: Princeton University Press, 1995.

Evans, P. , Rueschmeyer, D., and Skocpol, T. (eds), *Bringing the State Back In*, Cambridge: Cambridge University Press, 1985.

Falkingham, J., *Welfare in Transition: Trends in Poverty and Well-being in Central Asia*, London: Centre for Analysis of Social Exclusion, 1999. .

Feenstra, R., 'Integration of trade and disintegration of production in the global economy', *Journal of Economic Perspectives*, vol. 12:4, Autumn 1998, pp. 31–50.

Feldstein, M., 'Refocusing the IMF', *Foreign Affairs*, vol. 2, March/April 1998, pp. 20–33.

Feldstein, M. and Horioka, C., 'Domestic saving and international capital flows', *The Economic Journal*, vol. 90:358, June 1980, pp. 314–29.

Ferguson, N., *Colossus: the Price of America's Empire*, New York: Penguin Press, 2004.

Firebaugh, G., 'Growth effects of foreign and domestic investment', in M. Seligson and J. Passé-Smith (eds), *Development and Underdevelopment: the Political Economy of Global Inequality*, Boulder, CO: Lynne Rienner Publishers, 2003, 3rd ed., pp. 327–44.

Ford, J. L., *The Ohlin–Heckscher Theory of the Basis and Effects of Commodity Trade*, London: Asia Publishing House, 1965.

Frank, A. G., *Capitalism and Underdevelopment in Latin America: Historical Studies of Chile and Brazil,* New York: Monthly Review Press, 1967.

—— *Latin America: Underdevelopment or Revolution?*, New York: Monthly Review Press, 1969.

—— *On Capitalist Underdevelopment,* Bombay: Oxford University Press, 1975.

Frankel, J., 'Measuring international capital mobility: a review', *The American Economic Review*, vol. 82:2, 1992, pp. 197–202.

French, K. and Poterba, J., 'Investor diversification and international equity markets', *The American Economic Review*, vol. 81:2, May 1991, pp. 222–6.

Fukuda-Parr, S., 'The millennium development goals: the pledge of world leaders to end poverty will not be met with business as usual', *Journal of International Development* vol. 16, 2004, pp. 925–32.

Galati G. and Melvin, M., 'Why has FX trading surged? Explaining the 2004 triennial survey', *BIS Quarterly Review*, Basel: Bank for International Settlements, December 2004, pp. 67–74.

Garrett, G., 'Capital mobility, trade, and the domestic politics of economic policy', *International Organization*, vol. 49:4, 1995, pp. 657–87.

—— 'Global markets and national politics: collision course or virtuous circle', *International Organization*, vol. 52:4, 1998, pp. 787–824.

—— 'Shrinking states? Globalization and national autonomy in the OECD', *Oxford Development Studies*, vol. 26:1, 1998, pp. 71–98.

—— *Partisan Politics in the Global Economy*, Cambridge: Cambridge University Press, 1998.

——'Globalization's missing middle', *Foreign Affairs*, vol. 83:6, November/December 2004, pp. 84–96.

—— *The Three Worlds of Globalization: Market Integration, Economic Growth and the Distribution of Income in High, Middle and Low-income Countries.* February 2004. Online. Available http//:www.international.ucla.edu/profile/ggarrett (last accessed 11 June 2005), pp. 1–59.

Gattorna, J. L. and Walters, D. W., *Managing the Supply Chain: a Strategic Perspective*, Basingstoke: Macmillan, 1996.

Ghosh, J., *Christian Aid Policy Discussion Paper: Is India a Success Story of Economic Liberalization?*, Online. Available http://www.christian-aid.org.uk/indepth/505india/CA%20policy%20discussion%2001.pdf (accessed 12 March 2006).

Giddens, A., *The Nation-State And Violence: Volume Two of A Contemporary Critique of Historical Materialism*, Cambridge: Polity Press, 1985.

—— *The Consequences of Modernity*, Cambridge: Polity Press, 1990.

—— *Runaway World: How Globalisation is Reshaping our Lives*, London: Profile Books, 1999.

Gill, S., (ed.), *Globalization, Democratization and Multilateralism*, New York: United Nations University Press, 1997. .

—— 'The geopolitics of the Asian crisis', *Monthly Review*, vol. 50:10, March 1999, pp. 1–9.

Gilpin, R., *The Challenge of Global Capitalism: The World Economy in the 21st Century*, Princeton, NJ: Princeton University Press, 2000.

—— *Global Political Economy: Understanding the International Economic Order*, Princeton, NJ: Princeton University Press, 2001.

Gordon, D., 'The global economy: new edifice or crumbling foundations?', *New Left Review* vol. 168, 1988.

Gottschalk, P. , and Smeeding, T., 'Cross-national comparisons of earnings and income inequality', *Journal of Economic Literature*, vol. XXXB, June 1997, pp. 633–87.

Gray, J., *False Dawn: the Delusions of Global Capitalism*, London: Granta Books, 1999.

Greider, W., *One World, Ready or Not: The Manic Logic of Global Capitalism*, New York: Simon & Schuster, 1997.

Griesgraber, J. and Gunter, B., *World Trade: Toward Fair and Free Trade in the Twenty-first Century*, London: Pluto Press, 1997.

Griffith-Jones, St., Gottschalk, R. and Cirera, X., *The OECD Experience with Capital Account Liberalization*, Sussex: Institute of Development Studies, 2000. Online. Available http://www.ids.ac.uk/ids (accessed 17 December 2005).

Gunnell, B., 'Trade: what we want', *New Statesman,* 22.10.2001, pp. 23–4.

Hague, R., Harrop, M. and Breslin, S., *Comparative Government and Politics: An Introduction*, Basingstoke: Macmillan, 1998.

Hall, J. (ed.) *States in History*, Oxford: Blackwell, 1986.

Hall, S., Held, D. and McGrew, A., *Modernity and its Futures*, Oxford: Blackwell, 1999.

Halliday, F., *The Making of the Second Cold War*, London: Verso, 1986.

Harrison, D., *The Sociology of Modernization and Development*, London: Unwin Hyman, 1988.

Harvey, D., 'The geography of capitalist accumulation: a reconstruction of Marxism theory', *Antipode*, vol. 7, 1975, pp. 9–21.

Hay, C., 'Globalization's impact on states', in Ravenhill, J. (ed.), *Global Political Economy*, Oxford: Oxford University Press, 2005, pp. 235–62.

—— 'What's globalization got to do with it? Economic interdependence and the future of European Welfare States', *Government and Opposition*, vol. 41:1, 2006, pp. 1–22.

Hayward, J. and Page, E., (eds), *Governing the New Europe*, Cambridge: Polity Press, 1995.

Heckscher, E.,'The effect of foreign trade on the distribution of income' in The American Economic Association, *Readings in the Theory of International Trade*, London: Allen & Unwin, 1950, pp. 272–300.

Held, D., 'Law of states, law of peoples: three models of sovereignty', *Legal Theory*, vol. 8:1, 2002, pp. 1–44.

—— *Global Covenant: The Social Democratic Alternative to the Washington Consensus*, Cambridge: Polity Press, 2004.

Held, D. and Koenig-Archibugi, M., *Taming Globalization: Frontiers of Governance*, Cambridge: Polity Press, 2003.

Held D. and McGrew, A., 'Globalization and the liberal democratic state', *Government and Opposition*, vol. 28:2, 1997, pp. 261–87.

—— *Governing Globalization: Power, Authority and Global Governance*, Cambridge: Polity Press, 2002.

Held, D., McGrew, A., Goldblatt, D. and Perraton, J., *Global Transformations: Politics, Economics and Culture*, Cambridge: Polity Press, 1999.

Hettne, B., 'The Double Movement: global market versus regionalism', in R. Cox (ed.) *The New Realism: Perspectives on Multilateralism and World Order*, Tokyo: United Nations University Press, 1997, pp. 223–42.

—— 'Globalization and the new regionalism: the second great transformation', in B. Hettne, A. Inotai and O. Sunkel (eds) *Globalism and the New Regionalism*, Basingstoke: Macmillan, 1999, pp. 1–24.

Hettne, B., Inotai, A., and Sunkel, O. (eds), *Globalism and the New Regionalism*, Basingstoke: Macmillan, 1999.

Higgott, R., 'The Asian economic crisis: a study in the politics of resentment', *New Political Economy*, vol. 3:3, 1998, pp. 333–57.

Hinsley, F. H., *Sovereignty*, Cambridge: Cambridge University Press, 1986, 2nd ed.

Hirst, P. , 'The Global economy – myths and realities', *International Affairs,* Vol. 73:3, 1997, pp. 409–25.

Hirst, P. and Thompson, G., *Globalization in Question: The International Economy and the Possibilities of Governance*, Cambridge: Polity Press, 1996.

—— *Globalization in Question: The International Economy and the Possibilities of Governance*, Cambridge: Polity Press, 1999, 2nd ed.

—— 'Globalization in one country? The peculiarities of the British', *Economy and Society*, Vol. 29:3, 2000, pp. 335–56.

—— 'The future of globalisation', in J. Michie (ed.), *The Handbook of Globalisation*, Cheltenham: Edward Elgar, 2003, pp. 17–36.

Holsti, K. J., *Taming the Sovereigns: Institutional Change in International Politics*, Cambridge: Cambridge University Press, 2004.

Holton, R., *Globalization and the Nation-State*, London: Macmillan, 1998.

Hoogvelt, A., *Globalisation and the Postcolonial World: the New Political Economy of Development*, Basingstoke: Macmillan, 1997.

—— *Globalization and the Postcolonial World*, Basingstoke: Palgrave, 2001, 2nd ed.

Hummels, D., Ishii, J. and Yi, K., 'The nature and growth of vertical specialization in world trade', *Journal of International Economics*, vol. 54, 2001, pp. 75–96.

Hummels, D., Rapoport, D. and Yi, K., 'Vertical specialization and the changing nature of world trade', *Federal Reserve Bank of New York Economic Policy Review*, June 1998, pp. 79–99.

Hurd, I., 'Legitimacy and authority in international politics', *International Organization* vol. 53:2, 1999, pp. 379–408.

Hurrell, A., 'Power, institutions, and the production of inequality', in M. Barnett and R. Duvall (eds), *Power in Global Governance*, Cambridge: Cambridge University Press, 2005, pp. 33–58.

Hurrell, A. and N. Woods (eds) *Inequality, Globalization, and World Politics*, Oxford: Oxford University Press, 1999.

Huq, M., and Tribe, M., 'Economic development in a changing economy', *Journal of International Development*, vol. 16, 2004, pp. 911–23.

Hutton, W., *The State We're In*, London: Vintage, 1996. .

ICAC, *Annual Report of the International Civil Aviation Council*, Montreal: International Civil Aviation Council, 2001.

IMF, *Venezuela: Recent Economic Developments: IMF Staff Country Report No 98:117*, Washington D.C.: International Monetary Fund, 1998.

—— *Republic of Uzbekistan: Recent Economic Developments: IMF Staff Country Report No. 00/36*, Washington DC: International Monetary Fund, 2000.

Jackson, R., *Quasi-states: Sovereignty, International Relations and the Third World*, Cambridge: Cambridge University Press, 1990.

Johnson, C., *MITI and the Japanese Miracle: The Growth of Industrial Policy, 1925–1975*, Palo Alto, CA: Stanford University Press, 1982.

Joint European NGO Report, *EU Aid: Genuine Leadership or Misleading Figures?*. Online. Available http://www.eurodad.org (accessed 3 December 2006).

Jones, C., 'On the evolution of the world income distribution', *The Journal of Economic Perspectives*, vol. 11:3, 1997, pp. 19–36.

Jones, C. and Revenga, A., *Making Transition Work for Everyone: Poverty and Inequality in Europe and Central Asia*, Washington: World Bank, 2000.

Kaiser, K., Kirton, J. and Daniels, J. (eds), *Shaping a New Financial System: Challenges of Governance in a Globalizing World*, Aldershot: Ashgate Publishers, 2000.

Kaplinsky, R., *Globalization, Poverty and Inequality: Between a Rock and a Hard Place*, Cambridge: Polity Press, 2005.

Kentor, J., 'The long-term effects of foreign investment dependence on economic growth, 1940–1990', in M. Seligson and J. Passé-Smith·(eds), *Development and Underdevelopment: the Political Economy of Global Inequality*, Boulder, CO: Lynne Rienner Publishers, 2003, 3rd ed., pp. 345–56.

Keohane, R., *After Hegemony: Cooperation and Discord in the World Political Economy*, Princeton, NJ: Princeton University Press, 1984.

Keohane R. and Nye, J. S., *Transnational Relations and World Politics*, Cambridge: MA: Harvard University Press, 1972.

—— 'Power and interdependence in the information age', *Foreign Affairs*, vol.77:5, 1998, pp. 81–94.

—— 'Globalization: What's new? What's not? (And so what?)', *Foreign Policy*, vol. 118, 2000, pp. 104–19.

Khor, M., 'Preliminary comments on the WTO's Geneva July decision', *Third World Network*, 2005. Online. Available http://www.twnside.org (accessed 3 August 2005).

Kirsher, J., 'Keynes, capital mobility and the crisis of embedded liberalism', *Review of International Political Economy*, vol. 6:3, 1999, pp. 313–37.

Koenig-Archibugi, M., 'Mapping global governance', in D. Held and A. McGrew (eds), *Governing Globalization: Power, Authority and Global Governance*, Cambridge: Polity Press, 2002, pp. 46–69.

Kofman, E. and G. Youngs (eds), *Globalization: Theory and Practice*, London: Pinter, 1996.

Krasner, S., 'Compromising Westphalia', *International Security*, vol. 20:3, Winter 1995–6, pp. 115–51.

—— *Sovereignty: Organized Hypocrisy*, Princeton, NJ: Princeton University Press, 1999.

Krauthammer, C., 'The unipolar moment', *Foreign Affairs,* vol. 70:1, 1990, pp. 23–33.

Krugman, P. , 'Dutch tulips and emerging markets', *Foreign Affairs*, vol. 74:4, 1995, pp. 28–44.

—— 'Growing world trade: causes and consequences', *Brookings Papers on Economic Activity*, 1995, pp. 327–62.

Kuznets, S. 'Economic growth and income inequality', in M. Seligson and J. Passé-Smith (eds), *Development and Underdevelopment: the Political Economy of Global Inequality*, Boulder, CO: Lynne Rienner Publishers, 2003, 3rd ed., pp. 61–76.

Lall, S., 'The technological structure and performance of developing country manufactured exports, 1985–98', *Oxford Development Studies*, vol. 28:3, 2000, pp. 337–69.

Layne, C., 'The unipolar illusion: why new great powers will arise', *International Security,* vol 17:4, 1993, pp. 5–51.

Lee, S., 'The Political economy of the third way', in J. Michie (ed.), *The Handbook of Globalisation*, Cheltenham: Edward Elgar, 2003, pp. 331–46.

Leyshon, A., 'Annihilating space?: The speeding-up of communications', in J. Allen (ed.), *A Shrinking World?*, Oxford: Oxford University Press, 1995, pp. 11–54.

Lindhert, P. , 'Response to debt crisis: what is different about the 1980s' in B. Eichengreen and P. Lindhert (eds), *The International Debt Crisis in Historical Perspective*, Cambridge, MA: MIT Press, 1989, pp. 227–75.

McGrew, A., 'The globalization debate: putting the advanced capitalist state in its place', *Global Society*, vol. 12:3, 1998, pp. 299–322.

McGrew, A. and Poku, N., *Globalization, Development and Human Security*, Cambridge: Polity Press, 2007.

McLuhan, M., *The Gutenberg Galaxy: The Making of Typographic Man*, Toronto: Toronto University Press, 1962.

—— Carpenter, E., *Explorations in Communication*, Boston, MA: Beacon Press, 1966.

Maddison, A., 'The nature and functioning of European capitalism: a historical and comparative perspective', *Banca Nazionale Del Lavoro Quarterly Review,* vol. L:203, 1997, pp. 431–79. .

—— *The World Economy: a Millennial Perspective*, Paris: Development Centre of the OECD, 2001.

Mann, M., 'The autonomous power of the state', in J. Hall (ed.) *States in History*, Oxford: Blackwell, 1986, pp. 113–139.

Martin, H. and Schumann, H., *The Global Trap: Globalization and the Assault on Democracy and Prosperity*, London: Zed Books, 1997.

Mastanduno, M., 'Preserving the unipolar moment: realist theories and U.S. grand strategy', *International Security,* vol. 21:4, 1997, pp. 49–88.

Mead, W. R., *Power, Terror, Peace, and War: America's Grand Strategy in a World at Risk*, New York: Alfred A. Knopf, 2004.

Melhuish, M., *Energy and Sustainable Development in New Zealand*, New Zealand: Helio International, 2002. Online. Available http://www.helio-international.org/Helio/Reports/2002/English/NewZealand/NZtot.pdf (accessed 10 January 2007).

Michie, J., *The Handbook of Globalisation*, Cheltenham: Edward Elgar, 2003.

Milanovic, B., *Income, Inequality, and Poverty during the Transition from Planned to Market Economy*, Washington, DC: World Bank, 1988.

—— 'True world income distribution, 1998 and 1993: First calculation based on household surveys alone', *The Economic Journal*, vol.112, 2002, pp. 51–92.

—— 'Can we discern the effect of globalization on income distribution?', *World Bank Policy Research Working Paper 2876*, April 2002, pp. 1–22.

—— 'The two faces of globalization: against globalization as we know it', *World Development*, 2003, vol. 31:4, pp. 667–83.

Mittelman, J., 'The global restructuring of production and migration' in Y. Sakamoto (ed.), *Global Transformation: Challenges to the State System*, Tokyo: UNU Publications, 1994, pp. 276–98.

—— 'Rethinking the "New Regionalism" in the context of globalization', in B. Hettne, A. Inotai and O. Sunkel (eds), *Globalism and the New Regionalism*, Basingstoke: Macmillan, 1999, pp. 25–53.

Mohan, G., 'Globalisation and governance: the paradoxes of adjustment in sub-Saharan Africa', in E. Kofman and G. Youngs (eds), *Globalization: Theory and Practice*, London: Pinter, 1996, pp. 288–303.

Mosely, L., *Global Capital and National Governments*, Cambridge: Cambridge University Press, 2003.

Moxham, R., *Tea: Addiction, Exploitation and Empire*, London: Constable & Robinson, 2003.

Nierop, T., *Systems and Regions in Global Politics: an Empirical Study of Diplomacy, International Organization and Trade 1950–1991*, Chichester: John Wiley, 1994.

Nye, J. S., 'Soft Power', *Foreign Policy*, vol. 80, Fall 1990, pp. 153–71.

Obstfeld, M., 'The global capital market: benefactor or menace?', *The Journal of Economic Perspectives*, vol. 12:4, 1998, pp. 9–30.

Obstfeld, M. and Taylor, A., *Global Capital Markets: Integration, Crisis and Growth*, Cambridge: Cambridge University Press, 2004.

OECD, *OECD Historical Statistics 1960–1995*, Paris: OECD, 1997.

—— *OECD Historical Statistics 1970–2000*, Paris: OECD, 2001.

—— 'Intra-industry and intra-firm trade and the internationalisation of production', *OECD Economic Outlook*, vol. 71, Section 6, June 2002. Online. Available http://www.oecd.org/dataoecd/6/18/2752923.pdf (accessed 21 June 2003). .

—— *OECD Factbook 2006: Economic, Environmental and Social Statistics*, Paris: OECD, 2006.

Ohlin, B., *Interregional and International Trade*, Cambridge, MA: Harvard University Press, 1933.

Ohmae, K., *The Borderless World: Power and Strategy in the Global Marketplace*, London: HarperCollins, 1990.

—— *The End of the Nation-state: the Rise of Regional Economies*, London: HarperCollins, 1995.

—— 'Putting global logic first', *Harvard Business Review*, vol. 73:1, January–February 1995, pp. 119–25.

Oman, C. 'Globalization, regionalization and inequality' in A. Hurrell and N. Woods (eds) *Inequality, Globalization, and World Politics*, Oxford: Oxford University Press, 1999, pp. 36–65.

OSCE, *Public Social Expenditure by Main Category as a Percentage of GDP (1980–98)*, July 2002. Online. Available http://www.osce.org/publications (accessed 11 October 2002).

Oxfam, *Rigged Rules and Double Standards: Trade, Globalisation, and the Fight against Poverty*, London: Oxfam, 2002.

—— *Do the Deal*, London: Cafod, Action Aid UK and Oxfam, 2005.

—— 'Oxfam Background Briefing on South–South Trade and GSTP'. Online. Available http://www.oxfam.org.uk/what_we_do/issues/trade/downloads/south_trade.pdf (accessed 20 April, 2006).

Palma, G., 'National inequality in the era of globalization: what do recent data tell us', in J. Michie (ed.), *The Handbook of Globalisation*, Cheltenham: Edward Elgar, 2003, pp. 104–35.

Parry, R., 'Redefining the Welfare State', in J. Hayward and E. Page (eds), *Governing the New Europe*, Cambridge: Polity Press, 1995, pp. 374–401.

Pelagidis, T. and Papsotiriou, H., 'Globalization or regionalism? States, markets and the structure of international trade', *Review of International Studies*, vol. 28:5, 2002, pp. 519–35.

Perraton, J., 'The scope and implications of globalisation', in J. Michie (ed.), *The Handbook of Globalisation*, Cheltenham: Edward Elgar, 2003, pp. 37–60.

Perraton, J., Goldblatt, D., Held, D. and McGrew, A., 'The globalization of economic activity', *New Political Economy*, vol. 2:2, 1997, pp. 257–77. .

Petra, J. and Veltmeyer, H., 'Globalisation of Imperialism', *Cambridge Review of International Affairs*, XIV:1, 2000, pp. 32–48.

—— *Globalization Unmasked: Imperialism in the 21st Century*, London: Zed Books, 2001.

—— 'Age of reverse aid: neo-liberalism as catalyst of regression', *Development and Change*, 33:2, 2002, pp. 281–93.

Piven, F. 'Is it global economics or neo-laissez-faire?', *New Left Review*, vol. 213, 1995, pp. 107–14.

Pogge, T. and Reddy, S., 'How *not* to count the poor', March 2003, Online. Available http://www.columbia.edu/~sr793/count.pdf (accessed 6 June 2005).

—— 'Unknown: the extent, distribution, and trend of global income poverty', March 2003. Online. Available http://www.columbia.edu /~sr793 povpop. pdf (accessed 6 June 2005).

Polanyi, K., *The Great Transformation: The Political and Economic Origins of our Time*, Boston, MA: Beacon Press, 1944.

Prasaad, E., Rogoff, K., Wei, S. and Kose, M., *Effects of Financial Globalization on Developing Countries: Some Empirical Evidence*, IMF, March 2003. Online. Available http://www.imf.org/external/np/res/docs/2003/031703.pdf (accessed 3 April 2006).

Prerau, D. *Saving the Daylight: Why we Put the Clocks Forward*, London: Granta Books, 2006.

Puri, L., *Towards a New Trade 'Marshall Plan' for Least Developed Countries*, Geneva: United Nations Commission on Trade and Development, 2005.

Randall, V. and Theobald, R., *Political Change and Underdevelopment: A Critical Introduction to Third World Politics*, London: Macmillan 1985.

Ranger, S., 'Offshoring an "Unstoppable Force" says NHS IT Chief', Online. Available www. services.silicon.com/offshoring.html (accessed 20 July 2006).

Ravallion, M., 'The debate on globalization, poverty and inequality: why measurement matters', *International Affairs*, vol. 79:4, 2003, pp. 739–53.

Ravenhill, J. (ed.), *Global Political Economy*, Oxford: Oxford University Press, 2005.

—— 'Regionalism' in J. Ravenhill (ed.), *Global Political Economy*, Oxford: Oxford University Press, 2005, pp. 117–47.

Rhodes, M., 'The Welfare State: internal challenges, external constraints', in M. Rhodes, P. Heywood and V. Wright (eds), *Developments in West European Politics*, Basingstoke: Macmillan, 1997, pp. 171–88.

Robertson, R., *Globalization: Social Theory and Global Culture*, London: Sage Publications, 1992.

Rodriguez, F. and Rodrik, D., 'Trade policy and economic growth: a skeptic's guide to the cross-national evidence', *National Bureau of Economic Research Working Paper 7081*, April 1999, pp. 1–45.

Rodrik, D., 'Why do more open economies have bigger governments?', *NBER Working Paper Series 5537*, Cambridge, MA: National Bureau of Economic Research, April 1996, pp. 1–32.

—— *Has Globalization Gone Too Far?*, Washington, DC: Institute for International Economics, 1997.

—— *The New Global Economy and Developing Countries: Making Openness Work*, Washington, DC: Overseas Development Council, 1999.

—— *The Global Governance of Trade: as if Trade Development Really Mattered*, New York: UNDP, 2001, pp. 1–39.

—— *Comments on 'Trade, Growth, and Poverty'*, October 2000. Online. Available http://ksghome.harvard.edu/~drodrik/Rodrik%20on%20Dollar-Kraay.pdf (accessed 23 March 2006).

—— 'What's so special about China's exports?', 2006. Online. Available http://ksghome.harvard.edu/~drodrik/Chinaexports.pdf (accessed 23 March 2006).

Rodrik, D. and A. Subramanian, 'From "Hindu Growth" to productivity surge: the mystery of the Indian growth transition', March 2004. Online. Available http://ksghome.harvard.edu/~drodrik/IndiapaperdraftMarch2.pdf (accessed 23 March 2006).

Rosecrance, R., 'International security and the virtual state: states and firms in world politics', *Review of International Studies*, vol.28:4, 2002 pp. 443–55.

Rosenburg, J., *The Follies of Globalisation Theory: Polemical Essays*, London: Verso, 2000.

Roxborough, I., *Theories of Underdevelopment*, London: Macmillan, 1979.

Rudra, N., 'Globalization and the decline of the Welfare State in less-developed countries', *International Organization*, vol. 56:2, Spring 2002, pp. 411–45.

—— 'Re-assessing the relationship between globalization and welfare: welfare spending and international competitiveness in less developed countries' in S. Chan and J. Scarritt (eds), *Coping with Globalization: Cross-national Patterns in Domestic Governance and Policy Performance*, London: Frank Cass, 2002.

—— 'Openness, welfare spending, and inequality in the developing world', *International Studies Quarterly*, vol. 48, 2004, pp. 683–709.

Ruggie, J. G., 'International regimes, transaction, and change: embedded liberalism in the postwar economic order', *International Organization*, vol. 36:2, 1982, pp. 379–416.

—— 'Territoriality and beyond: problematizing modernity in international relations', *International Organization*, vol. 47:1, 1993, pp. 139–74.

—— *Building the World Polity: Essays on International Institutionalization*, London: Routledge, 1998.

Rugman, A., 'From globalisation to regionalism: the foreign direct investment dimension of international finance', in K. Kaiser, J. Kirton and J. Daniels (eds), *Shaping a New Financial System: Challenges of Governance in a Globalizing World*, Aldershot: Ashgate Publishers, 2000, pp. 186–200.

—— *The End of Globalization*, London: Random House Business Books, 2000.

—— 'Regional transnationals and triad strategy', *Transnational Corporations*, vol. 13:3, 2004, pp. 1–20.

—— *The Regional Multinationals: MNEs and 'Global' Strategic Management*, Cambridge: Cambridge University Press, 2005.

—— 'Globalisation and Regional Production', in Ravenhill, J. (ed.), *Global Political Economy*, Oxford: Oxford University Press, 2005, pp. 263–90.

—— 'Regional multinationals and the myth of globalization', *CSGR Annual Conference*, October 2005, pp. 1–31. Online. Available http://www2.warwick.ac.uk/fac/soc/csgr/activitiesnews/conferences/2005_conferences/8_annual_conference/rugman.doc (accessed 20 October 2006).

Sachs, J. and Warner, A., 'Economic reform and the process of global integration', *Brookings Papers on Economic Activity*, vol. 1995:1, 1995, pp. 1–118.

Sakamoto, Y. (ed.), *Global Transformation: Challenges to the State System*, Tokyo: UNU Publications, 1994.

Sala-i-Martin, X., *The Disturbing 'Rise' of Global Income Inequality*, Cambridge, MA: NBER, April 2002, pp. 1–65.

—— *The World Distribution of Income*, Cambridge, MA: NBER, May 2002, pp. 1–65.

Sassen, S., *Losing Control? Sovereignty in an Age of Globalization*, New York: Columbia University Press, 1996.

Saurin, J., 'Global environmental degradation', in C. Thomas (ed.), *RIO: Unraveling the Consequences*, Essex, UK: Frank Cass, 1994, pp. 46–64.

Scharpf, F., *Governing in Europe: Effective and Democratic?*, New York: Oxford University Press, 1996.

—— 'Economic integration, democracy and the Welfare State', *Journal of European Public Policy*, Vol. 4:1, 1997, pp. 18–36.

Scholte, J. A.,'Global capitalism and the state', *International Affairs*, vol. 73:3, 1997, pp. 427–53.

—— *Globalization: a Critical Introduction*, Basingstoke: Palgrave, 2000.

——'Governing global finance', in D. Held and A. McGrew (eds), *Governing Globalization: Power, Authority and Global Governance*, Cambridge: Polity Press, 2002, pp. 189–208.

—— *Globalization: a Critical Introduction*, Basingstoke: Palgrave, 2005, 2nd ed.

—— 'Global trade and finance' in J. Baylis and S. Smith (eds), *The Globalization of World Politics*, Oxford: Oxford University Press, 2005, pp. 599–620.

Schrim, S., *Globalization and the New Regionalism*, Cambridge: Polity Press, 2002.

Schumpeter, J. A., *The Theory of Economic Development: An Inquiry into Profits, Capital, Credit, Interest, and the Business Cycle*, Cambridge, MA: Harvard University Press, 1951.

Seligson, M. and Passé-Smith, J. (eds), *Development and Underdevelopment: the Political Economy of Global Inequality*, Boulder, CO: Lynne Rienner Publishers, 2003, 3rd ed.

Shannon, T., *An Introduction to the World-System Perspective*, Boulder, CO: Westview Press, 1992.

Shaw, M., *Theory of the Global State: Globality as an Unfinished Revolution*, Cambridge: Cambridge University Press, 2000.

So, A., *Social Change and Development: Modernization, Dependency, and World-system Theories*, London: Sage Publications, 1980.

Söderbaum, F. and Shaw, T., *Theories of New Regionalism*, Basingstoke: Palgrave, 2003.

Srinivasan, T., *Comments on Dani Rodrik and Arvind Subraimanian, From 'Hindu Growth' to Productivity Surge: The Mystery of the Indian Growth Transition*. Online. Available http://www.imf.org/external/pubs/ft/staffp/2004/00–00/sriniv.pdf (accessed 23 March 2006).

Stewart, F. and Berry, A., 'Globalization, liberalization, and inequality: expectations and experience', in A. Hurrell and N. Woods (eds), *Inequality, Globalization, and World Politics*, Oxford: Oxford University Press, 1999, pp. 150–86.

Stiglitz, J. and Charlton, A., *Fair Trade for All: How Trade Can Promote Development*, Oxford: Oxford University Press, 2005.

Stopford, J., 'Multinational Corporations', *Foreign Policy*, vol. 112, Winter 1998–9, pp. 12–24.

Strange, S., *Casino Capitalism*, Oxford: Blackwell, 1986.

—— *The Retreat of the State: the Diffusion of Power in the World Economy*, Cambridge: Cambridge University Press, 1996.

—— 'Globaloney?', *Review of International Political Economy*, vol. 5:4, 1998, pp. 704–10.

Sumner, A., 'Why are we still arguing about globalization?', *Journal of International Development*, 2004, vol. 16, pp. 1015–22.

Swank, D., *Global Capital, Political Institutions, and Policy Change in Developed Welfare States*, Cambridge: Cambridge University Press, 2002.

Tabb, W., 'The East Asian financial crisis', *Monthly Review*, vol. 50:2, pp. 24–38.

Tanzi, V. 'Globalization, tax competition and the future of tax systems', *IMF Working Paper*, IMF:Washington, DC, 1996, pp. 1–21.

—— 'Globalization and the Future of Social Protection', *IMF Working Paper WP/00/12*, Washington, DC: IMF, 2000.

Tanzi, V. and Schuknecht, L., *The Growth of Government and the Reform of the State in Industrial Countries: Working Paper WP/95/130*, Washington, DC: IMF, December 1995, pp. 1–39.

Taylor, A. and Thomas, C. (eds), *Global Trade and Global Social Issues*, London: Routledge, 1999.

Taylor, I., ' "Advice is judged by results, not by intentions": why Gordon Brown is wrong about Africa', *International Affairs*, Vol. 81:2, 2005, pp. 299–310.

Teeple, G., *Globalization and the Decline of Social Reform*, Toronto: Garamond Press, 1995.

Thomas, C. (ed.), *RIO: Unravelling the Consequences*, Essex, UK: Frank Cass, 1994.

—— 'Poverty, Development, and Hunger', in J. Baylis, and S. Smith, *The Globalization of World Politics*, Oxford: Oxford University Press, 1997, pp. 449–67.

—— 'Introduction' in C. Thomas and P. Wilkin (eds), *Globalization, Human Security and the African Experience*, Boulder, CO: Lynne Rienner Publishers, 1999.

—— 'Where is the Third World now', *Review of International Studies*, vol. 25:5, 1999, pp. 225–44.

—— *Global Governance, Development and Human Security*, London: Pluto Press, 2000.

—— 'Global governance, development and human security: exploring the links', *Third World Quarterly*, vol. 22:2, 2001, pp. 159–75.

—— 'Globalization and Development in the South', in J. Ravenhill (ed.), *Global Political Economy*, Oxford: Oxford University Press, 2005, pp. 317–43.

Thompson, D., *Europe since Napoleon*, Harmondsworth: Penguin Books, 1985.

Thompson, G., 'Globalization as the total commercialization of politics', *New Political Economy*, vol. 8:3, 2003, pp. 401–8.

—— 'Whither the "Washington Consensus", the "Developmental State", and the "Seattle Protests?": Can "managed free trade and investment" become an alternative developmental model?', *Problemas Del Desarrollo*, vol. 34:131, 2003, pp. 219–38.

—— 'The Supra-national regionalization of the International Financial System: How far and with what Prospects?' Presented at the GARNET Conference in Holland September 2006. Online. Available http://wi-garnet.uni-muenster.de (accessed 19 October 2006).

Traxler, F. and Woiteach, B., 'Transnational investment and national labour market regimes: a Case of "Regime Shopping"', *European Journal of Industrial Relations*, Vol. 6:2, 2000, pp. 141–59.

Tussie, D. and Woods, N., 'Trade, regionalism and the threat to multilateralism', in N. Wood (ed.), *The Political Economy of Globalization*, Basingstoke: Palgrave, 2000, pp. 54–76.

UNDIESA (United Nations Department of International Economic and Social Affairs), *Long-range World Population Projections: Based on the 1998 Revision*, New York: United Nations, 1999.

UNDP, *Human Development Report 1990: Concept and Measurement of Human Development*, Oxford: Oxford University Press, 1990.

—— *Human development Report 1998: Consumption for Human Development*, Oxford: Oxford University Press, 1998.

—— *Human Development Report 1999: Globalization with a Human Face*, Oxford: Oxford University Press, 1999.

—— *Human Development Report 2001: Making New Technologies Work for Human Development*, Oxford: Oxford University Press, 2001.

—— *Human Development Report 2002: Deepening Democracy in a Fragmented World*, Oxford: Oxford University Press, 2002.

—— *Human Development Report 2003: Millennium Development Goals*, Oxford: Oxford University Press, 2003.

—— *Making Global Trade Work For People*, Sterling, Virginia: Earthscan Publications, 2003.

UNICEF, *The Progress Of Nations 1999*, New York: United Nations International Children's Emergency Fund, 1999. .

United Nations, *International Trade Statistics Yearbook*, New York: United Nations, 1960.

—— *World Investment Report 1992: Transnational Corporations as Engines of Growth* (An Executive Summary), New York, United Nations Transnational Corporations and Management Division, 1992.

—— *World Investment Report 1995: Transnational Corporations and Competitiveness*, New York: United Nations Conference on Trade and Development, 1995.

—— *World Investment Report 1998: Trends and Determinants*, New York: United Nations Conference on Trade and Development, 1998.

—— *World Investment Report 2001: Promoting Linkages*, New York: United Nations Conference on Trade and Development, 2001.

—— *World Investment Report 2002: Transnational Corporations and Competitiveness*, New York: United Nations Conference on Trade and Development, 2002. .

—— *World Investment Report 2003: FDI Policies for Development – National and International Perspectives*, New York: United Nations Conference on Trade and Development, 2003.

—— *International Trade Statistics Yearbook*, New York: United Nations, 2003.

—— *Globalization and Development*, Geneva: United Nations Conference on Trade and Development, 2004.

—— *Trade and Development Report 2004*, Geneva: United Nations Conference on Trade and Development, 2004.

—— *World Investment Report 2004: The Shift towards Services,* New York: United Nations Conference on Trade and Development, 2004.

—— *Investing in Development: a Practical Plan to Achieve the Millennium Development Goals*, London: Earthscan, 2005.

—— *Trade and Development Report 2005: New Features of Global Interdependence*, Geneva: United Nations Conference on Trade and Development, 2005.

—— *World Investment Report 2006: FDI from Developing and Transition Economies*, New York: United Nations Conference on Trade and Development, 2006.

Väyrynen R., 'Regionalism: Old and New', *International Studies Review*, vol. 5, 2003, pp. 25–51.

Vidal, G., *The Judgement of Paris*, London: Heinemann, 1953.

Wade, R., *Governing the Market: Economic Theory and the Role of Government in East Asian Industrialization*, Princeton, NJ: Princeton University Press, 1990.

Wade, R., 'Disturbing Rise in Poverty and Inequality: Is it all a "Big Lie"', in Held, D., Koenig-Archibugi, M. (eds), *Taming Globalization: Frontiers of Governance*, Cambridge: Polity Press, 2003, pp. 18–46.

—— 'The Rising Inequality of World Income Distribution', in M. Seligson and J. Passé-Smith (eds), *Devlelopment and Underdevelopment: the Political Economy of Global Inequality*, London: Lynne Rienner Publishers, 2003, pp. 33–40. Online. Available http://www.imf.org/external/pubs/ft/fandd/2001/12/wade.htm (accessed 25 March 2005).

Wallerstein, I., *The Modern World System*, Vol. 1. New York: Academic Press, 1974.

—— *The Modern World System*, Vol. 2. New York: Academic Press, 1980.

—— *The Modern World System*, Vol. 3. New York: Academic Press, 1989.

Wallerstein, I. and Frank, A., 'Two Views of World History', *Review*, vol. XV:4, 1992.

Watkins, K., 'Debt Relief for Africa', *Review of African Political Economy*, vol. 62, 1994, pp. 117–27.

Watson, M., 'International Capital Mobility in an Era of Globalisation: Adding a Political Dimension to the "Feldstein-Horioka Puzzle"', *Politics*, vol. 21:2, 2001, pp. 81–92.

Weiss, L., 'Globalization and the Myth of the Powerless State', *New Left Review*, vol. 225, September–October 1997, pp. 3–27.

—— *The Myth of the Powerless State: Governing the Economy in a Global Era*, Cambridge: Polity Press, 1998.

—— 'Globalization and national governance: antinomy or interdependence?', *Review of International Studies*, vol. 25:5, 1999, pp. 59–88.

Wells-Dang, A., 'Having it Both Ways', *Foreign Affairs*, vol. 81:4, 2002, pp. 180–2.

Wiig, H., 'How much Globalization? Reassessing the Growth of International Trade and Investments in the OECD', *Norsk Utenrikspolitisk Institutt*, Report No.241. February 1999. Online. Available http://www.nupi.no/IPS/filestore/How_much_Globalisation. pdf (accessed 20 August 2006).

Wilensky, H., *Rich Democracies: Political Economy, Public Policy, and Performance*, Berkely, CA: University of California Press, 2002.

Winham, G., 'The evolution of the global trade regime', in J. Ravenhill (ed.), *Global Political Economy*, Oxford: Oxford University Press, 2005, pp. 87–117.

Wohlforth, W., 'The stability of a unipolar world', *International Security*, vol. 24:1, 1999, pp. 5–41.

Wolf, M., 'Will the Nation-state survive globalization?', *Foreign Affairs*, vol. 80:1, 2001, pp. 178–90.

—— *Why Globalization Works*, New Haven, CT: Yale Note Bene, 2005.

Woo, J., *Race to the Swift: State and Finance in Korean Industrialization*, New York: Columbia University Press, 1991.

Woo-Cumings, M., *The Developmental State*, Ithaca, New York: Cornell University Press, 1999.

Woods, N., 'The Role of Institutions', in D. Held and A. McGrew (eds), *Governing Globalization: Power, Authority and Global Governance*, Cambridge: Polity Press, 2002, pp. 25–45.

—— (ed.), *The Political Economy of Globalization*, Basingstoke: Palgrave, 2000.

—— 'Special issue: understanding pathways through financial crises and the impact of the IMF', *Global Governance*, vol. 12:4, October–December 2006.

World Bank, *World Development Report 1990: Poverty*, Washington DC: World Bank, 1990.

—— *The East Asian Miracle: Economic Growth and Public Policy*, Oxford: Oxford University Press, 1993.

—— *World Development Report 2000/2001: Attacking Poverty*, Washington, DC: World Bank, 2001.

—— *Globalization, Growth, and Poverty: Building an Inclusive World Economy*, Washington, DC: World Bank, 2002.

—— 'Growth is good for the poor', *World Bank Policy Research Department Working Paper No. 2587 (March 2002 Version)*. Online. Available http://www.imf.org/external/pubs/ft/fandd/2001/09/dollar.htm (accessed 25 March 2005).

—— *World Development Indicators 2004*, Washington, DC: World Bank, 2004.

—— *Inequality in Latin America and the Carribbean: Breaking with History?,* Washington DC: World Bank, 2004.

—— *Global Economic Prospects: Trade, Regionalism and Development*, Washington, DC: World Bank, 2005.

—— *World Development Report 2005: A Better Investment Climate for Everyone*, Washington DC: World Bank, 2005.

—— *World Development Report 2006: Equity and Development*, Washington DC: World Bank, 2006.

—— *Thailand and Malaysia at a Glance*, Online. Available http://devdata.worldbank.org/AAG/tha_aag.pdf (accessed 02 May 2006).

—— *China at a Glance*. Online. Available http://www.worldbank.org.cn/ English/Content/chn_aag02.pdf (accessed 28 March 2006).

—— *India at a Glance*. Online. Available http://devdata.worldbank.org/AAG/ind_aag.pdf (accessed 28 March 2006).

World Trade Organization, *Doha Declarations*, Geneva: WTO, 2001.

—— *World Trade Report 2003*, Geneva: WTO, 2003.

—— *International Trade Statistics: 2004*, Geneva: WTO, 2004.

—— *Selected Long-Term Trends*, Geneva: WTO, 2004.

Index